Phake

Phake

The Deadly World of Falsified and Substandard Medicines

Roger Bate

The AEI Press

Publisher for the American Enterprise Institute
WASHINGTON, D.C.

Distributed by arrangement with the Rowman & Littlefield Publishing Group, 4501 Forbes Boulevard, Suite 200, Lanham, Maryland 20706. To order, call toll free 1-800-462-6420 or 1-717-794-3800. For all other inquiries, please contact AEI Press, 1150 Seventeenth Street, N.W., Washington, D.C. 20036, or call 1-800-862-5801.

Library of Congress Cataloging-in-Publication Data

Bate, Roger.
    Phake : the deadly world of falsified and substandard medicines / Roger Bate.
        p. ; cm.
    Includes bibliographical references and index.
    Summary: "Drug trade, pharmaceutical industry, counterfeit drugs, product counterfeiting"—Provided by publisher.
    ISBN 978-0-8447-7232-5 (cloth)—ISBN 0-8447-7232-1 (cloth)—ISBN 978-0-8447-7233-2 (paper)—ISBN 0-8447-7233-X (paper)—ISBN 978-0-8447-7234-9 (ebook)—ISBN 0-8447-7234-8 (ebook)
    I. Title.
    [DNLM: 1. Counterfeit Drugs. 2. Fraud. 3. Drug Industry. 4. Drug and Narcotic Control. 5. Internationality. QV 773]

    364.16'68—dc23   2011046246

Printed in the United States of America

Contents

LIST OF ILLUSTRATIONS   xi

LIST OF ACRONYMS   xvii

PREFACE: A PERSONAL INTRODUCTION TO DANGEROUS MEDICINES   xxi

ACKNOWLEDGMENTS   xxv

INTRODUCTION   1

PART I: THE DEADLY WORLD OF DANGEROUS MEDICINES

1. HISTORICAL EXAMPLES OF DANGEROUS MEDICINES   11
   China-U.S. Heparin Scandal   11
   DEG: The Sweet, Syrupy Killer   17
   Tuberculosis: Poor-Quality Medicines Contribute
      to Drug Resistance   21

2. UNDERSTANDING THE PROBLEM   25
   What Are Dangerous Drugs?   26
   Guessing the Value of the Fake-Drug Market   30
   The Worsening State of Dangerous Medicines:
      A Growing Problem   34
   When Cheap Becomes Expensive: Why Quality Matters   35
   The Importance of Good Manufacturing Practice   36
   The Crucial Role of Medical Regulatory Authorities   42
   How Diversion Can Lead to Counterfeiting   45

3. OVERVIEW OF RESEARCH FINDINGS AND POSSIBLE SOLUTIONS   48
   Identifying Source and Target   49
   Field Research   52
   What Can Be Done?   55

PART II: DANGEROUS DRUG PROBLEMS BY LOCATION

4. AFRICA   60

    Counterfeit Malaria Treatments and
      Growing Drug Resistance   *61*
    Nigeria's Medical Regulatory Authority Steps Up   *64*
    Everyone Blames Foreigners   *67*
    NAFDAC's New Leadership   *69*
    Deploying New Technology   *76*
    Has Orhii Improved Drug Quality?   *78*
    A Shift to Local Production?   *88*
    Combating Corruption   *89*
    Political Will   *99*
    Changing Buying Behavior Takes Time   *105*
    Fraud and Theft: An Entry Point for Fake Drugs
      from East Africa to Nigeria   *106*
    East African Investigations   *107*
    Diverted Donor Drugs in Togo   *122*
    On the Trail of Stolen Medicines   *124*
    Post Hartcourt and Onitsha   *126*

5. INDIA   133

    Tracking the Counterfeiters   *144*
    Major Manufacturers   *152*
    Fake-Market Size   *156*
    Drug Production Oversight: The Ranbaxy Saga   *159*
    Whistleblowers and Informants   *167*
    Indian Exports to Africa   *168*
    International Networks   *171*
    Why India Should Favor More International Cooperation   *172*

6. CHINA   177

    Discovering the Source   *177*
    Locating the (Legal) Source of Substandard Ingredients   *183*
    The Battle against Counterfeiters in China   *187*
    Waking the Dragon: China Begins to Make an Effort   *188*
    Made in India, Faked in China   *196*
    The Way Forward for China   *198*

7. MIDDLE EAST 204

The Vicious Cycle Begins: Iraq 206
Dangerous Dealings: Fakes Infiltrate the Markets 207
The Smuggling Ring Expands: Syria and Jordan 208
Middle Eastern Governments Confront the
   Counterfeit Trade 211
Looking Ahead: More Challenges to Come 222
Conclusion 225

8. OTHER EMERGING MARKETS 227

Russia 227
Latin America 231
Southeast Asia 239
Turkey 242
Conclusion 245

9. THE ONLINE DRUG MARKET 246

The Case for Universal Jurisdiction 247
Internet Pharmacies: Are the Benefits Worth the Costs? 248
A Study of Credentials 249
Credentialed Sites Are Safe, but Buyer Beware
   (of Junk Mail) 250

PART III: DRUG-QUALITY ASSESSMENTS

10. FACTORS TO CONSIDER FOR RESEARCH 257

Bringing a Medicine to Market 258
Testing Drugs for Quality 259
The Minilab 261
Handheld Spectrometers 262
What We Procured from Where 263

11. RESULTS: WHAT WE FOUND 268

More Detailed Analysis with More Limited Datasets 270
The Role of Registration 271
Variability Analysis 278
Survey of Pharmacists 280

12. Results Broken Down for Africa, India, and Other Markets   283
      Africa   283
      India   291
      Remaining Cities Tested   294

13. Interpreting and Discussing the Results and Their Relevance   296
      Comparing Percent API in Various Failures:
         Breakdowns of the Data   298
      What Role Does Price Play in Quality?   299
      Further Price Analysis   310
      African Price Data   313
      Regulation, Income, and Literacy Rate: An Analysis
         of Possible Confounding Variables   313
      Regulation   315
      Macrolevel Analysis   317
      Counterfeit or Substandard?   318

Part IV: The Way Forward

14. Developing Medical Regulatory Authorities:
   The U.S. FDA as a Case Study   327
      Why an FDA? It Is All about Economics   328
      The Creation of the FDA   329
      Drug Regulation and the Market's Decisions   331
      The Massengill Massacre   332
      The FDA's Expanding Authority   334
      The FDA and China   336
      Challenges to MRA Development   340
      Limits to International Assistance   343
      Priorities for MRAs in Developing Countries   344
      The MRA Role in Protection through Registration   347
      Registration Is a Means, Not the End   348
      Challenges to Implementation   351

15. International Cooperation against Criminals
   and the Lethal Trade in Fake Medicines   356
      Counterfeit Medicines and International Law   358
      The Extent and Effects of Medicine Counterfeiting   362

Goals, Doctrines, and Proposals for a Counterfeit
Medicines Treaty *364*
Counterfeiting Crimes Are Widespread and Systematic *375*
WHO Authority to Negotiate a Treaty against
Medicine Counterfeiting *377*
A Call to Action *380*
Final Thoughts and Recent Developments *383*

16. A MARKET FOR PRODUCTS OF VARYING QUALITY AND
THE INTELLECTUAL PROPERTY DEBATE   387
Approaches to GMP *388*
In the End, It Is All about Endogenous Growth *392*

17. CONCLUSION   396

RELEVANT PUBLICATIONS BY ROGER BATE   401

NOTES   405

INDEX   423

ABOUT THE AUTHOR   457

List of Illustrations

Figures

1-1   Photograph of Real vs. Fake Artefan   2
1-1   Pharmaceutical Pill Production and the
        Supply-and-Distribution Chain   15
2-1   SET Diagrams   27
2-2   Total Percent Failures by City   32
2-3   Guesstimate of Global Fake Market Size (by $ Value)
        and Distribution   33
2-4   Counterfeit Drug Cases Opened by FDA's Overseas
        Criminal Investigation Department   35
2-5   Innovator Products versus Generics   39
2-6   LuMether Ad   45
2-7   Map of Donated Antimalarials to Africa and
        Their Subsequent Diversion   46
3-1   Plavix Packaging—Real vs. Fake   51
3-2   Plavix Pill—Real vs. Fake   51
3-3   Fake-Drug Trade Entry Points and Shipping Routes   53
4-1   Dora Akunyili Speaking at the American Enterprise
        Institute in 2007   65
4-2   Roger Bate with Paul Orhii at a Regulatory Seminar
        in London, May 2011   69
4-3   Nigerian-Impounded Chinese Fake of Indian Drug Lonart   74
4-4   Cell Receiving Text Verifying Authenticity   84
4-5   Sproxil Label   84
4-6   Artesunat Real   86
4-7   Artesunat Fake   87
4-8   NAFDAC Staff Being Trained on TruScan   88

4-9   Artesunate Front   *90*

4-10   Artesunate Back   *91*

4-11   Degraded Rimactizid   *91*

4-12   Results by Region and Size of Apparent Manufacturer   *96*

4-13   Fake Coartem   *103*

4-14   Operation Mamba Raids and Results   *111*

4-15   Operation Mamba Map—Expanding Cooperation   *112*

4-16   Antimalarial Drug Diversion   *118*

4-17   Flatpack Coartem   *120*

5-1   Aligarh Raid: Storage of Suspect API   *134*

5-2   Aligarh Raid: Unhygienic Fake Manufacturing   *134*

5-3   Ciprotab Fake Package   *136*

5-4   Ciprotab Back   *137*

5-5   Drug Control Officer after Raid   *140*

5-6   BCS Class Membership Risk Management   *142*

5-7   Former Delhi Police Chief Vijay Karan   *145*

5-8   Graph Comparing Sildenafil with Other Compounds   *147*

5-9   Falsified Viagra—Kamogra   *148*

5-10   Suresh Sati and Roger Bate outside Aligarh Market   *149*

5-11   Roger Bate outside Agra Market   *150*

5-12   Pill-Making Machine Captured in Raid   *153*

5-13   Delhi's Bhagirath Palace, Site of Legal and
           Illegal Medicine   *157*

6-1   Acetaminophen Synthesis   *182*

6-2   DNP Test vs. FBS Test   *201*

7-1   2007 Middle East Distribution Network   *219*

7-2   2009 Middle East Distribution Network   *221*

7-3   Amjad Markieh in Jail in Syria   *222*

7-4   Raed Abu Markieh in Jail in Syria   *222*

7-5–7-10   Syrian Customs Warehouse: Fake Products Destined
           for Iraq Recovered in Damascus   *223–224*

9-1   Fake Viagra Mailed from China   *251*

10-1   Roger Bate Learning to Use the Minilab in 2007   *262*

11-1   Quality Test-Drug Failures (Worldwide),
           Subcategorized by 0-Percent API, Visual
           Inspection Failure, and Degradation   *269*

11-2   Failure Rate by Registration Status   275

11-3   Failure Rate by Registration Status, Type, and Region   275

11-4   Breakdown of Registered and Nonregistered Drugs   277

11-5   Registered Drugs   277

11-6   Nonregistered Drugs   277

11-7   Pharmacy Survey: Percent Say Fakes a Problem   281

11-8   Pharmacy Survey: Percent Say Been Offered Fakes   281

11-9   Pharmacy Survey: Percent Offer Fakes Compared
            with Failure Rates   282

12-1   Quality Test Drug Failures (Africa), Subcategorized
            by 0-Percent API, Visual Inspection Failure,
            and Degradation   284

12-2   Drugs Failing Quality-Control Tests (India),
            Subcategorized by 0-Percent API, Visual Inspection
            Failure, and Degradation   293

12-3   Percent Failure by Drug Type, Pharmacies vs.
            Wholesalers   295

12-4   Drugs Failing Quality-Control Tests (Rest of the World),
            Subcategorized by 0-Percent API, Visual Inspection
            Failure, and Degradation   295

13-1   Testing Results by Region of Origin and Drug Type   299

13-2   Failure Rate by Country and City of Origin and
            Manufacturing Class   301

13-3   Failures with X Percent API   305

13-4   Box and Whisker Plot, Failures with X Percent API   305

13-5   Number of Failures with X-Percent API at Time
            of Testing: Africa   306

13-6   Number of Failures with X-Percent API at Time
            of Testing: India   306

13-7   Failures Grouped by API Concentration, as a Percentage
            of Total Failures: Africa   307

13-8   Failures Grouped by API Concentration, as a Percentage
            of Total Failures: India   307

13-9   Failures Grouped by API Concentration, as a Percentage
            of Total Failures: Rest of World   308

13-10 Fake Price Deviation from Quality Drug Price   311

13-11   Substandard Price Deviation from Generic Drug Price   *312*

13-12   Ratio of Input Costs in Retail Price   *314*

13-13   Modeling Poor Quality Drugs (IMPACT Data)
　　　　on Country Wealth   *318*

13-14   Fakes—Modeling Quality Based on Country/
　　　　City Wealth   *320*

13-15   Substandards—Modeling Quality Based on Country/
　　　　City Wealth   *320*

13-16   Both—Modeling Quality Based on Country/
　　　　City Wealth   *321*

13-17   All Together—Modeling Quality Based on Country/
　　　　City Wealth   *321*

13-18   Fake Artesunat Spectra vs. Real Artestunat Spectra   *322*

13-19   Spectra Analysis: Fake Artesunat Ingredients   *323*

14-1   Registration Timelines by Country   *350*

Tables

4-1   Spectrometry Testing Results by Region and Size
　　　of Apparent Manufacturer   *97*

4-2   Operation Mamba I, II, and III Summary Table   *112*

4-3   Average Drug Cost and Markup   *116*

4-4   Testing Results by Formulation and Presence
　　　of AMFm Logo   *117*

4-5   Summary of Results   *119*

9-1   Spectrometry Testing Results by Drug Type and Website
　　　Pharmacy Classification   *253*

11-1   Testing Results (Failures Recorded) by Country and City
　　　of Origin, and Registration Status   *273*

11-2   Testing Results (Failures Recorded) by Location of Origin
　　　and Registration Status and Medicine Type   *274*

11-3   Failure Rates by Registration Type   *276*

11-4   Failure Rates by Type of Producer   *279*

12-1   Drug Samples Failing Quality Tests (as a Percentage)   *288*

12-2   Drug Samples Failing Quality Tests   *289*

13-1   Testing Results by Region of Origin and Drug Type   *298*

13-2   Testing Results by Country and City of Origin
          and Manufacturing Class   *300*

13-3   Testing Results by Apparent Country of Manufacture   *302*

13-4   Testing Results by Region (and Size where Appropriate)
          of Apparent Manufacturer   *303*

13-5   Testing Results by Country and City of Origin and National
          Drug Registration List Status   *304*

Boxes

1-1   Pharmaceutical Pill Production and the Supply-and-
          Distribution Chain   *15*

2-1   Views on Fake Drugs   *27*

2-2   Innovator, Generic, and Copy Medicines   *38*

3-1   Plavix   *50*

4-1   Trovan and Polio: Nigeria vs. Pfizer   *70*

4-2   Punishment   *76*

4-3   Basic Testing Using the Minilab   *80*

4-4   Track and Trace   *82*

4-5   Holograms   *86*

4-6   Artesunat and Rimactizid   *90*

4-7   Local Production—A Solution to Local Access?   *92*

4-8   Ghana and PQM   *102*

4-9   Operation Mamba: Interpol's Multifaceted Attacks
          in East Africa   *110*

4-10   Subsidized Antimalarials: Is AMFm Working?   *114*

4-11   Diverted Medicines   *118*

5-1   Ciprotab   *136*

5-2   The Biopharmaceutics Classification System   *142*

5-3   Viagra   *147*

5-4   GSK Whistleblower   *164*

5-5   Rewarding Whistleblowers   *169*

6-1   Acetaminophen   *182*

6-2   Too Little, Too Late: China's Official Response to the
          Melamine Scandal—A Real Harm from China's
          Communism   *190*

6-3   Old Tests, New Tests, and Harparkash Kaur   *199*

7-1   Differences between Fakes in the Middle East and Africa   *218*

8-1   Thailand's GPO-vir   *240*

10-1   Raman Spectrometry   *264*

13-1   What Do Counterfeiters Put in the Fakes?   *322*

14-1   Medicines Transparency Alliance (MeTA)   *352*

14-2   Dangers of MRA Overreach   *355*

15-1   Strict Liability and the Issue of Intent   *378*

List of Acronyms

ACT   artemisinin-based combination therapies (e.g., Coartem), a cocktail antimalarial treatment, currently the most effective type of antimalarials on the market. To help prevent the further development of drug-resistant strains of malaria, the World Health Organization recommends that ACTs be used exclusively in all countries experiencing antimalarial drug resistance.

ADR   adverse drug reaction

AMA   American Medical Association

ANVISA   Agência Nacional de Vigilância Sanitária, Brazil's drug regulatory agency

API   active pharmaceutical ingredient

ART   antiretroviral therapy, the regime prescribed for HIV/AIDS patients.

ARV   antiretroviral drugs, a cocktail of medicines used to treat HIV/AIDS.

BRIC   "Brazil, Russia, India, China," the country-grouping used to reference the four largest and arguably most powerful emerging economies.

CAMEG   Centrale d'Achat des Médicaments Essentiels Génériques et des Consommables Médicaux, a Togolese agency responsible for the storage and distribution of antimalarial medications.

CDC   Centers for Disease Control and Prevention, the premier U.S. public health agency, involved in research and health advocacy in the United States and around the world.

CDSCO   Central Drugs Standard Control Organization, the regulatory body which oversees drug quality control in India.

CZSPL   Changzhou Scientific Protein Laboratories

DDOS   distributed denial of service

DEG   diethylene glycol, a poisonous organic compound often used as a solvent in chemical formulations. Prior to 1937, when DEG's toxicity was established, it was often used in pharmaceuticals.

EMA   European Agency for Medicines, the European Union's drug regulatory agency.

EU   European Union

FARC   Fuerzas Armadas Revolucionarias de Colombia (Revolutionary Armed Forces of Colombia)

FCTC   Framework Convention on Tobacco Control, the World Health Organization's first international treaty, which sets global standards on the regulation, sale, and use of tobacco products.

FDA   U.S. Food and Drug Administration, the regulatory body which controls all medical products and devices, food, cosmetics, radiation-emitting materials, and tobacco products in the United States.

GDP   gross domestic product

GMP   good manufacturing practice

GPHF   Global Pharma Health Fund

GSK   GlaxoSmithKline

HIV   human immunodeficiency virus

HPLC   high-performance liquid chromatography

IMF   International Monetary Fund

IMPACT   International Medical Products Anti-Counterfeiting Taskforce (World Health Organization initiative)

IP   intellectual property, refers to the body of law governing patents, copyrights, and trademarks

KEMSA   Kenya Medical Supplies Agency

MDC   Movement for Democratic Change, Zimbabwean political opposition party.

MeTA   Medicines Transparency Alliance

MHFW   Ministry of Health and Family Welfare, India

MRA   medical regulatory authority, e.g., the U.S. Food and Drug Administration.

NAFDAC   National Agency for Food and Drug Administration and Control, Nigeria

NIH   National Institutes of Health, primary agency responsible for biomedical and health-related research in the United States.

NMS   National Medical Stores, Kenya

OECD   Organisation for Economic Co-operation and Development

OSCS   over-sulfated chondroitin sulfate

PLA   People's Liberation Army, China

PQM   Promoting the Quality of Medicines

PQP   prequalification program, the World Health Organization's drug regulatory function.

SFDA   State Food and Drug Administration, China

SP   sulfadoxine-pyrimethamine, an older, monotherapy antimalarial drug.

TB   tuberculosis

TLC   thin-layer chromatography (Minilab)

UNICEF	United Nations Children's Fund
UNODC	United Nations Office on Drugs and Crime
USAID	United States Agency for International Development
USP	U.S. Pharmacopeia
WADRAN	West African Drug Regulatory Authority Network
WHA	World Health Assembly
WHO	World Health Organization
WIPO	World Intellectual Property Organization
WTO	World Trade Organization
XD-RTB	Extremely Drug-Resistant Tuberculosis

Preface

A Personal Introduction to Dangerous Medicines

In the autumn of 2004, I visited Bulawayo, Zimbabwe's second city. Like the rest of Zimbabwe, Bulawayo's one and a half million people were reeling under the weight of a collapsed economy, and sickness was widespread and often devastating. I spent the morning with Janice, a volunteer health worker, discussing the demise of the country's malaria-control program, which lacked the funds needed to procure insecticides, and the discussion left me depressed as I headed to lunch. Eating with Dr. Mark Dixon of Mpilo Hospital was even more upsetting: we discussed the problems he faced, from few ambulances due to a lack of fuel to an overflowing morgue due to the prevalence of human immunodeficiency virus (HIV). "It's not hard to find HIV-positive Zimbabweans," he lamented; "70 percent of my patients I treat for any reason carry the HIV virus."

I knew HIV patients were often malnourished, but as I toured the outskirts of Bulawayo, I was shocked by how emaciated most of these patients appeared. The majority of the people I saw would never receive any hospital treatment and were likely to die in their homes, some of which were nothing more than corrugated iron shacks. I conducted various interviews with doctors, patients, and city officials while I was in Bulawayo, and used these as the basis of an article for the *Wall Street Journal*. I wrote about Lucy—one of the lucky ones because she was receiving antiretroviral treatment—who told me, "If I had enough to eat I could take the adult dose." A thirty-four-year-old mother of two, Lucy was arguably fortunate to be in a suburb of Bulawayo where she was not likely to be ignored by local officials. Most of Bulawayo is run by the Movement for Democratic Change (MDC), a party that, in 2004, was in opposition to the ruling party of despotic president Robert Mugabe (as I write today, the MDC is in a very uneasy coalition with

Mugabe's party). Leading up to every election of the past decade, Mugabe's Zanu-PF party used food as a political weapon, limiting access to likely MDC voters. Much as doctors and social workers tried, they could not procure sufficient food for all of the HIV patients. Lucy was fragile, just able to lift her arm, but her social worker assured me I was seeing Lucy at her best. She was in a small, shabby house she shared with too many others in the unbearably poor peri-urban sprawl of Bulawayo.

I returned to interview Lucy the next year, but found that she had died. The medicines her doctor prescribed should have helped, but instead of improving, her health deteriorated, and she slowly slipped away as though she were not being treated. Dr. Dixon did not have time for lunch. As one of the few surgeons remaining in the country, he was operating around the clock. No other doctors had time to track down answers, but there were rumblings. Janice told me that quite a few patients had failed to respond to treatment, and Western pharmaceutical representatives I discussed it with in South Africa suspected the quality of the drugs was not good.

Drugs were supposed to follow a simple distribution chain from the Zimbabwean Department of Health directly to each clinic requiring them, but as with everything else in the country, health systems were not working properly, and drugs often either did not turn up or arrived late by circuitous routes. Since there were now no ambulances operating because fuel was rationed to Zanu-PF officials, it was not unusual to see patients and drugs arriving by horse-drawn cart. This was obviously not good for the patients, but it also meant that drugs were stored and transported in conditions likely to degrade sensitive HIV drugs.

In 2005, with rampant inflation and arbitrary violence, no one was particularly interested in investigating the source of poor-quality drugs, not least because patients had already taken most of the medicines and thrown away the packaging. The Zimbabwean government certainly was not interested, the doctors at Mpilo Hospital were already working to exhaustion, and the representatives of the Indian manufacturer—whose product may have been faked—showed no interest in discussing it. It was just another tragedy, another miserable fact, in the wretched lives of HIV-positive Zimbabweans.

But Lucy and so many others *should* have been saved. People were trying to help—money had been donated and drugs purchased—but a few greedy individuals were causing mayhem by exploiting urgent and enormous need where there was little vigilance over origin and quality. It is likely individuals were collecting discarded pharmaceutical drug packages and refilling them with what looked like the real drugs but contained nothing useful.

After returning to Washington, D.C., I kept thinking about this problem, and over the next few months, I decided to investigate drug quality more closely. My interest was reinforced by the chance watching of a movie. I'd already seen the classic film noir of 1949, *The Third Man,* but I mostly recalled the evocative zither music and the shadowy characters, rather than the plot. I had understood that the movie's central character, the likable rogue Harry Lime, played by Orson Welles, was trading in bogus pharmaceuticals, but I hadn't appreciated on first watching what an odious practice he was engaged in. The most heart-wrenching and rather overlooked scene is of discarded teddy bears piling up in a corner of a hospital ward. The bears signify the deaths from meningitis, ineffectively treated by the diluted penicillin, of numerous children who will no longer be around to play with them. The most famous scene from the movie is when Harry Lime explains to his friend Holly Martins (played by Joseph Cotten) from the top of a giant Ferris wheel why he has been stealing and diluting that penicillin in postwar Vienna: "Look down there," he says, referring to people on the ground. "If I offered you £20,000 for every one of those dots that stopped moving forever, would you really tell me to keep my money, or would you start calculating how many dots you could afford to spend—free of income tax?"

Although such stupendous profits, which would be measured in the multiple millions today, may be rare, hundreds, possibly thousands, of Harry Limes exist in the modern world, and they are plentiful enough that I have even met a couple. After all, in markets where counterfeiters are desperate enough to bother with such low-cost items as soaps, toothpaste, and shampoos, the margins on pharmaceuticals offer a highly attractive alternative.

Of course, in 2005 I didn't know any of this, but *The Third Man* made me angry, and so I decided to get involved. As a policy analyst I naturally began as any academic would, by reading the literature and talking to people, and much of what I learned in those interviews forms the basis of this book. During this process, I gradually realized I needed to know more than the limited literature would tell me. Who and where were the victims?

What was the source of the fake, substandard, or degraded drugs? I knew I would need to go to the field, sample, and test.

Beginning in mid-2007, my colleagues and I collected more than two thousand drug samples (mainly for treating bacterial infections and malaria) from nineteen cities in seventeen countries. We analyzed these drugs with multiple techniques and interviewed some of the drug sellers, some of the wholesalers, and, covertly, some members of counterfeit drug rings. In addition, in 2009 and 2010, we analyzed three samplings of Internet-sourced drugs, which were bought in or imported into the United States. Many of the results and analyses of these drug samplings were published in the scientific peer-reviewed literature from 2008 onward (a full list of publications is found at the end of this book), but some of the data and analyses are introduced here for the first time.

The people I met, the direct research I did, and the research of others left me convinced that there are thousands, maybe millions of Lucys; each has a story, some as tragic as Lucy's, but all involve worry, most involve fraud, and a lot immense suffering. It really is time to tackle this odious trade.

Acknowledgments

Many individuals and organizations have generously helped me; no private investigator did more than Suresh Sati, and no regulators did more than the two successive drug regulators from Nigeria, Doctors Dora Akunyili and Paul Orhii, both of whom have suffered death threats on account of their work (a bullet even grazed Dr. Akunyili's head). There are many more people to whom I owe a lot and without whom much of this book could not have been written. I would like to acknowledge them, but many would not thank me for compromising their anonymity in the intelligence community, which is increasingly vital for combating the traders of dangerous drugs.

Dr. Patrick Lukulay of United States Pharmacopeia taught me a great deal and introduced me to the Minilab system, developed by the Global Pharma Health Fund for use in developing countries where funds were tight and laboratory capacity limited. The Minilab provides a relatively inexpensive method for assessing basic drug quality, and we used it for most of the drugs we tested. Tom Woods, an African specialist and former deputy assistant secretary at the State Department, introduced me to Ahura Scientific, now part of ThermoFisher Ltd., which produced the TruScan, a handheld spectrometer that is incredibly useful for rapidly identifying and authenticating drugs in the field. Many people at Ahura were helpful, but spectroscopist Bob Brush spent hours training me on the TruScan's use and interpreting much of the data my research team generated. Independently, I came across the brilliantly named Phazir, a near-infrared spectrometer manufactured by a different company, Polychromix, now, like Ahura, taken over by the large company Thermo-Fisher, which we also deployed.

Two colleagues deserve immediate recognition for helping with drug testing and other analysis in support of this work over the years: I thank Kimberly Hess and Lorraine Mooney, both of Africa Fighting Malaria. In addition, Africa Fighting Malaria's director, Richard Tren, and Amir Attaran of Ottawa University have provided wonderful intellectual support.

My research assistant for two years during this project, Karen Porter, did much additional and valuable research. Carlos Odora, Franklin Cudjoe, Thompson Ayodele, Greg Starbird, Aimé Mutembe, William Awagu, Rajesh Singh, their staff, and other covert shoppers who would prefer not to be named, provided invaluable help in the collection of drugs studied. Sujat Khan and Barun Mitra helped identify locations from which random pharmacy selection occurred in India, interviewing shop owners and assisting with the initial drug collections. Numerous others deserve mention but would prefer that I not name them. To those in the security services, the police, private investigation, medical, and myriad other professions, I thank you all. I wish I had met Dr. Harparkash Kaur of the London School of Hygiene and Tropical Medicine sooner, because her knowledge and boundless enthusiasm might have improved my investigations; as it is, I am indebted to her for her analysis of our degraded and diverted and otherwise suspicious and hence interesting products. Paul Newton, Facundo Fernandez, and Aline Plançon also deserve mention for the insightful help and advice they gave. I would also like to thank Julissa Milligan, my current research assistant, and Olivia Joan Madrid, Andrew Brown, and Alex Rued, my recent interns, for providing valuable research for this book. They, Victoria Andrew, Kathy Swain and Dale Swartz provided editing of the manuscript. I owe an enormous debt to my bosses and backers. None of my research could have been undertaken without the support of AEI, Dany Pletka and Arthur Brooks in particular, and the financial backing of the Legatum Group. The Searle Freedom Trust funded the first Internet collection.

In the rest of this book I will refer to my actions in most instances in the singular, because I was often alone when I did them, but in some instances, particularly those involving drug collections and testing, I was with a research team. To simplify the narrative, I will not always explain which team members were with me. They know who they are, and they know the gratitude I feel toward them. Without their help this would be a far more limited book. Naturally, all errors are my own.

Introduction

While researching this book, I met several private investigators, including many based in India. If there was a unifying theme to their motivation, it would be one, well known among pharmacologists, that "while dying from a disease may be inevitable, dying from a medicine never should be." Yet dying from bad medicines is what happens to thousands of people every year.

In May 2008 in Delhi, one such investigator posed as a medical representative to buy counterfeit medicines from a wholesaler. He did it to show me how easy it is to procure dangerous products. He bought underdosed copies of popular drugs offered wholesale from a cheaper price list. He also received "helpful" advice that when selling to the public, he should take the substandard product he had just bought and mix it in with his regular stock at a rate of about 25 percent. That way, if an inspector called, refused a bribe, and insisted on taking samples for testing, he could claim he must have been sold a faulty batch. Pharmacists and others in the distribution chain procure fake products—often intentionally—but without evidence of obvious intent to harm, prosecuting those trading dangerous products is difficult.

The counterfeit industry excels at adapting to new conditions. Around the same time the private investigator easily procured poor-quality drugs from the wholesaler, India's drugs controller general had been proposing a national survey of drug quality, which the government promised would be a covert operation. Because fake-drug traders would have been exposed in such a survey, counterfeiters began printing "Physician's Sample: Not for Resale" on the foil of blister packs containing the pills, in the hope that an investigator would ignore any such samples he found on a pharmacist's premises.

Criminal reaction to government decisions to improve medicine quality is not unique to India; I've encountered creative responses to attempts

1

FIGURE I-1

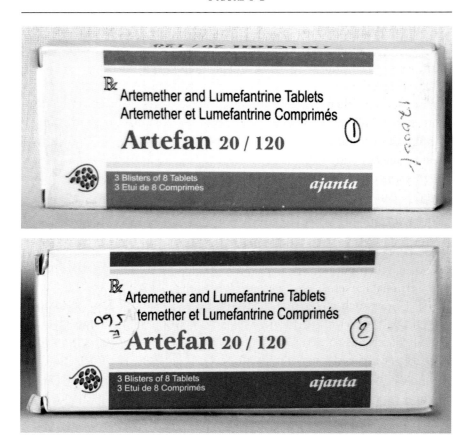

Photograph of real (top) vs. fake (bottom) Artefan

to combat fakes in every country I've investigated. Such actions create a dangerous environment, especially for consumers of these medicines, who almost certainly won't be able to differentiate the real drugs from the fakes. Figure I-1 shows two boxes of an antimalarial drug; the one on the top is real, made by Indian generic company Ajanta, and the one on the bottom is a fake. There is no obvious difference in the packaging. After four years of studying these types of products, I knew they were different only after chemical tests of the pills. The real and the fake drug both sold for less than five dollars.

A child suffering from malaria who took the drug on the right might die in forty-eight hours because the malaria remains untreated. With such a lethal outcome, one would think that action against counterfeiters would be global and swift. Yet counterfeiters are not actively pursued in more than half the countries in the world, and few countries entirely agree about what should be illegal or otherwise deterred. Without agreement on the severity of the offense, or even if there is an offense, extradition to a country that would prosecute is rare. This can make legal recourse for internationally traded counterfeits almost impossible; in addition, local prosecution is a legal headache, and other regulatory and civil actions are inconsistent and unpredictable.

In some countries, the law insists that a drug must cause harm before anybody can be prosecuted. If the child given the drug on the right above recovered from malaria (and most incidents of malaria do not result in fatalities), no action would be possible against the fake drug seller in these jurisdictions. Because malaria kills quickly, it may be possible to catch the fake drug seller, but how can ambiguous and weak laws address the patient with terminal leukemia who was shortchanged in life by a drug that did not work? Under such circumstances, giving a falsified drug to a sick patient may be the perfect murder weapon, because foul play is rarely suspected and almost impossible to prove—the patient was not expected to live and probably swallowed the evidence.

As we will see throughout this book, part of the reason that legal and medical experts have problems determining what type of dangerous product they are encountering is that the source of bad drugs may be anything from a chicken shed or garage to a state-of-the-art facility operated by international organized crime networks in a licensed production facility. Some drugs fail because a licensed producer at an otherwise legal factory cuts corners; others because of inevitable mistakes that just happen and cannot be attributed to cutting corners. As one can imagine, rectifying such a diverse set of problems can be difficult. It is less of a problem today in rich countries, but control was not as good even fifty years ago. Indeed, as I discuss in chapters 1 and 14 explicitly and imply at other times, today's problems in emerging markets mirror many problems the United States faced in the last century.

But perhaps the most intractable aspect of the problem is that many people—and not just the poorest and least educated—keep buying drugs they probably *know* are not real but that they believe are better than nothing. As I discuss in part III of this book, no one buys a drug believing it will not work, but people do buy cheaper drugs because they cannot afford more expensive ones, even when they know there is a nonnegligible risk that the cheaper one will not work properly. In some instances, fake versions of products, such as the one shown in the above figure, might be sold at lower price to the consumer, but this is rare as it tacitly tells the buyer that this is lower quality. This means that price is an unreliable indicator of quality. A fake Rolex is a tiny fraction of the price of the real watch because the buyer is party to the fraud. That is not the case with medicines. But of course not all poor quality products are fakes, and for substandards price may be a more reliable indicator of quality (part III discusses my original research on this important topic).

At this point I would have liked to present photos of two different legally made drugs, one that is routinely well made and one that is some-times made well. However, to do so would leave me open to legal action by the second manufacturer. Some companies routinely make more poor-quality products for markets they know will not be inspected. Many of these companies are *capable* of making good products; they simply cut costs to make more profit. But you can bet that their better samples are the ones sent to medical regulatory authorities when getting their products regis-tered. And even though I can present evidence that a particular sample is not up to standard, this could be due to reasons outside the manufacturer's control (such as wholesalers or retailers storing the product poorly so it has degraded). Such legal difficulties are faced by regulators, doctors, and ultimately patients every day, and it is an important reason why more is not done to prevent substandard medicines from reaching the market.

Part I, chapter 1 introduces three differing examples of dangerous drugs; chapter 2 describes some of the important and often contentious terms used in the discussions of poor-quality medicines: *degraded, substan-dard*, and *counterfeit* (or *falsified*). It also provides some examples of the kinds of problems we will encounter throughout the book and the entities and processes essential to preventing dangerous drugs from reaching patients. I also present a few estimates of the size of the market for these myriad deadly drugs. Chapter 3 introduces my extensive scientific field research, which was undertaken to try to understand the nature of the market in dangerous drugs. I conclude Part 1 with an outline of key policy responses worth considering to combat the menace of dangerous drugs. In that sense Part 1 can be seen as a lengthy summary of the book.

Part II provides geographical studies of deadly drugs, allowing me to dive into far more detail about the problem, those responsible for it, and those doing their best to improve drug quality. These chapters (4–9) do not always discuss the same problems in each location and not always the same problems from the same perspective. Given the varied nature of drug-quality problems, this is to be expected. As a result, some of the chapters have an unavoidably different feel to them compared to the others.

Nigerian authorities have been most forthcoming, even welcoming, of exposure of the problems and possible solutions in Nigeria. In contrast, the Indian authorities are generally quite hostile to independent researchers who expose their domestic problems and query official statistics, and since I have been doing both for quite some time, I have not had much luck convincing the Indian authorities to discuss the problem with me. India does have a fine network of private investigators who provided invaluable support to my research and helped me meet counterfeiters from two gangs. Both Nigeria and India had experts and doctors prepared to talk in depth. These chapters (4 and 5) discuss the varied problems of drug quality, but particularly of counterfeit drugs.

Corruption is a widespread and major problem in most of the emerging markets I investigated, but especially so in East Africa (discussed in chapter 4). Investigators are quite scarce, but some officials did talk on the record, and some investigators were very helpful. The sections on East Africa focus primarily on product diversion, for while diverted products (legal products stolen and reintroduced into the distribution chain by criminals) are generally high quality and not the subject of this book, they are also often traded by the same people who trade fakes. Indeed, diversion is in many locations the gateway to the counterfeit trade. Furthermore, given the billions of dollars in health aid sent to East Africa and the amount of product diversion I saw, it is perhaps the most significant problem this region faces. We meet a trader working on the borderline of legality in Tanzania and learn how diverted and fake drugs make it from East to West Africa.

In China (chapter 6) the problems are more varied than anywhere else in the world. The authorities are more reticent, the police more unapproachable, private investigators more frightened, and the doctors and other health professionals more cowed than anywhere else. Most would not talk on the record. But because China is the source of much of the world's counterfeit chemicals and finished products, what I did unearth is interesting. From American and European points of view, this chapter is also the most worrying because we discover how many APIs, active pharmaceutical ingredients, for legitimate Western companies come from unknown Chinese sources and, anecdotally, how many production plants are not up to good standards. We also see the interesting interactions between U.S. and Chinese officials around the heparin scandal that probably caused the death of 149 Americans (also discussed later in this book in chapter 14).

The chapter on the Middle East (chapter 7) is the first to discuss the major criminal gangs that pervade drug trading. A Jordan- and Syrian-based smuggling ring turned to the fake-drug trade when the chaotic situation in Iraq in 2003 provided an opportunity to make vast profits. Working initially with fake products from China, the gang sold bogus drugs into seven countries, with most tragic consequences in the Palestinian territories.

We then encounter unusual problems and solutions from five countries in chapter 8. In Russia we encounter a criminal politician causing mayhem with fake drugs. Brazil actively condones products of unproven quality, and Peru registers products that also are not proven; both have dangerous consequences, but Brazil proposes a novel solution for developing countries. In Turkey we find no fakes but typical battles over what technology should be introduced—and at what cost—to prevent fakes from entering from abroad. In Thailand we encounter the same types of local production-quality problems we also saw in Africa, but with less fatal results.

Chapter 9 in part II discusses online drugs. I tested the online pharmaceutical market, and this chapter not only outlines the many dangers of this market but also discusses how to safely purchase drugs sold on the Internet. This chapter finds many actors at their worst—criminals acting with impunity, impotent regulators unable or unwilling to act, grasping pharmacists selling bogus products for a few extra dollars, and the Western pharmaceutical industry misleading people about the dangers of the Internet.

Part III (chapters 10–13) discusses all the original data my research team generated from nineteen cities and the Internet. The results largely confirm most of the more anecdotal findings of other researchers and my own travels, but these data also show complexities about what should be a priority for poor countries and where there is little they can do without broader socioeconomic development.

Part IV builds on the country-level discussions and the data from part III and leads me to the policies that should be enacted to improve the drug-quality situation. Chapter 14 outlines how developing countries can learn from the U.S. Food and Drug Administration (FDA), both its current status and its history, as they work to build effective medical regulatory authorities. It discusses the political realities that affect an international ability to create better laws and a workable consensus on legal policy and puts forward priorities that are politically realistic, but not necessarily the most ideal, if all actors were acting rationally (chapter 15). Chapter 16 addresses medium-term solutions for developing countries that are not going to be able to make a leap from unregulated markets to Western standards overnight. Chapter 17 concludes the book with a plea for far stronger and more cooperative action against dangerous drugs. Following the final chapter, there is an appended list of my relevant published academic research on this subject. The book's accompanying online resource; the website http://www.phake-meds.org includes many more anecdotes about dangerous drugs around the world and other additional information.

PART I

The Deadly World of
Dangerous Medicines

1

Historical Examples of Dangerous Medicines

There are myriad problems with dangerous drugs, and to illustrate a few of them, this chapter offers three examples of drugs gone wrong. The evidence presented in this book demonstrates that drug quality is far worse in poorer nations, but we are all at risk, and the first example shows that the cleverest criminals can penetrate even the best-regulated markets in the world. It is about the recent heparin contamination in the United States and is a warning to us all. The second example is of diethylene glycol (DEG). The tragedy of DEG contamination is illustrative: it shows that even a well-known method of contamination that first killed patients over seventy-five years ago in America goes on killing today in emerging countries because of greedy criminals, lazy corporations, and weak regulations or regulators (box 1-1 shows where these two examples fit into the medicine supply and distribution chain). The third example shows how disease can bite back if we do not take the problem of fake drugs seriously. Treatments for tuberculosis (TB) are failing due to naturally acquired drug resistance; this resistance is accelerated by counterfeit and poor-quality products. While TB kills far more in poor countries than wealthy ones, the rich are not immune, as we have seen recently in the United States.

China-U.S. Heparin Scandal

In January 2007, the U.S. Food and Drug Administration (FDA) received news that three patients had died from reactions to heparin, a blood-thinning drug. For the entire previous year there were only three such deaths total, so officials quickly raised an alert. Between January 2007 and

May 2008, heparin had led to adverse effects, including breathing difficulties, plunging blood pressure, nausea, and excessive sweating, and, in a shocking 149 cases, death.[a]

The supplier of the dangerous heparin, Baxter International Inc. of Deerfield, Illinois, was the first to declare its product was contaminated, although a dozen firms in as many countries have since been affected. Baxter's laboratories ran tests that were more sensitive than those required by the FDA and found the contaminant: over-sulfated chondroitin sulfate (OSCS). Further tests confirmed that OSCS likely caused the symptoms described. OSCS is not used in any legitimate medicines and costs nearly one hundred times less than heparin.

Baxter's supplier of the active pharmaceutical ingredient (API), heparin, was another American company, Scientific Protein Laboratories, of Waunakee, Wisconsin. Scientific Protein Laboratories had a joint U.S.-Chinese branch called Changzhou Scientific Protein Laboratories (CZSPL), which purified pigs' intestines to make heparin. (Heparin is derived from animal mucosal tissues, almost exclusively from pigs.) In China, many small firms harvest basic heparin material by cooking and drying pig intestines. These firms are often run by small-scale farmers and are subject to almost no regulatory scrutiny.

In February 2008 the FDA was given permission to inspect CZSPL by the Chinese government. The FDA issued a warning letter the following month after finding many failings in good manufacturing practice (GMP), including the use of dirty and unsuitable equipment, a failure to ensure that impurities were removed effectively during processing, unverified quality tests, and a failure to adequately evaluate both the suppliers of heparin and the heparin itself.

CZSPL testified to the FDA that it followed current GMP and pointed out (correctly) that the contaminant (OSCS) could not have been detected

---

a. Throughout this book I will refer to 149 deaths related to the heparin tragedy; however, the actual number could be lower or higher than this because there is no entirely accurate estimation. For example, it is possible some of deaths were due to allergic reactions not attributable to contaminated heparin. The Pew Trust report "After Heparin" suggests the death toll is at least 178. See Pew Trust Group, "After Heparin: Protecting Consumers from the Risks of Substandard and Counterfeit Drugs," July 12, 2011, http://www.prescriptionproject.org/assets/pdfs/Pew_Heparin_Round4b_SinglePgs_b.pdf.

with the then-approved tests.[b] In other words, CZSPL passed the FDA's heparin requirement at the time. However, CZSPL's overall approach fell short of required FDA GMP standards.

One reason CZSPL had not been inspected and its GMP failures noted earlier is because it had a license only as a chemicals manufacturer, not as a pharmaceuticals manufacturer. This distinction put it outside the purview of China's State Food and Drug Administration (SFDA). The SFDA had no authority to investigate CZSPL's products, and other competent Chinese authorities neither inspected nor took action against the company. In fact, the U.S. FDA found that CZSPL bought, used, and shipped materials to the United States that came from a workshop the firm itself had designated unacceptable. The FDA recommended an import ban on all of the firm's products until CZSPL could show that all quality failings had been fully corrected.

Researchers working in collaboration with the U.S. FDA and supported by the U.S. National Institutes of Health found suspect samples from six companies associated with the contamination event. Twenty-eight additional samples manufactured between 2004 and 2007 contained contaminants and impurities that came from by-products of the purification process. These findings show that heparin had been contaminated with chemically modified heparin (including OSCS) by-products since 2004, and the findings support the theory that the contamination product came from a common source. To isolate the contaminant, however, the researchers had to develop a new test using highly sophisticated (magnetic resonance) techniques that had not previously been designated by any pharmacological or regulatory body as a test for heparin. The standard testing equipment used by companies importing API into the United States before this incident was high-performance liquid chromatography (HPLC), which yields highly accurate and reliable results when used properly. Still, even the $50,000 HPLC equipment could not distinguish between pure and adulterated heparin, which prompted the researchers to say their

---

b. According to Roger Williams, CEO of U.S. Pharmacopeia (USP), the organization that establishes standards for testing, the identification test used at the time was simply a flame test for the presence of sodium. This has since been changed to more robust tests (personal communication with the author, March 14, 2011).

findings strongly suggested that the contamination was very deliberate and amazingly sophisticated; it seemed to have been designed to beat the tests performed on the drug.

Industry sources estimate that the profit the Chinese rogues made in the Baxter case could have been as little as $1 million. Even ignoring the tragedy of 149 deaths, the economic costs of product recalls, investigations, and especially damage to reputations, exceeded the profits hundreds of times over.

Chinese authorities eventually acknowledged that heparin produced in China contained OSCS, but they still do not accept that it caused the adverse deaths attributed to the drug. Nonetheless, the link is indisputable. Once Baxter's OSCS-contaminated heparin was pulled from the market, reports of otherwise unexplainable adverse reactions ceased.

The contaminated heparin episode, which is essentially a case of counterfeiting—passing OSCS off as heparin—demonstrates that even the most rigorous regulatory system is vulnerable to clever fraud and may be left playing catch-up when people start to die. Interestingly, there were no recorded deaths in Europe from contaminated heparin. The explanations for this conflict slightly. Roger Williams, chief executive officer of U.S. Pharmacopeia (USP), says that European Pharmacopoeia had a better identification test, enabling an Irish official to spot the bad heparin so that it was not distributed. In contrast, Guy Villax, chief executive officer of the Portuguese pharmaceutical company Hovione, told me that contaminated heparin did cause deaths in Europe before it was discovered, but the European Union (EU) data are "badly recorded," so deaths may not have been attributed to it.

In many of the poorest countries, regulations and the legal systems are so weak or corrupt and fraud is so easy to perpetrate that patients take a risk every time they use a health care product, but in the richest countries of the world, such sophisticated and lethal frauds are rare. Private brand protection and enforced regulation prevent most of the dangers of poor-quality drugs. But given that probably 40 percent of America's drug components come from China, the heparin contamination provides a stark example of the potential risks to the U.S. drug supply (for more information on production supply lines, see box 1-1 below). Pharmacist Cynthia Reilly, a director of the American Society of Health-System Pharmacists, says chemicals coming from China put the United States at risk. In April 2011, she told me,

Box 1-1
Pharmaceutical Pill Production and the Supply-and-Distribution Chain

The figure below outlines the supply and distribution chain for pharmaceuticals, and presents some examples of how fakes can infiltrate the system.

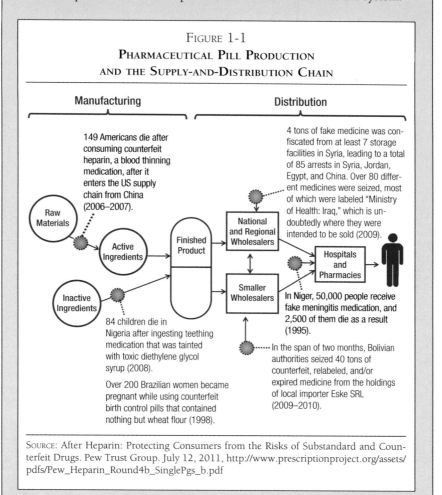

Figure 1-1
Pharmaceutical Pill Production and the Supply-and-Distribution Chain

Manufacturing

Distribution

149 Americans die after consuming counterfeit heparin, a blood thinning medication, after it enters the US supply chain from China (2006–2007).

Raw Materials

Active Ingredients

Finished Product

National and Regional Wholesalers

4 tons of fake medicine was confiscated from at least 7 storage facilities in Syria, leading to a total of 85 arrests in Syria, Jordan, Egypt, and China. Over 80 different medicines were seized, most of which were labeled "Ministry of Health: Iraq," which is undoubtedly where they were intended to be sold (2009).

Hospitals and Pharmacies

Inactive Ingredients

Smaller Wholesalers

84 children die in Nigeria after ingesting teething medication that was tainted with toxic diethylene glycol syrup (2008).

Over 200 Brazilian women became pregnant while using counterfeit birth control pills that contained nothing but wheat flour (1998).

In Niger, 50,000 people receive fake meningitis medication, and 2,500 of them die as a result (1995).

In the span of two months, Bolivian authorities seized 40 tons of counterfeit, relabeled, and/or expired medicine from the holdings of local importer Eske SRL (2009–2010).

Source: After Heparin: Protecting Consumers from the Risks of Substandard and Counterfeit Drugs. Pew Trust Group. July 12, 2011, http://www.prescriptionproject.org/assets/pdfs/Pew_Heparin_Round4b_SinglePgs_b.pdf

(continued)

Box 1-1 (*continued*)

**PHARMACEUTICAL PILL PRODUCTION AND THE
SUPPLY-AND-DISTRIBUTION CHAIN**

Basic chemicals and other materials are procured from chemical plants by pharmaceutical manufacturers and sent to a site for the synthesis and production of the active pharmaceutical ingredients (APIs), which are the key ingredient in any medicine, but may only make up 15 percent of the actual pill by weight. Since API dosing must be precise, any medicine allowances for variations in APIs are the least tolerated by regulatory bodies.

APIs will usually be shipped to another location where they will be mixed with inactive ingredients, usually called excipients, and often provided by other suppliers. Excipients, such as dyes, coatings, sweeteners, and binding agents, are important to ensure a medicine doesn't degrade or crumble too quickly or too slowly and hence delivers the API the patient requires. Excipients often make up the bulk of any pill. The finished pill will be packaged and sent for distribution, where over weeks and months it may pass through numerous brokers and wholesalers, repacked with different inserts (often for language requirements of countries), until it arrives at hospitals and pharmacies, where it is dispensed to patients.

Problems can occur at any of the production stages to make a drug substandard, and fake versions of the intermediary or final products may be inserted anywhere along the supply chain. And as more and more APIs and finished products are imported into the United States every year monitoring chemical quality and entry points for fake versions is harder and harder.

"There are more heparins occurring every day, not through lethal products, but because quality is lower, causing far more product recalls, and, hence, drug stockouts." She claims this is leading to increasing morbidity and even mortality in American patients.

China will appear many times in this book as a source of dangerous products. China is developing many of the institutions of a modern economy at breakneck speed and often seems incapable of preventing widespread fraud. Many of the problems it has today mirror the problems America faced in the earlier parts of the last century, when Americans were vulnerable to cavalier attitudes toward safe manufacture. The precursor of the U.S. FDA was the Bureau of Chemistry, which sprang from the Department of Agriculture; its main focus was the adulteration, contamination, and dilution of food products, as these had been problems for centuries.

Late nineteenth and early twentieth century surveys of products in the U.S. market found numerous examples of animal parts or animal infestations in food and pharmaceuticals. The U.S. Bureau of Chemistry reported around 1900 that the drug supply was "unreliable, the purity suspect, the price high and variable, and the corrupted substances sometimes fatal."[1] Modern parallels were seen as recently as 2010, when a batch of counterfeit Viagra, whose major ingredients were bat and bird droppings, was seized in New Zealand. According to Dallas Mildenhall, a New Zealand government scientist, other intercepted medicines have been found to contain whole insects, dust mites, hair, charcoal, and heavy metals, including arsenic and mercury.[2]

Although allowing such disgusting contamination of products is never acceptable, it is surely worse to add an ingredient known to be toxic simply to make a bit more money. This leads to the next example, just one of many possible instances where bad practices are echoed globally again and again, and often with distressingly similar results. Tragically, we see the same problems Americans encountered more than one hundred years ago appearing today in other countries.

DEG: The Sweet, Syrupy Killer

The first antibiotics had scarcely been invented before they were misused with fatal consequences. In 1937 the newly developed sulfonamides were wildly popular, and a resulting "sulfa craze" prompted experiments with hundreds of formulations. One of these included an even newer compound, diethylene glycol, a sweet-tasting, syrupy solvent. Chemists at the highly respectable, long-established drug company S. E. Massengill Company of Bristol, Tennessee, mixed sulfanilamide with DEG to make an elixir easier for patients to swallow than the pill formulation.

The problem? DEG is fatally toxic.

Massengill's chemists had taste-tested the syrup in the not particularly scientific way of simply swallowing a tiny amount. They found it sweet, odorless, and nearly translucent; that is, well suited to their needs.

Fortunately for those doing the testing, they did not ingest enough to cause harm. Others were not so lucky.

In December 1937, *Time* magazine reported that seventy-three deaths had been attributed to Massengill's elixir. In the end, the elixir probably caused 105 deaths. Harold Watkins, the company's chief chemist, took his own life.[3] The company settled civil suits while fighting prosecution for criminal carelessness. There were no specific regulations requiring toxicity tests at the time, but several papers had been published in medical journals explaining the risks of DEG.

The FDA could prosecute Massengill only for mislabeling its product: an elixir should have contained alcohol, and this one did not. The company was fined $26,000 (about $240 per death), the largest fine the FDA had imposed to that time. Public outcry over the incident broke a congressional deadlock on increasing the power and scope of the FDA, and on June 15, 1938, the Federal Food, Drug, and Cosmetic Act was signed into law. Among other things, the law required companies to perform product-safety tests prior to marketing.

The disaster drove public support for the watchdog role of the U.S. regulator. The changes had immediate and long-term ramifications for companies. The incident provided immediate scientific lessons, provoked media discussion within weeks, and sparked discourse and dissemination of data in academy and business circles within months. Yet, even after DEG's danger became known globally, the push for political changes to prevent its use really occurred only in the United States and a few other rich countries. The bigger tragedy tied to this incident is that DEG continues to kill in almost the same way—a toxin adulterating health care products—over seventy years later. Today, the cause is deliberate cost-cutting by unscrupulous manufacturers who put their greatest entrepreneurial efforts into maximizing profits regardless of the danger to patients and absolving themselves of any accountability to victims.

DEG costs about half as much as glycerol (glycerine), which is safe for use in pharmaceuticals, skin care products, and foods. DEG has many industrial uses, including as a solvent for oils, resins, and dyes; as a humectant in printing inks and tobacco; and as a component in brake fluid, lubricants, and heating oil. It has been used as a coolant and anti-freeze, but ethylene glycol is more common. Even now, however, there are limited data on its exact toxicity in humans, although researchers suspect that a lethal human dose when ingested may be as low as 0.1 percent of body weight.[4]

Despite Massengill's highly publicized disaster, DEG continues to pose a global threat. In 1969, seven children in Cape Town, South Africa, died of kidney and liver damage after being treated by their parents with an over-the-counter sedative contaminated with DEG. In Spain in 1985, five patients receiving medical treatment for burns died because the ointment being used contained DEG.[5] [c]

In 1986, twenty-one patients died of kidney failure in Bombay, India, after being treated with hospital supplies of glycerol contaminated with DEG. India saw tragedy again in 1998 when thirty-three children, all between two months and six years of age, died of kidney failure in Gurgaon, near Delhi, after being prescribed a cough mixture by local, private medical practitioners. The medicine was made by a local company, and, as in the Massengill case, the active ingredient (acetaminophen in this case) was genuine; the problem was in the solvent syrup, which was contaminated with DEG.[6]

Nigeria has been badly affected twice, and both incidents caused deaths of children. In 1990, forty-seven children died after being treated with cough syrup. The syrup had been contaminated with DEG by wholesalers supplying local, small-scale pharmaceutical manufacturers. The second incident, as recent as 2008, is the last major recorded event of DEG poisoning. A baby-teething syrup containing DEG caused the deaths of eighty-four children between the ages of two months and

---

c. When a weak grape harvest failed to produce wines of sufficient sweetness and body in the mid-1980s, Austrian wine producers struggled to fulfill massive supermarket contracts to supply the German taste for sweet white wines. This prompted a conspiracy among producers, their chemists, and their shipping agents to adulterate the wines with DEG, which produced the desired results. A scandal broke after routine postmarketing lab testing in Germany found the wines had been contaminated. Most samples contained only trace amounts (well below toxic levels), but one bottle of this Austrian wine contained enough DEG to kill an adult. During the subsequent prosecutions, one convicted producer committed suicide, and the whole Austrian wine industry collapsed. The industry did not rebound to pre-1985 levels of production until 2001; see John Tagliabue. "Scandal over Poisoned Wine Embitters Village in Austria," *New York Times,* August 2, 1985; web, July 11, 2011, http://www.nytimes.com/1985/08/02/world/scandal-over-poisoned-wine-embitters-village-in-austria.html.

seven years. The National Agency for Food and Drug Administration and Control (NAFDAC), Nigeria's drugs regulator, traced the source of DEG contamination to an unlicensed local chemical dealer who had sold DEG to a pharmaceutical manufacturer.[7]

Incidents in Bangladesh and Argentina around 1992 were both traced back to adulteration by local manufacturers. In Bangladesh, it took two years and 339 cases of kidney failure in children to isolate the cause as acetaminophen syrup contaminated with DEG.[8] In Argentina, a traditional remedy, propolic, had been dissolved in glycerol contaminated with DEG; ninety-two people died before the cause was identified.[9]

Many of the recent incidents have involved fraudulent or poorly regulated manufacture of pharmaceutical ingredients in China. When children started dying of kidney failure in Port-au-Prince, Haiti, in 1995, epidemiologists identified acetaminophen syrup made by a local producer as the likely cause. Because this producer had close links to the government, samples were sent to the U.S. Centers for Disease Control (CDC) for analysis. The glycerol had been contaminated with DEG. In this case, the U.S. FDA took up the investigation and tracked the supply through two European traders to a chemical factory in Dalian in northeastern China. The U.S. Embassy in China spent eighteen months seeking the permission of the Chinese government to inspect the factory; by the time approval was granted, the factory had been shut down and stripped empty.[10]

In 2006 the FDA and CDC became involved when patients treated in a hospital for hypertension and diabetes in Panama City, Panama, started to develop contradictory symptoms, reminiscent of the Haiti case. Some elderly patients taking blood-pressure medications had developed a cough, and it was a scarcely remembered treatment with contaminated syrup that ultimately killed at least 145 people. This shipment was traced back to China via agents in Panama and Spain, who were prosecuted. At the request of the U.S. FDA, Chinese authorities investigated the manufacturer, Taixing Glycerine Factory, which it subsequently closed. The Chinese agent, CNSC Fortune Way, which is government owned, was never sanctioned and is still trading. Its website claims it to have a "sound reputation for the best quality and competitive prices, achieving significant growth over the past four years." As of March 2011, no one in China has been held accountable for the deaths in Panama.[11]

The Chinese response to the world outcry over contaminated tooth-paste in 2007 was more encouraging. Thirty brands, some of which were counterfeited (including Sensodyne sold at private garage-type sales in the United Kingdom, and Colgate-Palmolive brands found in dollar discount stores in the United States), were found in thirty countries. At first, China claimed the level of DEG used was within safe limits, but China's SFDA later banned all use of DEG in toothpaste. The U.S. FDA now tests all imports containing glycerol for DEG.[12]

From the Massengill disaster in 1937 to the last documented case in 2008, 750 deaths in ten countries have been attributed to drugs contaminated with DEG. These cases involve a mixture of criminal counterfeiting and negligent production of substandard medicines. The guilty nearly always escaped sanction.

Through the research I have conducted, I have come across many examples of manufacturers, traders, and even pharmacists and doctors who think only about increasing profits by any means they can get away with, as if making, selling, or prescribing substandard medical products were no different from faking designer-clothing labels. Although today most examples occur in emerging markets, some issues still arise in the richest countries, reminding us that no country is immune or can regulate its way to complete safety.

Tuberculosis:
Poor-Quality Medicines Contribute to Drug Resistance

About a third of the world's population, concentrated in poorer regions of the world, may be infected with TB, which generally lies dormant until the carrier's immunity is impaired by another disease (often HIV infection). Without treatment, about half of the patients with active TB will die. According to World Health Organization (WHO) estimates, TB claimed 1.7 million lives in 2009, most of them in Africa.[13]

Standard treatment for TB is long and complicated; it requires that patients take four different antibiotics at different times in different combinations, amounting to fifteen to twenty pills per day over a six-month period. The side effects of treatment are unpleasant, including fever, vomiting, jaundice, and blurred vision. If treatment is stopped too soon or skipped, the bacteria that are still alive can become resistant to the drugs taken, leading to a form of TB that is much more dangerous and difficult to treat. Drug-resistant strains of TB can quickly become fatal, especially if a patient's immune system is already compromised. Resistance-driven drug failure is believed to be due largely to patient noncompliance with the drug regimen prescribed. When people start to feel better, they often stop taking the medicine before the TB is completely overwhelmed by the drug. As a result, the still-living strain develops resistance to that drug regimen.

This problem is not unique to the developing world. The same process is the main reason Western health care systems are plagued by "superbugs." In poorer locations, though, patient negligence is compounded by irregular supply, stockouts, and inferior medicines that fail even when the patient completes the course of treatment. My research team's samplings of drugs in nineteen cities from seventeen countries usually included TB medicines. In some locations, up to 30 percent of TB drugs were substandard; they either were underdosed in some way or had degraded, being sold after expiry in some cases. An aggregate failure rate of about 8 percent across all samplings shows this is a significant problem. Such a failure rate surely means a portion of the cause of the failure of TB drugs is because patients have taken substandard treatments.

Rifampicin is a key anti-TB treatment. Fake versions of real rifampicin drugs are readily available in India. Rifa i6 Kid is a children's treatment for TB, and, unfortunately, there are fake versions of it too. Such a treatment is likely to be administered at home, often without a prescription, which makes detection of fake TB drugs harder. A doctor at a clinic might see enough similar cases to recognize treatment failure due to fake drugs, but a mother has almost no chance. Many mothers choose to treat their children for TB at home because it is less expensive, but they also do it because TB carries a stigma as a poor person's disease and a mother may be too humiliated to admit her child has TB. In some circles, if a child has TB, society sees it as the mother's failing and not just a medical problem. The symptoms of TB are well recognized, and most mothers are able to buy familiar brands over the counter. Buying without a prescription is not allowed under Indian law, but my research team's surveys showed that all of the seventy pharmacies we sampled from in Delhi, Chennai, and Kolkata dispensed medicines without a prescription.

The Rifa i6 Kid TB treatment sample was procured for me by a private investigator in Delhi. It was underdosed, containing about two-thirds of the required API, and partly explains why TB treatment failure continues to grow in the developing world.

Aside from the health burden, the financial costs of TB are astounding. The total drug costs for standard treatment, known as first-line treatment, are about $60, reasonable even for many of the poor in many countries. Second-line treatment for resistant cases (multidrug-resistant TB) consists of a bigger range of less-effective drugs with more severe side effects for a period of two years; the treatment costs no less than $15,000.[14]

Even if a patient with TB is able to afford such extensive and expensive care, treatment may fail again, resulting in extremely drug-resistant TB (XDR-TB). As the name implies, XDR-TB is effectively untreatable for many patients. In 2006 an outbreak of newly infected XDR-TB was reported in South Africa; that is, patients who had not previously been treated for TB had been infected first by an already extremely resistant strain. Fifty-three patients were admitted to the hospital, and fifty-two died. South Africa is the most affluent country in Africa and had the resources to treat XDR-TB; had the extent of drug resistance been known earlier, fewer lives would have been lost. Even so, subsequent outbreaks in South Africa have claimed the lives of two-thirds of those infected.[15] Given a cost of at least $15,000 per patient and treatment requiring hospitalization (preferably in isolation), many diagnostic laboratory tests, access to all available TB drugs, and considerable expertise in TB treatment, it is not surprising that few people are properly treated, even where staffing is available. Generally, patients are kept in isolation and treated with medications that fail most of the time; as a result, most patients infected with XDR-TB die.

Although most TB deaths occur in poor nations, a TB epidemic hit New York City between 1984 and 1994, centered on the poorer immigrant areas, particularly Harlem. Patient compliance was low and drug resistance high; at its peak in 1992, there were 441 cases of multidrug-resistant TB. Eventually, the city was able to control the epidemic, but the total cost far exceeded $1 billion.[16] At such cost, it is easy to see why few patients in the developing world receive adequate treatment for resistant strains.

All the major killers currently subject to international attention—HIV, malaria, and TB—are infectious diseases caused by pathogens that regularly mutate, thereby protecting themselves from attack by drugs. Moreover, drugs have been counterfeited, falsified, or manufactured so poorly that they do not work for all of these diseases. Substandard drugs can be fatally poisonous or fatally useless, and the enhancement of drug resistance can make effective drugs obsolete; yet the problems of the poor-quality drugs are somehow not serious enough to build political consensus on allocating enough resources to fix them. Herein lies a major cause of the failure to put an end to the market for dangerous drugs.

This chapter has introduced three different types of problems—counterfeited heparin, substandard (sometimes intentionally substandard) products made with DEG, and substandard and degraded anti-TB medicines—to demonstrate just a few of the wide-ranging dangers that exist. It is now time to define the problems so that it is easier to understand how to combat each.

2

Understanding the Problem

Ineffective drugs take lives, waste money, and make precious cures useless. Drugs have been recycled after their expiry date; they have been contaminated with fatal toxins; they have been made too weak or with no active ingredient at all. From the evidence I have seen over the last few years, new ways to falsify medicines are invented every week to squeeze out more profits. Often, the victims are the world's poorest people: the rural and urban poor struggle to afford treatments for deadly diseases such as malaria, tuberculosis, and bacterial infections, only to find out that the medicines it cost so much of their meager resources to purchase are useless or even toxic. There is growing recognition and agreement about this, but beyond the basic details, the issues related to counterfeit and substandard pharmaceuticals are mired in disagreement.

Medicines may not cure as expected for several reasons. For the majority of the world's population this is exacerbated because they so often diagnose and treat themselves because doctors are scarce and expensive, especially in the vast rural areas of many poor countries. The cheapest tests for malaria are more expensive than the cheapest drugs, so patients may choose to self-treat for malaria even though the fever may have another cause. Even good drugs affect people differently, and the threat posed by poor-quality drugs makes the practice of self-treatment even more dangerous. Identifying bad drugs takes considerable training and skill; self-treating patients have little chance of recognizing that a drug is of poor quality before the damage—sometimes fatal—is done.

Only the vaguest estimates of the size or spread of the problem exist, and they have been hotly contested. There is controversy even about how to define these dangerous drugs because some are cheaply made pills with ersatz ingredients pretending to be something they are not (falsified or counterfeit), others are just shoddily produced (substandard), and still others are degraded. These may have been stored or transported badly—some require cold-chain storage, which many developing countries are far from able to guarantee—or they may have been offered for sale in less than optimal conditions, such as after being inadvertently baked out in the open by a tropical sun. There is also a flourishing trade in drugs at or near expiration, which—instead of being destroyed or returned to the distributor—are sold on the black market with new expiration dates.

What Are Dangerous Drugs?

Definitions of "dangerous drugs" are far from exciting, but lack of agreement on how to define terms is part of the reason there is insufficient political will to combat the problems discussed in this book (see box 2-1).

Three main types of drugs are dangerous to consume. The most universal are degraded products. Most people have come across these: any drug past its expiration date is technically degraded. If you have Tylenol, Panadol (or any brand of acetaminophen) in your bathroom cabinet that has expired, throw it away. Some products degrade slowly and may be useful after expiration, sometimes years after, but others, such as acetaminophen, can be lethal. Unexpired products that have been stored badly in transit or at their final location may decay before their official expiration date. This problem is considerable in the poorest locations; from my team's samplings, about 2 percent of the drugs procured in Africa were degraded versions of the correct medicine.[a] However, our protocol limited covert buyers to sampling only from formal pharmacy premises. This was necessary to ensure we used a standard methodology in all of the cities we sampled from, to allow us to compare our findings. In the poorest places, the poorest people cannot afford pharmacy prices and instead buy from street markets, kiosks, hawkers on buses and trains, and quacks traveling from village to village selling drugs from the back of a bicycle. To my knowledge, nobody has systematically surveyed these outlets in more than one location, but from what we do know, the quality of products sold is likely to be frighteningly low, because all of the factors that make drugs dangerous are likely present in these informal settings.

---

a. In testing the drugs procured for other studies, we found that one drug in particular, Coartem, an antimalarial, seemed to work well even after its shelf life had passed.

Box 2-1
VIEWS ON FAKE DRUGS

FIGURE 2-1
SET DIAGRAMS

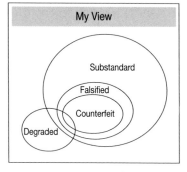

My View

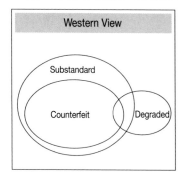

Western View

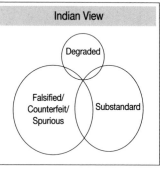

Indian View

The first SET is how I view the problem. Degraded drugs are a separate issue and to the side and largely an emerging market problem. Counterfeits are a significant problem and make up the majority of, but not all, falsified products (if one assumes counterfeits must include a trademark violation). Given that one cannot be sure of *any* drugs that have false data about their provenance, all of these products are within the subset of substandard drugs. There are many substandard products that are not falsified.

(continued)

Box 2-1 (*continued*)
VIEWS ON FAKE DRUGS

The second SET represents the opinion of an average Western businessman. The main point to note here is that most substandard drugs are counterfeits and there is no discussion of the distinction between falsified and counterfeit drugs. (My opposition to this is that it underplays the vast amount of substandard drugs on the market; in addition, there is ignorance of non-counterfeit falsified products.)

The third SET is broadly that of a quintessential Indian trader. The main point to note here is that there is overlap between substandard and falsified products, but there are falsified, even counterfeit, products that are not substandard. (My main opposition to this is the notion that there are any falsified or counterfeit drugs that can be considered of standard quality.)

The second category of dangerous drugs is substandard products, that is, those products that, generally speaking (and there are gray areas, as we shall see), are *unintentionally* made poorly. Most people in the West have never come across these products because of good quality controls, but they are prevalent in poorer locations.

The final category of dangerous drugs—and the main subject of this book—is falsified medicines: these are products intended to lead buyers to believe a product is something it is not. These are found in every country in the world, and the deception can range from repackaging discarded expired medicines to intentionally producing cheap drugs without caring about quality. In this book, I generally use the words "counterfeit" and "fake" interchangeably with "falsified," for they all mean the same thing to me: intentionally mislabeled medicines.[b] "Falsified medicines" is the least controversial term in legal circles, but "counterfeit" is the more common term. A few combative Indian businessmen tell me some drugs Western companies would call counterfeit are simply good copies of brand-name

---

b. However, if one defines counterfeit as a subset of falsified to say that counterfeit includes a trademark violation, then I am happy to go along with this distinction (see fig. 2.1 for a graphical representation).

pharmaceuticals that have been manufactured hygienically, with the correct ingredients, and in the correct proportions. Many of these drugs breach intellectual property rights but are not inherently dangerous as long as they are perfect copies. These businessmen may be right, but in many unfortunate cases, the motivation for counterfeiters is short-run profits, not reliable products with sustained repeat business. Most illegal drug manufacturers are more inclined to perfect the packaging of their products than the contents, and they then try to pass their dangerous wares off as the real thing. And it is surely too much to assume that any company that will lie about the provenance of a drug can be trusted to make a drug that will always work. So for the purposes of this book, I assume all counterfeits/falsified medicines are substandard.

The problem in combating all of these dangerous drugs is that the remedies for each category often differ greatly, and the myriad interests involved in addressing policy promote their particular concerns above others, which can lead to stalemate. Conflicting interests have often led to an impasse in efforts to control dangerous drugs. Figure 2-1 shows some of the beliefs (including my own) about how dangerous drugs should be viewed.

Dangerous drugs cause problems in at least four ways. First, the drugs may be contaminated with pathogens (fungi, bacteria, viruses, or parasites) or with heavy metals or other toxic elements (such as drugs contaminated with DEG or the suspect heparin products described in chapter 1). Second, drugs that do not contain the correct ingredients or the correct ratio of ingredients will not treat the conditions or diseases for which treatment was prescribed, and death may result (as is the case with the TB drugs described in chapter 1). Third, drugs that contain some of the right active ingredients but are badly formulated may lead to death because the drugs are not biologically available; that is, they may not be absorbed in the gastrointestinal tract, so they are not taken into the blood stream (this is a major problem for many suspect antimalarial drugs I encountered in my research). Fourth, even fairly well-formulated drugs made by legitimate firms can contribute to drug resistance across the population if the formulation is reasonably good—such that it partially cures or prevents immediate death—but is not completely right and encourages the most robust bugs to become resistant. This renders even the very best quality drugs useless, as the XDR-TB example in chapter 1 demonstrates.

Public health professionals everywhere, but especially in emerging markets, bitterly resent the loss of faith bad drugs cause among their patients; they spend much of their energy trying to steer patients away from hocus-pocus remedies toward (much more expensive) Western medicine, only to have the rug pulled out from under them by the fake-drug trade.

These drugs directly or indirectly cause thousands of deaths every year. One not particularly scientific estimate produced by the International Policy Network in London claims poor-quality drugs kill 700,000 people a year, but the true figure is not known.[1]

Unfortunately, solutions have been piecemeal so far, partly because of legitimate arguments over definitions, but more often because arguments are used to cover vested interests or rekindle old battles. Part IV, which addresses the way forward, will examine these battles in more detail.

Guessing the Value of the Fake-Drug Market

There are almost no real estimates of the number of substandard and degraded products, and measures of counterfeits are not based on any proper, scientifically rigorous estimation method. One oft-repeated estimate puts the value of the counterfeit-drug market at $75 billion a year.[2] Although the damages to life and health from poor-quality drugs can hardly be overstated, this dollar figure is almost certainly too high. I say this having examined drug types failing quality-control tests. When the fake-drug market size was forecast to be $75 billion by 2010, it was based on the expectation that the fake market is approximately 10 percent of the total pharmaceutical market, and the total global market for 2010 was estimated to be approximately $750 billion. In fact, the global market for pharmaceuticals was valued at $837 billion in 2009, but the fake-drug market is almost certainly worth less than $83.7 billion. First, the 10 percent figure is imprecise and undoubtedly wrong. It is attributed to WHO, but no published WHO document claims such a figure. The figure of 10 percent was based on various comments by WHO staff at public meetings, mistakenly reported as though a comprehensive scientific study had been undertaken, when in fact they were mere speculation.

According to 2009 data from IMS Health, the sum value of the thirteen largest pharmaceutical markets (which obviously have fewer poor-quality medicines than 1 percent of the market) is $652.45 billion, more than three quarters (77.9 percent) of the value of the worldwide pharmaceutical market ($837 billion).[3] If we add the market value of the thirteen remaining Organisation for Economic Co-operation and Development (OECD) countries, whose failure rates are also likely to be less than 1 percent, the total value of the pharmaceutical market that has a fake-drug prevalence rate of less than 1 percent is between three-fourths and four-fifths of the world total.

The combined market of Brazil, Russia, India, and China (the BRIC countries) is roughly $90 billion, and failure rates for all four of these countries are certainly considerably less than 10 percent, and often much less if my research team's samplings are anything to go by. More accurate estimates of the prevalence of drugs failing quality-control tests (counterfeit, substandard, or degraded drugs) in poor countries range from a few percent to over half of the market in a few particularly poorly governed countries in sub-Saharan Africa.

To calculate an approximate value of the fake-drug market in the countries studied for this book, I began with the city-level data I collected on drug quality as proxies for the countries as a whole (the data collection and research findings are explained in more detail in part III). Using data on the size of the market from IMS Health for the countries from which we took samples, we found that the total size of the pharmaceutical market in the areas studied was $106.5 billion in 2009.[4] If we assume the city-based failure rates for the drugs in our sample are representative of their respective countries (a stretch, to be sure, especially because rural rates are probably higher), then because most of the countries with the larger market sizes, BRIC countries in particular, have lower failure rates, the total estimated value of the drugs failing tests is $5 billion. Our proxy markets make up about 12 percent ($106.5 billion) of the total global market for 2009 (as mentioned above, $837 billion). Simply extrapolating from our sample by market size ($5 billion times 0.12 or 12 percent), we find that the value of the fake-drug market comes out to $40 billion. That number is far too high an estimate, however, as the failure rates for the majority of the global market are far lower than those of my sample, which is heavily biased toward low-income markets. Figure 2-2 summarizes the percent of total drug failures by city, according to my sampling.

FIGURE 2-2
TOTAL PERCENT FAILURES BY CITY

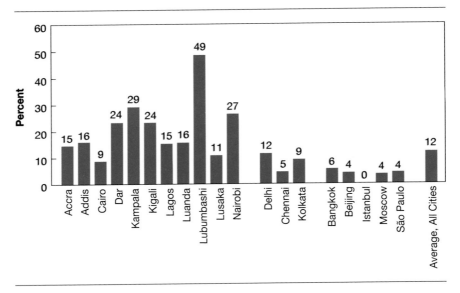

To approximate a global value for the fake-drug markets, it is probably right to add at least another $3 billion to the $5 billion approximated from my data for the vast number of mid- and lower-income countries for which I did not collect data (totaling $8 billion). These countries' total markets approximately equal the value of the total BRIC market, the roughly $90 billion mentioned previously.

Estimating a failure rate of 1 percent for the developed world's market valued at nearly $600 billion (which, by my team's Internet-based estimates, is quite high), we add $6 billion, indicating a total global fake-drug market value of $14 billion, or roughly one-fifth of the widely quoted estimate. But given that failure rates in the wealthiest markets are considerably below 1 percent, a more reasonable estimate[c] of a fake-drug

---

c. Even one-sixth of 1 percent (0.167 percent), based on my research and conversations with investigators at the FDA, seems quite high: it would mean roughly five million Americans receive fake drugs a year, which seems highly implausible because one would have expected that adverse drug reactions would have exposed patterns of poor drugs.

FIGURE 2-3

GUESSTIMATE OF GLOBAL FAKE MARKET SIZE (BY $ VALUE) AND DISTRIBUTION

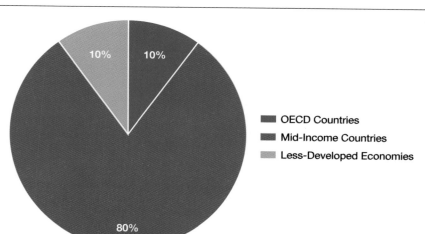

market value would be $1 billion for the developed world (a failure rate of one-sixth of 1 percent), making the total global fake market value nearer $10 billion (see figure 2-3).[d]

The greatest harm of the poor-quality drug market may be to patients in the poorest countries, which overwhelmingly have the worst drugs, but if the premise of the back-of-the-envelope calculation above is correct, the most valuable fake-drug market is in mid-income countries. These countries have increasing wealth but poor private brand enforcement and weakly enforced public regulations. The market in developed countries is not large and is where most of the economic value of the legitimate market remains.

---

d. This may appear to be a back-of-the-envelope calculation, and it is. I have data for only specific cities and for only three important classes of drugs while ignoring numerous other product categories. Without better, more comprehensive data there is little point in creating a more compelling analysis using impressive statistical techniques. I do the above because the forecast figure of $75 billion in 2010 is widely quoted, and although well intentioned, it was not really based on any reliable evidence. I explain how my figures have been broadly calculated; the reader may decide their value.

That said, there are two opposing measurement concerns with many drug-quality failures found in my samples from poorer countries. The first is that we suspect there would be more failures in rural areas, so the estimation underestimates the problem of fake drugs. Opposed to this is the fact that failures may be due to substandard or degraded products and not just fakes (perhaps half of poor-quality drugs in Africa, the worst affected region, could have been the result of poor-quality manufacturing).

Although my guesstimate of the economic value of the products may be lower than what many suspect, even if this is correct the cost to patients is high, especially in poorer countries.

The Worsening State of Dangerous Medicines: A Growing Problem

Although data in developing countries are poor and limited, and pharmaceutical companies everywhere are reluctant to publicize the faking of their products because their brands may suffer as a result, we are confident that there has been a sharp increase in drug seizures and investigations of counterfeiting rings. The rising numbers of seizures and prosecutions suggest a growing global problem. In 2006 the European Commission reported that customs agents intercepted 2.7 million counterfeit drugs at EU borders, an increase of 384 percent from a year earlier.[5] The U.S. FDA opened seventy-two criminal cases against pharmaceutical counterfeiters in 2010, more than ten times the number of cases in 2000 (see figure 2-4).[6]

The Pharmaceutical Security Institute, which is funded by the pharmaceutical industry, compiles a database of incidents involving seizures by customs and law-enforcement agencies, illegal diversions, and theft. By its reckoning, incidents have increased steadily from 196 in 2002 to 2,003 in 2009. The institute acknowledges that increased attention and vigilance have contributed to these numbers, but the value of the seizures has also increased. The proportion of incidents involving a "commercial" amount (defined as more than one thousand dosage units) increased by 7 percent year-on-year until 2009, when 48 percent of the total 978 seizures made by customs officials, police, or health inspectors were of commercial size.

For much of the past two decades, lifestyle drugs—erectile-dysfunction medicines, painkillers, diet pills, and antianxiety medicines—were the most common knockoffs, particularly in rich countries. But in the past few years,

FIGURE 2-4

COUNTERFEIT DRUG CASES OPENED BY
FDA's OVERSEAS CRIMINAL INVESTIGATION DEPARTMENT

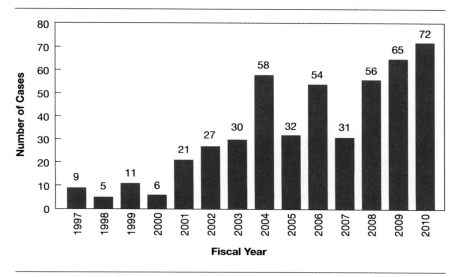

SOURCE: www.fda.org.

counterfeiters appear to have moved into far more life-threatening fake pharmacology; they are now manufacturing drugs used to treat such things as cancer, HIV/AIDS, and serious heart conditions.

When Cheap Becomes Expensive: Why Quality Matters

Fighting counterfeiting is a constant and interminable struggle. Currency counterfeiters make money for (nearly) nothing, diminishing the welfare of a nation; some have even used counterfeit money as a weapon of war.

Luxury-brand consumer products create aspirations to ownership often beyond ability to pay, and look-alike goods of inferior quality will appear on the streets overnight like mushrooms after rain. This diminishes the cachet of luxury brands, which is significant enough to warrant companies spending significant portions of their revenue on protecting their brands from counterfeiting. Financial losses for some products are economically important, but the general public probably would not feel the inflationary pressure resulting from forged banknotes, and is unlikely to feel moral outrage when a luxury-goods provider faces losses because a counterfeiter imitates its label for jeans or a watch.

There is a distressingly prevalent view that the same goes for expensive pharmaceutical brands—that companies are simply charging a premium for fancy packaging or unnecessary extra ingredients, like sugar coatings to ease swallowing—and that there really is no harm in reducing some of these attributes a bit, especially if the product is expensive. In short, many people believe drugs can be produced more cheaply without endangering patients or decreasing quality. Many of the problems discussed in this book arise from this lacuna of ignorance because, although some products can be made cheaper, cutting too many corners can be lethal.[e] (See the next box for many examples of the problems of cheap cost-cutting drugs.) Competition in the drug market, as in any market, is generally a good thing. It lowers prices and enables more consumers (patients in the case of medicines) to be supplied. But this is only the case where competitors trade in products of equal efficacy and safety, and unfortunately that is increasingly not the case in many parts of the world.

The Importance of Good Manufacturing Practice

To make sure pharmaceuticals are safe and work as designed (that is, to re-create the product in the form that gained initial regulatory approval by a stringent agency like the U.S. FDA), manufacturers must make them according to a strict protocol. All major regulatory agencies demand, and leading pharmaceutical manufacturers have developed and implemented, a comprehensive set of safeguards and procedures known as good manufacturing practice. GMP is designed to ensure, among other things, that the medicine is appropriately soluble, any trace impurities are minimized, variations in the amount of API are small, API is sustained at the requisite levels prior to expiration, and any degradation occurring

---

e. It is not just poor consumers who view counterfeit drugs much like other counterfeit products; most of the academic literature on counterfeiting takes a similar line, which is, of course, legitimate in the sense that it reflects much public perception, but that perception is wrong and dangerously so.

prior to expiration is not dangerous. Errors and mix-ups in formulation or packaging and other possible mistakes can be deadly. The protocol also regulates the condition of the building, qualification, and training of staff, cleanliness and sanitation, monitoring, supervision, and many other aspects of medicine production.

GMP also has to be revised regularly in line with new scientific findings. GMP from the 1980s would not pass today, and no doubt today's GMP will look inadequate in 2040. GMP is established by national regulators, and it varies by location: passable GMP in Kenya or Peru is not as stringent as GMP regulations in the United States or Switzerland. Most pharmaceutical experts would agree that it is appropriate for GMP standards to tighten over time, but I suspect that some, maybe most, would not accept that there should be different GMP standards based on location. Although purists might be correct from a pharmacological standpoint, that is, that there should not be different standards of GMP at any one time, in actuality there are. And disagreements about what constitutes GMP contribute to disagreements about what is considered a dangerous drug.[f] After

---

f. In the grayest of gray areas in this regard, think about how many Indian firms have copied Western products over the past few decades and whether GMP is perfectly followed. A Western company has filed a patent for a drug, providing detail of the APIs, excipients, and other details in the product monograph. But it does not publish every tiny procedure, every process, and all the minutiae as to how it arrives at the product. An Indian firm will reverse-engineer the product. In working out how to develop it, the Indian company may hit on every single procedure and thus make the drug identically, but it might develop slightly different ones; it might even use different excipients. As long as the chemical is bioequivalent to the original drug (that is, as long as it works in exactly the same way) in a dozen patients, it is considered absolutely fine, and it is seen as a huge advance for the poor if it is half the cost. But what if it has harmful side effects to one in three thousand people when the original was harmful to one in ten thousand? Does that mean the GMP of the Indian product is inferior, even if one cannot be sure how it caused a slightly worse tolerance in patients? Probably yes, but it is the kind of difference that will be ignored, probably by everyone except the originator company, which will continue to complain about it.

More serious deviations from GMP occur regularly; in these cases bioequivalence is not established. In other words, the profile of the copy version is further from the original, but this deviation may also be tolerated in some locations, so the notion that GMP means the same thing everywhere is simply false. Having said this, most violations we come across in this book are significant, not marginal, and there are undeniably base GMP processes that all legitimate manufacturers could agree on, regardless of location. But above that base level of agreement, however, there is debate.

Box 2-2
Innovator, Generic, and Copy Medicines

Once the patent of an innovator drug has expired, other manufacturers are allowed to produce the same medicine after providing evidence that the new drug is bioequivalent to the original; these drugs are known as generics. Proving bioequivalence is not a trivial procedure and requires high-level technical expertise. A pill is a delivery device for an API, so it must not only transport the API but also ensure that it dissolves and is absorbed correctly in the patient. Excipients ensure that both solubility (the API dissolving into our aqueous bodies) and permeability (transportation between the cells) occur in the same way as in the original drug. Even small variations may affect patients differently. In the 1970s, Australian regulators noticed that a simple change in a generic antiepileptic drug's excipients made it less effective in some patients and caused side effects not associated with the original drug in others.

According to a large study of data spanning more than a decade, in the United States the average variance in generic absorption against the originator brand is only 3.5 percent.[1] For most medications, this difference will not affect the drug's efficacy, but this is not the case for all.

The following examples demonstrate that medications copying innovator products may vary in both structure and efficacy.

Glivec. Glivec® is an innovator drug used to treat chronic myeloid leukemia. In the last two and a half years, case studies involving comparatively well-off patients from middle-income countries have demonstrated that copy drugs are ineffective in treating chronic myeloid leukemia in some patients. These copy medications are not proven generics and are not required to pass stringent bioequivalence tests prior to use in hospitals and pharmacies. Some of these medications, such as imatinib, are produced by large, reputable pharmaceutical manufacturers—in this case India's Cipla, whose pharmaceuticals regularly pass FDA inspections and meet international regulatory standards. While Glivec® has demonstrated a "high hematologic, cytogenetic, and molecular response rate and favorable long-term safety profile," five reported case studies suggest that copy versions, which

---

1. B. M. Davit et al., "Comparing Generic and Innovator Drugs: A Review of 12 Years of Bioequivalence Data from the United States Food and Drug Administration," *Annals of Pharmacotherapy* 43, no. 10 (2009): 1583–97.

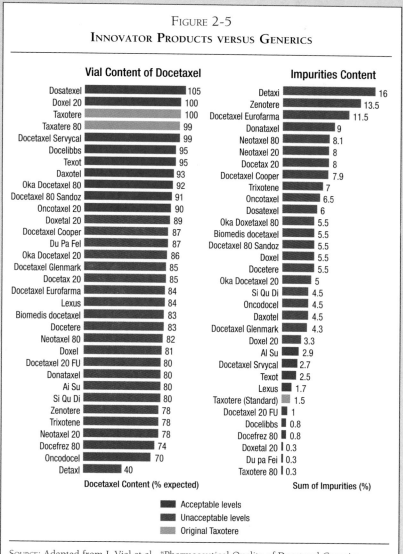

Figure 2-5
Innovator Products versus Generics

Vial Content of Docetaxel

Product	Docetaxel Content (% expected)
Dosatexel	105
Doxel 20	100
Taxotere	100
Taxatere 80	99
Docetaxel Servycal	99
Docelibbs	95
Texot	95
Daxotel	93
Oka Docetaxel 80	92
Docetaxel 80 Sandoz	91
Oncotaxel 20	90
Doxetal 20	89
Docetaxel Cooper	87
Du Pa Fel	87
Oka Docetaxel 20	86
Docetaxel Glenmark	85
Docetax 20	85
Docetaxel Eurofarma	84
Lexus	84
Biomedis docetaxel	83
Docetere	83
Neotaxel 80	82
Doxel	81
Docetaxel 20 FU	80
Donataxel	80
Ai Su	80
Si Qu Di	80
Zenotere	78
Trixotene	78
Neotaxel 20	78
Docefrez 80	74
Oncodocel	70
Detaxl	40

Impurities Content

Product	Sum of Impurities (%)
Detaxi	16
Zenotere	13.5
Docetaxel Eurofarma	11.5
Donataxel	9
Neotaxel 80	8.1
Neotaxel 20	8
Docetax 20	8
Docetaxel Cooper	7.9
Trixotene	7
Oncotaxel	6.5
Dosatexel	6
Oka Docetaxel 80	5.5
Biomedis docetaxel	5.5
Docetaxel 80 Sandoz	5.5
Doxel	5.5
Docetere	5.5
Oka Docetaxel 20	5
Si Qu Di	4.5
Oncodocel	4.5
Daxotel	4.5
Docetaxel Glenmark	4.3
Doxel 20	3.3
Al Su	2.9
Docetaxel Srvycal	2.7
Texot	2.5
Lexus	1.7
Taxotere (Standard)	1.5
Docetaxel 20 FU	1
Docelibbs	0.8
Docefrez 80	0.8
Doxetal 20	0.3
Du pa Fei	0.3
Taxotere 80	0.3

Legend:
- Acceptable levels
- Unacceptable levels
- Original Taxotere

Source: Adapted from J. Vial et al., "Pharmaceutical Quality of Docetaxel Generics versus Originator Drug Product: A Comparative Analysis," *Current Medical Research and Opinion* 24 (2008), 2019–33.

(continued)

Box 2-2 (*continued*)
INNOVATOR, GENERIC, AND COPY MEDICINES

---

contain a slightly different version of the active ingredient, are ineffective in some cases.[2] In all five studies, the patient experienced a relapse after switching from the original to the generic medication and then improved again when put back on the original drug. In one case, an older patient in fragile condition was unable to recover and died even after the reintroduction of the innovator drug.

Cyclosporine. Kidney-transplant patients are normally given cyclosporine to minimize the risk of organ rejection, but studies on particular copy products have shown them to be far less effectual than the original.

Psychotropic Drugs. There is a marked effect in psychotropic drugs in particular. A major literature review of reported adverse events following the switch from an original to a generic drug advised that patients being switched to a generic drug should be closely and individually monitored throughout the transition.

In another study of 260 epileptic patients who were switched from an original to a generic, 105 (42.9 percent) experienced increased seizure frequency or other negative side effects, including headaches, fatigue, and aggression. The patients who experienced adverse results were switched back to the innovator drug, and the symptoms went away. Multiple reports suggest that antiepileptic drugs are susceptible to variations in bioavailability.

---

2. Inas Asfour and Shereen Elshazly, "Changing Therapy from Glivec® to a 'Copy' Imatinib Results in a Worsening of Chronic Myeloid Leukemia Disease Status: Two Case Reports," *Cases Journal* 2 (December 17, 2009).

---

all, a Dutch regulator might reject a Chinese import based on European-quality rulings of which the Chinese company falls short. Such differences can lead to trade tensions, limiting international cooperation; this point is discussed at length in part IV.

Sticking to Western-standard GMP is expensive and—especially where a manufacturer or regulator has only a rudimentary understanding of pharmacology—can be seen as an unnecessary indulgence.

In a number of examples, epilepsy sufferers reported increased seizures when they switched to a generic, but they regained control after taking the original drug. In a report on the generic schizophrenia medication clozapine, researchers found that 40 percent of patients reacted negatively to the copy product, even though they could find no difference in the concentration of the drug in the bloodstreams of affected patients. In similar antidepressants studies, researchers found that switching from an innovator to a generic caused a resurgence of former symptoms, new symptoms, or side effects. Switching between different generics caused a resurgence of symptoms and an increase in the drug's side effects, including diarrhea, nausea, and itching. Another study verified that two chemically indistinguishable generics dissolved at different rates in laboratory testing; one matched the dissolution rate of the originator brand, but the other did not.

Diabetes Drugs. Different formulations of a popular diabetes drug, which had all been approved and registered, were found to have "different bio-availabilities, even within drug classes and within countries."[3] A detailed analysis of various generic preparations of the anticlotting drug streptokinase revealed "wide variations in the activity, purity, and composition of the available streptokinase preparations." Finally, different production methods used by a generic manufacturer can change the form of a drug or introduce impurities.

------

3. Horst Blume et al., "Pharmaceutical Quality of Glibenclamide Products: A Multinational Postmarket Comparative Study," *Zentrallaboratorium Deutscher Aptheker* 19, no. 20 (1993): 2713–41.

Sometimes, poor quality is caused by willful negligence; cheaper ingredients and laxer processes are substituted for what is required to ensure consistently good quality. This is more likely in emerging economies, where young companies, afraid of losing nervous or impatient backers, may take advantage of lax oversight and skip important steps in the regulatory process to move drugs to market quicker and cheaper. The table in box 2-2 shows myriad poorly performing versions of a cancer drug—Docetaxel.

Some of these versions are so poor that in a tragic irony they are likely to be highly carcinogenic.

The Crucial Role of Medical Regulatory Authorities

To combat those who might cut corners in GMP, to help identify those selling fake drugs, and to address myriad other issues related to pharmaceuticals, countries benefit from developing a fully functioning medical regulatory authority (MRA). A functional MRA is a mighty administrative body; its competences and responsibilities reach into many aspects of modern life. A glance at the U.S. FDA's home page shows that the organization covers an enormous range of topics in great detail. As I look while writing this, there is a campaign warning against fraudulent weight-loss "dietary supplements," while in the news section a manufacturer of a heart-lung bypass machine is going through its licensing process.

The U.S. FDA's major departments cover food, drugs, medical devices, vaccines, blood and biologics, animal and veterinary, cosmetics, radiation-emitting products, and tobacco products. Each has its own research, communications, regulatory, and legal specialties, all demanding extremely high levels of education, training, and expertise.

For this book, we are interested in only four of those functions—the strictly medical ones—but even so, the requirements are demanding. An MRA is responsible for ensuring the safety, efficacy, and quality of imported and locally produced medicines in both the public and private sectors, and its primary duty is to register medical and health care–related products for sale. This means much more than keeping a list (although it is also necessary to keep a publicly available, up-to-date list), as the MRA must satisfy itself that any product has passed appropriate scientific trials, including ensuring toxicological and clinical bioequivalence; that it performs as claimed; that it contains the right ingredients; that it has been manufactured to required standards and in a manufacturing plant also up to standard; that the product will remain stable throughout its shelf life; that the prescribing leaflet is accurate and easy to understand and correctly lists all ingredients and their amounts; that the packaging is sufficient to protect the product; and that the packaging lists the batch number, expiration date, and correct physical address of the manufacturer.

The manufacturer applying for registration must submit a complete dossier allowing the MRA to assess all of these factors and more, and the manufacturer must include a pharmacopeial monograph (a statement of the kind and amount of drug, how and when it should be used, and when it should not be used); a comprehensive chemical analysis, along with the methods used; and an exhaustive record of each stage of manufacture. This is not all. For example, physical inspections must be made, and once all this and more information is gathered together, the dossier is reviewed by a committee of experts. The recommended composition of this committee is as follows: a senior clinician from a major teaching hospital; a pharmacologist from a university, research institute, or hospital; a regulator from the national MRA; a general or community practitioner; a community pharmacist and expert on good manufacturing practice; a pediatrician; and a representative from consumer groups.

And this is not a full list of the processes needed *for registration* under a fully functioning MRA.

The responsibilities of an MRA continue with licensing pharmaceutical establishments, such as manufacturers, importers, distributors, wholesalers, and retailers. Each of these will be governed by their own specific regulations and requirements for good practice and each must be inspected regularly to ensure compliance. Ideally, this should be credibly enforced, by fines or revocation of license, and so on. Similarly, an MRA must be prepared to amend or revoke registration of products if they are found to be of unacceptable quality, safety, or efficacy, and this should also be supported by enforcement. It is also crucial that an MRA maintain an adverse-drug reporting system supported by a practicable and timely recall procedure to remove dangerous products already in the market.

Even the best-run MRA will conduct postmarketing surveys to try to identify unsafe products that have slipped through the system (or bypassed it by being smuggled into the country). This involves making covert purchases of certain products in randomly selected retail establishments, which is exactly what my research teams did to gather the information on drug quality presented in part III; in fact, we followed the methods recommended for MRAs by U.S. Pharmacopeia. Clearly, more gaps in regulatory procedure lead to the presence of more substandard products, and important postmarketing surveys provide useful intelligence for the MRA.

It also falls to the MRA to control how medicines are promoted and advertised. False advertising is a constant threat in all societies—witness the FDA campaign against spurious claims for weight-loss products—but in societies less familiar with Western medicines and with low education and literacy levels, the consequences can be tragic when worthless products claim to cure AIDS or malaria, or even when products oversell what they can do. LuMether, a copy of the most important antimalarial drug, provides an example of the problems that overpromising causes (see figure 2-6). The manufacturers claimed it was much more effective than it was; when my research team tested it, it seriously underperformed.

The risk that medicines are inappropriately promoted is also present in every society, and the line between corporate hospitality and bribery can be a narrow one.

Finally, the national MRA is the body responsible for approving clinical trials. This is an essential function in developed economies, which undertake most of the clinical research and development in the world. It is less imperative to maintain the requisite level of expertise within the MRA of an emerging country, but that is not to say there should be a free-for-all, and controversy has arisen in the past about the appropriate standards that should be applied. This question has yet to be resolved satisfactorily, and at present it creates a barrier to the development of medicines for diseases that really affect only developing countries.

Though the processes described here represent quite a small part of what the U.S. FDA does, they place demands on developing countries that are not easily met. In part IV, I suggest how functions may be prioritized in developing countries based on recommendations made by U.S. Pharmacopeia.

In this chapter I have introduced some of the key concepts that are important to be borne in mind when analyzing more detail and data in later chapters. We've encountered the different types of dangerous drugs, a rough estimate of the size of the market of these drugs, why product theft is important for the fake drug trader, why MRAs are important to prevent fakes and those who trade them, and why MRAs are equally vital to limit sloppy manufacturers from making substandard products. Before I move on to the next chapter and discuss my research findings, there is one small topic linked to bad-quality drugs, and that is good-quality drug theft.

Figure 2-6

LuMether ad

Notes: There are at least three errors/lies with this advertisement. First, there is an error on the amount of ingredients in the drug (the second picture for LuMether Junior indicates it contains far too much lumefantrine—this may only be a typo, but it shows lack of attention to details in a public advertisement). Second, and far more important, this product is not approved by the WHO, whereas others are. Third, there are always side effects with medicines.

How Diversion Can Lead to Counterfeiting

Diversion is the polite word for drug theft, and in emerging markets it usually begins when drugs are stolen from government stores and ends with the drug's sale in private markets, often outside of the country where the drugs were stolen. Diverted drugs are typically essential drugs governments have purchased or that have been donated or sold at a low cost to an aid agency. This is a particularly acute problem in East Africa, where trade routes for stolen public supplies cross borders across the region (see figure 2-6). In our survey of pharmacies in 2007 in Nairobi, Kenya, we found supplies of the best-available malaria treatment, Coartem, in distinctive packaging, which Novartis, the manufacturer of the drug, told us indicated these treatments had been donated to Nigeria. There are also problems in West Africa, such as in Togo, which I also cover.

I do not discuss the issue of diversion in depth in this book because these are not poor-quality drugs. On the contrary, diverted drugs are usually the very highest quality, and one could make a case that diverted drugs

FIGURE 2-7

MAP OF DONATED ANTIMALARIALS TO AFRICA
AND THEIR SUBSEQUENT DIVERSION

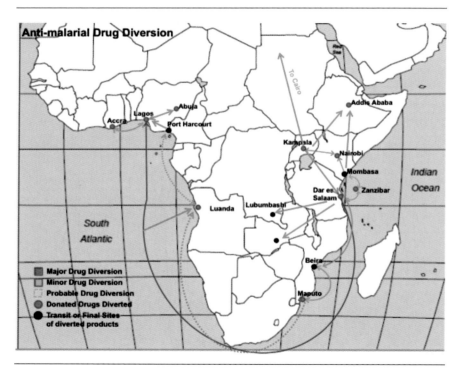

SOURCE: Roger Bate, Lorraine Mooney, and Kimberly Hess, "Medicine Registration and Medicine Quality: A Preliminary Analysis of Key Cities in Emerging Markets," *Research and Reports in Tropical Medicine* (December 13, 2010).

NOTES: Over the past five years, vast quantities of antimalarials have been donated to Africa. A lot of these drugs (probably tens of millions of treatments) have been stolen from their intended recipients and reappeared in private markets, often in countries hundreds of miles away. This map shows the diversion we unearthed in our investigation of the problem.

still provide the medical benefit for which they were intended. However, the side effects of this perversion of good intent are damaging.

First, diversion denies assistance to the people who were supposed to benefit from subsidized medications. If they are lucky, an equivalent product will have been substituted, or at least a copy product with the right ingredients will be available, so they at least have access to some form of treatment. If they are unlucky, diversion will leave no medicine at the clinics for them unless they can afford an extra "fee" for the nurse, who can go to a nearby pharmacy to buy the requisite drugs. Stockouts, often the result of theft rather than a pure mismanagement of supplies, are common in East Africa and can foster drug resistance by interrupting treatment.

Second, what begins as trade and smuggling of genuine products morphs over time into outright criminal traffic in dangerous substandard drugs. This is a major problem in the Middle East and is increasing in Africa, too. Unfortunately, the trade routes of stolen genuine drugs and of counterfeit drugs—and in some instances the traders themselves—are identical.

In addition, because drug theft is a pharmaceutical crime, it is often lumped in with trade in fake drugs, so many media reports discuss illegal trade without fully distinguishing between the two. Figure 2-7 above presents a rough sketch of drug diversion routes in Africa.

3

Overview of Research Findings and Possible Solutions

As long as products have existed, cheats have sought to undercut the legal market. Inferior medicines have been passed off as the real thing for decades. Registered manufacturers and government regulatory bodies seek to thwart these cheats, but there are no systematic data about their prevalence. Anecdotal evidence suggests that substandard and counterfeit producers have been gaining ground in recent years.

But there is disagreement among interested parties on the scale of the problem and what types of problems dominate. Groups such as Oxfam insist that the major problem for poorer nations is substandard products, whereas the Western pharmaceutical industry focuses primarily on counterfeit products. How bad is the dangerous drug problem? Do counterfeits or substandard products dominate?

My research team and I have studied drugs in both the developed and the developing world to present the most comprehensive picture of the problem available. We followed rigorous and uniform scientific methodology, but some of our data were more limited than others because of the nature of the task. This chapter provides an overview of the findings of the study we conducted, and part III contains an in-depth explanation of this research as well as other relevant data.

In addition to the aggregate-drug quality study we conducted, my research included interviews with pharmacists, legal analysis of counterfeiting, econometric analysis establishing a price-quality nexus, and chemical and spectrometry assessments of inferior products. This research has led to more than a dozen research papers published in the peer-reviewed scientific, legal, and economic literature (see appendix A for a full list of my publications and working papers on this topic).

Identifying Source and Target

Whether you live in a rich country or a poor one, it is inevitable that one of your countrymen, someone, somewhere, is producing counterfeit medicines. For while most may not make the final product, making good fake packaging is ubiquitous (see box 3-1 on Plavix for a dangerous version of a key medicine used by the wealthy in rich and poor nations). But the majority of fake products seem to originate in China and India, with the former providing most of the suspect active ingredients and a great deal of bogus packaging and the latter providing a significant number of fake finished products. Recent evidence suggests that many fake "Indian-made" drugs are actually produced in China, and some of these involve substantial criminal networks.

Most people focus on the criminal part of organized crime, but I'm equally concerned, even impressed, by the organized part. In many places criminals' distribution systems are better than the government's, although in others, most obviously North Korea and its Riajin trade zone, organized crime is backed by the government, so the two are indistinguishable. When I lived in Hong Kong in 1989, Chinese triads were the groups to fear. Today the people to be wary of are certain actors within the police and the Chinese state. To paraphrase Deng Xiaoping, it doesn't matter if the economy is criminal or legal, as long as it makes money.

According to Misha Glenny, author of the book *McMafia,* most major organized syndicates are made up of clusters of dozens of minor conspiracies that move a product or service a little farther down the chain of distribution.[1] The vast majority do not entail Mafia-type organizations.

The more successful fake-drug traders have learned from the Colombian narcotics cartels. Where the more famous Pablo Escobar and his Medellin cartel turned Medellin and Bogota into abattoirs, the Cali cartel acted in a quieter, more systemic way, bribing or otherwise perverting every significant public and private official to ensure business could continue, even establishing their own banks. Cali even funded the presidency of Ernesto Samper in 1994. To make tons of cocaine requires tons of precursor chemicals, so Cali established a chain of pharmacies to cover its chemical purchases.

Cali was not a centralized organization but a dispersed grouping, and when the heads of Cali were arrested, there was little change in the price of cocaine in the United States, a significant indication of little change in

---

Box 3-1

PLAVIX

Counterfeit and substandard drugs are to be found even in northern Europe, particularly in Ireland, Finland, and the United Kingdom. Strict regulation and enforcement in many of these countries close much of the legal markets to fakes, but criminal organizations routinely exploit lax transit laws and weak supply chains to import illegal drugs into even the highly regulated United Kingdom. Many of the illegal drugs purchased in northern Europe are bought via Internet pharmacies.

Though fake drugs undoubtedly pose the greatest threat in this region, substandard paracetamol and tuberculosis drugs have also been reported in northern Europe.

In the United Kingdom in recent years, criminals have shifted focus from using the Internet to sell small quantities of fake (predominantly lifestyle) drugs to individuals, to targeting pharmaceutical wholesalers, especially those that supply public entities such as hospitals or aid organizations. In the summer of 2007, British authorities were forced to issue drug alerts to health-care professionals for Plavix (see figures 3-1 and 3-2 of fake and real Plavix), a blood thinner; Zyprexa, a treatment for schizophrenia; and Casodex, a hormone treatment for prostate cancer. By targeting wholesalers, counterfeiters are able to capture larger and more lucrative markets efficiently. The wholesale price for a pack of twenty-eight Casodex pills in Britain is £160 ($260), which yields a wide profit margin to a counterfeiter for such therapeutic drugs.

---

supply. The same is true of some fake-drug rings today. The loss of leaders will not affect the price or availability of fake products.

Like narcotics traders, substandard drug peddlers and outright fake-drug trading criminals take advantage of anti-American sentiment in many people in countries as diverse as Brazil, India, and China. Whether they believe it or not, traders argue that it is a moral duty for them to sell local, often inferior, copies of all sorts of American products, including medicines. Like the Cali cartel, these traders have corrupted powerful defenders in positions of power.

The executive director of the United Nations Office on Drugs and Crime (UNODC), Antonio Maria Costa, says that "collusion between corrupt

FIGURE 3-1

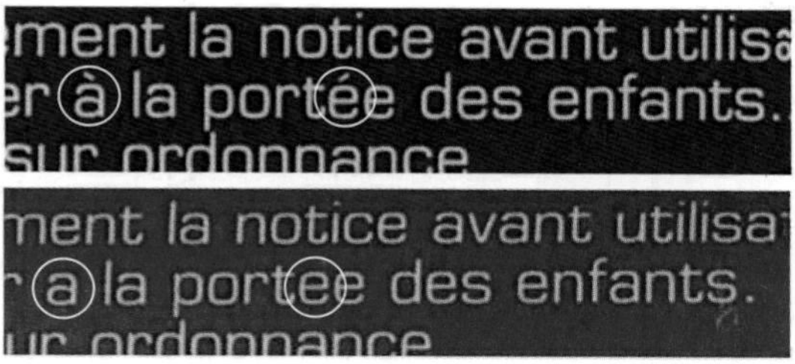

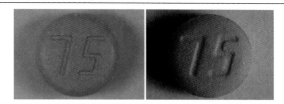

Plavix packaging—real vs. fake

NOTE: The real packaging is on the top; the fake packaging is on the bottom. The fake packaging does not have accents in the text (see circled letters).

FIGURE 3-2

Plavix pill—real vs. fake

NOTE: The real pill is on the left; the fake pill is on the right. The fake pill has deeper indentations.

elites and opportunistic criminals enriches the few, impoverishes the many, and undermines public institutions. States are being hollowed out from the inside. Democracy and development falter, while crime and corruption flourish."[2] And the problem isn't limited to the developing world, as box 3-1 demonstrates.

In addition to the intentional counterfeiters, India and China are home to many substandard drug producers, as is Africa. National government policies encourage local drug production but do not provide the requisite regulatory environments to ensure products are consistently of high quality. In fairness to India and China, these two countries combined house

80 percent of the world's manufacturing capability for APIs, so they provide most of the legitimate chemicals used in pharmaceuticals in addition to most of the dangerous ones. Americans and Europeans want Indian and Chinese products because then the costs of medicines are lower (maybe 30–50 percent less) than would otherwise be the case. As the CEO of GlaxoSmithKline (GSK) said in 2007 as the pharmaceutical boom in the East really took off, "If we can buy it cheaper than we can make it, then of course that's what we're going to do."[3] In 2010, the United States imported over $85 billion worth of pharmaceutical products, an almost threefold increase over the $30 billion imported in 2000.[4]

Field Research

Over the course of the past four years, my research team and I sampled drugs from nineteen different cities in seventeen countries, as well as from the Internet. The following is a brief overview of the samples procured by region. We tested the samples we collected for quality. Research findings are explained in detail in part III.

Drugs we sampled that failed quality tests did so for various reasons. All failing drugs were substandard, but only a subset of these could be considered counterfeit products (drugs we considered "counterfeit" contained zero API or were obvious visual fakes or were confirmed as counterfeit by the legitimate manufacturer—if a trademarked product had been faked and that company replied to requests for information). The trend in the percentage of counterfeit drugs in a market approximately follows the trend in the percentage of total failures, which means countries that struggle to regulate their drug markets will have both a greater share of poor-quality drugs overall and a proportionally greater share of fake drugs in the market.

Africa. We sampled drugs from ninety pharmacies in nonslum areas in eleven large African cities in four separate samplings. The sampling methods were the same for each assessment; however, a couple of key variations ought to be noted. First of all, there was some regional variation in the drug samples we were able to procure. Researchers purchased three classes of drugs: antimalarials, antibiotics, and antimycobacterials (drugs to treat

FIGURE 3-3
FAKE-DRUG TRADE ENTRY POINTS AND SHIPPING ROUTES

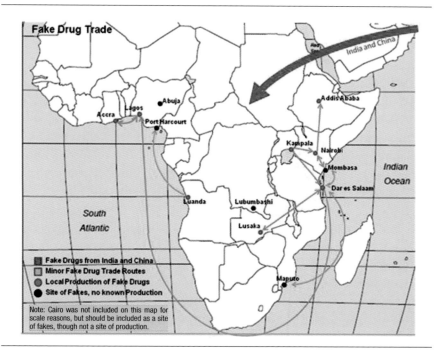

TB). Within drug classes, some brands were found in many places, whereas others were unique to one city. Second, our sampling took place over the period of four years, and hence available products changed.

The above map of Africa (figure 3-3) shows the production sites of fakes I came across in my own research, and nearly every one of these cities had fake or substandard drugs imported from India and China.

India. Sampling from India revolved around three separate procurements from seventy pharmacies in 2008 and 2009 in three cities. A portion of the Delhi pharmacies was sampled again in 2010. We used the same methodology as in the African cities, but the malaria drugs we bought were often different because Indian mosquitoes generally carry a different strain of malaria than that which dominates in Africa, and therefore the treatments are different.[a] Sampling in India also included an assessment of the same five drugs from four wholesalers in one major location in Delhi, Bhagirath Palace.[b]

Other Emerging Markets. We also sampled from fifty pharmacies in five cities scattered throughout the rest of the developing world, but these data are inherently unreliable even as snapshots of the cities in question, let alone of the rest of their respective countries. However, the exercise gave me some insights into pharmacy operations, problems for drug-quality control, and the myriad ways dubious drugs infiltrate different markets. The samples—from Bangkok, Thailand; Beijing, China; Moscow, Russia; Istanbul, Turkey; and São Paulo, Brazil—were collected between December 2009 and February 2010.

The Internet. Any reasonably priced small-scale procurement (fewer than several thousand samples) from Western pharmacies, where the drug-supply system is well regulated and quality is consistently high, is not worthwhile—anticipated failure rate would be so low as to be of little value. However, drugs purchased over the Internet are often considered dangerous. The WHO has stated that 50 percent of drugs bought over the Internet from sources hiding their location are fakes. To tentatively test the WHO's statement and assess other types of websites, we procured five commonly purchased innovator-brand drugs from a total of fifty-five online pharmacies. Each pharmacy was grouped into one of four stratified categories based on an assessment by Western regulatory authorities.

---

a. One failing in this sampling is that we did not consider the time of year for procurement, and malaria in parts of India is seasonal. It is possible we would have procured a wider variety of antimalarials in Delhi, in particular, if we had sampled during a different season.

b. Obtaining a representative sample of wholesale drugs is much more difficult than procuring the corresponding drugs from a retailer. A Delhi native can walk into a pharmacy and purchase drugs for personal or family use without suspicion. But most wholesalers do repeat business with drug traders and are more likely to be skeptical of a procurement request from an unknown source. In order to avoid the wholesaler's suspicion, we contracted a local trader to procure drugs for us. Because the trader we contracted already had an established business relationship with the wholesalers sampled, it is likely our data from the wholesale evaluation do not reflect the true magnitude of the counterfeit trade.

While part III presents the results of this study and discusses the implications, it is worth noting a few summary results at this stage, so that the reader can contemplate the scale of the problem, and what can be done about it, as we encounter counterfeiters and their deadly trade in the next few chapters.

Africa has the worst problem with poor-quality drugs, while India, China, and other emerging markets are doing better than in Africa, but a lot worse than the richest countries. Poverty and corruption are significantly associated with weaker drug quality, but the link is not that strong, and certainly not unbreakable, as we will see. Africa has a smaller share of fakes as a percentage of all failures, and combating substandard drugs is as much a priority for them as combating counterfeits, whereas for richer nations (including India), combating counterfeits may be the greater requirement. More precisely, my data indicate that substandard drugs are a bigger problem than counterfeits until income reaches an annual level of approximately $10,000 per person; after that, counterfeits are more dominant.

What Can Be Done?

While the poor are more likely to be affected by dangerous drugs, they can limit their exposure to dangerous drugs and avoid the worst excesses of those trading these products if they and their governments adopt a few sensible policies. Nigeria is a beacon of hope in this regard.

The rest of this book discusses the detail of the problems and outlines possible solutions, but it is worth mentioning a few here to demonstrate that all is not lost. There are things individuals can do to help curb the problem. Given a sufficient understanding, individuals can pressure the government and litigate through the courts; however, if their government provides no forum for citizens to address such issues, there is little they can do.

Where trademark violations are considered illegal, courts can provide legal redress for wronged companies, and individuals may be able to use common-law actions, such as negligence, especially if that comes with the power of injunction (stopping a company from manufacturing). The great value of civil action under English common law is the demonstration effect and restitution (other legal systems have similar forms of restitution).

Former British colonies have similar legal systems, so the remedies can be profound. As well as injunction, legal costs could be paid in addition to compensation, in effect requiring a responsible company to make real restitution to the victims and their families. Fines paid to an MRA do nothing to compensate victims.

Helping countries develop strong MRAs is surely a good policy, but where governance is poor, it may be futile or counterproductive to hand vast funds to a nascent and possibly corrupt MRA. After all, Western countries addressed corruption over the course of gradual development caused by economic growth and a cultural demand for safety, and it has taken about one hundred years to get to this point. Fortunately, myriad solutions have been tried and tested, so countries looking at MRA development as a new issue can choose what suits their needs, adapting methods as they like, but without having to go through all of the pain of trial and error themselves—some errors and failure of course are inevitable. Unfortunately, some countries lack even basic governance, and these countries may not appreciate external efforts encouraging them to establish an MRA, which ultimately may have to fight corruption within the government.

Because poor countries are often incapable or even unwilling to combat dangerous drugs effectively, the question of definitions takes on more global significance; it would be fine for countries to have their own definitions if they took effectual action on their own soil and had cooperative arrangements with other countries, such as extradition treaties. Western countries are frustrated by a capacity imbalance: most poor-quality drugs come from countries with inadequate rules and no ability to act, while Western countries have strong laws but lack the power to act. An international convention could increase the visibility of the importance of bad drugs in all countries without dictating paternalistic approaches for the poorer locations.

From top to bottom, here is a cursory list of what is needed to combat dangerous drugs: define fake drugs in international and national laws; enforce drug-quality laws through good communication between the police, customs, and MRAs; and equip MRAs with the authority and incentive needed to ensure they aggressively assess the products on the market, registering the good while exposing and preventing the bad. Although intellectual property rules can be useful in combating goods that violate trademarks (counterfeits), they often do little to remove substandard products from the market, and, therefore, for the poorest nations their enforcement should not be seen as a priority. (Nonetheless, laws should be in place to help companies take private actions, which can improve drug safety and provide them recourse.) Donors and other potential partners should assist with the above.

Doing the above should not be that difficult, and indeed it would not be if there was agreement on the importance of all of these factors. Unfortunately, as this book will show, disagreement exists to varying degrees on all of the above points and prevents necessary action.

PART II

Dangerous Drug Problems by Location

Nineteenth-century French novelist Honoré de Balzac is reputed to have said that "behind every great fortune there lies a great crime."[1] While most of those trading dangerous drugs are not wealthy—indeed, many are pathetically poor—many fortunes are certainly made by the worst criminals in the world of fake drugs.

In this part of the book, we encounter the trade and traders in counterfeit drugs. We will see the diverse ways in which they operate, the similarities and differences in their operations, and, in rare instances, read interviews with them. By nature of the subject, this is far from a complete assessment. Some places where counterfeits are made and traded are simply inaccessible or too dangerous for me to explore. In others, the underground nature of the business makes it largely impossible for an outsider to find useful information, even when one is actually in the right place.

I am constantly impressed by the drive and determination of those trying to stop counterfeiters; some of these individuals are discussed at length. A few, particularly security personnel in countries and companies who would not want to be acknowledged, form a large part of the reason I have any good stories at all. Indeed, most of the detailed stories below are from personal and professional contacts and, in some instances, from being in the right place at the right time. Most of the investigators I have come across epitomize those most likely to benefit from "chance." They often make me think of the great golfer Gary Player and brilliant chemist Louis Pasteur: both believed that hard work and expertise create the best framework to take advantage of new opportunities.

The journey begins in Africa.

4

Africa

Although this chapter addresses several countries in Africa, the primary focus will be Nigeria. That Nigeria might have a problem with fake drugs should be no surprise to anyone with experience of the country. Many state offices have little legitimacy and appear to exist for the sole purpose to siphon off money for personal gain. From the moment one arrives at Lagos airport the corruption begins. Informal traders sell access to the fast track at the airport for $10, and those not paying the bribe regret it immediately as immigration and customs officials, working in tandem with the touts, work so ponderously as to make $10 a bargain. And the corruption accelerates from there.

Counterfeit drugs were first reported in Nigeria in 1968, eight years after the country's independence from Britain. Until that time, Crown Agents, a private company founded in 1749 that dealt with, among other matters, drug procurement and management, had a monopoly on drug importation and supply into Nigeria. From all accounts, Crown Agents did a fine job of controlling safety, but because Crown Agents also focused on supplying drugs to the white minority, the black majority had only sporadic and limited access to these medicines. It is likely there were some adulterated and fake medicines in Nigeria prior to 1968 in both white and black communities, but these were unrecorded. Following independence, some regulations were repealed while others were not enforced. This occurred partly to encourage local businesses but also to ensure that the black majority benefited from greater access to medication. However, this more lax regulatory environment compromised safety. The problem grew enormously over the next three decades: Nigeria experienced an oil boom followed by bust and a bailout from the International Monetary Fund, while a background of "political patronage" awarded, among other things, pharmaceutical licenses and access to foreign pharmaceutical exchange to people who knew nothing about the pharmaceutical industry except that great profits were possible.

In response to these events, the legitimate supply-and-distribution chains became dysfunctional, corruption reigned, and good-quality drugs became scarce, at least for the majority of the population. Criminals took over parts of the distribution chain in Nigeria, further pushing legitimate suppliers out of the market. They filled the void with counterfeits, many originating from overseas. Paired with the general population's lack of understanding about medicines, major problems followed.

Andreas Seiter, the leading medicine expert at the World Bank, has made numerous general insights about the state of knowledge in many developing countries when it comes to drugs, but the following statement is particularly apposite for Nigeria: "Most education systems fail to provide the general population with basic knowledge about medicines and drug treatment, so in many countries a naïve belief in the possibilities of drug treatment persists, along with a 'more is better' attitude. Patients may expect a doctor to prescribe three or four drugs per visit. Injections are viewed as more powerful, even if there is no rational basis for this belief, and in fact, the rate of potential complications is much higher than for oral treatment. Such perceptions influence physicians' behavior as well; a physician who resists a patient's irrational expectation may fear losing the patient to another doctor."[2]

With such lack of appreciation of the appropriate use of medicines and the free-for-all that existed in Nigeria, it is of little surprise that a study conducted for a pharmaceutical firm in Lagos, Nigeria, in 1990 by Adeoye Lambo, former deputy director general of the WHO, found that an average of 54 percent of drugs in major pharmacies were fake.[3] By 2000, some estimated the figure had risen to 80 percent.[4]

Counterfeit Malaria Treatments and Growing Drug Resistance

In the summer of 2008, I went to Nigeria to investigate the case of fake drugs. I was lucky to have Dr. Andrew Azikiwe, a local doctor in Abuja, Nigeria's capital, as my guide. "I'm just like a Western doctor. Many of my patients have minor ailments," he told me as we walked through the crowded reception area to his office. But along with the broken bones and common colds, Dr. Azikiwe sees more and more patients with malaria, a mosquito-borne disease that kills nearly one million Africans each year, most of them children.

Most Nigerians administer their own malaria treatment. They know the symptoms: high fever and aching joints. They know the time-tested remedy: chloroquine, which can be purchased from a local pharmacy or street trader. Unfortunately, chloroquine's effectiveness has deteriorated over the years as the malaria parasite has mutated and developed resistance to the drug. Chloroquine now fails most of the time it is administered.

The second line of defense for malaria includes stronger drugs with strange names and uneven track records. Some of these drugs are excellent, while others made by legitimate firms have significant problems, including encouraging drug resistance and exhibiting side effects or poor performance against the disease. Complicating this new world of malaria treatment is, of course, a well-established industry of fakes, forgeries, and pseudo-pharmaceuticals with suspicious provenance. A sick patient who has tried what she thinks is chloroquine and who shows up in the doctor's office needing further treatment now presents a puzzle, and it is a dangerous and perplexing one.

If what she took was an outright fake, made of something like chalk or even fever-reducing aspirin (to which the malaria parasite is impervious), she may yet respond to genuine chloroquine. But if she has taken a poor-quality copy or counterfeit containing some chloroquine but not enough to kill all the parasites, then only the newer, much more expensive artemisinin-based combination therapy (ACT) will do. In the worst case, a patient may have received a dose of artemisinin—perhaps in a diluted medicine with a phony label—too weak to kill the parasite. Under those circumstances, the parasite may develop some immunity to artemisinin. Treating such a patient presents a problem even for well-qualified, well-resourced doctors, who are available only to the few "fortunate" Nigerians. The intertwined challenges Dr. Azikiwe faces are both social and medical: a hardy, drug-resistant strain of malaria and a corrupt, poor, and inconsistent health infrastructure constantly reinforce each other to the detriment of patients. The effects are often disastrous for children under five, who make up the majority of Africa's malaria victims and require more delicate care than adults.

While researchers and pharmacologists around the world work to develop new drugs, their efforts are complicated by opportunists faking legitimate products. In an environment where every sale puts a patient's life in peril, the market, which encompasses traditional commerce as well as financial aid and in-kind donations, has broken down in the deadliest of ways. This version of the black market not only distorts prices and causes inefficiencies, as one might expect with knockoff DVDs or Fabergé eggs; it kills children.

The UNODC says that there are 83 million cases of malaria in West Africa, of which more than half occur in Nigeria, and they suspect that perhaps up to half are treated with counterfeit medication, which "would represent a fake malaria drug market worth just under a half billion dollars."[5] To arrive at this figure means assuming a drug price of just under $10 a treatment, which, as we will see in part III, is probably manyfold too large, but the UNODC is right that the harm to patients is still significant.

One type of domestic counterfeiting particularly favored by Nigerians is the dilution of critical products, and, as has been known for nearly a century, dilution can be lethal. The practice in reality is quite similar to that fictionalized in *The Third Man,* the movie I discussed in the preface.

Of the pharmacies I visited in Abuja and Lagos in 2008, I could not pick out the counterfeits, diluted real drugs, or entirely bogus ones. As a white face asking about malaria drugs, I was offered the most expensive treatments with prices for a full course ranging from 1,250 to 1,750 naira (approximately $10 to $14 at that time). The best treatment on the market in 2008 was Coartem, an ACT produced by the Swiss company Novartis. It has been tested and approved by EU and Swiss regulatory agencies and is produced in both the United States and China. Of the twenty pharmacies my colleagues and I visited, thirteen stocked Coartem, six had heard of it but did not stock it, and one claimed no knowledge of it whatsoever.[a] But the drug's high cost ensures low sales (see box 4-10 on AMFm on page 114 for the latest attempt to increase access to Coartem and similar drugs). Patients tend to opt for older, cheaper drugs; because of drug resistance, many of these are ineffectual even when made well. But often drugs in

---

a. These visits were not part of the sampling in part III.

Africa are manufactured without consistent or effective quality assurance, making buying drugs a lottery in some places.

Back at his clinic, Dr. Azikiwe showed me a package called Salaxin, which claims on its packaging to be an antimalarial medicine produced in Belgium by a company called Saphire Lifesciences. Salaxin does not work, and it is not because Saphire Lifesciences is incompetent. Rather, the firm's address does not exist; nor is there a drug company of that name in Belgium.

Nigeria's Medical Regulatory Authority Steps Up

In a poor country like Nigeria, where the market is inundated with poor-quality drugs, a competent regulatory body becomes even more important. In most of the countries I visited, governmental bodies were not particularly helpful, and they often seemed to make little effort to improve the general drug-quality situation. Most health departments deny they have a significant drug-quality problem and particularly resent its exposure by independent foreigners. Of course, that is not to say officials want fake drugs; most countries are members of Interpol and work to varying degrees with it and related police, customs, and health agencies. National MRAs and police may not like to discuss the problem, but when confronted with a specific crime, and especially if offered a solution, they generally act; where evidence exists that they do not, it is presented in this book.

Nigeria, surprisingly, was the exception to this rule. Though the country struggles with corruption, it has discovered leaders who actively improve drug quality. I found many Nigerian government officials to be helpful, welcoming, and open. Indeed, they were more so than in any other country. They were willing to discuss the type, scale, and danger of the problem openly with researchers such as me. Dr. Azikiwe, among many others, praised certain officials, particularly those in the National Agency for Food and Drug Administration and Control.

Nigeria is still combating the fake-drug market, but the tide turned for the better in 2001, when its ineffectual MRA was dissolved and relaunched with[b]

---

b. NAFDAC was formed by Decree No. 15 of 1993 as a separate agency overseen by Ministry of Health; prior to that time, medicines were controlled by the Department of the Ministry of Health.

FIGURE 4-1

Dora Akunyili speaking at the American Enterprise Institute in 2007

Dora Akunyili (see figure 4-1); the agency's first director general who was to make impressive strides in combating the illegal drug trade. Akunyili was not only a pharmacy professor well versed in the problem of quality assurance in pharmaceuticals but also had a personal motivation for fighting drug counterfeiters: her sister Vivianne died in 1988 from an infection left untreated by a fake antibiotic, which she required because she had taken fake diabetes drugs. While in office from 2001 until accepting a new post in December 2008, Akunyili collected volumes of shocking tales about phony drugs and government complicity. "People have been dying in this country from fake drugs since the early 1970s," she told me.

Akunyili says that at the peak of the fake-drug problem, corrupt Nigerian officials would extort money from legitimate drug manufacturers in exchange for access to the market. She explained that some companies refused to bribe inspectors on ethical grounds and that others did not do so because tight profit margins did not allow for excess spending. With fewer legitimate suppliers and high demand, officials started accepting bribes from counterfeiters in exchange for legal protection when they introduced their dangerous drugs to the market.

Controls were so lax that few in government likely knew which products in the local market were authentic. Government officials and the wealthy purchased their drugs abroad or from suppliers sourcing from abroad.

Willful ignorance of the problems in the local market led to a major disaster in 1995, when the Nigerian government attempted to help neighboring Niger. Niger had launched a vaccination campaign to combat a meningitis epidemic. It received a donation of 88,000 vaccines from Nigeria, courtesy of pharmaceutical companies Pasteur Mérieux and SmithKline Beecham. It was not until after the immunization campaign had begun that workers from Médecins Sans Frontières noticed the vaccine behaved oddly when dissolved. Upon investigation it was discovered that the real vaccines, which had left the donor companies, had been substituted with perfect-looking fakes before reaching their destination. These contained no active ingredient. By the time the investigation determined the vaccines were fake, 60,000 people had been "inoculated," and some 2,500 patients died as a result.

A joint survey by NAFDAC, the UK Department for International Development, and the WHO, taken across Nigeria in 2001, revealed that between 40 and 70 percent of drugs for sale were fake or substandard; a follow-up survey in 2005 found that the number of such drugs had dropped to 16.7 percent. My first small survey of seven Lagos pharmacies showed a 32 percent failure rate for antimalarial drugs in 2007. In subsequent samplings in Lagos in 2009 and 2010, I found that the failure rate had fallen to roughly 17 and 10 percent, respectively (both larger samplings and from eleven pharmacies). These were significant reductions, and the credit goes to the leaders of NAFDAC.

Akunyili made impressive strides in fighting counterfeit drug rings in the country Transparency International once ranked as the most corrupt on earth.[c] NAFDAC's public awareness campaigns had notable successes; tip-offs from the public led to $16 million worth of fake drugs being seized or voluntarily handed over in 2005. NAFDAC also secured the convictions of more than sixty counterfeiters in Akunyili's first few years and had more than sixty open cases when I spoke with her in 2007. In 2006 her office shut down a market in the southeastern city of Onitsha in a raid that netted more than eighty truckloads of counterfeit drugs, most with no proper ingredients and nearly all with convincing labels and packaging.

Akunyili successfully pushed for harsher punishments for counterfeiters. Prior to her taking office, drug counterfeiters faced at most an $80 fine and three months in jail. Most of the accused never saw the inside of a courtroom, let alone a jail cell, because they paid off the police. By the time she resigned in 2008, the penalties still did not rival those for dealing in

---

c. The health minister between July 2003 and May 2007 was Eyitayo Lambo. When interviewed by me about a specific fake-drug problem reported in 2004, he dismissed it as his predecessor's problem. He was the last health minister to ignore or deflect concerns about fake drugs.

narcotics or even penalties for fake-drug trading in many other countries, but fines had increased. Many now exceed $1,000, and jail time is occasionally measured in years, not months. Equally important, more cases are actually prosecuted: tough laws are useless if they are not enforced. This is "not good enough, but a lot better than before," she says. And she is right: the drug market where at least one in ten drugs may be lethal is still disturbing.

I am not convinced that any quality estimates I have heard are that accurate or helpful, though. Even accurate aggregate numbers can hide major variations, and this assumes data are collected systematically by the same methodology across the country. In fact, data have not been collected properly, systematically, or with the same methodology, which is why Akunyili's figure of 10 percent fake drugs in Nigeria made me uneasy. Visiting a couple of rural markets around Kano and seeing drugs distributed in the cities in informal settings, such as at kiosks and general stores, and hearing that trade also occurs with street traders and in public transport, I got the distinct impression most of the figures are simply guesses; they may be educated guesses, but they are still guesses. This is not to imply that fake-drug rates have not fallen or that Akunyili was misleading anyone: I am sure fake rates have dropped and that quality has improved—at least in Lagos and Abuja—but even the best estimates are based on small samples. In fact, as quality improves it becomes more difficult to estimate overall quality: surveys have to be larger and even more rigorous to capture the full picture.

As will be seen in the next chapter on India, even governments that attempt to systematically measure drug quality run into problems if even one apparently small aspect is faulty—such as the sampling methodology. India should be praised as the only emerging market that has even attempted to measure quality.

Everyone Blames Foreigners

Most people have a pretty strong sense of positive national identity. We may quietly admit the failings of some of our country's citizens, but by and large we tend to be positive about our country's inhabitants. For those in positions of authority who represent their country, it must be especially difficult to openly criticize citizens, even more so if they harm fellow countrymen. Foreigners have been involved in most cases I have heard about that involved fake and otherwise dangerous drugs, but there is little doubt that nationals of each country in question were involved in the sale of these dangerous products, too. Yet, in nearly every case, authority figures will first focus criticism on foreign participants. Thus, when Akunyili identified preventing the importation of fake drugs as essential, I wondered how much was because they were to blame and how much was an indirect method to protect the reputation of her country.

Akunyili suggested that NAFDAC officials must inspect factories anywhere in the world "before we register their drugs, cosmetics, food, and other regulated products to ensure GMP compliance." She faced a daily battle during her time in the post, especially in dealing with officials from India and China, the two countries that supply most of her country's fake (as well as their real) pharmaceuticals. "Neither government is really trying to stop [the] production and export of fakes," she said. She sought funds from the central government to pay for NAFDAC analysts in India, China, and Egypt; they would recertify locally approved drugs before they could be exported to Nigeria. She also told me it is mandatory that preshipment information be provided by all importers before their drugs arrive. Having a NAFDAC clearance permit is a requirement for Nigerian banks to process any financial documents for drug importers. In addition, before an imported drug can be registered in Nigeria, a "certificate of free sale" signed by a minister of trade or industry from the exporting country must be provided and authenticated by a Nigerian embassy or any Commonwealth mission in a country without a Nigerian embassy.

These legislative requirements may be useful as long as government officials do not act in perverse ways, either by delaying product approval in the hope of seeking bribes or, worse, by approving products they know to be suspect and possibly fake because they were offered financial or other inducements. Even if officials properly comply with regulations, such regulatory controls tackle only registered products passing through legitimate intermediaries and approved points of transit; they do nothing to curtail smuggling, and they increase the bureaucratic costs. Furthermore, these requirements do not address the problem of home-grown fakes or substandard drugs, an issue about which Akunyili, like every drug authority figure I have met, was reticent. I suspect that at least a few senior officials

FIGURE 4-2

Dr. Paul Orhii
NAFDAC Nigeria

Roger Bate with Paul Orhii at a seminar with African regulators, May 2011

of the government are behind local drug companies in many cases, making Akunyili's job even more difficult.

Regardless, there is no denying that her actions against domestic traders of fake drugs were significant. She was successful even in the face of massive personal risk. In 2003 her car was ambushed, a bullet grazed her head, and a member of her staff was killed. The following year, her offices were burned down, leading to a decision to keep bodyguards with her around the clock.

Until the trade is significantly abated, Akunyili believes it is better to go without medicine than to consume drugs that might be counterfeit. Perpetuating the counterfeit trade will cause more deaths in the long run than forgoing improper treatment now. Her final words to me when I saw her last, in 2008, continue to make me think: "Better to have lack of access [to drugs] than access to counterfeits and substandard medicines."

NAFDAC's New Leadership

Akunyili was succeeded by Paul Orhii (see figure 4-2), whose task, although still huge, benefited greatly from his predecessor's work. Orhii is extraordinarily well qualified for this work, as he is a medical doctor and a lawyer and he holds a PhD in pharmacology. Orhii is well connected politically. He spent a stint as a legal practitioner in Texas, returning to Nigeria to support the Nigerian government's case against the U.S. company Pfizer. Pfizer conducted a clinical trial of Trovan, an antibiotic being tested against meningitis, during an epidemic of the disease in Nigeria in the 1990s (see box 4-1, "Trovan and Polio," on page 70). The company was accused of improperly conducting the trial, which ultimately led to an undisclosed settlement.[6] Critics claim Orhii was awarded the NAFDAC job as a reward

---

Box 4-1
TROVAN AND POLIO: NIGERIA VS. PFIZER

It was a good case for Orhii to be the plaintiffs' lawyer. There is little doubt at least one Pfizer employee acted very badly by backdating or inventing patient (and patient's guardians') acceptance forms for treatment with Trovan (Pfizer's meningitis drug). Simply for doing that, major damages would probably have been awarded had the case not been settled. At the same time, it is hard to say from looking at the data that a single child died because of Pfizer's actions. Children did die when taking Trovan, but across the patient population slightly more died taking other treatments. Meningitis is a killer disease, and a lot of children died, but many more were saved because of drugs and other treatments administered by Pfizer, charitable groups, and the Nigerian government. During the case, I suspected that if it remained as bitter and protracted as seemed likely, it would discourage investment or more clinical trials from taking place in Nigeria, which would ultimately be the worst outcome for the country. This seems to have become true. The case may have also furthered distrust of modern medicine and sent at least some people back to more traditional methods of treatment.

Polio vaccination is a miracle. There is no need for an injection: you just suck on a vaccine-encrusted sugar cube, and you are protected for the next decade. Yet, in Kano, Nigeria, it is not uncommon to see muscular upper bodies moving with acrobatic abilities on their hands—a novelty until you realize they have no legs. These are the crippling results of polio. How did this come about?

---

for his role in extracting funds from Pfizer. He says he just did his part to help Nigeria and expected no reward.

Orhii says he has one aim for his time at NAFDAC: to ensure that anybody can buy quality-assured drugs from any pharmacy in Nigeria. He wants to reduce the prevalence of forgeries to the level of Western countries—less than 1 percent—and to achieve this, he is taking action on several fronts. He revived plans for and formed a Federal Task Force on Counterfeit Drugs. His task force has raided premises and impounded suspect products in Abuja and other cities. In August 2010, he told me he hopes to extend activities to rural areas, but budgets are

When a WHO campaign was launched in 1988 to eliminate polio from the 123 countries still afflicted, it almost succeeded. By 2003, only seven countries still had cases, and the end was in sight. But clerics in Kano counseled parents against the vaccination, proclaiming it an American plot to sterilize Muslim youth and give them HIV. When Muslim parents obeyed, the southern-based and largely Christian Nigerian government refused to demand vaccination in the north, because it did not want to create religious tension. Today, Nigeria has over 70 percent of the world's polio cases and is rapidly exporting the disease. After the boycott, polio moved from Nigeria to Ivory Coast, from West Africa to Sudan, then across the Red Sea into Saudi Arabia and Yemen—which had been polio free for a decade; it even jumped continents to surface in Indonesia. Since the 2003 boycott, about twenty-five countries previously declared polio free have been reinfected.

Authorities in Kano State blamed the Pfizer/Trovan controversy for the widespread suspicion of government public health policies. State prosecutor Aliyu Umar said in court documents that the polio vaccine boycott "by citizens of Kano State is a direct consequence of the 1996 actions" of Pfizer. Religious leaders and government agencies are complicit in the deaths of orders of magnitude more children than Pfizer, but this is revisionist history to bolster a legal case against a foreign corporation. At the time the polio vaccinations were suspended, the governor of Kano State cited a belief that the polio vaccine itself was harmful, and did not mention Pfizer.

limited. Laboratory facilities are being upgraded to meet WHO international standards so they can be used for research, particularly for the creation of a databank of all drugs registered for sale in Nigeria. He says, "NAFDAC will undertake a survey and audit of all drugs on sale with the aim of building a databank of brands, identification marks, and differences between fake and genuine drugs." Under his leadership, NAFDAC is working to "encourage private businessmen to build drug wholesale hubs to 'ease out' existing open drug markets and to sanitize chaotic distribution channels." From what I can see, he is making progress, but it is painfully slow.

NAFDAC Partnerships. Orhii was eager to accept help from outside, and one of his first moves was to partner with the U.S. FDA, which trained NAFDAC officers in the best-available technology and advised NAFDAC on how to elicit help from state governors in Nigeria, especially those whose poorer and less-educated people are easy targets of counterfeit vendors. Orhii also sought help from the governments of India and China, where NAFDAC knows large quantities of fakes originate. He continues the work Akunyili did in this regard, and I got the impression relations between Nigeria and both Asian nations are better now than they were in the mid-2000s.

Negotiations with India, China, and Egypt have finally led to the presence of Nigerian agents who check all NAFDAC-registered exports from these countries for quality and proper documentation before they are loaded, as Akunyili had proposed. The NAFDAC officials work with appointed laboratories in India and China to test medicines before they are shipped to Nigeria. Orhii differentiates between India and China. Unlike Akunyili, who met intransigence and stonewalling from both India and China, Orhii encountered a more willing Indian government, whose position seemed to have changed sometime between 2007 and 2009. Like many experts, he sees great potential in India's vibrant industry and their genuine desire to improve drug quality, whereas China basically says, "Buyer beware."

Indeed, Samir Udani, chairman of Mecure Industries and a member of the Indian Pharmaceutical Importers in Nigeria, said he has been pleased with Orhii's openness. He also said he has been impressed by Orhii's efforts to ensure only good-quality Indian drugs are imported. Udani does have some critiques; he says NAFDAC needs to deploy more staff, particularly in northern Nigeria, and he is worried about increasing charges for imports from India and the slower speed of product-approved passage through customs. There are no simple solutions to these concerns, as part of the increase in delays at ports is due to increased inspections. Though these do increase costs for the innocent, and also, I'm told, the possibility of bribes being demanded, they pay off in terms of catching the guilty. A June 2009 bust led to a massive haul of oncology drugs, some of which had been concealed in men's boxers and duvets. Adetoun Olamuyiwa, NAFDAC's director of Ports Inspectorate, wants the airlines to pay more attention, too (particularly the Chinese air carriers). "If you bring fake products, the products will not only be seized; the aircraft will be impounded. [The airlines] should insist that all required NAFDAC documents are made available by importers before accepting [the] consignment," she says. Despite the delays and increased costs, the overall improvement in Nigerian-Indian relations heralds better-quality products, which, indirectly, probably worries Nigerian importers from China.

The partnership with China has been more complicated. Reading internal NAFDAC documents led me to the conclusion that the Chinese Chamber of Commerce realizes its reputation is bad for business and bad for brand China. Orhii says China is slowly beginning to act; after all, 25 percent of Nigeria's drugs come from China. But there is a conflict between China's stated desire to become the third-largest drug exporter by 2013 and its apparent lack of interest in fighting counterfeits. Orhii suggests it is in both Chinese and Nigerian interests to stop the fake-drug trade: the Chinese have a reputation for substandard products, but the Nigerians primarily suffer the health consequences.

Paul Orhii alerted me to the astonishing Chinese criminal counterfeiting drug networks his teams had unearthed. The networks are run from China and employ Nigerians and people of many other nationalities. They have successfully infiltrated the entire supply-and-distribution chains, from producer to patient, and across continents. Dr. Orhii said they either bribe employees of customs departments or, in numerous instances, their own personnel obtained jobs in places ranging from Nigerian and Chinese customs to Emirates airline, which was unwittingly transporting the fakes from China to Nigeria.

Each compliant official had responsibility at key parts of the distribution system, from manufacture in the Shenzhen free-trade zone until the drugs arrived in Lagos, Nigeria's largest city.

Dr. Orhii told me there are numerous cases of Chinese-made fakes being passed off as Indian generics. In 2009 my Nigerian colleague Thompson Ayodele came across another fake of an Indian drug, this time an antibiotic. Later we found out it too had been made in China.

Orhii's NAFDAC has been at the forefront of an unexpected fight between pharmaceutical interests in Beijing and Delhi. In early 2010, NAFDAC intercepted Lonart antimalarial drugs, allegedly made by GVS Labs of India (see figure 4-3). Lonart is a generic version of Coartem (Novartis's innovator product). GVS is one of the few Indian manufacturers approved by the WHO prequalification system to supply international donors. But the drugs actually came from China and were fake.

NAFDAC found out about this because of its whistleblower scheme, another of Orhii's ideas, which rewards informants with up to $2,000

FIGURE 4-3

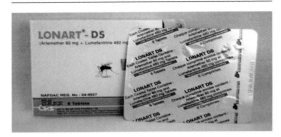

Nigerian-impounded Chinese fake of Indian drug Lonart

if their tips lead to prosecutions. "Someone called us about Indian fake meds coming into the airport, but once we opened the container we saw they were originally from China," he told me. In an effort to placate Nigeria and to show resolve, the Chinese authorites sentenced to death the six Chinese nationals complicit in this particular counterfeit drug trade (the sentence had not been carried out at the time of this writing).

Sentencing for Counterfeiters. In her term as director general, Akunyili was able to lengthen sentences a little and increase fines for counterfeiters; now, Orhii is working to make punishments much more severe (see box 4-2, "Punishment," on page 76 for discussion of the benefits and costs of this). He has consulted with legal scholars to create a new anticounterfeiting law that is working its way—"too slowly," he insists—through the sclerotic Nigerian political system. Under the law, counterfeiters would serve lifetime jail terms, their assets would be confiscated, and the value of their assets would go toward compensating victims and their families.

He originally promoted the notion of the death sentence for counterfeiters, saying, "When armed robbers catch you on the road and point a gun to your head, they demand either your money or your life. They give you an option, and most of the time, when they take your money, they let you go; they spare your life. But in this case [sellers of lethal fake medicines], these people take your life, they take the little money you have while they allow the disease to kill you slowly. So to me, they are worse offenders than even armed robbers, which in Nigeria . . . are executed by firing squad."

The issue of the death sentence is but one factor contributing to the difficulty of forming an international agreement on combating fake drugs. One astute observer is Ade Popoola, CEO of the Nigerian chain Reals Pharmacy. He explained that the "death sentence on drug fakers may be difficult for the [Nigerian] House of Assembly to approve since there are other very serious offences [for which] this country has cancelled the death sentence. What I think the National Assembly would rather do is increase the jail terms and increase the fines of drug fakers." He makes some interesting, even cryptic, criticisms of Dr. Orhii, saying that a lawyer looks at the law; other leaders look at power. "Dr. Paul Orhii stayed for so long in the Western world [which] could serve as an inhibition or area of weakness because [the West] is an environment where every law or legislation must be followed to the letter."

I wasn't entirely sure if Popoola was saying that Dr. Orhii will assume legislation is being followed and hence is naïve or that Dr. Orhii will not abuse his power, even when Popoola thinks he should, to catch or punish criminals, because he has become Westernized and will obey the letter of the law. But I think he meant the latter. In any event, he says that a few people have taken advantage of the transition from Akunyili to Orhii.

NAFDAC's own documents say it is "embarrassing" that the Chinese participants in a counterfeit drug ring exposed in 2009 faced far more serious punishments in China (six were ultimately sentenced to death) than the Nigerians involved. As NAFDAC stresses, China sentenced its participants even though the intended victims of the fake drugs were all Nigerians. "A Nigerian who committed the same offence in China sneaked back into the country and was arrested and charged in court by NAFDAC, but he was soon back on the streets as a free man as he was granted bail," said Orhii. NAFDAC uses these egregious discrepancies to demand that a "law review seek to impose stiffer penalties for offenders." Such statements are eagerly reported in the Nigerian media, which seems to support Orhii's aim.

Joseph Odumodu, CEO of pharmaceutical company May and Baker Nigeria, commented on how we should view NAFDAC investigative actions: "Generally, emphasis should now be not on the amount of fake products seized or destroyed but on what happened to owners of such products. That is why we applaud the DG [Orhii] on his determination to prosecute offenders and punish them according to the law. Though we appreciate that some of the laws are weak on punishments, it is necessary to use some

---

Box 4-2
PUNISHMENT

In many places such as Nigeria and even the United States, the maximum punishment for counterfeiting of drugs is too low, measured in a few months and three years, respectively. But while stiffer penalties are warranted for such a dangerous, potentially lethal activity, they do not help significantly if not backed up by other actions. As will be discussed in part III of this book, those countries with the strictest penalties actually have worse counterfeit drug problems. This is not a perverse result; it can be explained by these countries' efforts to demonstrate toughness against a problem they recognize as significant. But while sentences should be tough, that alone will never solve the counterfeiting problem. As Randy Barnett, a law professor at Georgetown University and a former criminal prosecutor for the Cook County State's Attorney's Office in Chicago, explains, the deterrent power of potential punishment is a function of both its severity and the rate of prosecution (that is, the likelihood of getting caught and convicted).

A government's first response to counterfeiting often involves an increase in fines, periods of incarceration, and other forms of punishment. Although a strong step, the stiffer punishment may not have the desired effect. By increasing penalties, a government may unwittingly decrease the likely rate of prosecution, thereby canceling or even reversing any added deterrence. In the United States, for example, convictions in criminal trials demand evidence "beyond reasonable doubt"; verdicts in civil trials permit a less rigorous

---

people as deterrent to others. To me, I do not subscribe to outright death sentence. I believe there are other ways to kill a criminal. If, for instance, a convicted person has twenty houses, and the state seizes them, and he is left with nothing after serving his jail term, believe me, he has been made to die slowly. There can be no other agony of death than seeing all that you have worked for being taken away from you and reducing you to nothing."

Deploying New Technology

Despite NAFDAC's continuing efforts, many distributors still push fake and substandard products through the numerous open-air markets, even in Lagos. Lanre Familusi, chairman of the Lagos chapter of the

"preponderance of the evidence." In criminal trials for serious offenses, where punishments may be severe, the evidence hypothetically is held to the highest standard. Even when a criminal is successfully prosecuted, punishment in high-stakes cases may be delayed, further weakening the penalty's deterrent power. Harsher penalties also increase incentives for counterfeiters to resist capture and prosecution. Potential defendants may bribe or intimidate officials, especially customs agents. If a trial seems likely, they will pay for better lawyers and may invest in buying off witnesses. While some potential counterfeiters may be deterred, those who remain will tend to be more organized and more violent.

Making punishment more severe is usually a step in the right direction, but only when it is joined with strong enforcement. Although the United States, Nigeria, and other nations should increase sentencing for counterfeiting of drugs, a key reason that the United States has a very low problem is because of the considerable enforcement effort of its customs agents, companies, police, FDA, and other agencies.

Sources: Randy Barnett, *"Fighting Crime without Punishment," The Structure of Liberty: Justice and the Rule of Law* (Oxford: Oxford University Press, 2004), chap. 11; Barnett, personal communication with author, October 2004.

Pharmaceutical Society of Nigeria (which opposed Orhii's nomination to head NAFDAC because he was not a pharmacist), made a very prescient point in the November 30, 2009, issue of the magazine *Nigerian Newsworld*. He expressed disappointment in the proliferation of drug markets across the country, claiming that it leads to "chaotic drug distribution channels," notably from the open-air drug markets that exist in many key locations throughout Nigeria. "No matter what NAFDAC does to arrest drug faking, as long as the open drug markets are allowed in the drug distribution chain, nothing meaningful would come out of the effort," Familusi says.

Foreign security experts tell me up to seventy importers and traders without any real pharmaceutical knowledge operate with impunity on Lagos Island; they contribute to the fake-drug problem but are not stopped by NAFDAC. Colleagues of mine, such as Thompson Ayodele of the Initiative for Public Policy Analysis, tell me stories of the plethora of general traders not licensed to trade in drugs and, therefore, outside NAFDAC's jurisdiction; they routinely trade in drugs, especially in open markets.

Has Orhii Improved Drug Quality?

In discussions with the various interested parties, I was struck by the fact that even in 2011 no one was sure how bad the fake-drug situation was in Nigeria. Though I think most estimations are just good guesses, I put the question to Orhii at different times and venues—not so much to trick him into different answers, but because he was making educated guesses, and those guesses may change over time with new information. The last time I spoke with him at the end of summer 2011, he reminded me that the last official assessment had been made in 2005, when NAFDAC and the WHO reported the rate at 16.7 percent. In 2011 he believed the failure rate was "less than 10 percent in cities, closer to 5 percent in most, but I suspect [there is a] higher rate in rural areas, where we are going to investigate now." Orhii knows it will be difficult to improve quality where products cannot be assessed properly.

Given budget constraints, Orhii decided deploying technologies such as bar scanners—which require major systems and logistical support—to track and trace products through the distribution chain was simply not viable for most of Nigeria (box 4-4 on page 82 discusses track and trace technology). He has deployed some Minilab test kits, which nonexperts can use after only basic training to analyze suspicious drugs (see box 4-3, "Basic Testing Using the Minilab"). These fast-testing, portable laboratory systems analyze samples within a few hours and are being used at various NAFDAC sentinel sites around Nigeria. Although useful, however, the Minilab is not fast or easy enough to be deployed widely in rural areas, so testing has been limited outside of the cities. Furthermore, the Minilab has not deterred as much criminal activity as Orhii would have liked.

NAFDAC also suffers from too few staff to undertake its job. With over six thousand companies to be inspected in Lagos, a city of twenty million people, and only three NAFDAC vehicles for inspection, much of possible investigation time is spent in transit. Interminable traffic restricts NAFDAC to inspecting only three companies a day. "We only have 1,500 staff for the whole of Nigeria to cover drugs, but also food and chemicals, [and] there are 774 administrative areas," Orhii says. Track-and-trace technologies, outlined in box 8 below, may be able to help.

NAFDAC needed to upgrade its technology in an effort to deter drug counterfeiting and to identify counterfeiters more efficiently. As a result, Orhii was a proponent of and very excited by the deployment of the TruScan, a Raman spectrometer first used in Nigeria in January 2010. The TruScan allows users to assess products while they are still in situ in the field, and hence it is far faster than other technologies. In fact, it can provide a result instantaneously. It is also easy to use; anyone with a moderate education can be trained to operate it in an hour. Although they are expensive (about $50,000 each), Orhii bought six TruScan devices. Because these spectrometers can identify fake drugs in a matter of seconds, people selling fake products can be questioned and even arrested on the spot.

Of nearly one thousand press clippings about NAFDAC in 2009, at least twenty referred to the TruScan as a new technology that would help save people's lives. Given that the technology had yet to be deployed, this was considerable coverage. The stories slightly exaggerated how successful the TruScan would be (as I will show in part III, the TruScan has limitations that media coverage often overlooks). If counterfeiters believed those news stories, which appeared in every major news outlet in the country, some likely changed their activities. Knowing NAFDAC would deploy the TruScan in the cities first, it is possible counterfeiters curtailed some of their activities in the cities. This may have contributed to the fall in counterfeit drugs that NAFDAC, I, and my colleagues in key Nigerian cities witnessed. However, counterfeiters may have simply shifted their activities to rural areas where controls and technology deployment were weak. Still, Orhii believes at least some counterfeiters are backing off. The "fake rate could maybe be down to 1 percent in two to three years," he says.

It may seem odd that a relatively poor country deploys such an expensive technology, but it makes sense. Although one U.S. State Department official I spoke with called this akin to using a "nuclear device to crack a nut," Orhii may have been correct to deploy such devices precisely because alternative, cheaper methods require logistical support absent in most parts

Box 4-3
BASIC TESTING USING THE MINILAB

The Minilab is a self-contained mobile laboratory designed by the Global Pharma Health Fund that provides the essential lab ware, chemicals, and reference materials to quickly screen for medicine quality in nonlaboratory settings. The Global Pharma Health Fund (www.gphf.org) is a charitable organization initiated and funded exclusively by donations from Merck Darmstadt, Germany.

Working within international development assistance initiatives, the Global Pharma Health Fund aims to improve health care and medicines supply, supporting the fight against counterfeit and substandard-quality medicines' proliferation by using their Minilab test kits. The kit's great value is in enabling robust basic quality testing in places where formal laboratory facilities are not available. It enables health facilities responsible for drug purchase, storage, and distribution to protect themselves and patients against the danger of counterfeit medicines consumption.

In 2011 Nigeria received 20 Minilabs, which means at least 420 Minilabs are being used in over 70 countries of Africa, the Asia-Pacific, and Latin America. "The key is that our Minilabs are reaching people where protection against counterfeit and substandard quality medicines is needed instantly, hence, in countries and drug supply organisations where appropriate testing capacities are still lacking." says Richard Jähnke, project manager at the Global Pharma Health Fund. The first Minilab went to a hospital in Mindanao run by Doctors for Developing Countries (a charity also based in Darmstadt, Germany) in the Philippines in 1999. However, the concept of the Minilab really gained momentum when WHO's Roll Back Malaria

of Nigeria, not to mention the even poorer parts of Africa. A handheld spectrometer is more important in a resource-constrained environment than it would be in a middle-income country such as China, because basic logistical drug-delivery systems, which we take for granted in the West and which could be deployed in China, are simply not deployable in most of Nigeria due to illiteracy and woeful management. A stand-alone, rapid technology is deployable anywhere, though, including in the most backward and corrupt places. This makes sense, for although technology can do only so

Partnership programs assessed and used more of them in the sub-Saharan, Mekong, and Amazon regions.

Over one hundred Minilabs have been deployed by technical assistance programs of the United States Pharmacopeia alone. This helped in boosting testing capacity, identifying harmful counterfeit or substandard-quality medicines, and protecting public health and patient safety in about twenty countries.

USP's program, Promoting the Quality of Medicines (PQM), has provided Minilabs at field data collection facilities, called sentinel sites, allowing personnel at the local/community/hospital/health program levels to regularly test medicine quality in the marketplace. PQM staff train users in basic testing methods (visual/physical inspection, disintegration, and thin-layer chromatography [TLC]) developed and validated specifically for the Minilab for antimalarial, antituberculosis, antiretroviral, and some antibiotic medicines. With the monographs PQM developed on oseltamivir phosphate and oseltamivir capsules, the Minilab can also be used to test the quality of medicines for avian influenza. Prior to testing the medicines, PQM staff conduct training in proper sampling procedures.

Elsewhere, minor initiatives are deploying Minilabs at medical stores and drug supply organizations, allowing them to conduct due diligence in quality assessment. The Minilab's method inventory has been extended and now covers fifty-two active pharmaceutical ingredients, the bulk of them being anti-infective agents to treat malaria, TB, and AIDS. Another supplement is scheduled for 2011, which will cover five more compounds from the same treatment categories.

much, it sends subliminal and powerful messages to fakers that NAFDAC is modern and sophisticated and waiting to pounce (as I explain in part III, simply introducing the TruScan had a statistically noticeable impact on drug quality in Lagos).

The TruScan had an immediate impact, assisting in the above mentioned interception of fake Lonart. NAFDAC used the TruScan to detect a whole container load of imitation Lonart (see figure 4-3), providing evidence that made it easier to arrest culprits on the spot. And as I saw

Box 4-4

TRACK AND TRACE

"Track and Trace" technologies are automated tracking systems used to monitor the location and authenticity of drugs as they move from manufacturer to patient. Innovative technology certainly has the potential to improve our ability to detect fakes, but lack of resources and difficulties in scalability make it uncertain how useful it can be

A manufacturer "tracks" each lot, batch, or unit dose by embedding the package with a unique electronic identification code that can be detected when the item is scanned. The drug is "traced" when a manufacturer, regulator, retailer, or consumer scans the item, which automatically generates an electronic record including the batch number, drug details, and scan location. This process requires three unique and interconnected technologies. First, it requires an electronic chip that is embedded in the unit-dose packaging at the time of manufacture. Second, all members of the supply chain must have access to a scanning device to read the electronic encryption. Finally, the scanning device must be connected to an electronic database that provides the purchaser or regulator with the drug's origination information and stores the scan location for the manufacturer's later use.

There are two main types of Track and Trace technology, unit-dose bar codes and radio frequency identification (RFID). Unit-dose bar codes are, as their title indicates, visible electronic codes encrypted on the unit-dose packaging. These are cheaper than the RFID technology, but can be challenging to monitor because each product must be scanned individually. It is doubtful that regulators charged with inspecting and tracking shipments containing thousands of individually marked drugs will be able to scan and trace each package, so these are not ideal tools for monitoring large international shipments. However, they may be useful at the retail and consumer level if the scanning technologies are easily available in countries where the regulatory system is of low capacity.

RFID encoding, which includes batch and lot number as well as unit-dose identification, creates a reliable electronic record of the drug's movements and allows for rapid recall of batches if required, but still has some significant limitations. RFID technology is more expensive and less reliable than the simpler bar coding. A pilot study report by Cardinal Health indicates that interference between the different chips' frequencies may hamper the scanner's ability to read the encrypted data, and 15 percent of the chips in the pilot were unreadable by the time they reached the pharmacy level.[1]

Imbedding the unique electronic identifier on each individual unit-dose, whether it be a bar code or an RFID chip, is a significant expenditure for the pharmaceutical company, and it is unlikely that companies will be willing to do this without significant monetary incentives. In order for these technologies to become operable on a large scale, either they must generate profits equal to the cost of identification chips, or companies must face expensive legal penalties for failing to do this.

To overcome these obstacles, two firms, Sproxil and PharmaSecure, have taken a technology of mPedigree of Ghana and developed an interesting option. They print a code on the package, which the consumer can text to the associated phone number, also printed on the package, to verify authenticity. Within minutes, their cell will receive a text that verifies or denies the authenticity of the medicine. While Sproxil, a firm based in Nigeria, prints codes under a scratch-off label, India's PharmaSecure uses the cheaper (albeit less clandestine) method of printing directly onto a range of packaging materials in tamper-proof ink (see figures 4-4 and 4-5, below). Because each code can only be verified once, counterfeiters would not profit from producing imitation batches.

In order to recoup the costs of the program, these start-up firms collect market data and cell numbers when a user texts in the drug number. They then provide the manufacturer with the data and contact information, and the companies are able to advertise to consumers with promotional offers via text message. To date, Sproxil has sold over five million unique scratch-off labels to major clients such as GlaxoSmithKline (for its antibiotic Ampilox) and Johnson & Johnson (for Nizoral antifungals). PharmaSecure has sold seventy million codes to drug manufacturer Unichem. Despite the low cost and scalability of the mobile verification method, it has its downsides as well. First, the systems, like all systems heavily reliant on technology, are vulnerable to glitches in

(continued)

---

1. "Nigeria Reaffirms Efforts to Eliminate Fake Drugs," Xinhua General News Service, February 13, 2003, reporting on survey by the Nigerian government's Institute of Pharmaceutical Research.

Box 4-4 (*continued*)
TRACK AND TRACE

the database and attacks from hackers, including direct manipulation of the database, DDoS attacks, and rerouting of the phone number to a number that automatically verifies any code. Second, this system provides no information to regulators concerning where the drugs are coming from or the location of sale, a major selling point for the RFID tracking system.

FIGURE 4-4
CELL RECEIVING TEXT VERIFYING AUTHENTICITY

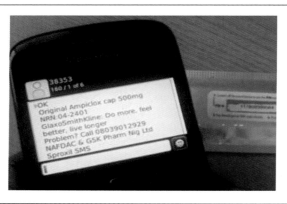

FIGURE 4-5
SPROXIL LABEL

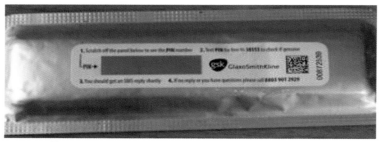

Scratch-off label, self-adhesive

in my research, the TruScan is having a major impact in other ongoing investigations. Finding fake versions of drugs such as Artesunat, a Vietnamese antimalarial, is also made easier using the TruScan (see figures 4-6 and 4-7 in box 4-5).

Elizabeth Awagu of NAFDAC chuckles when she recalls how traders' eyes open very wide when they see the TruScan being deployed and people arrested immediately. "It sends a powerful signal," she tells me. Arrests and new technologies are eagerly reported in the media (and NAFDAC enjoys being able to show that it uses an advanced U.S. technology no other country uses in such a systematic way; to the local media, NAFDAC presents itself as "the only regulatory organization in the world" deploying the TruScan [see figure 4-8]).

Orhii uses the TruScan spectrometer in many ways, but he broadly follows a protocol so results can be comparable. A NAFDAC vehicle sits outside a store NAFDAC staff members are going to investigate. Their procedure resembles a scene from CSI: first, a covert inspector is sent to procure drugs, which are then whisked outside to be tested with the TruScan; if the drugs are fake, NAFDAC has probable cause, and the staff members proceed to interview and possibly arrest the pharmacist and test more of the drugs. This practice caught the eye of experienced news icon Dan Rather in September 2010, and won a spot on his U.S. television show *Dan Rather Reports*.

In addition to good TV, it is also scientifically interesting that, according to Orhii, the TruScan results agree with the more detailed laboratory analysis NAFDAC has undertaken. Although most scientists I have spoken with think the TruScan is useful, some are unsure of how it stands up to these more detailed laboratory tests, so Orhii's statements are anecdotal validation of the technique. At some stage I hope to analyze the NAFDAC data in full. From what I have seen, it will be the largest and most comprehensive fake-drug database of any country where fake drugs are a consistent and dire problem.

NAFDAC officers have been testing the products in markets and arresting, prosecuting, and jailing traders in fake drugs. Kindsley Ukungwu of Onitsha was arraigned July 1, 2010, before the federal high court in Awka for trading fake drugs. This kind of NAFDAC action is now expected and understood by criminals, who, it is expected, have adapted their behavior

Box 4-5
Holograms

Holograms have been used by manufacturers to help prevent counterfeiters from perfectly copying legitimate packaging. Holograms are costly to manufacturers, but they are widely considered worthwhile so as to increase the cost to the counterfeiters of having to emulate complicated ones. In addition, holograms are useful for spotting fake packaging. Note the Artesunat samples below. The one on the right is the fake, and one can see that the hologram does not appear as bright or detailed as the real to the left. Interestingly, it looks better to the naked eye and looks very similar to the real hologram. Photography accentuates the fake's flaws for some reason. Another advantage is that fake holograms provide law enforcement with even more data to work with in order to find the counterfeiters.

Figure 4-6

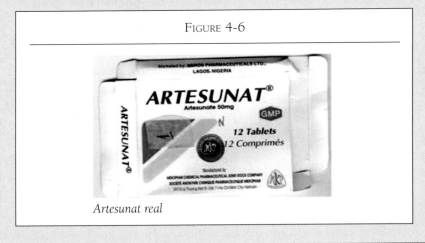

Artesunat real

accordingly. The chairman of the Onitsha Drug Dealer Association, Emeka Ezeanyika, who attempts to ensure good-quality trade takes place in Onitsha, commends NAFDAC head Paul Orhii. Even away from the major cities of Lagos and Abuja, dealers like Ezeanyika were aware of "the introduction of the new fake-drug detecting machine."

But although NAFDAC's clampdown and deployment of the TruScan means some may no longer conduct criminal actions, others will just change the form of their lethal fraud. So although NAFDAC's action is certainly

The downside, of course, is that patients and pharmacists and others in the legitimate distribution chain have to know what the real hologram looks like or that a hologram should be present (note box 5-1 on Ciprotab; the fake doesn't have a hologram on the back, but the pharmacist from whom it was bought and our covert buyer didn't know one was required). My research team did not notice the flawed hologram in the below Artesunat fake until *after* the drug had been tested. Once we realized it had zero API, we examined the packaging more closely and found the flaw in the hologram.

FIGURE 4-7

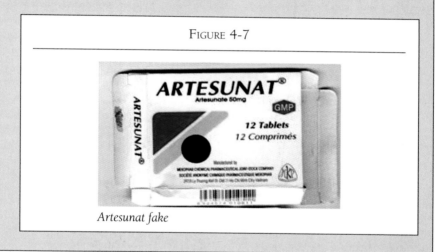

Artesunat fake

good, several expert investigators I spoke with suspect the larger fake traders are now avoiding most of the major markets and selling stolen products directly to smaller-scale traders, who sell to roving salesmen, who then sell to consumers on buses and through kiosks. Many of the stolen and fake drugs will be shipped from Onitsha down the Niger River to other African countries or by road to northern Nigeria, where current NAFDAC activities are not quite as well targeted. "As the more formal settings are cleaned up, illegal actors move to less formal ones," a local pharmacist I spoke with said, echoing the investigators' arguments. Although happy about NAFDAC's actions, he suggested there was only so much one agency could do with rampant corruption in the entire region.

Of course, sometimes one doesn't need to use TruScan to spot a bad product; sometimes the drugs are so degraded that anyone who knows what to look for can spot these drugs immediately. Unfortunately, degraded drugs are often sold as though they're fine, with tragic consequences (see box 4-6, "Artusenat and Rimactizid").

FIGURE 4-8

NAFDAC staff being trained on TruScan

A Shift to Local Production?

Orhii expects that a decline in the rate of counterfeiters will be the result of new, local drug producers, who will make good products to displace suspect imports. Currently, Nigeria imports from India and China 70 percent of drugs required by the population. "Most [Nigerian] companies will have WHO certification by [the] end of 2011. . . . It will be easier for us to oversee local production than travelling far and wide to oversee the drugs Nigeria imports," he says. "I envision a situation where at least five indigenous drug companies can access the Global Fund after attaining WHO prequalification through NAFDAC's guide."

Nigeria has a massive potential market of over 150 million people, and its local firms want to supply this market. But there can be all sorts of problems with locally produced drugs in infant industries. First, economies of scale mean these drugs are nearly always more expensive than imported drugs. Second, the quality is more variable (see figure 4-5 for a comparison of Western and Indian drugs with those made in Africa), leading to more substandard products. Third, when either of these two problems arises, supporters of local companies—often politically powerful support-ers—pressure officials to ignore these concerns. Indeed, like his predeces-sor, Orhii does not want to discuss the problems local production might cause. He just wants to focus on the positive and hopes donors will invest in Nigerian pharmaceutical businesses. But although NAFDAC routinely arrests company representatives who break the rules, there is no doubt that Nigeria's pharma industry is still a long way from operating universally at a strong ethical level. Olumiyiwa Akintayo, who is a pharmacist and an employee of a Lagos-based pharmaceutical company, was trading in faked drugs, replacing his companies' products with the fakes before selling into markets in Ibadan. Such incidents are not isolated (see box 4-7 on page 92 for more detail on the advantages and problems of local production).

Orhii does acknowledge that NAFDAC does not have the staffing to do proper assessments of all of the products produced locally. Indeed, he says, "We're not funded enough to have well-trained staff for all locations," even for the job of monitoring fake drugs on the market. Take Kano State with its 9.5 million people, he says. "Kano State has forty-four government areas; we-have two vehicles and one is not functioning. How are we going to effectively cover those forty-four areas?" He shrugs. "Ideally we should be present in every local government area."

But with the focus on finding dangerous products and catching those selling them, he acknowledges that his department is slow to register new legitimate products, and this causes opportunities for fake traders. He told Nigeria's *Leadership* magazine on February 13, 2009, "When it takes too long to register genuine products that have been certified to be safe and allowed to get into the market, the smugglers have the market and because when you have very light penalties, just a slap on the wrist for violators, then there are incentives because the profit margin is high for them, the incentives are there." Orhii told me NAFDAC had registered 15 percent more products in 2009 than in 2008. This was probably due to an increase of 332 staff over the same period.

Combating Corruption

Like in other locations in Africa, many public-sector products are stolen and diverted into private-sector distribution systems in Nigeria. Like the issue of

Box 4-6
Artesunat and Rimactizid

In the pictures below, the box of Artusenat is obviously degraded. One can see the buckling of the blister pack because of exposure to sustained and significant heat. The product was bought in Nigeria and failed quality control tests, so its use could have led to the nontreatment of malaria.

The drug pictured below is Rimactizid, a TB drug bought at a pharmacy in Delhi. One can see the most degraded product bottom right.

Figure 4-9

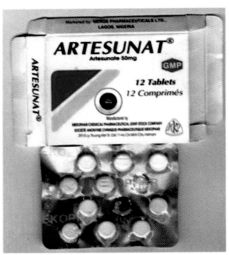

Artesunat front

Figure 4-10

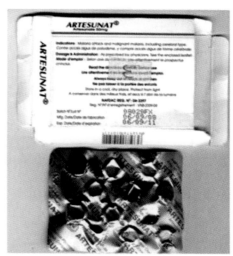

Artesunat back

Figure 4-11

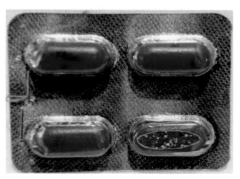

Degraded Rimactizid

Box 4-7

LOCAL PRODUCTION—A SOLUTION TO LOCAL ACCESS?

The local production of pharmaceuticals refers to the production of drugs or other treatments by firms located in (and/or owned by) a country that are specifically tailored to meet the demands of the market in that country (e.g., Ugandan pharmaceutical firms that produce antimalarials specifically for the Ugandan market). The term "local," however, can take on several meanings depending on whether a strict ownership or economic perspective is adopted in considering production, so local producers may include national firms, with sale activities strictly within the country, or multinational firms, which carry out only part of the production process within the country. As each of the three levels of pharmaceutical production (primary, secondary, and tertiary) can be undertaken locally, local production includes a variety of products: primary production includes the manufacture of active pharmaceutical ingredients and intermediates; secondary production includes finished dosage forms; and tertiary includes the packaging and labeling of products.[1]

There are many reasons why a government might want its own companies to make essential medicines rather than have to buy from abroad, including the following: unreliable suppliers; questionable drug quality (from other developing-country producers); avoidable costs (i.e., transportation costs); and difficulties involved in forecasting demand when preordering supplies.[2] In theory, local production seems like an attractive solution to many of these problems—and it is one donors seem to want to support. For example, the German government is funding pharmaceutical companies in Bangladesh (Squire Pharmaceutical), Cameroon (Cinpharm), Ethiopia (Sino-Ethiop), Kenya (Cosmos LTD), and Tanzania (Shelys Pharmaceuticals).[3] Rhetorically, supporters of local production refer to "health security" much like supporters of agricultural subsidies do of "food security." Secondary, more industrial, reasons for a developing country wanting to promote local production might

---

1. "An intermediate is a material produced during steps of the processing of an API that must undergo further molecular change or purification before it becomes an API." Kaplan, W. L., and R. Laing, *Local Production: Industrial Policy and Access to Medicine--An Overview of Key Concepts, Issues, and Opportunities for Future Research.* HNP Discussion Paper, World Bank, Human Development Network, page 4. Available at www.worldbank.org/hnp.

2. Ibid, p. 1.

3. Ibid, p. 6.

also include the desire to create a new employment base, increase transfers of technology and knowledge, enter a new export market, cut dependency on foreign suppliers, and better manage otherwise negative foreign exchange flows.[4] Though local pharmaceutical production can have industrial benefits for developing countries, the extent to which it can provide increased access to medicines varies considerably from country to country.

For local production to be successful and competitive, it requires a constant supply of inputs, such as organic chemicals and biological agents like enzymes, as well as constant energy, clean water, skilled expertise, and advanced technology; without reliable supplies, the manufacturing of local drugs can lead to shortages and when produced be of inconsistent quality; in some cases, dangerous. Even if the drugs are of acceptable quality, local producers must still be nearly as efficient as foreign suppliers in order to succeed, or they will fail in the face of competitors offering lower prices for the same product. Often, when nascent pharmaceutical companies lack the capacity needed to compete in the international market on their own, their respective governments will protect them from more efficient foreign producers. Such action can result in higher drug prices and lower access because there are fewer cheap foreign drug supplies.

A World Bank study compiled a series of indices helpful for predicting the pharmaceutical production capability of a given country.[5] Using statistical analysis and data from a variety of countries, the Bank report assesses the strength of the association between local production and several independent variables, such as population size, gross domestic product, total health care expenditure, and level of human resources; all were factors that had strong positive associations with high pharmaceutical production capacity. The report concluded that the ability for developing countries to be successful in local production varied greatly, because "to be globally competitive as a producer of pharmaceuticals requires a combination of factors that only a few developing countries can approach. There is a critical mass of industrial and

(continued)

---

4. Ibid.
5. Ibid, p. 18.

Box 4-7 (*continued*)
LOCAL PRODUCTION—A SOLUTION TO LOCAL ACCESS?

---

socioeconomic development in human and technical resources that must be reached before any indigenous pharmaceutical industry can survive."[6]

Looking at some of the indicators mentioned above, we can see why some developing countries have been successful, notably India. India has a good variety of raw materials for pharmaceutical production and export.[7] India's vast population also provides significant demand for locally produced pharmaceuticals, and the location of the country facilitates access to markets around the world. Furthermore, as a significant absolute number of its total population is enrolled in secondary and tertiary education, India has a large pool of highly skilled and qualified workers necessary for a viable pharmaceutical industry, which most other developing countries do not have.[8] All things considered, India has the industrial capacity and resources necessary to make local production efficient, competitive, and beneficial in practice.

Most developing countries, however, lack the combination of factors that makes local pharmaceutical production viable. This is particularly true for many countries in sub-Saharan Africa. In Africa, a variety of these barriers are already well known, including a general shortage of skilled labor, lack of advanced technologies, weak flows of foreign direct investment, dependence on foreign aid, weak legal and regulatory systems, poor educational systems, poor infrastructure, unreliable energy supply, and concerns over a lack of domestic tax base, inflation, and corruption, among other things.[9,10] It is because of these problems that even agencies that are incentivized to promote local production, such as the United Nations Conference on Trade and Development (UNCTAD), caution: "It therefore may not make sense for all LDCs [least-developed countries] to aspire to be scaling up their local production

---

6. These factors might include: "GDP greater than about $100 billion, population greater than about 100 million, sufficient numbers of the population enrolled in secondary and tertiary education, a net positive pharmaceutical balance of trade, and a competitiveness index greater than about 0.15," Kaplan & Laing (2005) p. 26.

7. Ibid, p. 15.

8. Ibid, p. 25.

9. Ibid, p. 12.

10. "The Business of Health in Africa: Partnering with the Private Sector to Improve People's Lives," International Finance Corporation (IFC) Report, World Bank Group (2007) p. 77.

of medicines." UNCTAD's report also points out that "many LDCs do not require evidence of bioequivalence for generic medicines."[11]

If local production is inefficient, there is the temptation for governments to enact legislation to protect local firms from the more efficient foreign producers. In Tanzania, the government implemented a 10 percent tax levy on imported medicines to keep local producers competitive, and in Nigeria the government banned the importation of many drugs manufactured locally, so much so that local industry now supplies more than 30 percent of medicines in the country.[12] As the International Finance Corporation, the World Bank's private sector lending arm, noted, although "in general these protectionist policies aid the domestic competitive position of sub-Saharan African pharmaceutical manufacturers . . . whether these policies will improve access to more affordable drugs or create the right incentives to improve drug quality is debatable," and results thus far have been mixed.[13]

As the South African coordinator for the WHO's Drug Action Programme, Martin Auton, explained, "Every little country wants to manufacture ARVs [antiretrovirals], [and] a lot of it's about national pride—but you have to make sure it's economically viable, and not just producing for the sake of producing."[14]

Generally, drugs produced by smaller companies are more expensive than those produced by larger companies because they cannot benefit from economies of scale (whereby a producer's average cost per unit falls as scale is increased). Consequently, African manufacturers generally produce at a cost disadvantage to bigger generic manufacturers, particularly in India. "Although conversion cost scale efficiencies generally plateau around 1.0–1.5 billion tablets in blister packaging per year, production at most sub-Saharan African formulation sites is far below that level."[15] Local African

(continued)

---

11. "The evolution of Drug Production in Nigeria," National Agency for Food, Drug Administration and Control (NAFDAC), available at http://www.nafdacnigeria.org/drugproduction.html.

12. "A Case for Local Manufacturing of Pharmaceuticals," Uganda Pharmaceuticals Manufacturers' Association (UPMA) Report (2007) p. 5.

13. IFC Report, p. 78.

14. "AFRICA: Local manufacture—competition key to cheaper ARVs," PlusNews (September 2005), available at http://www.irinnews.org/InDepthMain.aspx?InDepthId=12&ReportId=56079.

15. IFC Report, p. 77.

Box 4-7 *(continued)*
LOCAL PRODUCTION—A SOLUTION TO LOCAL ACCESS?

manufacturers in places such as Ghana are estimated to bear a 30–40 percent cost disadvantage compared with larger Indian manufacturers, and almost a third of this is attributed to scale.[16]

Not only do small African producers struggle to compete in price against larger foreign companies, but often their drugs cannot compete in quality. As the International Finance Corporation notes, "While several manufacturers in the region are seeking [WHO] prequalification, it is a difficult process for most of them—it requires renovation of production facilities, familiarity with qualification requirements and processes, and a dossier of product efficacy and safety tests that meets with regulatory bodies' requirements. Given the prevalence of small manufacturers in the region, the above requirements represent too high an economic burden, and, at the same time, often exceed the limited technical capability of the management teams."[17]

Consequently, firms not meeting international quality standards miss out on a significant part of the pharmaceutical market in developing countries, namely, the donor market, estimated at up to $1 billion annually.[18] Currently,

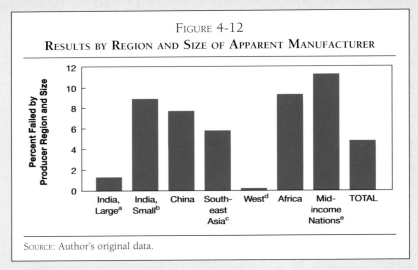

FIGURE 4-12
RESULTS BY REGION AND SIZE OF APPARENT MANUFACTURER

SOURCE: Author's original data.

---

16. Ibid.
17. Ibid.
18. Ibid.

local manufacturers only capture a small segment of the donor market in sub-Saharan Africa, as "donor-funded contracts generally require product prequalification from stringent regulatory bodies such as the WHO or the USFDA."[19] Therefore, the activity of these companies is largely restricted to the smaller, private sector in developing countries where, as mentioned in previous sections, products of local producers are up against the low drug prices of larger producers and the low prices of donated drugs leaked from the public market and sold into the private sector.

Unproven quality and cost disadvantages, as well as a general lack of other important factors, make pharmaceutical manufacturing largely inefficient across much of Africa.

TABLE 4-1

**SPECTROMETRY TESTING RESULTS BY REGION
AND SIZE OF APPARENT MANUFACTURER**

	Total samples tested	Total samples failing Raman spectrometry	Percent failed
India, large[a]	471	6	1.30
India, small[b]	327	29	8.90
China	169	13	7.70
Southeast Asia[c]	69	4	5.80
West[d]	438	1	0.20
Africa	302	28	9.30
Mid-income nations[e]	62	7	11.30
TOTAL	1,838	88	4.80

SOURCE: Author's original data.

19. Ibid.

a. More than $300 million in annual revenue.
b. Less than $300 million in annual revenue.
c. Countries include Thailand and Vietnam.
d. Countries include those within European Union, as well as Switzerland and the United States.
e. Countries include Brazil, Turkey, and Russia.

poor-quality local production, Orhii does not really want to discuss this topic either. He deflects my assertion that diverted drugs are a problem in the country. Of course, his staff can only do so much. It may be a rational decision to not prioritize shutting down local producers who might occasionally sell something bad, or to go after thieves who steal small amounts of medicines. But because drug-industry insiders I have spoken with think diversion and other forms of corruption are a concern across Nigeria, diversion may be another critical problem largely ignored. Ultimately, NAFDAC is essential to stopping corruption in medicines, but to date, it has not begun addressing this problem. One drug executive who declined to be named because he routinely works with the Nigerian government said he thought NAFDAC was not able to pay attention to it because "other senior political actors are involved."

"General corruption in the country is a problem; our staff [members] do not come from heaven; we are not immune of the corrupt practices," Orhii bemoans. "Counterfeiters and others try to compromise my staff, and we have to use a lot of resource to police our own staff. We try to improve general service conditions, pay, office space, sometimes I give a double promotion immediately [to someone catching a counterfeiter]. Sometimes we give monetary rewards, too." On March 8, 2009, the *Independent Newspaper* made allegations of corruption against the NAFDAC chief of the directorate of administration and finance, but this was the only example of NAFDAC corruption I was able to find in the local press. In a country as corrupt as Nigeria, with a divergent and relatively free press, this is a good record.

Orhii wants more and better staff, but he is concerned when a potential employee comes too highly recommended, for example in one recent incident by up to "ten politically powerful people." He is wary because he suspects—based on historical precedent—that these people are being planted by the politically connected and will be the ones who make sure the fakes pass through customs freely.

In researching this book, I found that Orhii was not the only government employee worried about this type of problem, but he was the only one to openly discuss it. Perhaps this was because in Nigeria there was corrupt pressure from many sides, and Orhii knows how important it is that his staff remains focused. His staff know Orhii will not tolerate the kind of everyday bribery and corruption that is a regular occurrence in Nigeria. And it seems to be working.

His team busted a criminal network bringing in drugs via Qatar airline flights from India and China. The bust illustrated how corrupt officials had contributed to the trade. Orhii said that within two weeks of breaking into this crime ring, they "saw how the ring had bypassed customs in China and paid off people in Nigerian customs, too. Syndicates actually place people to be employed in all the agencies they want . . . Chinese customs, Nigerian customs, the airlines, the warehouses, even the security agencies, the list goes on." Sometimes Orhii's team intercepts fake products where the security personnel of the Nigerian government or those from legitimate drug companies are complicit.

Andreas Seiter, a pharmaceutical expert at the World Bank, backs up Orhii's assertions. He told me that the bribing of regulators and other officials is a major problem. As he put it: "A $500 bribe makes a $60,000 investment in security useless."

Political Will

The Nigerian author Chinua Achebe says that "Nigerians are corrupt because the system under which they live today makes corruption easy and profitable; they will cease to be corrupt when corruption is difficult and inconvenient. . . . The trouble with Nigeria is simply and squarely a failure of leadership. There is nothing basically wrong with the Nigerian character. I am saying that Nigeria can change today if she discovers leaders who have the will, the ability and the vision."[7] Achebe's view of Nigeria, written in 1984, is probably shared by most foreigners who visit the country.

With a wry smile Orhii told me that "counterfeiting is like a sexually transmitted disease—if you have it you don't want to publicize the fact." Yet, to fight sexually transmitted diseases (or fake drugs), one needs to be open about the problem, something at which NAFDAC succeeds. Denial is the first response to many health-related problems with awkward public-relations implications, but recognizing the problem can make all the difference. In the 1990s, Festus Mogae, the former president of Botswana, took a risk and said Botswana had an HIV epidemic that had to be addressed. As a result, it was addressed. Nigeria's leaders have decided to admit the country has a fake-drug scourge, and they are trying to address it. No other African country has taken on the challenge with such gusto. And it helps Orhii that some provincial governors are big supporters, too, such as Gabriel Suswam of Benue State, who publicly reminds people that fake drugs kill his constituents, especially those in rural areas. NAFDAC officials have considerable power to act, and in 2010 Darlington Chukwu was sentenced to five years in jail for impersonating a NAFDAC officer with the intent to extort.

Tom Woods is a former U.S. State Department official who specializes in African policy and has been helping NAFDAC and other agencies of the Nigerian government. Woods has traveled in ministerial convoys with the ministers of defense and commerce, as well as with Orhii. He says security for Orhii is far greater than for the other ministers. I doubt that the head of the U.S. FDA requires as much security as people such as U.S. Secretary of State Hillary Clinton. In fact, I have visited FDA offices just outside of Washington, D.C., and while there is security, it is light in comparison with the security for the State Department or for the Department of Defense. But in Nigeria, NAFDAC has real influence, and those opposed to it are dangerous, so Orhii requires a major security detail.

While Orhii has escaped any direct harm, a few of his staff have not been so lucky. NAFDAC officer Emeka Obi Mwolie of the Port Harcourt office was shot dead in May 2010. Then four officers attending his funeral were abducted, and a ransom of 12 million naira ($750,000), a vast sum in Nigeria, was demanded for their release. All four were eventually released, the lone female employee first and the three male NAFDAC officers found abandoned and blindfolded on a roadside in Rivers State. And these are far from isolated incidents. Other NAFDAC officers have been beaten, abducted, and otherwise harassed, so much so that one NAFDAC PR official, Anselm Okonkwor, said that "the lives of our officials are no longer safe."

NAFDAC carries on, defying the threats with strong rhetoric. In addition, the use of the TruScan is one way to demonstrate, and not just say— as so many leaders like to do when it comes to counterfeit drugs—that the Nigerian government takes the matter seriously. But Nigeria plays its part in the talk, too; Orhii says, "Nigeria is at the forefront of building [an] international coalition against counterfeit drugs through WADRAN— [the] West African Drug Regulatory Authority Network—and the World Health Organization's IMPACT [International Medical Products Anti-Counterfeiting Taskforce]."

Akunyili was the first chair of WADRAN, a forum for heads of MRAs in West Africa to share strategies and experiences and help each other along in the fight against drug counterfeiters. Akunyili explained its role to the European Parliament in 2007, not long after its inception by NAFDAC. It was understood that when things were made difficult for counterfeiters in Nigeria, they relocated to other West African countries and tried to carry on their trade there. So collaboration across West Africa is vital, as Ghana seems to be acting (see box 4-8, "Ghana and PQM"); if other regional countries also take action, traders will be left with access only to the poorest rural areas, which would likely hurt their profits. Although I discussed this possibility, and people politely nodded that WADRAN may provide a partial solution, no one seemed optimistic.

Still, Orhii is doing what he can to get other countries, particularly those exporting drugs to his country, to act as well. Every May in Geneva, Switzerland, health officials convene for the World Health Assembly. Orhii spoke with the Brazilian and Indian representatives at the 2010 World Health Assembly, hoping to get a stronger international agreement on combating drug counterfeiting. "I thought we had agreed, but when we went back to the floor they opposed it," he said. As will become clear when we revisit the political problems preventing more active opposition to counterfeit drugs, not all countries are acting in concert.

One means of developing political will across nations would be to establish an international convention against counterfeit medicines. The Chirac Foundation was set up by Jacques Chirac, former president of France, to pursue access to quality medication and health care in the poorest countries of the world. At the inauguration of Benin's Ministry of Health's National Pharmaceutical Quality Control Laboratory, in the capital Cotonou on October 12, 2009,[d] Chirac called for support to establish an international convention to tackle counterfeit medicine.[8]

Chirac invited heads of states and governments, heads of international organizations and nongovernmental organizations, and industrial leaders to come to Geneva in 2010 for a global conference aimed at establishing

---

d. The lab is designed to have the capacity to test marketed pharmaceuticals and drugs available in hospitals, dispensaries, and pharmacies in Benin.

Box 4-8
Ghana and PQM

Joint efforts by international monitors, domestic regulators, and the local citizenry have been effective in many parts of Africa, as noted below in the discussion on recent Interpol operations. A collaborative program between U.S. Pharmacopeia and local Ghanaian regulators has aggressively sought to educate and involve the local people and has been similarly successful. Recognizing the increasing risk posed by fake and substandard medicines in emerging markets, USP created a program in 2009 to help developing nations monitor their drug supply. "The Promoting the Quality of Medicines (PQM) Program, a $35 million cooperative agreement, will serve as a primary mechanism to help assure the quality, safety and efficacy of medicines that are essential to USAID's [U.S. Agency for International Development's] priority health programs."[1] Ghana launched a new initiative, the Medicines Quality Monitoring Program, in 2008, joining the local knowledge of the Ghanaian Food and Drugs Board with the intelligence and technological capacity of the PQM program. The program gained international accolades first in 2009 when officials discovered a counterfeit version of Coartem (see figure 4-13). Given that the African market for Coartem is over eighty million treatments a year, it was inevitable that eventually it would be counterfeited. The imitation was discovered when a vigilant patient noticed an abnormality in his medication and alerted the authorities to the potential problem. Upon investigation, the regulators found that the pills contained no active ingredient and were clearly fakes. In a November 8, 2010, USP press release, Dr. Opuni noted the twofold danger these types of drugs pose in developing nations:

> Few people fully realize the devastation that distribution of substandard or counterfeit medications can wreak on vulnerable populations.
> . . . The individual patients taking the drugs get no relief, and drug resistant strains of malaria may grow stronger. In addition, people lose confidence in the efficacy of medicines and may be reluctant to seek medical help when they need it.[2]

The program continues to succeed, thanks to surveillance conducted periodically by the regulators of the Medicines Quality Monitoring program

---

1. *The Standard.* Vol. 8, Issue 2, Winter 2011.

2. U.S. Pharmacopeia. Last modified November 8, 2010. http://us.vocuspr.com/Newsroom/ViewAttachment.aspx?SiteName=USPharm&Entity=PRAsset&AttachmentType=F&EntityID=108443&AttachmentID=0d02b0fc-5718-4ba1-8c5f-084d4b7128dd.

FIGURE 4-13

Fake Coartem

Notes: The fake package (above) displays three different packaging errors, first discovered by the Ghanaian MRA & USP. The package has an incorrect German spelling, it does not list artemether or lumefantrinepyrimethamine 7mg/tab, pollen suggests eastern Asia, Dacrydium pierrei in genuine competitors. Additionally, the yellow line on the white tab to the side is missing from the top tab. Compare to the real package, below, which contains the yellow line on both white tabs.

(continued)

> Box 4-8 (*continued*)
> **GHANA AND PQM**
>
> and the involvement of local citizenry. In October 2010, sentinel site staff of the Ghana Food and Drug Board found thirteen different brands of poor-quality medicines, including substandard drugs and counterfeits of legitimate brands, across the Ghanaian countryside. Fakes were discovered in public hospitals, private pharmacies, and other drug retail outlets. Taking a tough stance against the counterfeiters, government officials recalled all suspect medicines and publicly announced the names of the locations at which the poor-quality versions had been discovered, equipping patients to make better-informed decisions when purchasing their medications. Dr. Patrick Lukulay, director of PQM, applauded the program's success in seizing fake antimalarials, but noted that there is a long battle ahead against substandard and counterfeit medicines across all drug categories.[3] If the program continues to effectively team international and domestic resources as it has until this point, Ghanaian patients will be able to gain increasing confidence in the efficacy of their medications.
>
> ———
> 3. Ibid.

the basis of international action.[e] Orhii welcomes such attention to the problem and possible solutions. In part IV, I discuss the possibility of such a convention.

Such high-level political talk shows considerable hope for the future, but changes will take time. For now, those who fight counterfeiters are at risk. As I left Azikiwe's clinic in Abuja in the summer of 2008, he wished me

———

e. Among other things, Chirac urged these leaders to acknowledge that the manufacturing and marketing of counterfeit medicine is a crime and a breach of peace and to decide at the national level how best to apply the strict application of legislative and regulatory texts in states where they are already available. He advised the creation of a legislative and regulatory framework where there is none, on-the-field implementation of effective instruments against the traffic of counterfeit medication with trained personnel and repressive systems adapted to its realities, the reinforcement of health officials' capacities to prevent and fight counterfeit medicines, and the implementation of public awareness and information campaigns on the detrimental effects of counterfeit medication.

well and told me to watch my back: "There are many people who gain from the current climate, so don't make yourself a target." He had been threatened before when he exposed a dealer trying to sell fake drugs at his clinic.

Changing Buying Behavior Takes Time

Azikiwe thinks the problem of fake drugs will persist because people are not aware of why one should buy from registered pharmacists and not from street traders with no knowledge of pharmaceuticals. This may seem odd to anyone with experience of buying drugs only at Western pharmacies. Our buying habits have changed over time, but today, people in rich countries are more cautious than ever before. Westerners will buy a newspaper from someone on the street, perhaps a T-shirt at a concert; they may pay someone to wash their car windows at a traffic light, but buying food or drink is less common, and I do not know any Westerner who would buy medicine from a stranger on the bus. Probably because I am a Westerner, in the two bus rides I took, no one offered me drugs and I did not see any being sold, but my West African colleagues assure me it happens all the time.

Perhaps it is best to explain such buying behavior with the words of someone who buys medicines on buses or the street. The April 15, 2009, *Nigerian Compass* published interviews with people buying from unreliable sources (known as "hawkers") of drugs. Dauda, a middle-aged builder, said, "I buy drugs from these sellers because I don't need to go out and search for drug shops, since they can either come to my place of work or pass in front of my house in the evening. . . . The drugs are cheaper compared to what you buy from the shops. They give you different types of drugs at a very cheap amount."

Ease of use and cost seem to persuade many to ignore the alarm bells NAFDAC and doctors like Azikiwe are ringing about fake drugs. Ayodele tells me that perhaps as many as 10 percent of Nigeria's drugs are traded informally. I shake my head and am about to say something smug and superior about Western buying habits, but I catch myself as I realize that of course Westerners do buy drugs this way; they are known as narcotics. We may not buy aspirin or antimalarials from a street dealer, but some of us will buy cannabis and cocaine (and, increasingly, painkillers and Viagra). Many Western adolescents try narcotics usually with the full knowledge that they have no idea what they are actually taking. They know what they think they are buying, but they cannot be sure. Regular users of narcotics end up relying on certain trusted traders because they understand the risks of adulterated supply; they may even have had a bad reaction to one supply, or they know someone who has. Occasional users try to score drugs from those friends who use more regularly, because they are less likely to be ripped off or be made sick. But with no large businesses with reputations to defend supplying the drugs and no regulatory structures behind them, buying Ecstasy at a night club in London is arguably more risky than buying aspirin from a bus in Lagos. Of course, I suspect if Ecstasy was sold in pharmacies in London, most people would buy it there, but some would still stick to the back streets, especially if the products being sold worked most of the time and were noticeably cheaper. Nigerian buying habits are not that different from our own. My Western smugness on hold, I left Abuja for the airport.

While I was probably in no danger while visiting Dr. Azikiwe or while openly discussing the fake-drug trade with other Nigerians, my colleagues who procured a lot of drugs for me possibly were, although none of them reported any interference from traders or officials to me. Of course, those who are trying to stem the tide of counterfeits definitely are in danger. There was the attempt on Akunyili's life and, in 2010, an attempt on Dr. Orhii's life, too; apparently he was shot at while traveling to work. One reason that the danger has increased is that enforced punishment for fake drug operations in Nigeria has been increased and might soon rival that for dealing in narcotics—and, as is well known, organized crime fights dirty.

Fraud and Theft:
An Entry Point for Fake Drugs from East Africa to Nigeria

Sadly, it is sometimes true that those with the responsibility of delivering medical supplies are letting patients down. An important cause of the amount of fake products in a market is the culture under which drugs—in fact, all commodities and finished products—are traded in a particular location. If corruption, fraud, and theft are encouraged and not prosecuted, fake drugs will likely be prevalent. Those profiting from illegal operations may be happy to expand their product lines to include fake drugs. This thesis is broadly tested in this book, and it is worth documenting some of the examples where drug fraud causes poor public-health outcomes and leads to counterfeit drug infiltration. For the most important recent problems in this regard, I went to East Africa.

East African Investigations

Health workers in many East African countries have long complained of stockouts of essential drugs. Local press reports tell many tragic stories of desperate patients seeking treatment from public-health facilities whose overstretched, undertrained workers charge for "extra costs" so they can provide drugs, syringes, latex gloves, IV equipment—everything, in fact, except the bed.

The last time I was in Kenya, reports of stockouts of medicines, particularly antimalarials, and medical supplies in government facilities were widespread. In part, this was because the government had agreed to purchase (with donor funds) over seven million treatments of an antimalarial drug called Artefan made by the Indian firm Ajanta. The firm is approved by the WHO, and from what I have seen and my colleagues have tested, its drugs are fine. But the company was unaccustomed to providing such large orders, and it failed to deliver on time. The resulting stockouts forced donors to purchase expensive emergency drugs to fill the void and allowed fake drugs a new entry point for infiltrating supply chains.

This illustrates one specific incident in what is a widespread problem with stockouts in the region. Numerous stories document patients arriving at the hospital to find empty pharmacy shelves. If patients pay, nurses can quickly obtain supplies from nearby private chemists, a practice that has led to charges against nurses of hoarding and theft, and opens patients to fake drugs from the private suppliers. Strong security systems in a hospital dispensary are useless if most patients are supplied outside of the dispensary. The nurses argue that they are accused because they make an easy target, and they claim the real culprits are government ministries. Luke Kodambo, a spokesman for the National Nurses Association of Kenya, points to mismanagement at the two ministries that share the responsibility for drug oversight: the ministries of Public Health and of Medical Services. In February 2010, suppliers suspended orders until unpaid bills from 2008–2009 were cleared. The shortage was attributed to a budgetary deficit at the Ministry of Medical Services. Although the ministry received a $20 million bailout, there was a delay of some months before stocks were expected. At the same time, a ministry directive allowing the Kenya Medical Supplies Agency to buy drugs from new, untried local producers prompted nurses' concerns about the quality of the drugs. Kodambo was worried that they "might end up having patients given expired drugs."[9] Such disarray encourages other, less-official sources of drug supply, including counterfeit products.

Kenya's national medical stores were shaken up in 2008, and policymakers attempted to implement a budgetary policy for drug procurement and distribution. Insiders consider that implementing the policy will go a long way toward ensuring that health facilities have the medicines they need, but there are concerns that some people want this policy to fail so that they can continue doing things their own way. Locals tell me of mismanagement at district health facilities, where stock either runs out or expires on shelves because the staff is unable to anticipate demand. Although it is the National Drug Authority's responsibility to monitor the destruction of expired stock, there is neither a system in place nor a budget available to separate, load, or transport expired stock to an approved incineration facility. This glaring gap in the security of the drug supply is worse because the single approved incinerator in the country belongs to the military, which does not allow straightforward access for the health department, and hence delays occur, increasing temptation for theft of expired drugs. That expired drugs often are not destroyed and existing stocks are monitored only erratically is worrisome enough, but the system contains even greater flaws, which allow fake products to flood in.

Such problems are not confined to Kenya. Moses Kamabare, general manager of the Uganda Medical Stores, insists that "there is totally no theft here at the [national] medical stores," but many reports suggest his confidence is misplaced. According to stories in local Ugandan papers, including the *Monitor*, the Global Fund to Fight AIDS, Tuberculosis, and Malaria (Global Fund) suspended grants worth $367 million in August 2005 over mismanagement by the Project Management Unit after an audit found that about $1.6 million had been stolen. Although this occurred before Kamabare's time, the commission set up by the government to investigate the theft found that up to 373 officials in government and civil society were involved. As of March 2010, only eight, most of them low-level participants, had been prosecuted. The government faced pressure to repay the money and to accept conditions attached to future grants.

Drug theft and corruption enable fakers to enter the market, too. Through intelligence gathered in Dubai and from analysis of the Artesunat products procured in East Africa, my investigator contacts learned the following about one criminal ring in 2009. A Chinese supplier delivered intermediate drug chemicals to an entity in Dubai that was run by a man of Nigerian and UAE descent. These chemicals arrived from Shanghai by ship and were pressed into pills, either in Dubai or at some other location outside of China and before arrival in final locations in Africa. The Nigerian supplied at least two traders, one in Kenya and another in Nigeria, with Artesunat monotherapies that primarily contained talc and the constituents of Excedrin (acetaminophen, aspirin, and caffeine)—see box 4-9 for one of the rare international successes in combating fake drug rings.

The nearly identical compounds were found in seven samples of three "brands"—one Indian, one Chinese, and one Vietnamese—in four Nairobi pharmacies. Two similar samples of these brands were found in a single pharmacy in Lagos, Nigeria, too.

I would like to tell you that all of these players will no longer be trading lethal products into Africa, but not a single prosecution resulted, due to lack of evidence.

In April 2010, the auditor general of Uganda reported that Uganda's national medical stores failed to deliver drugs in a timely manner, meaning health centers incurred high costs by purchasing drugs (some of which were probably fake) from the private sector while the national medical stores allowed drugs to expire. Expired drugs are a notorious problem in Uganda. As Moses Kamabare admits, "We know stocks have accumulated over the years; people talk of fifteen years of expired drugs, and expiration of drugs is a common thing."

Between July 2005 and June 2008, the costs amounted to at least $22 million in lost sales while drugs worth $3.3 million expired. The national medical stores spent $18,000 every month to store these expired drugs and another $350,000 to destroy them.

Box 4-9

OPERATION MAMBA:

INTERPOL'S MULTIFACETED ATTACKS IN EAST AFRICA

While East Africa certainly faces significant dangers from counterfeit and substandard drugs, three major Interpol operations in the region over the past three years have demonstrated that the governments of many East African nations are getting serious about combating the illicit drug trade.

In September and October of 2008, Interpol conducted its first "Operation Mamba" in Uganda and Tanzania. Interpol provided logistical, training, and information expertise to local customs officials, drug regulators, and policemen. These groups collaborated in both countries to consolidate the information necessary for the series of raids that regulators and enforcement officials carried out between September 29 and October 5 of 2008. The raids resulted in the seizure of more than one hundred different brands of unregistered or substandard drugs, sixty-five investigations, and at least four arrests. The effort was hailed as such a success that the Kenyan government joined the group and local investigators working with international intelligence officials orchestrated a second investigation, which culminated in Operation Mamba II the following August. The results from the second raid were astounding: more than five tons of medicines were seized from the 270 shops that were investigated. By this point, the raids had drawn international attention, and another operation was planned for the following year. Rwanda, Burundi, and the sultanate of Zanzibar (a major shipping port that is part of Tanzania but was not included in the 2008 investigations) joined the team to increase the scope of the operation further. Operation Mamba III, conducted in July and August of 2010, led to eighty prosecutions and the seizure of more than ten tons of substandard pharmaceuticals (see figure 4-14).

The widespread success of these operations has been hailed by Interpol offices throughout Africa as a model for using global intelligence sources such as Interpol in conjunction with local regulatory authorities to crack down on international criminal rings. Observers noted that Interpol effectively drew on local resources and provided clear communication chains between various interested parties in order to effectively coordinate these actions. Some argue that an organization such as Interpol can use these investigations to help build local capacity among governments whose internal communication and monitoring structure might otherwise be too weak to effectively combat the problem.

Following the success of Operation Mamba III, Interpol experts and local government officials from all countries involved in the raids met in Zanzibar to reiterate their commitments to fighting unregistered, substandard, and fake medicines. They agreed to a regionwide information-sharing agreement, and they committed to continuing the process begun by the first three Mamba raids. In February of 2011, Interpol officials initiated another meeting in Sudan, including all participants in Mamba III as well as Sudan, Ethiopia, Djibouti, Eritrea, the Seychelles, and Somalia. The meeting provided a larger forum at which to discuss issues pertinent to the entire East Africa region and provide a base of support for future operations. Interpol officials are optimistic that the governments of the broader East African region will continue to increase communication and cooperation on future investigations to target regionwide problems, specifically including the fake pharmaceutical industry.

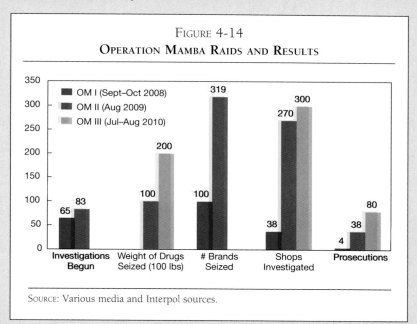

FIGURE 4-14

OPERATION MAMBA RAIDS AND RESULTS

SOURCE: Various media and Interpol sources.

(continued)

Box 4-9 (*continued*)
OPERATION MAMBA:
INTERPOL'S MULTIFACETED ATTACKS IN EAST AFRICA

TABLE 4-2
OPERATION MAMBA I, II, AND III SUMMARY TABLE

	OM I (Sept–Oct 2008)	OM II (Aug 2009)	OM III (Jul–Aug 2010)
Investigations Begun	65	83	
Weight of Drugs Seized (100 lbs)		100	200
# Brands Seized	100	319	
Shops Investigated	38	270	300
Prosecutions	4	38	80

SOURCE: Various media and Interpol sources.

FIGURE 4-15
OPERATION MAMBA MAP—EXPANDING COOPERATION

■ Participated in OM I, II, III
■ Participated in OM II, III
■ Participated in OM III
■ Participated in Broader East African police chiefs meeting

NOTE: Interpol has successfully orchestrated three raids of increasing size and scope in East Africa. The most recent meeting in Sudan hopes to expand the circle of cooperation against criminals even further.

Denis Rubahika Kinungu of the National Malaria Control Programme in the Ministry of Health says its key donor, the Global Fund, set conditions that were strict and not easily met (see box 4-10 on page 114). As Uganda sought to meet increased regulatory requirements, it failed to manage procurement properly and the country's supplies of Coartem were erratic. According to the *Ugandan Independent*, to avert stockouts, Uganda needed "$44 million for purchasing Coartem" for all health centers in the country per year. But given that the country only spent "$0.93 per person on Essential Medicines and Health Supplies" and the Coartem was more expensive than this, "it was impossible for the Health Department to afford Coartem without relying on donors."[10]

Uganda has also had to address the theft of donor funds. In July 2009, Annaliza Mondon and her aunt, Elizabeth Ngororano, were sentenced by a Kampala court to five years in prison for embezzling HIV- and malaria-treatment grants worth over $15,000 through their company, Value Added Health Ltd.

Mondon and Ngoroano are not alone; donated funds and, more importantly, donated drugs are being diverted by multiple actors, creating a cyclical spiral. Stockouts encourage medicine theft to fill the gaps and lead to more diversion of life-saving medications and more stockouts; this creates an opportunity for fake drugs to infiltrate the system and fill the void. Both government agencies and private individuals are guilty of perpetuating this deadly cycle.

The effects of shortages are widely reported in Uganda and to a lesser extent across the rest of East Africa. In May 2010, Uganda's *Sunday Monitor* reported that notices posted in several hospital maternity, surgical, and general wards advise patients that upon admission they would have to buy syringes, urinary catheters, bandages, gauze, cotton, and IV fluids.[11] Although Uganda may seem to have worse conditions than some of the other countries because of the number of incidents reported, this is because its government appears to be trying harder to prevent the problem and because it has a relatively free press to report incidents.[12] Uganda's government has also tried to enact a whistleblower scheme; even if this does little to alleviate the problem, it should be seen as a positive step and one that should help shift attitudes. As a brief aside, I note that it is important that donors support such positive efforts, because they are so easily undermined. If donors

Box 4-10
SUBSIDIZED ANTIMALARIALS: IS AMFM WORKING?

In 2010, the Global Fund launched a new program to subsidize artemisinin-based combination therapy (ACT) antimalarial treatments in an effort to push older and less effective therapies off the market. Older treatments, like chloroquine and sulfadoxine-pyrimethamine (SP), are dangerous to weak patients and those who contract a resilient strain of malaria and can contribute to the development of artemisinin resistance.

The Global Fund's Affordable Medicines Facility–malaria (AMFm) program is a financing mechanism designed to increase access to ACTs in the public and private sector. The Fund subsidizes the wholesale drug purchase, and the lower costs are supposed to be passed on to consumers. The subsidies are targeted at lowering ACT prices to chloroquine and SP price levels.

AMFm Phase 1 pilot is currently being implemented in Cambodia, Ghana, Kenya, Madagascar, Niger, Nigeria, Tanzania, and Uganda. At the end of 2012, it will be reviewed through an independent evaluation, after which the Global Fund Board will determine whether to expand, accelerate, modify, terminate, or suspend the AMFm.

My research team and I undertook a study to assess the price and quality of a small sampling of AMFm ACTs, non-AMFm ACTs, and artemisinin monotherapies in Ghana and Nigeria. We also sampled in Lomé, Togo (a country not participating in the AMFm) to assess whether AMFm drugs have been stolen and diverted.[1]

We sampled antimalarial drugs from 22 pharmacies in Lagos, Nigeria (62 drugs) and 15 pharmacies in Accra and Ghana (77 drugs) and tested them using standard protocol.[2]

Our sampling yielded worrying results. One in eight (12.5 percent) AMFm ACTs failed basic quality testing. While the failure rates for non-AMFm drugs were higher, AMFm failures are particularly worrisome because these products were produced by innovators and leading generics producers. The U.S. Government and security experts on the ground privately

---

1. This previous study suggests medicine diversion could be a very significant problem. http://www.dovepress.com/antimalarial-medicine-diversion-stock-outs-and-other-public-health-pro-peer-reviewed-article-RRTM.

2. For standard methods, employed in previous peer-reviewed published research, see http://www.dovepress.com/antimalarial-medicine-diversion-stock-outs-and-other-public-health-pro-peer-reviewed-article-RRTM.

suggest entire batches of drugs have failed quality control tests and have been returned, causing severe shortages. If these reports reflect a systemic problem, then drug companies are cutting corners to deliver the 100 million treatments already ordered for Ghana and Nigeria.

Equally alarming was the fact that ACT prices were on average higher than monotherapies, notably in Lagos, and all AMFm drugs were marketed at higher prices than AMFm's suggested retail price. So while AMFm ACTs are cheaper than non-AMFm ACTs, monotherapies are still cheaper overall. Another objective of the AMFm is to increase use of ACTs in vulnerable populations, including children under 5 years of age.[3] We found that all child treatments cost more than the suggested price; some cost 10 times the suggested retail. The results in both categories are summarized in tables 4-3 and 4-4 below.

Investigations in Lomé, the capital of Togo, unearthed another danger. Evidence of diversion is limited from our brief and cursory investigation, but there is no doubt that that at least five separate products were stolen from Ghana and Nigeria and diverted into Togo. The scale of diversion could be significant; drugs were found in both official and unofficial markets in Lomé. Perhaps even more worrying, 30 percent of the samples collected failed quality control tests, and all failures had non-zero API contents. These types of drugs (almost certainly degraded) are most likely to cause arteminisin resistance.

The Global Fund and AMFm funders should be commended for exploring innovative solutions to increase access to safe and effective malaria medicines, including working with the private sector. However, this study suggests AMFm drugs are still susceptible to quality problems; they are still more expensive than monotherapies in progam cities; children's therapies are still unusually expensive; and some drugs are being diverted across national borders. It is not obvious that the AMFm represents the best use of scarce public funds, and it is possible that the beneficial effects could be achieved at lower cost.

(continued)

---

3. "Eighteenth Board Meeting: Report of the Affordable Medicines Facility—Malaria ad hoc Committee" The Global Fund, 7–8 November 2008. Available through: http://www.theglobal fund.org/en/amfm/background/.

Box 4-10 *(continued)*
SUBSIDIZED ANTIMALARIALS: IS AMFM WORKING?

TABLE 4-3
AVERAGE DRUG COST AND MARKUP

Formulation		Non-AMFm drugs[a]		AMFm drugs[b]	
		Adult	Child	Adult	Child
Artesunate-amodiaquine fixed-dose combination and co-formulation	Overall Average Cost	$4.04	$3.29	$2.49	$1.52
	Overall Average Markup	N/A[c]	N/A	2.96	6.3
	Average Cost in Lagos	$3.19	N/A	$2.34	$1.60
	Average Markup in Lagos[d]	N/A	N/A	3.06	8.33
	Average Cost in Accra	$4.21	$3.29	$2.76	$1.50
	Average Markup in Accra[e]	N/A	N/A	2.8	5.71
Artemether-lumefantrine	Overall Average Cost	$4.32	N/A[i]	$2.32	$2.00
	Overall Average Markup	N/A	N/A	2.83	6.53
	Average Cost in Lagos	N/A[f]	N/A	$2.47	$2.08
	Average Markup in Lagos	N/A	N/A	3.22	3.61
	Average Cost in Accra	$4.32	N/A	$2.02	$1.97
	Average Markup in Accra	N/A	N/A	2.05	7.5
Artesunate mono-therapy[g]	Overall Average Cost	$2.03	N/A[j]	N/A[h]	N/A
	Average Cost in Lagos	$1.87	N/A	N/A	N/A
	Average Cost in Accra	$3.62	N/A	N/A	N/A

SOURCE: Bate et al. "The Global Fund's Malaria Medicine Subsidy: A nice idea with nasty implications." *Africa Fighting Malaria working paper*, September 2011.
a. Includes collected antimalarial drugs lacking an AMFm logo on packaging.
b. Includes collected antimalarial drugs containing an AMFm logo on packaging.
c. No markup available for antimalarial drugs lacking an AMFm logo on packaging.
d. Markup based on expected price of 120N/adult course and 30N/child course[1] (90N was used for 2 child courses of 18 pills/pack).
e. Markup based on expected price of 1.5 GHS/adult treatment[2] and 0.40 GHS/child treatment.
f. No samples of artemether-lumefantrine lacking an AMFm logo on packaging were collected in Lagos.
g. No markup available for artesunate monotherapy.
h. No samples of artesunate monotherapy containing an AMFm logo on packaging were collected in either Lagos or Accra.
i. No samples of artemether-lumefantrine child treatment lacking an AMFm logo on packaging were collected in Lagos or Accra.
j. No samples of artesunate monotherapy child treatment lacking an AMFm logo on packaging were collected in Lagos or Accra.

TABLE 4-4

TESTING RESULTS BY FORMULATION

AND PRESENCE OF AMFM LOGO

Formulation	Test	Non-AMFm drugs[a] Failure rate			AMFm drugs[b] Failure rate		
		Accra	Lagos	Total	Accra	Lagos	Total
Total TLC		17.4%	19.0%	18.2%	0%	5.4%	3.2%
		(4/23)	(4/21)	(8/44)	(0/39)	(3/56)	(3/95)
Total TLC &/or HPLC		21.7%	19.0%	20.5%	12.8%	12.5%	12.6%
		(5/23)	(4/21)	(9/44)	(5/39)	(7/56)	(12/95)

SOURCE: Bate et al. "The Global Fund's Malaria Medicine Subsidy: A nice idea with nasty implications." *Africa Fighting Malaria working paper,* September 2011.
a. Includes collected antimalarial drugs lacking an AMFm logo on packaging.
b. Includes collected antimalarial drugs containing an AMFm logo on packaging.

continue to supply funds and drugs that can be reasonably assumed will be stolen, they tacitly damage Uganda's efforts at transparency and account-ability (in addition to the text below, see box 4-10 on the malaria medicine subsidy scheme and box 4-11 on diverted medicines).

Angola has also suffered under similar circumstances. The country lost over $642,000 in diverted antimalarial drugs provided by USAID between January 2008 and June 2011. The loss was the result of four thefts of Coartem; the amount stolen would have treated over 534,000 people with malaria, and the theft undermined the U.S. president's Malaria Initiative. According to an audit report by USAID's Office of Inspector General, the thefts occurred because "USAID/Angola did not ensure a quick and proper delivery of the drug from the airports and because it relied on a distribution system with significant control weaknesses managed by the Government of Angola."[13] The fourth theft occurred in May 2009, while the drugs were under the control of the Angolan Ministry of Health and after enhanced control procedures had been put in place. The audit also revealed $14,900

Box 4-11
DIVERTED MEDICINES

Background: Antimalarial medicine diversion has been seen across numerous African markets and can lead to serious stockouts in the public sector, which can be dangerous to countries with high burdens of disease. The map below builds off of a study we conducted to assess the degree to which antimalarial medicines were being diverted across Africa. The study results are presented below.[1]

Methods: A total of 894 samples of antimalarial medicines were covertly purchased from private pharmacies in eleven African cities from late 2007 to early 2010. All medicine packages were visually inspected for correctness,

FIGURE 4-16
ANTIMALARIAL DRUG DIVERSION

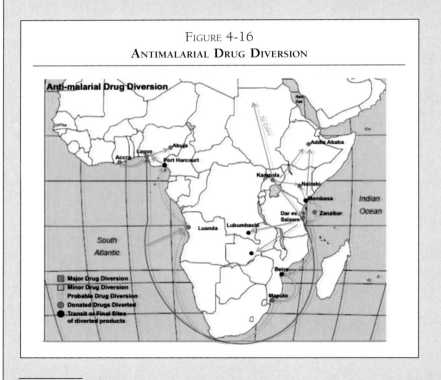

---

1. Roger Bate, Kimberly Hess, and Lorraine Mooney. *Antimalarial medicine diversion: stock-outs.* Research and Reports in Tropical Medicine 2010. http://www.aei.org/docLib/ Antimalarial-drug-diversion-stock-outs-and-other-public-health-090210.pdf.

in line with the protocol established by the Global Pharma Health Fund e.V. Minilab®, as well as for signs of diversion.

Results: Overall, 6.5 percent (58 out of 894) of collected antimalarial medicines were found to be diverted, comprising 2.4 percent (5/210) of medicines collected in 2007 from six African cities, all of which were ACTs; 2.3 percent (3/129) of medicines collected in 2008 in Lagos, Nigeria, two of which were ACTs; and 9 percent (50/555) of medicines collected in 2010 in ten African cities, thirty-five of which were ACTs. ACT was by far the most diverted

TABLE 4-5

SUMMARY OF RESULTS

Sampling	Older therapies[b]	Artemisinin monotherapies	ACTs	Total
Accra 2007	0% (0/13)	0% (0/16)	0% (0/8)	0% (0/37)
Nairobi 2007	0% (0/24)	0% (0/14)	50% (2/4)	4.8% (2/42)
Dar es Salaam 2007	0% (0/16)	0% (0/17)	0% (0/1)	0% (0/34)
Kampala 2007	0% (0/29)	0% (0/28)	0% (0/9)	0% (0/66)
Kigali 2007	0% (0/6)	(0/0)	100% (3/3)	33.3% (3/9)
Lagos 2007	0% (0/8)	0% (0/7)	0% (0/7)	0% (0/22)
Lagos 2008	1.7% (1/59)	0% (0/65)	40% (2/5)	2.3% (3/129)
Accra 2010	0% (0/23)	0% (0/24)	10% (1/10)	1.8% (1/57)
Lagos 2010	10% (3/30)	0% (0/47)	52.9% (9/17)	12.8% (12/94)
Addis Ababa 2010	0% (0/20)	0% (0/16)	33.3% (2/6)	4.8% (2/42)
Cairo 2010	0% (0/25)	0% (0/19)	20% (2/10)	3.7% (2/54)
Luanda 2010	10% (2/20)	0% (0/17)	25% (2/8)	8.9% (4/45)
Lubumbashi 2010	26.3% (5/19)	0% (0/14)	50% (3/6)	20.5% (8/39)
Lusaka 2010	6.5% (2/31)	0% (0/21)	0% (0/9)	3.3% (2/61)
Kampala 2010	7.4% (2/27)	0% (0/18)	35.3% (6/17)	12.9% (8/62)
Nairobi 2010	4.3% (1/23)	0% (0/19)	37.5% (6/16)	12.1% (7/58)
Dar es Salaam 2010	0% (0/12)	0% (0/16)	26.7% (4/15)	9.3% (4/43)
TOTAL	4.2% (16/385)	0% (0/358)	27.8% (42/151)	6.5% (58/894)

NOTES: a. Percentages are supported by number of samples diverted/total samples collected.
b. Includes amodiaquine, mefloquine or sulphadoxine–pyrmethamine.

Abbreviation: ACTs, artemisinin-based combination therapies.

(continued)

Box 4-11 (*continued*)
DIVERTED MEDICINES

treatment in this study: 15.6 percent (5/32) of ACTs collected in 2007, and 30.7 percent (35/114) of ACTs collected in 2010.

Conclusion: The number of diverted ACTs over the thirty-three months covered by this study is probably related to the laudable provision of vast amounts of donated or low-priced ACTs across African nations and the actual increase in diversion of these medicines into the private sector. The small sample sizes in this study might exaggerate any problem, but a potentially serious problem may well exist. To the extent that diversion of medicines exacerbates stockouts, this is a public health problem and a perversion of donor intent, but there are other possible harms of diversion, such as increased trade in counterfeit and expired and otherwise substandard medicines.

FIGURE 4-17

Flatpack Coartem

Notes: The flatpack Coartem in the background is designed purely for the public sector and was diverted into private pharmacies, where we bought them. The box of Coartem in the foreground is the private-sector packaging, which is the only package that should be found in pharmacies.

in missing USAID-funded bed nets from the Ministry of Health's warehouse.[14] The warehouse supervisor explained that the nets had been lent to another malaria campaign, but there was no record of this loan.

Concern is growing that in addition to the inefficiencies in stock ordering and distribution systems throughout East Africa—which alone provide an opportunity for fake drugs to enter the supply chain—corrupt officials are diverting life-saving medicines into the private sector and across borders, making it even more likely that criminal gangs (some maybe even working under the control of politicians) will gain control of key distribution pathways. Willis Akwhale, an official at the Kenyan Ministry of Health, alerted me to this problem in February 2005. At that time, I was looking for evidence of a link between increasing drug resistance and the proliferation of fake malaria drugs, so I didn't realize the full significance of his complaint about the burgeoning black market in antimalarial drugs; after all, I thought, these weren't counterfeits.

But Akwale has been worrying about drug theft for awhile. He expressed concern that medicines in government storage facilities were being stolen and diverted by those directly involved in storing and distributing medical supplies. These products are increasingly being removed from the public supply and sold to those willing to smuggle them across borders to supply the black market. Drugs have always been stolen; for example, in 2004 antiretrovirals distributed as part of Kenya's HIV-medicine program were found on the streets of Nairobi. Similar incidents have been observed in Uganda and Cameroon, where government health workers sold public-sector antimalarial drugs to retail shops. An article in *Lancet* also documents this problem, stating that "some reports suggest it is common practice for public-health workers to divert drug supplies to private facilities." But what Akwhale was worried about was the massive diversion of tens of thousands of drugs every month, and, unfortunately, that is what we've seen since 2005.[15]

Stephen Malinga, the Ugandan health minister, told me in 2009 that those stealing drugs "are murderers, causing the deaths of hundreds of children" in Uganda. Malinga has been bold enough to point the finger at the role of corrupt officials, although he insists the problem is at the local level rather than in the central government. "We are beginning to realize [the stockouts] are not genuine stockouts. The medicines we have in the country should be enough. The drugs are transported from what we call the national medical stores in lorries to districts and regional hospitals. We discovered that in some cases these drugs were not being delivered. They [the thieves] are selling those drugs to South Sudan."[16]

In April 2010, Uganda's *New Vision* newspaper reported that antimalarial drugs donated by the Chinese government and meant for hospitals were diverted to private companies, local schools, and individuals.[17] Allegedly, the drugs had been requisitioned unlawfully by three senior Ministry of Health officials in charge of the malaria program in Uganda; these officials have since been charged with corruption and mismanagement.

Diverted Donor Drugs in Togo

The West African francophone nation of Togo has a population of about 6.5 million people and had nearly 900,000 reported incidents of malaria in 2008, the last year for which data are available. Togo typifies the problem malaria's scourge causes in sub-Saharan Africa: 2,663 deaths from malaria were registered in 2008, while many more likely were unreported. Roughly a quarter of all child deaths in Togo are attributed to malaria.

Togo's gross domestic product (GDP) per capita using purchasing power parity is only $900, and the government budgets only $70 per person per year in health spending. With half of the population surviving on less than $1.25 per day, antimalarials are prohibitively expensive for thousands of ill Togolese children without donor-subsidized medicines. In 2005 the Global Fund awarded Togo a grant of $10,694,981 to purchase and distribute antimalarial drugs and train health workers. Most of this money has been spent on Coartem. As of September 28, 2010, the publicly available Global Fund grant performance report indicated that $4,770,451 had been spent on pharmaceuticals. Global Fund donations are channeled through United Nations organizations, which procure medications with CAMEG, the Togolese distribution agency. CAMEG is responsible for the storage and distribution of antimalarial medications throughout Togo.

According to Global Fund statistics, more than three million people have been treated for malaria with ACTs and other drugs since 2005. The Global Fund has procured more than two million ACT treatments for Togo. Although available data do not indicate a reduction in disease prevalence, on the surface at least, more people are receiving treatment, giving the appearance of a moderately successful use of donor funds.

However, in July 2010, CAMEG CEO Mamessile Assih reported to the Togolese government that ACTs had been stolen from government stores. A subsequent internal government audit revealed that from roughly two million donated ACT treatments, 544,161—well over a quarter of those donated—had been diverted and sold for profit. My colleagues' investigations indicated that these drugs were widely available in street markets throughout the country. These markets sold ACTs for several dollars per treatment. At this price, the Global Fund's intended beneficiaries, the poorest of the poor, are unable to access high-quality treatment. Furthermore, street markets provide no control over drug-storage conditions. Some of the diverted ACTs were likely degraded due to improper storage, which, as mentioned earlier, will reduce drug efficacy and contribute to the development of ACT-resistant strains of malaria.

On October 29, 2010, Komlan Mally, Minister of Health, warned Togo's Council of Ministers that the situation may be worse than anticipated: antimalarial medicines provided by the Global Fund and worth about $1.59 million had been stolen. In connection with this theft, CAMEG's chief financial officer and four other CAMEG officials face allegations of corruption and are currently under investigation. Several remain in custody because they are potential flight risks.

The Togolese government has been relatively open; Mr. Assih of CAMEG deserves particular recognition for exposing corruption of high-level officials and initiating swift action in this case. Togolese police and other agencies have recovered some of the stolen drugs from illegal markets, but many simply disappeared (possibly overseas) after street traders realized the government was investigating the thefts.

The Global Fund has also demonstrated a commitment to transparency, but the organization probably took too long to initiate action in Togo; by the time the fund stepped in, the trail had grown cold, and most of the diverted products had long since disappeared.

In addition, the Global Fund is like so many other donors in prioritizing the obvious delivery of drugs into a country (an input measurement) rather than whether the drugs not only lower disease rates (an outcome measurement) but also don't disrupt other systems or relationships in the country and thereby cause long-run harm. And this means the fund is reactive to cases of fraud and corruption and drug diversion, because these are secondary to their main concern of getting funds approved and drugs procured.

In the summer of 2011, I visited Togo as part of an effort to analyze where donated drugs were being diverted. Even while drug diversion was rampant in Africa, the Global Fund pushed ahead with a malaria drug subsidization scheme, under the acronym AMFm (see box 4-10 for its progress), costing hundreds of millions of dollars. In West Africa, Nigeria and Ghana took part in the scheme, but Togo and Benin (sandwiched between these two geographically) did not. Yet going to several open-air markets in Lomé, Togo's capital, I discovered that it was easy to find ACTs, which had been supplied to Ghana and Nigeria, being sold there. Not only do Nigerians and Ghanaians not get the full benefit of the drugs they are supposed to, but criminals are making money from the diversion and undermining the legitimate sellers in all countries, including Togo. Such downstream problems never make it into the reports or promotional documents of the Global Fund.

On the Trail of Stolen Medicines

Other countries suffer from the same problem as Togo but at arguably greater magnitude: in Tanzania, it appears hundreds of thousands, and maybe millions, of drugs have been stolen from central stores and sold in locations as far afield as Nigeria. Anecdotal evidence suggests that drugs near expiration tend to disappear rather than be incinerated. It is easy to imagine how poor stock-keeping can seed a lethal trade. My research suggests this is a recent development; three years ago, my investigative team did not find any obviously stolen and diverted medicines in our survey of important markets in West Africa, but in February 2010, 9 percent of our samples appeared to have been diverted. (Even more significant, just under 30 percent of the most donated, best, and most expensive types of antimalarials—the ACTs—had been diverted.) The packaging indicated that most had been diverted from Tanzania, Zambia, Uganda, and Kenya—all countries that are a considerable distance from the West African markets surveyed. Figure 4-1 shows where drugs that were diverted originated and, in some instances, where they went. Dar es Salaam, Tanzania, appears to be the main hub. In June 2010, I found evidence suggesting how some of these diversions occur and started tracking stolen medicines, discussed in box 4-11 on page 118.

Felipe Muñoz is a sailor with a small coastal trading operation. He runs cargoes mainly between Tanzania's free-trade zone on the nearby island of Zanzibar; Dar es Salaam, Tanzania's major commercial city and port, where I met him; and Maputo, the capital of Mozambique, where he was born. Muñoz suggested we meet in Kunduchi, where I was staying, and we drove back into downtown Dar. He told me his story first over a beer and then as we drove. His business is mainly in small-scale commercial shipments or domestic goods—furniture and the like—and his dealings are generally casual. Although he appears honest in manner, corrupt officials and the constant fear of pirates can make his trade profitless and dangerous. "I don't always pay costs [tariffs or other charges] on the goods I transport; nobody does," he shrugs. He tells me this, with no hint of irony, as we drive past the Marine Police headquarters on our right and the High Court on our left. I feel a little nervous, even guilty, like you do when you're driving slightly over the speed limit and see a police car, but he seems entirely relaxed.

Toward the end of 2007, Muñoz agreed to take a small consignment of what he identified as Coartem malaria pills up the coast to Mombasa, Kenya's main port, for a Tanzanian trader he called William. After several successful trips, William introduced Muñoz to a Nigerian trader also based in Dar es Salaam who had a very different proposal: to transport a larger shipment of the same type of cargo to Port Harcourt, in Nigeria.

Muñoz's operation is small; his main craft not really suited to the 5,000-mile trip around Cape Horn, but he suggested contacts in larger firms. The Nigerian was not interested, and it became obvious to Muñoz that not only was he looking for someone to smuggle the drugs but also that the drugs were stolen. Muñoz politely withdrew. About a year later he met a competitor and acquaintance with a larger ship who had taken the job and transported perhaps half a million treatments in several shipments before being hustled off the trade by a Nigerian-registered ship whose "crew had threatened my competitor's crew at Port Harcourt," Muñoz said.

According to drug investigators, Nigerian traders primarily in the Niger Delta region have been smuggling good-quality donated products for years, but recently they have become more creative. As NAFDAC has recorded in the past few years, counterfeiters are faking the packaging and relabeling aspirin or chalk as antimalarials. Still, trade in stolen products, rather than counterfeits, may be just as significant in the region.[f]

Because it was not possible for me to follow any of the shipments of drugs from Dar es Salaam directly, I left Tanzania and returned to Nigeria, where I suspected the drugs were probably being brought in and shipped to all parts of Africa's most populous state. From my own research team's assessment, I knew vast amounts of stolen drugs were appearing in many Nigerian states, but local informants indicated most went to Rivers State and were centered around Port Harcourt and Onitsha on the Niger River.

Port Harcourt and Onitsha

With a population of 1.6 million people, Port Harcourt is not a particularly large town, but the area of the delta that feeds into the harbor and town is vast. The total population of the greater Port Harcourt area is a more significant 5.7 million. Political patronage is more obvious in Africa than anywhere else, with so many streets named after recent or even incumbent presidents. So it was no surprise that I found myself driving down Olusegun Obasanjo Way, past the Olusegun Obasanjo Police Station, which appeared deserted. My driver turns onto Ikwere Road and then on to Wharf Road; as we get closer to the wharf, that unmistakable harbor smell pervades my nostrils.

There are numerous tributaries and creeks around the delta, some navigable by large craft, others only by small craft, and some not at all. The rainfall in the delta is pretty high, and the subsequent humidity will accelerate degradation of medicines, making a mockery of expiry dates.

The small expatriate white and largely oil-industry-employed community lives behind concrete walls and wire fencing and with private security on tap. Having spent a lot of time in South Africa, I know this is nothing

---

f. And theft can be so significant because most donors are turning a blind eye to such activities. Exasperated investigators wonder if it is possible for U.S. citizens donating funds and drugs that are stolen to be prosecuted for infringing the U.S. Foreign Corrupt Practices Act. Lawyers doubt this is feasible or warranted, but it shows the annoyance investigators feel toward those supplying money and products into corrupt environments.

new, nor are rich areas in proximity to squalor, which are without electricity or running water, with the very obvious awful sanitation, too. But the palpable anger in the delta is astounding, far worse than anything South Africa has to offer except in time of conflict. In the poorest communities we drive by, I don't think I've ever seen as much buckled corrugated iron for roofing, or muddy streets with detritus everywhere.

It is especially disheartening that these conditions occur in a delta that provides more oil than all but the very largest oil producers, over two million barrels a day. Patterson Ogon of the Niger Delta Development community said that "official corruption" by central and regional governments had ensured that the local people remained poor, living on a dollar a day on average. The locals have no property rights to speak of, and in the past fifty years things have gotten worse in a legal sense and probably in every sense since the time of Ken Saro-Wiwa's execution in November 1995 (I didn't notice much improvement from my previous visit in 1996 when I wrote about oil and the delta for the *Wall Street Journal*[18]). At least that is what Asume Osuoka of the Oil Watch Africa Network believes to be the case.

The benefits of the oil are not finding their way to the poor. Indeed, the corruption sustains the status quo, continuing to undermine the rights of the local poor. I don't see a better option, but what currently passes for business as usual is unpalatable, to say the least.[g]

Outside of OECD countries, there are few oil-producing nations that aren't either dictatorships or where corruption isn't rampant. Nigeria may be typical of these regions. Perhaps it shouldn't be a surprise that the Niger Delta is a hub for massive amounts of stolen and counterfeited products.

---

g. The UNODC says of oil theft in Nigeria: "The wide range of players involved in bunkering and the complex web of their alliances make it difficult to discern the victims from the perpetrators. The loss of oil revenues—perhaps one third of the income on which 80 percent of the Nigerian national budget is based—means that, aside from a few well-placed individuals, the Nigerian public is the net loser." P4 UNODC West Africa trafficking report, 2008. Available at: http://www.unodc.org/unodc/en/data-and-analysis/WDR-2008.html. Nigeria has over half the population and 60 percent of the GDP of the region. And since it loses a third of its oil, it is effectively operating at two-thirds capacity (2mb per day, instead of 3), p.20, same report. Much of the oil is taken out of the country by barges or "Cotonou boats," where there is a man at each end of the boat, one steering the other as lookout; the rest of the boat is literally awash in oil. Theft for the domestic market is generally transported in drums via trucks.

The delta is replete with small land masses and myriad small islands, like Yellow and Bonny. Indeed, Bonny has a small port itself that, according to investigators, is where a lot of the illegal traffic is dropped off (probably not at the central port itself, but close by, perhaps literally dropped into small boats near the port). Several communities were moved from or relocated within Bonny Island when the Nigerian Liquefied Natural Gas Plant was built there, and parts of the Finima community are wretched.

Numerous foreigners have been kidnapped from this area; a few simply disappeared, never to be heard of again. Kidnapping has been the main publicity (and possibly fundraising) tool for the Movement for the Emancipation of the Niger Delta. The photojournalist Ed Kashi captured their plight and fight back in his book *Curse of the Black Gold*. One can see from his pictures and videos the bristling anger of the masked young men carrying AK-47s in the creeks, which they patrol and where they are the law, when government patrols are not around. And it's not just in creeks where the Movement for the Emancipation of the Niger Delta has influence; it has shut down significant amounts of the oil production in the delta at times.

Fighting fake or stolen pharmaceuticals would not be my priority if I worked or lived here, and it is of little surprise that everything illegal flourishes. Why would the locals care about the relatively quiet trade in fake products, even if they kill far more people, especially children, than direct violence, when there is barely the rule of law, and violence is so obviously an everyday part of life and a far scarier daily reality? And this is another reason why NAFDAC has such a tough job. It is quite likely that some of those trading the bunkered oil are also trading fake antimalarials, and victims have nowhere to turn. The central government is detested by the locals because it is seen as being complicit, and to a great degree it is complicit, with the conditions under which these people have to live. Elf, Total, and Shell, among other companies, are here to exploit oil. Following Saro Wiwa's execution, the Western pressure on these companies pushed them to do more for the local community, but they are still distrusted by local leaders. While the government does nothing to protect local rights and has squandered so much oil revenue over the last forty-five years, there is little that company staff can do.

Onitsha is about 120 miles from Port Harcourt, and the journey took the better part of four hours. I was glad to get out of Port Harcourt and be on my way to what I expected would be one of the main trading locations for fake drugs. Traffic was bad and eventually, after winding our way past some incredibly poor areas we ended up at the main market where drugs are freely traded. Three million people dwell in its narrow streets and dismal alleys, and although most are poor, I was told that a substantial number of the wealthier traders owned Blackberry-type devices.

I knew I would not be able to get out and ask detailed questions about the source of the drugs the sellers had on display. From experience in other markets, both in Nigeria and in other African markets, I knew that traders could often become hostile, especially when supported by their colleagues. But although aggressive stares were all one got in many places, I might well get jostled here and even attacked.

That, at least, was the opinion of George Babangida, who was born in Port Harcourt but now lives in Onitsha, and is a thirty-four-year-old former policeman. I asked him what he is today, and he said he does not know; I suggested he is a security consultant, but he laughed because he does not really know what that term means. He has a laconic attitude of "you can call me what you want." I hired him as both bodyguard and guide, hoping he would share knowledge about the region. He seemed entirely relaxed as he entered the market and procured specific antimalarial drugs and antibiotics for me. It was not a proper sampling—after all, the locals may have known who he was—but he is not associated with NAFDAC, so I assume all the fakes would not be pulled from stalls as soon as he entered the market.

Most of the drugs he collected were key antimalarials in private- and public-sector packaging, such as Coartem. He also procured some fake products; though their packaging indicated manufacturing locations as varied as Vietnam, India, and Belgium, they were probably produced in China. A lot of Cotexcin was available; it is an artemisinin monotherapy the WHO has discouraged the production of for many years, even in the legitimate version. Of the five samples we procured of this specific drug, one failed tests for the active ingredient. Using a TruScan, we tested the drugs bought in Onitsha and found that roughly one in ten failed quality tests, which was actually much better than I had expected. NAFDAC's efforts should be credited at least for part of the lower-than-expected failure rates. I mentioned the result to one experienced foreign security consultant, and he shook his head and went on to explain that many of the worst traders have bypassed the main market in Onitsha because they know it is being watched.

The ethnic background of the traders in the market was overwhelmingly Nigerian, as one would expect, but there were a couple of Indians trading alongside the locals. Compared to East Africa, where the Indian diaspora accounts for much of the wholesale and some of the retail drug trade (legal certainly and maybe illegal too), it doesn't obviously account for any of the trade in the Niger Delta. However, much trade in the delta revolves around Indian and Chinese products, which, from an imprecise eyeballing of drugs bought in Onitsha's market, appear to account for about half the antimalarial products on sale. For ex-policeman Babangida, NAFDAC director Orhii, and the other investigators I spoke with in Nigeria, organized crime rings from China are the main culprits in the fake-drug trade. This conclusion is echoed in East Africa, too.

David Nahamya is a senior inspector with Uganda's National Drug Authority. He has been investigating the criminals behind the trade in diverted and fake drugs for several years—to him it is "organized crime." He almost shows admiration for the discipline of these gangs, which sell only to trusted intermediaries, lowering the chances of being caught. Through working with Interpol, though, the Ugandan police succeeded in infiltrating an illegal-trade ring and uncovered the trade in expired and fake antimalarials; a drug called Duo-Cotexcin, an ACT that had been donated by the Chinese government to Tanzania, had expired; its expiration date simply had been removed from the blister packaging. But it is not just Chinese producers, but also those in India who have been implicated in the manufacture of fake drugs (as we will see in the next chapter). But overall, more and more investigators implicate China, and more and more of the fake products are made in China or traded by Chinese in Africa and elsewhere.

Fake traders and their products are infiltrating legitimate markets, and through their skill, however disreputable, they gain access. In Africa, the normal distribution systems are so poor and public-sector drugs are so often stolen and diverted that it is difficult to analyze the environment and full scope of the problem. This also means the best solutions are not simply to ramp up enforcement action against the fake-drug trade. While counterfeiters always deserve to be investigated and prosecuted, in East and West Africa they are enabled by a dysfunctional system of drug distribution and oversight, and combating that system is, or should be, a top priority.

5

India

Although I'd come across the final location of many fake drugs, met a few unfortunate victims of the trade, and generally seen the distrust such drugs bred in the health systems in Africa, I had not found any production locations of the fakes. So in January 2008, I went to India, where after months of planning and expectation, I was finally on my way to a fake-drugs factory. I had driven with private investigator Suresh Sati, who had masterminded the whole affair, ninety miles south of Delhi into Uttar Pradesh. We were only five miles from the city of Aligarh, but we had spent nearly an hour bouncing along a rutted track to reach our destination. Knowing that international trade in counterfeit medicines was worth many billions of dollars per year, I was expecting some James Bond–type covert operation run by SPECTRE, or at least a man with a disfiguring scar or a hook for a hand. What I saw instead was a small, shabby shack. It was pathetic, really.

The eight or nine people working in the "factory" were too poor to venture outside the village; Sati said they had probably never even been as far as Aligarh. They likely were illiterate and had no idea what good pharmaceutical manufacturing practice would entail. Their working conditions were wretched. They used an industrial cement mixer to blend ingredients shoveled in from ripped sacks on a dusty floor (see figures 5-1 and 5-2). The place was dirty. Rat droppings, the occasional cockroach or beetle, and a variety of unidentifiable bugs were the main evidence of wildlife (better known as contamination) at this production site.

While production took place in disgusting conditions and the products may have been lethal, the people working in this factory were arguably innocent (they may even be considered victims of the fake-drug trade). They may have known they were primarily mixing chalk and pressing it into pills, but they likely did not know these pills would

FIGURE 5-1

Aligarh raid: storage of suspect API

FIGURE 5-2

Aligarh raid: unhygienic fake manufacturing

be taken on to another location and put into packaging claiming the contents were painkillers. Local investigators tell me these poor-quality products will probably be "good enough" only to be sold on the street, or more likely the backstreets, of towns and villages. The buyers will be India's poor. In part III of this book, I discuss the drugs we procured in India, most of which were from legitimate pharmacies. Even from these pharmacies, drugs are often dispensed in handmade envelopes instead of in pill containers or aluminum blister packs. The rural poor, who often buy solitary pills, never see Western-style dispensing hygiene. If they are lucky, the makeshift envelopes made out of old newspaper will at least keep their pills dry.

At Sati's office, a suite of rooms in the basement of an unassuming house in a Delhi residential area, he showed me what he was up against. He laid out the samples of phony drugs he collected from recent clandestine purchases and the previous week's raid. He placed two vials of liquid erythromycin, an antibiotic similar to penicillin and used to treat bacterial infections, in front of me. One vial contained the real thing; the other contained water from a Delhi tap. "Which one is the fake?" Sati quizzed me. I could not say. They looked identical.

As I have come to learn, the best fakes are indistinguishable to everyone but trained experts from the particular company that made the real product. It once took a month for a sample I sent to a company to be identified as the real thing; the package had been exposed to sunlight and had faded to such an extent that it looked wrong, though it was actually correct. Spotting packaging errors often comes down to noticing minor differences in the folds of the packaging or in the fonts or inks used in printing. To be able to spot any flaw, one must have a legitimate version for comparison and know what to look for. Problematically, no one under normal purchasing conditions has a comparable legitimate product at hand and the knowledge and patience to search out a bogus copy. Even looking at a legitimate version beside a fake, you can see the mistakes only after you are shown the difference, and sometimes not even then (see the pictures in box 5-1 as examples). In reality, under normal conditions a nonexpert has a zero chance of spotting the best fakes.

These drugs that Sati showed me, and ones like them, fall into the category of deceptive counterfeiting; to patients, they look identical to and

Box 5-1
CIPROTAB

The figures in this box show two versions of a well-known Indian-brand generic medicine, Ciprotab. Ciprotab is marketed by Fidson, a Nigerian company working with the producer, the Indian company VS International. Fidson's product is a generic version of ciprofloxacin, a powerful antibacterial drug.

Figure 5-3 below shows an example of a fake package that is virtually indistinguishable from the original, even to trained observers. In the photos of the back of the packages, the fake is on the bottom; one can see a hologram on the real product. Our covert shopper and the pharmacist who sold him the product did not know that the product was supposed to have a hologram. Tests revealed the fake to be a mixture of baby (talcum) powder, glass, and other potentially dangerous substances.

According to Vidhyut Shah, the managing director of VS International of Mumbai, "Ciprotab is one of our leading brands and also the No. 1

FIGURE 5-3

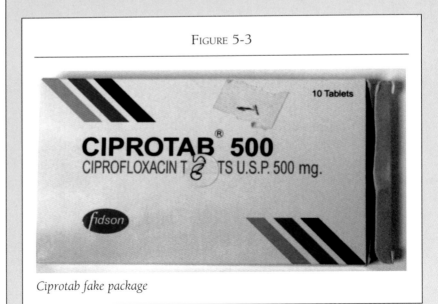

Ciprotab fake package

FIGURE 5-4

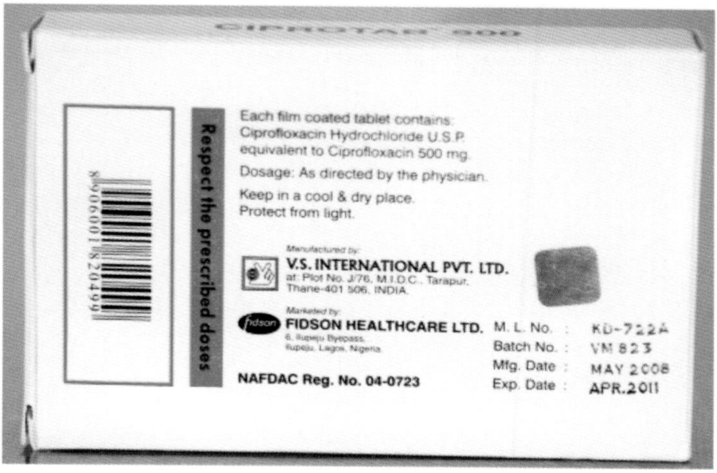

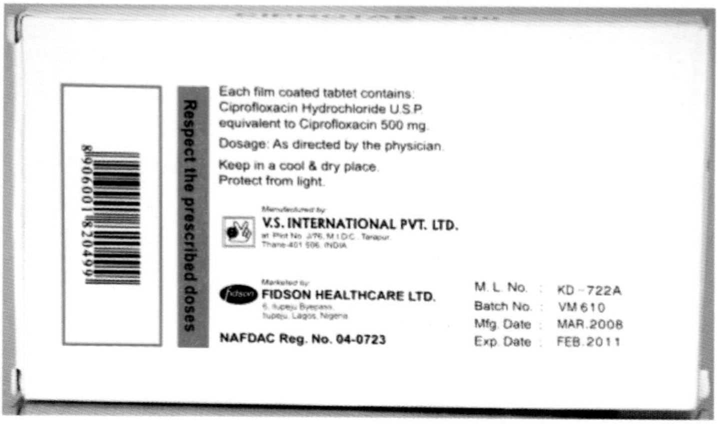

Ciprotab back

(continued)

Box 5-1 (*continued*)
CIPROTAB

---

brand of ciprofloxacin in Nigeria. We are aware that the product is being faked, and consequently we have incorporated a number of anti-counterfeit measures to protect the integrity of the product and to ensure that only the original product reaches the consumer."[1] According to Dr. Shah, the fake version has a correct batch number but not when matched with the manufacturing date.

When brands such as Ciprotab are faked, the reputation of the company and of Indian generics as a whole may become compromised. The trademark could be faked by counterfeiters within India or from elsewhere (we suspect those from China). It is important that VS International and other companies producing brand pharmaceuticals be able to protect their brands and take action against those who infringe them.

---

1. Personal communication on June 25, 2009.

---

are sold at the same price as their legitimate counterparts. There are also other types of counterfeits, though, that are not truly deceptive to at least some patients or are not classified as deceptive to economists. Although the patients who buy them may not understand GMP or that the products they have bought do not comply with it, such fakes are less deceptive in the sense that they are noticeably cheaper than ostensibly comparable (and better) products on the market. Patients may knowingly purchase these knockoffs because they are cheap. While patients may feel deceived when the drugs do not work as they expected, the drugs' prices should convey some information about quality. The price analysis in part III discusses to what extent price was a reliable indicator of quality in our data—on average, pricier medicines are better quality, but that doesn't mean that an expensive medicine will always work.

Whether priced as a legitimate product or an easily spotted fake, some of the fake drugs on the market are lethal, and Sati has a huge job. A large and cheerful man from a small town in the foothills of the Himalayas in northeastern India, Sati has been hunting down counterfeit and otherwise suspect goods for thirty years. From the moment I met him, I could tell that he enjoys his work. We set off down the road toward one of Delhi's sprawling markets to make his rounds, and Sati smiled nostalgically as he recalled his first anticounterfeit raid, back in 1980, on a small-scale outfit manufacturing knockoff TV antennas. These days, Sati runs a company called The Protector SS, which investigates intellectual-property fraud and orchestrates raids for a wide range of domestic and international corporate clients. His bread-and-butter work is in personal care products—shampoos, body lotions, and the like—but his passion is hunting for fake drugs, because, he says, "somebody's got to do it."

India's counterfeiters come in all shapes and sizes. They have a long history of copying anything they can sell. Pharmaceutical counterfeiting is a newer trend that has gained momentum in recent years. Sati tells me the fake-drug industry works in much the same way as the counterfeiting of designer handbags or DVDs of the latest Hollywood blockbuster. Counterfeiters provide a superficially reasonable imitation of the real product, manufacture fakes in vast amounts, and price their products often just above the cost of production. Unless the counterfeit enterprise is vast and vertically integrated, counterfeit manufacturers are unlikely to sell directly to consumers and—assuming that those along the distribution chain know they are buying fakes—profit for the manufacturers is made in high volume. Where the enterprise is vertically integrated, or where the manufacturer can hoodwink the legitimate supply chain, fake products may sell well above the cost of production and make far greater profits. The gold mine for a drug counterfeiter is to be able to fake a valuable, essential medicine for next to nothing and infiltrate the legitimate distribution chain that assumes the products are real and pays normal high prices. This also means the counterfeiter's products are dispersed far and wide, so patterns of the clinical failure that result may remain unobserved. In this way, counterfeiters can make high, sustainable profits. Fortunately, very few counterfeiters likely achieve this goal, and those who do tend not to be able to maintain such infiltration for very long. Some manufacturers will not even try to infiltrate the legitimate supply chain because the chances of being caught in doing so may be considerable. They often sell their products to the same criminal middlemen who deal in other knockoffs.

The difference in the case of counterfeiting drugs is that these fake products often carry a significant human price tag. High production standards and good products are found in all industries, and sloppy versions exist in all industries, too. Handbag designers for Louis Vuitton undoubtedly are outraged when bags made with inferior materials and stitching are passed off as their products. But while fake bags still perform their primary function of carrying contents and provide some real value to their buyer, fake versions of drugs do not function properly and can cause real harm to their users and to efforts to combat diseases worldwide. Because they are not likely to be bioequivalent to the real version, fake drugs have zero or even negative value, but outside of pharmaceutical circles this point is largely lost. Businessmen, economists, traders, consumers, and most government officials tend to view fake drugs like other fake products, inferior but having positive value. That most fakes are harmful and not just inferior is a point I did not truly appreciate until I had been investigating fake drugs for some time. I think that partly explains why Sati and his colleagues have such a tough time convincing people to take the subject more seriously.

Sati tells me many producers market chalk as aspirin or lactose as Viagra, and they put extreme care into faking a medicine's packaging so the drugs can be sold in stores or exported to foreign markets. More sophisticated counterfeiters add small amounts of the right active ingredients so their drugs pass simple chemical tests; when such drugs are tested with authorities' cheapest methods, they will pass and enter the distribution chain. Other counterfeiters make drugs of pretty high quality, some of which may even work perfectly well. Of course, where subterfuge is involved, safety is something of a lottery.

FIGURE 5-5

Drug control officer after raid

Some counterfeits are produced by legitimate, licensed pharmaceutical firms in addition to their legitimate products. Rogue owners, managers, or even employees make production runs at night, after official business has ended, using stolen or substandard substitute ingredients. Sati drove me by one such production location, near one of Delhi's main arterial roads, but we did not stop. "It's much harder to close these operations," he said, because not only are they legitimate firms most of the time, their directors—some of whom may be entirely innocent of any wrongdoing—are politically connected and prefer to discredit those investigating their plants rather than unearth wrongdoing by their staff. Sati seems depressed by such operations, but is rational enough to realize that because they are politically and legally untouchable, he must focus his efforts elsewhere.

A classic method to further cheapen the production process of some drugs is to skimp on the recommended time that the ingredients spend in the centrifuge mixer, which reduces the quality but does not affect appearance. Sati says he knows of some firms that do this where the managers and directors of the firm—not just some renegade staff—are certainly involved. The firms are legitimate by day and make knockoffs of their own brands to sell in low-value markets by night. They squeeze prices and compromise quality, in part because lowering price increases the chance of winning state and federal government drug tenders. Cheapening production means more drugs that will be harmful to patients. As box 5-2 demonstrates, some drugs must be made to the highest standards or they will fail to treat properly.

Harinda Sikka, senior executive of prominent Indian drug firm Nicholas Piramal, is on record as saying that no reputable company even bids on most government tenders, as they cannot supply good quality at the rock-bottom prices demanded. Of those companies that do, he asserts that some are operating out of their garages while forging quality-control documentation.

In some respects these firms are quite clever. They segment the markets where they sell products, knowing that inferior, low-priced products, often for poor rural clinics, are not likely to mix with the higher-priced, GMP-quality products sold in richer, private urban pharmacies. For this market segmentation to work for counterfeiters, it is also essential that enough buyers are ignorant of the dangers of cheap, low-quality medicines, believing that the drugs will still do the job, if not as well or as quickly as the

Box 5-2

THE BIOPHARMACEUTICS CLASSIFICATION SYSTEM

The Biopharmaceutics Classification System (BCS) is used to broadly classify each drug into one to four ratings as shown below.

A rating of I is best and IV is worst. Any drug qualifying as a I has both good solubility and permeability, and hence bioequivalency is not required.

FIGURE 5-6

BCS CLASS MEMBERSHIP RISK MANAGEMENT

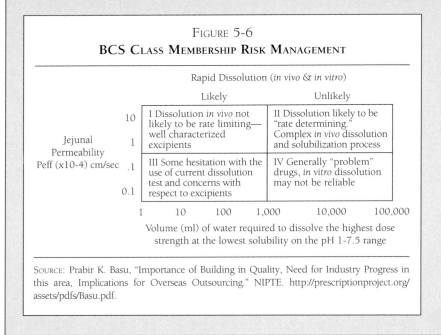

		Rapid Dissolution (*in vivo* & *in vitro*)	
		Likely	Unlikely
Jejunal Permeability Peff (x10-4) cm/sec	10 / 1	I Dissolution *in vivo* not likely to be rate limiting— well characterized excipients	II Dissolution likely to be "rate determining." Complex *in vivo* dissolution and solubilization process
	.1 / 0.1	III Some hesitation with the use of current dissolution test and concerns with respect to excipients	IV Generally "problem" drugs, *in vitro* dissolution may not be reliable

1   10   100   1,000   10,000   100,000

Volume (ml) of water required to dissolve the highest dose strength at the lowest solubility on the pH 1-7.5 range

SOURCE: Prabir K. Basu, "Importance of Building in Quality, Need for Industry Progress in this area, Implications for Overseas Outsourcing." NIPTE. http://prescriptionproject.org/assets/pdfs/Basu.pdf.

expensive ones, which are beyond their reach. Sati and others tell me this opinion is pervasive.

Historically, pharmaceutical company executives have complained about India's lax intellectual-property and pharmaceutical-crime laws. But even with Indian law as it is, owners of some of these companies, ignorant of their staff's afterhour activities, may well be guilty of gross negligence. At the very least, owners who do not properly monitor drugs leaving their premises allow their staff to skim company profits by substituting cheaper

From the drugs we will encounter and that my research team tested for basic quality, mefloquine and lumefantrine (both antimalarial drugs) are category I. Examples of category III products (which have low permeability but high solubility) also generally don't need bioequivalency; they include isoniazid (a TB drug) and ciprofloxacin (an antibiotic). Examples of category II include chloroquine, pyrimethamine, and quinine (all antimalarials) and rifampicin (a TB drug), which have good permeability but low solubility, and most probably do require bioequivalency testing. Drugs with low solubility and permeability—category IV—include erythromycin, which requires bioequivalency testing.

But it is not just drugs we think of as cheap that can escape bioequivalency; some complex antiretrovirals, such as zidovudine, no longer require bioequivalency.

Most people procuring and testing a drug will focus on the active ingredients because they are by definition the key component of any medicine. But the other components of a product, the "excipients," are important too. As Dr. Prabir Basu, director of the U.S. National Institute for Pharmaceutical Technology and Education, says: "The nature of pharmaceutical manufacturing problems is complex and multifaceted, but a shared and key aspect spanning manufacturing problems is the lack of understanding of properties of excipients and how these products influence product functionality."[1]

---

1. Prabir K. Basu, "Importance of Building in Quality, Need for Industry Progress in this area, Implications for Overseas Outsourcing." NIPTE. http://prescriptionproject.org/assets/pdfs/Basu.pdf.

or illegitimate supplies and selling them under the company's name—a trick long practiced in the bar and pub trade.

Sati is not particularly interested in discussing these firms. He tells me he knows less about these products because their markets are often overseas, particularly in Africa but also in some developed nations, and he cares less as a result. His business is stopping fakes within India. I will return to these businesses later in this chapter when discussing the whistleblowers who sometimes risk everything to expose the malfeasance of their colleagues.

Tracking the Counterfeiters

Later in his office, Sati showed me vials of morphine—all well-packaged fakes—recovered from a raid. He had established that they were made by a local company producing bulk pharmaceutical ingredients. These samples were only one-half to two-thirds the strength the drug should have been. He was convinced this finding suggested an established supply line for the deliberate production of substandard (in this case deliberately understrength) drugs: the producer of the active pharmaceutical ingredient was likely willing to make special orders for trusted domestic customers. This opinion was supported by former Delhi police chief Vijay Karan. Karan, a dapper dresser with a penchant for Burberry ties, told me over a long lunch at a Chinese restaurant in downtown Delhi that he was concerned such drugs were undermining therapeutic products in the Indian market and even those destined for Europe and the United States (see figure 5-7). Until this point I had assumed only the poorest African markets were affected by such understrength, substandard products, but Karan indicated they proliferated across several markets. "The North [of India] has a worse problem than the South since more fake drugs are made in the North," he said, and many of these fake drugs often are not transported very far. The segmentation of markets by the counterfeiters and illegal traders is interesting; while some specialize in trading globally, others have far more limited range, and inside India, fake drugs do not seem to travel that far.

It is a difficult problem for Sati. It is obvious from his actions and attitude that he cares about the people harmed by all sorts of fake and substandard products, but most of his clients are businesses that want to prevent theft of their intellectual property. Sati is hired to find examples where this is happening and expose and stop such theft. If a local business is selling substandard drugs but not marketing them as if they were name-brand products, it is taking market share from a competitor (perhaps one of Sati's clients), but it is not Sati's paid work to investigate these producers.

Although it is the job of the MRA to unearth substandard drugs, there is little private interest in doing so. With a substandard drug, no third-party company's intellectual property is stolen, and in many places around the world, including in India, private-sector efforts are the most effective at combating counterfeiters. For sure, MRAs and other agencies often become

FIGURE 5-7

Former Delhi police chief Vijay Karan

involved, but with notable exceptions, such as the U.S. FDA and NAFDAC, public-sector agencies do not drive much of the action. Without private-sector involvement, an MRA is left on its own to expose and sanction substandard producers. Because many of these producers are protected by political systems more concerned with the jobs these companies provide than with the harmful products they sometimes make, action is rare.

In addition, in some locations substandard drugs are not even illegal; deliberate production of bad medicines requiring criminal intent—*mens rea*—must be proven before action will be taken against producers. In other words, while it is often difficult, but not impossible, to catch counterfeiters, local producers of substandard drugs have almost total immunity. Furthermore, while the gray areas of negligence are complex in Western countries where at least actions are taken (though of varying success), negligence is never, or rarely ever, even addressed in middle-income and poorer countries.

Sati sat forward and was generally more engaged when I returned the conversation to fake drugs and the Indian market he knows most about. He was even more alert when I brought up the final stage of production: packaging and presentation. This is a topic on which he has become an expert. It is at this final step in the production process that drug counterfeiters take the most care. Modern computer graphics, ink matching, and printing capabilities make it relatively easy to duplicate packaging; even holograms designed as security devices are reproduced with seemingly little trouble. The copy holograms are often far from perfect, but they easily fool undiscerning pharmacists and patients. Each technological advance in packaging protection costs the counterfeiter time and money, so these devices are still very useful, especially for certain brands. Ultimately, however, technology has proven inadequate to stop counterfeiters altogether, especially in the poorer markets where options are limited.

According to Sati and other investigators, probably 50 to 70 percent of the costs of fake-drug production are in the packaging. Indian drugs are the cheapest in the world; when over half of the costs are used to create packaging, it is clear how little is spent on the actual drug production (see box 5-3). From the counterfeiters' perspective, money for packaging is money well spent. Without sophisticated packaging, they can penetrate only the poorest-value markets, usually only those in proximity to where the drugs were made. Better packaging enables counterfeiters to sell their drugs more widely and to insert them into legitimate distribution channels. Large criminal networks have their own distribution channels, including the ability to create bogus paper trails, bills of lading, certificates of drug-quality approval, and even fake customs stamps. With these, they are able to infiltrate legitimate wholesaler and distributor systems. A smaller-scale counterfeiter is able to sell to rural traders and may have access to a few pharmacies and smaller wholesalers and may even be able to sell to a larger criminal enterprise.

Packaging is important, but producers of the hardest-to-spot fakes do not always evade arrest. Sometimes skillful producers and packagers simply do not have the connections required to infiltrate legitimate supply chains, and when they try to branch out they may unwittingly sell to undercover investigators. Once investigators have evidence of a counterfeit operation, they often provide information and a dossier to the police and encourage the police to raid the premises. Sati works with his clients—Western and Indian drug companies—in this way, often making covert "buys" from traders, to find those infringing his clients' rights; he routinely provides this information to the police.

The most successful criminal networks initially do not need to make the best product, but they do need to have the best distribution chains. As some counterfeiters succeed and others fail, they buy out, threaten, or otherwise take over the makers of the best packaging. If they are smart, as most are, they keep production and packaging at separate facilities to limit the likelihood of exposure. And they always provide what the market wants.

Sati explains that for most of the past decade richer markets had been flooded with copies of lifestyle drugs: erectile-dysfunction medicines (notably Viagra), painkillers (especially Vicodin and OxyContin), diet pills, and antianxiety medicines (notably Valium). By 2008, though, numerous

BOX 5-3
VIAGRA

To understand why Viagra is one of the world's most faked drugs, you have to grasp how packaging trumps product in counterfeiters' profit margins. In both China and India, a kilogram of sildenafil citrate, the active ingredient in Viagra, can be produced for $60. Name-brand Viagra will contain 100 percent of the active ingredient; the knock-off blue pills might have 100 percent, but some contain far too much, which has led to heart attacks, and others none at all. Formed into thousands of fake pills and sold in the United States, that single kilogram can be sold for about $200,000. That's a higher markup than cocaine, with lower penalties for getting caught. And if one uses chalk or sugar instead of the proper ingredients, the markup is even greater. Even with the best fakes, the typical Viagra counterfeiter will spend more than half of his overhead on packaging; where chalk is used, maybe 85 percent of production costs are packaging.

FIGURE 5-8
GRAPH COMPARING SILDENAFIL WITH OTHER COMPOUNDS

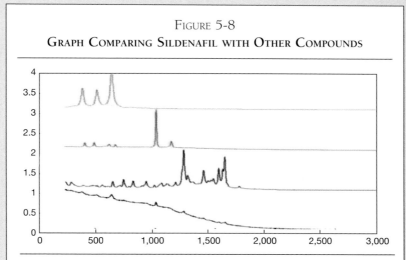

Note: Top three spectra are of key ingredients of Viagra—the bottom is a fake version but with actual sildenafil citrate API. The fake operation making this product—Kamogra (see figure 5-9)—probably hopes for repeat business.

(continued)

Box 5-3 (*continued*)
VIAGRA

It is widely believed that if pharmaceutical companies would simply lower their prices on drugs, counterfeiters would have less incentive to make fakes. Intuitively, it makes sense; smaller profit margins should be a deterrent. Unfortunately, it rarely works that way. Counterfeiters can accept tiny margins on each product sold—as long as they move millions of pieces of merchandise. Take a Johnson's bar of soap, like one I saw in 2008 in a Delhi market. The genuine product can be bought for just 60 cents, but the soap on sale that day was a fake. The bar itself was low-quality soap, not up to Johnson's standards, but the packaging was nearly identical to the real thing. If counterfeiters will go to this much trouble to fake a bar of soap, the cost of genuine drugs—no matter how cheap—will always make it worth their time.

FIGURE 5-9

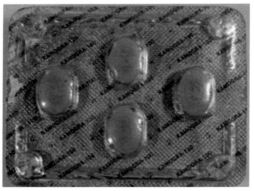

Falsified Viagra—Kamogra

counterfeiters had moved into far more life-threatening fake pharmacology, manufacturing drugs used to treat cancer, HIV/AIDS, malaria, tuberculosis, and serious heart conditions. Drugs for these therapeutic categories had been faked a lot before, but it was accelerating. Indeed, most of the fake drugs Sati showed me from recent raids were for dangerous conditions or potentially lethal diseases.

FIGURE 5-10

Suresh Sati and Roger Bate outside Aligarh Market

Sati, Karan, and other Indian investigators are convinced that, hampered by a lack of resources, most Indian states find the problem overwhelming, and they suspect that in other poor parts of the world the situation is worse. Indeed, Sati's personal battle against fakes never stops. The first day I spent with him started at seven in the morning and finished just before midnight. He is fighting a losing battle. "For every faker we shut down," he says, "another two or three start up." Still, Sati keeps going; if anything, the circumstances make him even more eager to go after the major players. He showed me where they are based.

The market in Aligarh is fairly nondescript, made more interesting and dangerous by the penchant of some traders to arm themselves with a *kutta,* which is a homemade pistol found among the underground of Uttar Pradesh. It has a barrel with a tendency to blow up. The first shot usually works; after that it may not function and is sometimes lethal to the user. But because most traders will never fire their weapon, it is mainly a deterrent (see figure 5-10). According to Sati's colleagues, who monitor this market on a daily basis, perhaps 10–20 percent of the trade at this market is in fake products.

The city of Agra, best known as the home of the Taj Mahal, has gained notoriety among insiders as the center of India's drug-counterfeit trade in recent years. Of the three main wholesale markets where fake drugs are traded in Agra, the largest is Mubarak Mahal, which spans three floors and houses around five hundred small drugstores. The market is easy to miss; it has a narrow entrance accessible only by a narrower lane (see figure 5-11). It is impossible to enter unnoticed; my white face was scrutinized by a dozen traders, but even Sati and his Indian colleagues were eyed suspiciously. Although one could perhaps enter surreptitiously, I imagine raids cannot catch store owners far from the entrance by surprise.

Shutters would be down and the bogus products removed before police could penetrate the deeper recesses of this market.

According to Uday Shankar, a pharmacist with the Agra Government Hospital and one of the many contacts I made through Sati, fake drugs comprise 20 percent of store sales, a trade valued in excess of $5 million per day. Everything is on sale in the market, from hypertensives to antimalarials to painkillers to antibiotics; even anesthetics are available. Stories of fake anesthetics alarm me more than others; incidents of patients waking up during procedures seem more disconcerting than even the deaths some products cause. Early in 2009 at Osmania General Hospital in Hyderabad, a patient given an underdosed fake anesthetic woke up thirty minutes into a two-hour procedure. It is possible the image of patients writhing in pain on the operating table trumps death, and it is an image I cannot shake, and I have to really try to focus in order to listen to Dr. Shankar, for whom the story is old news. He says he "wouldn't be surprised if Agra supplied" a lot of the problem drugs we have seen over the past few years.

Agra suppliers were implicated in a series of raids conducted in November 2009 by Uttar Pradesh authorities; the raids occurred over a fifteen-day period across fourteen state districts. Counterfeit and substandard drugs at hospitals are rampant, and earlier in 2009, fake antidepressants, painkillers, and insulin—many of which had only 11–12 percent of API—were found at Danapur Railway Hospital in Bihar State. Fake anesthetics were also found in March 2010, when the Maharastra police raided a company manufacturing counterfeit IVIGLOB-EX, an injection used to treat cancer and AIDS patients. Officials seized 324 bottles of the injection, which they found resembled the chemical properties of another, cheaper brand of injection also used to treat terminally ill patients. Officials believe fake labels were printed and placed on bottles of the cheaper injection for resale.[1]

FIGURE 5-11

Roger Bate outside Agra Market

These dangerous drugs may not have all come from Agra's markets, but Agra's dangerous drugs are going somewhere. Shankar says there are hundreds of Indians taking dangerous, potentially fatal pharmaceuticals made or traded through his hometown at any given time.

Although Shankar is not alone in exposing and otherwise fighting fake drugs in Agra, he does not have many allies. Anyone interested in combating fake drugs can feel isolated in India. Given that whistleblowers are generally not liked, those who are combating fake drugs tend to associate with each other, partly to provide physical protection and partly to defend one another's reputations. I asked each of them many of the same questions and one in particular: are there any good-quality fake drugs? That is, are there drugs with falsified labels pretending to be a more expensive brand, but that have the correct contents in the correct formulations? These people, who are working to combat drug counterfeiting, usually looked at me quizzically, as though the question was absurd, and none believed there are well-made fakes. Yet, some businessmen in India do.

Shankar took me around all the drug-trading areas, or at least the parts that sell dangerous products. Within a few hundred yards of the Mubarak Mahal market is the Fountain market, with at least fifty stores primarily trading generics. Some of its traders offer illegal and hard-to-distinguish copies of generics for sale. Some of those copies may work, but most will not. The few drugs I saw were superficially fine, they were not tested for quality, but Sati showed me some definite fakes that had been bought at that market just one week before.

Not far from the Fountain market is an even less formal market, near the Sarojini Naidu Medical College, where at least 180 drugstores operate. Shankar tells me that this college market has one of the highest percentages of fake drugs. "Many doctors at the college will tell patients to buy drugs from particular vendors within the market," Shankar says, "some to ensure that these patients buy drugs of decent quality, but others to intentionally direct them to pharmacists supplying fakes." Shankar believes doctors are receiving kickbacks for referring their patients; he told me pharmacists routinely expect to pay the prescribing doctor 15–20 percent of the sales price of the drugs. I told him I was surprised at his openness, his willingness to criticize doctors in his home city, but he says he is largely ignored and no threat to them. Until the authorities decide to act, Shankar is an irritation at most. As I left Agra I wondered whether I would ever be able to think of the Taj Mahal again without contemplating the lethal trade happening a few miles away. I also wondered whether I would see Dr. Shankar again, because if and when Agra officials start to take fake drugs more seriously, the illegal traders may fatally target those exposing them.

Major Manufacturers

Some of the bad drugs on sale in these Agra markets are from relatively large fake-drug manufacturers. Operations run by Rajesh Sharma, also known as Rajesh Dua, are quintessential producers for these types of markets. Sharma is a well-known and increasingly influential counterfeiter from the state of Haryana, northwest of Delhi. Sharma specializes in producing fake drugs to order, allowing the buyer to set the percentage of active ingredient to be included, with a sliding cost scale depending on how much is required. I saw one of his factories in the stifling heat of an Indian summer. Although these facilities were far from good manufacturing standards, they were not the backstreet, rundown operations we saw outside Aligarh.

Some of the drugs he produces will be chemically similar to brand-name antibiotics and painkillers, but other versions will be little more than dust, chalk, and road paint with excellent packaging. It all depends on what the buyer wants and is willing to spend.

Investigators tell me Sharma employs more than forty people and moves tens of millions of dollars of merchandise each year. His business is growing and mobile, with production facilities in several locations around Delhi. So far, businessmen like him have been able to operate freely.

Pavel Garg runs seemingly respectable pharmaceutical businesses, Combitic Global and Unisule. The Combitic website lists Garg as the proprietor, gives the company address, and states its business as "Manufacturers & Exporters of Pharmaceutical & Allied Products—Antibiotics, Antispasmodics, Antimalarials, Analgesics, Antipyretics & Antiaides [sic], Vitamins Preparation in form of Capsules, Tablets, Parentrals [sic] & Liquid Dosage form." When a reporter from Mumbai's *Daily News and Analysis* tried to contact Garg there in April 2009, however, he found the address was actually that of Capital Insurance Brokers Pvt. Ltd. Dinesh Gupta, its director, said, "We [moved] here one-and-a-half years ago and keep getting mails for Combitic

FIGURE 5-12

Pill-making machine captured in raid

Global. We don't know where the company or its proprietors are."[2]

Nevertheless, Garg manages to maintain enough credibility to provide cover for his more "creative" activities. His illicit operations produce millions of fake pills each day, and a BBC undercover crew once caught him on camera bragging that he wanted to "spread the wealth around," which he accomplished by bribing the chief minister of Haryana Province with a Bentley.[3] This is a sound strategy for Garg to follow. By rewarding those providing the permissive environment in which he operates, he gives officials a positive reason to want to help him, while also making them legally complicit, an important point of leverage, should external political pressure compel them to act. As recently as May 2011 a journalist, Gethin Chamberlain, posing as a drug buyer, told me he walked around Garg's new company premises. Garg appears to have expanded his business, because this is a quite sizable operation. His "semi-legal" business, as he describes it himself, is obviously flourishing.

During his time as Delhi's chief of police, Karan amassed more than enough evidence to bring Garg to justice (see, e.g., figure 5-12, above). He told me that when his officers went to arrest Garg, officers of the Haryana State Police were protecting Garg, resulting in a standoff between the two police forces. Because the raid and attempted arrest were in Haryana, Karan's Delhi police had to withdraw, a failure this normally cheerful man still appears bitter about. But even in Haryana State, effective officials do operate. Rakesh Dahiya, the district drugs control officer, seized vast quantities of bogus antibiotics in 2008, but he is a rarity.

The seemingly unstoppable Garg has a wide repertoire of questionable business activities. In 2007 he sent a large shipment of pharmaceuticals to a Russian firm; for anybody familiar with fake-drug trafficking, this fact alone is enough to ring alarm bells. Garg claimed the shipment never arrived, so he filed a claim on a $2.5 million policy with the New India Assurance

Company. The claims were repudiated by the insurance company on the grounds that Garg was trying to dupe the company. Later, this decision was overturned by a consumer commission, which awarded him $1.245 million.[a] Despite the significant media attention his activities have drawn, Garg's counterfeit drug business continues to flourish. In fact, Sharma and Garg are being joined by others taking advantage of the profits to be made selling drugs of questionable quality to overseas markets.

An Indian investigator working at my request approached Sharma's network posing as a buyer for a southern African pharmacy chain, and he was offered rifampicin, at 15 percent strength. That level of API is "enough to pass color dye tests and much cheaper than 100 percent," Sharma told my investigator. Although this may make sense from the point of view of the sophisticated faker, at that strength the pill would do little to help the patient and likely contains just enough API to allow the bacterium to become resistant to future drug treatments. This is exactly the kind of operation that endangers life and threatens entire classes of good-quality drugs by building dangerous drug resistance.

To find Sharma's newest factories or packaging colleagues, anticounterfeit investigators must often rely on anonymous—and lucky—tips. Smart operators move production at regular intervals to avoid discovery. Even shoddy operations, such as the factory I visited near Aligarh, are only discovered by chance. In the case of the factory near Aligarh, a conversation between one of Sati's agents and a villager's friend alerted Sati to the

---

a. If that does not sound dubious enough, in 2006 Garg and two other business colleagues founded and funded a political party. In India, contributions to political parties are tax exempt. The Electoral College claims Garg's company made contributions of $400,000. The party had only one candidate, and he attracted so few votes that he lost his deposit. In India and the United Kingdom, for example, to prevent frivolous attempts to undermine the political system, candidates have to deposit a small amount of money, which they forfeit if they do not get a reasonable number of votes (usually measured in the hundreds of votes, not an onerous task for a serious candidate, but difficult if the exercise is a farce or, in Garg's case, a tax-avoidance cover). The party moved out of its office a few months after the election, and the office is now occupied by a chartered accounting firm, which also made donations to the party. The party has since renamed itself and moved out to Sonepat in Haryana, to the same address as another donor. *Express India,* "Forum Awards Rs 5 Cr to Pharma Company," October 3, 2007, available at http://www.expressindia.com/latest-news/forum-awards-rs-5-cr-to-pharma-company/223844/ (accessed July 11, 2011).

possible counterfeit manufacturing site. To hunt down these operations, Sati has developed loose contacts with hundreds of people who hang around markets all over northern India; he pays them if they provide useful information (he pays the more important and successful informants a retainer, too). Following the Aligarh tipoff, he and his team spent months building a case against the owner of the operation that Sati hoped would lead to a prosecution. When I asked him about the case in early 2010, he told me that the fake-drug operation had closed down, but the perpetrators were at large and could easily have set up somewhere else. Even if it had gone to court, he said it was unlikely to lead to a conviction because he had no evidence of direct harm to anyone from the drugs produced.

Sati faces an uphill battle even when he has presented authorities with substantial evidence of counterfeiting and even after a raid has occurred, in part because fakers often infiltrate the police. While I was with Sati in his office one day, a uniformed senior police officer arrived to escort him to a police station where, some months earlier, he had filed a complaint of counterfeiting following a successful raid. Sati knew what to expect and hinted delicately to me that this policeman had been convinced by the defendant to persuade Sati to drop the case. When I saw him a few days later, I asked how it went. With a characteristic shrug, he explained that a lawyer who sometimes helps him in these situations came along and pressured the policeman to let things stand. "It's ridiculous, I know, but that's how we have to do business in India," he lamented. I later stumbled across an Indian website, www.ipaidabribe.com, established by anticorruption activists. The site exposes an astonishing array of graft across India, from small bribes to policemen to register complaints about thefts, to larger amounts when dealing with tax authorities and corrupt regulators.

Sati doesn't dismiss all authorities as corruptible—far from it: he could not get anywhere if there were not good people in charge. He relies heavily on some key officers in the police and in other investigative branches of the law. His boss, company CEO R. B. Pathak, is a former police inspector. Also, Karan is a widely sought-out consultant on the topic. He deserves the fees he is earning and seems to enjoy his new advisory role. Still, for all the goodwill and efforts of men such as Sati, Karan, and others, they have little influence and have to operate in small geographic areas; they face a constant uphill battle.

Fake-Market Size

It is difficult to know how many poor-quality drugs are in the market in India, not least because regulation is divided between the central government in Delhi and the various state governments. While the central government sets standards, the states oversee quality and issue manufacturing and retail licenses with varying degrees of rigor.

In 2003 the government of India's Central Drugs Standard Control Organization (CDSCO) conducted a survey estimating that 11 percent of drugs in the national market were substandard and 0.4 percent of drugs were spurious. In 2009 CDSCO undertook another survey, but this time was reticent about providing details of the findings. In fact, the government did not release the report for nearly a year after first leaking information of the study to the news media in the fall of 2009. It provided no details other than a headline figure that 0.03 percent of the market had been deemed spurious. "Spurious" is a particularly Indian term capable of many interpretations, but the most consistent definition is that spurious drugs are those that contain no active ingredient at all, that is, counterfeit and totally substandard products. Eventually, after ten months of leaks about the results, CDSCO released the "Report on Countrywide Survey for Spurious Drugs" in July 2010. The report, conducted over a period of seven months in 2009, found that of 24,136 samples, 11, or 0.045 percent, were spurious.[4]

CDSCO took pains to point out that its results flatly contradicted reports over the past decade from scholars and industry groups claiming fake-drug rates ranging from 3 to 35 percent of the national market. Indeed, CDSCO expressed a clear aim to overcome the "apprehensions about the availability of safe and genuine medicines in India."[5] Little wonder: the Indian government is rightly proud of its pharmaceutical market, worth $25 billion a year. Surinder Singh, drug controller general and head of CDSCO, claims that a child is vaccinated in the world using an Indian-made vaccine every second and says 45 percent of India's pharmaceutical production is exported to more than two hundred countries.[6]

The CDSCO report's results fail to pass even the most cursory of inspections. Not only are there discrepancies with international studies, but there are also unexplained internal inconsistencies that undermine the findings. For instance, the report claims that its authors had no useful information

FIGURE 5-13

Delhi's Bhagirath Palace, site of legal and illegal medicine

about areas known for counterfeit drugs. This is inconceivable: despite being a foreigner, I know that New Delhi's Bhagirath Palace (see figure 5-13) and certain markets in Agra and Aligarh are major locations of the fake-drug trade. More important, the report claims repeatedly that only 3 samples of 2,976 (0.101 percent) were found to be substandard, but only 305 samples were subject to chemical analysis (implying complex testing for impurities), which means the failure rate was actually 1 percent—ten times what the report touts. Confusingly, the report later implies that only basic API analysis was performed on all 2,976 samples, which means many substandard drugs likely went undetected. In addition, the quality assessments were actually undertaken by Indian pharmaceutical companies, which have a direct interest in hiding any substandard versions of their own products or fakes made by other criminal enterprises.

Previous annual government assessments of many thousands of samples showed the number of drugs failing quality-control tests at about 10 percent in the 1990s and 7 percent over most of the last decade. In an assessment of more than 700 samples in 2008 and early 2009 in three Indian cities, Delhi in the northwest, Chennai in the southeast, and Kolkata in the east, just over 8 percent of my research team's samples failed tests (69 samples failed out of 782), which concurs broadly with the government's larger samplings. There were differences across the cities in our study; samples from Delhi failed more often (11.5 percent) than those from Chennai (5 percent) and Kolkata (9 percent). The details of these and other research findings are discussed in depth in part III.

It is also likely the 2009 CDSCO report generated untrustworthy findings because the samples were biased. Karan told me many pharmacists are routinely aware of when and by whom government surveys are undertaken.

The report itself notes retail pharmacists in cities "refused to sale [sic] . . . the schedule drug without prescription." Of the seventy Indian pharmacies we visited for our research, none demanded prescriptions. Either pharmacists voluntarily and drastically changed policy just for the government sampling, which seems unlikely, or they were alerted to who the covert buyers were and reacted by following the letter of the law instead of usual practice.

Conducting covert surveys requires following a careful protocol. In my team's peer-reviewed studies for the *Public Library of Science One* journal, reviewers grilled us about how interviews were conducted because poor sampling might have biased the results. Yet, the CDSCO report includes only a single sentence on the importance of sampling protocols. Nowhere in the report is the drug-collection protocol actually discussed. Although less important, the report also contains glaring typographical and reporting errors, as in the first table, where samples are referred to as "Not of Sub-Standard Quality," when the authors mean "Not of Standard Quality."[7] The 2009 CDSCO report is a well-conducted analysis of dubious data, making the results useless. If this were a minor report, the error might be passable, but given the life-threatening nature of fake drugs, this is not something the government should tolerate. A Pew poll in August 2010 found that 54 percent of Americans distrust drugs made in India.[8] This comes as no surprise.

Indian products dominated the markets in all countries where my research team sampled drugs, domestically and in other developing countries, particularly across Africa. Table 4-1 contains summaries of a subset of these data, and a full discussion of our research methods can be found in part III.

Of course, India's government is proud of the country's spectacular growth in the pharmaceutical market, which managed a 30 percent annual increase even during the recent world recession. Still, my own data attest that substandard and otherwise fake products are a small but significant problem for India's drug makers. Ironically, Indian insiders seemed the least shocked by the CDSCO results, not because they believed them, but because they expected underhand actions from their government. But fake-drug whitewashes like the CDSCO report are counterproductive. They increase distrust of Indian medicines, and they undermine the great work of people such as Sati and Karan by making it seem like the problem of low-quality drugs does not exist. If the report is believed, those fighting the fake-drug problem come to be considered scaremongers or, worse, doing the bidding of Western companies trying to trash Indian manufacturers' reputations. Perhaps the worst outcome of the CDSCO whitewash is that it scares those who might otherwise have been prepared to take risks to expose bad behavior. Without government support, people who could expose criminal drug traders would end up risking their lives for nothing. Nevertheless, there are brave souls who continue to risk their lives to expose illegal and dangerous activities, often within legitimate firms.

Drug Production Oversight:
The Ranbaxy Saga

Under the right conditions, those working within illegal operations may be prepared to expose their organizations. Whether an entire operation is criminal or just one part, informants, or whistleblowers, often form the most important information source for investigators. As good as external investigators can be, they are not as well informed about operations as those actually working within them. India was not the first place I came across informants, but it was the first place where one contacted me directly.

This particular story starts back in 2004. Legitimate drug approvals by stringent agencies like the U.S. FDA are slow and expensive because the aim is to ensure, as far as possible, that only safe and effective new or imported products are approved for sale. Because the costs are high, especially for young and small firms in middle-income countries, the WHO created a drug-regulatory function of its own—the prequalification program—with the aim of approving good-quality generic products made by firms practicing GMP but based in middle-income countries. The WHO does not have full regulatory authority, but it can review data, often provided by companies (and independent laboratories with which they contract) seeking approval for their products. In 2004 the prequalification program was a work in progress; I analyzed the approval system at the WHO and found it wanting.[9] The WHO had approved copies of innovator (branded) HIV drugs but did not establish that these drugs were true generics—that is, bioequivalent to the innovator product. (Other stringent drug regulatory authorities such as the FDA and the European Medicines Agency demand evidence of bioequivalence before approving generics for their markets.[10])

Since that time, the bioequivalence deficiencies in the prequalification program, as well as other minor concerns, have probably been resolved—at least there are no obvious manifestations of approved products failing quality-control tests.

Nonetheless, as a result of my initial analysis and subsequent publications, a whistleblower from Ranbaxy, the largest Indian drug company at the time and one of the most respected, contacted me with allegations that the company was falsifying data on product stability. If he was correct, Ranbaxy was fabricating a crucial part of the quality-assurance assessment for critical HIV medications destined for Africa. He hoped I would expose this bad practice without betraying his confidence. He said he had contacted me because he did not trust the Indian authorities and thought only foreigners would punish Ranbaxy effectively and, by so doing, protect HIV patients from potentially dangerous drugs. GMP dictates, among other things, that companies record the degradation of a product over time to show that a product works when it is first made and throughout its approved shelf life. The documents the whistleblower gave me showed identical degradation data for HIV products examined after nine months and twelve months. Given that the readings were reported to several decimal places and that products inevitably degrade over a three-month period, at least part of the data were almost certainly incorrect and had been approved by managers who were not even in the plant on the critical days. Internal Ranbaxy e-mails I saw also revealed staff concern that such data would be a red flag to inspectors, lowering the chance that Ranbaxy would win a procurement order for HIV medicines from the United Nations Children's Fund.

Had a small data-transfer error occurred, or was the entire production line compromised? Were some of the managers at this Ranbaxy plant incompetent, or were they cutting corners on a wide scale, resulting in potentially dangerous products coming off the line?

I realized the significance of the data and tried to meet with the whistleblower, but he said he was scared for his life. I don't normally think of India as being a dangerous place for business espionage and contract hits. This was the stuff of Le Carré novels, Bourne and Bond movies, and real-life Mafioso-type activities. But when I asked a few drug-industry insiders in India about his fears, they did not dismiss them. If illegal activity was taking place at Ranbaxy, they did not rule out the possibility that any illegal, even lethal, action might be taken to prevent its exposure. Most thought it likely the problem was at a relatively low level, but one did not dismiss the possibility that more senior personnel might have known of the data manipulation.

I remained skeptical, and without a face-to-face meeting, I was concerned I was being misled. What better way to discredit me than having me expose a false problem? My criticism of the WHO had irked some of its staff, and Michael Riggs, one of their staff and later a consultant to the WHO, told me several years later that he had been instructed to do what he could to discredit me and my writings by claiming to the media that I was simply "hostile to WHO." In any event, I was not about to trash the reputation of a respected Indian firm without better information. Instead of writing about the subject, I forwarded the data to the WHO and the FDA in late 2005 and to the U.S. Department of Justice in mid-2008, with the expectation that they would act. The whistleblower had also said he was sending information to the WHO and the FDA, and he showed me his e-mail exchange with Lembit Rago, head of the prequalification program, which had approved the Ranbaxy HIV medicines in question.

The FDA closely examined Ranbaxy's production. In a June 2006 warning letter to Ranbaxy, the FDA recommended "withholding approval" of new drugs and API manufactured at the company's Paonta Sahib plant until certain deficiencies were corrected. Nearly a year later, Ranbaxy's counsel admitted that "it had not yet addressed all of [the FDA's] concerns."[11] Nonetheless, the FDA did not hesitate to approve eighteen new drug applications from Ranbaxy, suggesting that the problem was likely one of record keeping rather than quality.

In July 2008, the FDA and the Department of Justice made their concerns public, announcing they were investigating Ranbaxy for fabricating bioequivalence and stability data to support applications to market new generic drugs in the United States and to sell drugs to the U.S. President's Emergency Plan for AIDS Relief. Quality assurance supervisors were absent from the plants when they were supposed to be on duty, and risks of cross-contamination of products was significant, too, including in the manufacture of antibiotics. "Allegations from reliable sources and supporting documents indicate a pattern of systemic fraudulent conduct," the Justice

Department wrote in its July 3 brief. "Evidence suggests that Ranbaxy uses API from unapproved sources, blends unapproved API with approved API, and uses less API in its drug than had been approved by the FDA." In September 2008, the FDA issued an import ban on more than thirty generic Ranbaxy products.[12]

Ranbaxy claimed that "except for issues that have already been fully aired with the [U.S.] government, [it knew] of no evidence to support" the allegations. It pointed out that the FDA collected more than two hundred samples of Ranbaxy products and believed that the "FDA's testing of these samples did not uncover any product failures."[13]

In September 2008, the Department of Justice dropped its case after Ranbaxy provided it with a tranche of requested documents, but the import ban remained. In February 2009, the FDA announced that Ranbaxy had indeed falsified laboratory tests for drugs approved for sale in the United States. In mid-May, company CEO Malvinder Singh announced his resignation, and the FDA received a "corrective action plan" from the company.[14]

What is of particular interest to U.S. patients is that Ranbaxy was chosen to be the sole generic supplier, for six months after patent expiry (December 2011), of Lipitor (atorvastatin), the world's most valuable medicine. It is expected that in the six-month period Ranbaxy will earn $600 million, but of possible concern is that the drug is due to be manufactured at the Paonta Sahib plant, where some of Ranbaxy's false data were found. Given the problems that Ranbaxy has had, the FDA has delayed its decisions over whether Ranbaxy will be allowed to make Lipitor for the U.S. market. As a result, Mylan, a U.S. generic manufacturer, sued the FDA in April 2011 because it claims that the FDA's prevarication will delay the launch of its own generic version of Lipitor.

All of these downstream and wide-ranging problems derive from lax behavior by a few staff in one or two locations in India.

What can be learned from the Ranbaxy saga? FDA inspections of manufacturing plants—both foreign and domestic—routinely identify GMP shortcomings similar to those alleged to have occurred in the Ranbaxy plant. The FDA often takes punitive action, including halting all new drug approvals, even when there is no evidence that a product is actually dangerous. (The FDA did not issue a recall for any of Ranbaxy's products.) The FDA has to weigh repeated GMP infractions against the quality of the products seen and the impact on the market (and on access to medicines) of a ban. The FDA generally makes the right decisions for the American people. It is more precautionary than other agencies, but it can and should act proactively because Americans can afford—and demand—the highest level of quality compliance when it comes to their pharmaceuticals. Not all agencies have the same precautionary approach. Even in the United States and Europe, standards are not always kept. As box 5-4, "GSK Whistle-blower," describes, a Puerto Rican plant of the British firm GSK has failed in significant ways to control quality.

In the Ranbaxy case, the U.S. FDA acted because Ranbaxy's drugs were being exported to the United States or procured by the U.S. government for distribution in poor countries. But what happens to oversight in cases in which the FDA does not have a direct interest? Both Ranbaxy and GSK export drugs that are sent to other countries but not sent to the United States. During the period that Ranbaxy was under investigation by the FDA, the WHO also inspected Ranbaxy's Paonta Sahib plant several times and took a slightly different view. In May 2007, it concluded that the plant was operating at an "acceptable level of GMP," although noncompliance with WHO guidelines "needed to be addressed by the manufacturer and verified."[15] In November 2008, the WHO commissioned a special inspection team composed of itself, the Therapeutic Goods Administration (Australia), the Medicines and Healthcare Products Regulatory Agency (United Kingdom), and Health Canada. The team concluded that Ranbaxy was "operating at an acceptable level of compliance with WHO GMP guidelines."[16]

It seems the U.S. FDA operates to higher standards than the WHO and possibly higher than any other stringent MRA. This led me to wonder whether standards should be identical across nations of varying wealth and development. After all, while cutting corners has risks for patients in terms of efficacy and safety and for the broader population in terms of increased resistance risks, there may be conditions under which doing so is warranted. Is it possible that while both the WHO and the FDA reacted differently to the Ranbaxy problem, both acted appropriately, given their remit?

The Ranbaxy affair puts issues about the various demands for drug quality for developing countries into perspective. There can be no doubt

Box 5-4
GSK WHISTLEBLOWER

Cheryl Eckard was a quality control manager at GlaxoSmithKline with the job of inspecting pharmaceutical plants and ensuring that drugs were being produced with the correct ingredients and potency and met government standards for purity.

In 2002 GSK assigned Eckard to help lead an investigation of one of their largest plants in Cidra, Puerto Rico, following a report by the FDA that cited violations. Eckard's quality assurance team discovered many more problems than the FDA investigation; they also found that drugs produced at Cidra were being contaminated with bacteria by poor employee manufacturing practices and tainted water. Eckard also learned that production line failures at the plant were producing drugs with the wrong potency, mislabeling bottles, and mixing up powerful drugs of different types and doses in the same bottles; for instance, Paxil 30mg tablets (antidepressants) were found in the same bottle as Avandia 4mg tablets (a diabetes drug).

According to Eckard, she immediately alerted three senior vice presidents about the violations and recommended immediate action. She suggested that GSK stop shipping all products from the Cidra plant, stop manufacturing product for two weeks in order to investigate and resolve the issues raised and the impact on released batches, and notify the FDA about the product mix-ups.

Unfortunately, GSK took none of her recommendations. GSK assigned Eckard to a longer-term project at the plant to work on correcting its compliance problems. Eckard believes her superiors were covering up the violations because they feared the FDA would not consider approval for two new treatments if their concerns about the plant were not reported as corrected.

After eight months of reporting problems at Cidra, Eckard sent a summary of her findings to seven GSK executives that detailed the nine high-risk areas at the plant (mix-ups, water contamination, sterility problems, etc.) and warned that if the FDA knew what the company knew, the factory would be closed.

Weeks later, Eckard was reportedly fired; GSK claimed it was due to "down-sizing."

Then, after multiple attempts to meet with GSK executives about Cidra were ignored, Eckard reported the company to the FDA. Three weeks later, the FDA launched its own investigation; federal agents searched the plant and confiscated defective drugs worth hundreds of millions of dollars, and the plant was eventually closed.

In 2010 GSK pleaded guilty to the felony charges of manufacturing and distributing adulterated drugs, including Kytril, Bactroban, Paxil CR, and Avandamet and received a criminal fine of US $150 million.

Eckard, however, filed her lawsuit under the Federal Whistleblower Law, claiming that GSK defrauded the U.S. government by selling hundreds of millions of dollars worth of adulterated drugs to Medicaid programs, which are funded by U.S. taxpayers. To resolve this civil settlement, GSK paid $600 million to the federal government and states. Under the Federal Whistleblower Law, Eckard was rewarded a percentage of the government's total recovery—the largest payout under this law to date—$96 million.

GSK denies any reports of adverse reactions from patients. But Eckard claims the company covered up adverse reactions, citing the example of an eight-year-old patient whose pharmacist reported an adverse reaction after the child received what was labeled Paxil 10mg but was really Paxil 25mg, or two and a half times the amount he was prescribed. Eckard assigned one of her investigators to the case and found that both Paxil doses were made on one production line at Cidra. Her theory was that there were still 25mg pills left in the filling hopper when the bottles and labels were switched out, causing the first batch of bottles that went through to be labeled Paxil 10mg but filled with the leftover Paxil 25mg tablets.

She took her findings to the same vice president (Steve Plating) as she had months before. He reportedly covered the incident up and filed a report with the FDA stating that the mix-up wasn't real. The vice president is no longer with GSK, but the company still denies Eckard's allegations that it lied to the FDA.[1]

Mistakes can be made, but cover-ups must not be allowed to go unpunished, or they may be repeated. For all of GSK's mistakes and criminal acts, the problem has been resolved.

---

1. "GlaxoSmithKline Whistleblower Wins Record £61m Payout," *Guardian*, October 27, 2010, available at http://www.guardian.co.uk/business/2010/oct/27/glaxosmithkline-whistleblower-wins-61m; U.S. District Court for the District of Massachusetts, Case 1:04-cv-10375-JLT Document 65, filed 10/17/08, available at: http://i.bnet.com/blogs/gsk-comp-07ce69a66c.pdf.

that it is expensive for companies to keep products registered with various authorities. In April 2007, Ranbaxy voluntarily withdrew four of its HIV/AIDS drugs—eleven formulations, including one manufactured in its Paonta Sahib plant—saying that "the demand generated through WHO Prequalification Status" had "been minimal and not commensurate with the concomitant administrative mechanism required to sustain it."[17] HIV patients who receive subsidized, donated, or insurance-covered medications would doubtless demand, as I would, that Ranbaxy's products be taken off the market, but I suspect many patients who struggle to procure their own HIV medications or those who need treatments for acute infections would accept the risk in purchasing these products if that risk meant they could afford the medication.

I have personal experience of the choices made under the pressure brought on by sickness. In March 2009 I was visiting Chennai, the main port of southeastern India. I was sickened by what was probably a very aggressive virus. At the time, however, I worried it might have been a nasty bacterial infection, which potentially could have been serious. I already had rehydration salts and potable water at hand, but I was getting worse. Through a friend, I obtained a treatment course of the drug Cifran—the brand name of ciprofloxacin manufactured by Ranbaxy—in a matter of hours. I checked the packaging and the pills as closely as a sick patient could (years of researching the dangers of substandard and counterfeit medicine have taught me to do this with any drug), and I did not hesitate to take them. I even knew of a counterfeiter called Minhu Bhati who routinely made a fake of this product with only 50 percent API. I got better in a few days, probably because the virus left my system. But I have no doubt that the Cifran would have knocked out any bacteria, too. Ideally, I would have taken a Western product, but Cifran, for all I knew made at the Paonta Sahib site, was my only option. Yes, the Cifran could have been dangerous, but the odds were low, and I took the chance—a chance most Indians and even more Africans take every day.

I certainly don't mean to draw a parallel between my relative discomfort and the acute and dangerous sicknesses afflicting many of the world's poor. The point is more that I could have afforded far more expensive medication, but there was simply no choice available—and lack of choice is a reality for the majority of the world's population.

Whistleblowers and Informants

When a large and legitimate company such as Ranbaxy can illegally breach GMP by aggressive cost-cutting, it is easy to see how smaller companies without well-trained and well-rewarded management cannot monitor illegal after-hours operations or other procedural breaches. Understanding the problems at Ranbaxy made me think more about the companies on which Sati cared not to focus. I can understand how the directors of some of those businesses, which sometimes operated on the edges of legality, might have had the wool pulled over their eyes if companies as astute as Ranbaxy were unable to stop all illegal activity.

It is not just the oversight, or lack thereof, that is of interest. It is instructive to view how the whistleblowers were treated in the Ranbaxy case and in the GSK case. In the former, the man too afraid to go public received no reward for his actions. In the latter, whistleblower Cheryl Eckard did not hesitate in reporting issues with the GSK plant in question; she has become famous, was the star of a *60 Minutes* episode, is respected for her integrity, and has been rewarded with nearly $100 million dollars compensation. Because Ranbaxy's products were not shown to have caused any significant harm (perhaps because most of the locations where it sells its drugs will not have adverse drug reaction data available), Indian authorities did not take the company's action seriously.[b] A case could be made that out-and-out criminal entities should be actively pursued as the priority, especially for a relatively poor country with limited resources. I think most objective observers would agree that would be a sensible approach. Unfortunately with brazen counterfeiters such as Pavel Garg running around free, it really is only the small-time traders who actually get prosecuted. If India is ever to have the reputation for quality equal to that of the United States, whistleblowers are essential for a whole raft of producers making terrible products, and they must be supported by the police and a legal system that does not

---

b. India's drug manufacturing sector has advanced enormously in the past decade, and as a piece of industrial policy it is entirely understandable that the Indian government would support, rather than criticize, Ranbaxy. Many countries look to India as an example of how to develop a drug industry; industrial policy trumps health policy in India, which leads to a significant number of poor producers making suspect products that get left on the market in numerous countries.

turn a blind eye to bad actions. Fortunately, in 2009 the Indian government enacted a scheme to reward whistleblowers who give evidence against the makers and traders of dangerous fake medicines. The details of this can be found in box 5-5. Early reports indicate that the system is not working well, but it is encouraging that India is trying to implement a system to support and encourage whistleblowers at all.

Indian Exports to Africa

Mumbai, on India's west coast, is the most populous city in India and the business capital of the country. Geographically, it is well placed to trade with Africa, and it is also the center of the pharmaceutical industry in India, with at least five thousand producers based there. It is not surprising that Mumbai is the major trading port for Indian drug exports en route to Africa. India suffers from a persistent shortage of competent inspectors, and many suspect producers and dealers appear to operate with impunity inside the country. The regulatory situation for exporters, those applying for permits and sometimes financial guarantees from the government, is even more lax than the domestic market; controls are rarely applied on exports.

Evidence gathered in Mumbai by Michel Koutouzis, a European expert on potentially lethal pharmaceuticals, was featured in a 2006 French documentary called *Trafic Mortel [Deadly Trade]*. It shows a sophisticated network of wholesalers, producers, and exporters all willing to produce drugs to whatever standard a buyer wants and smooth the way of shipments through customs. Posing as a buyer of substandard drugs destined for Africa, Koutouzis is allowed to inspect a factory that seems to have high manufacturing standards. This factory takes orders from huge multinational drug companies and is licensed to produce its own brand of generic products; it will also produce counterfeits to order. *Trafic Mortel* shows examples of fakes of popular malaria medicines licensed for production only in Belgium and China. The factory manager proudly indicates their attention to detail: the packaging is perfect, batch numbers are from an original product, even the correct sales-tax stamps are in place. Apparently, no detail is overlooked to ensure ease of passage into African markets.[18]

Box 5-5
REWARDING WHISTLEBLOWERS

The Indian Ministry of Health and Family Welfare states: "Public health is one of the major objectives of Government," and "medicines are the most essential component to fight various diseases prevalent in the country. It is, however, important that the drugs so available are not only of standard quality but are safe, potent and efficacious."

The ministry continues with a veiled attack on illicit Chinese businesses: "Internationally, the vested interests are supplying spurious medicines manufactured by them but with 'Made in India' label. Allegations of marketing and circulation of spurious or fake drugs within the country also are raised from time to time by the media, consumer associations, NGOs as well as in legislative forums. The volume of the pharmaceutical market and stakes involved in it makes it easy for the people to fall prey to the lures of money and indulge in various malpractices. The manufacture and sale of spurious drugs is a clandestine activity generally indulged in by anti-social elements and carried out by unlicensed manufacturers which exploit the confidence enjoyed by certain fast selling drugs by making their imitations.

"The manufacture and sale of drugs is looked after by the State Drugs Control Authorities appointed by the State Governments while imports, market authorization and new drugs are the responsibility of the Central Government. The Central Drugs Standards Control Organisation (CDSCO), under the Ministry of Health and Family Welfare, with the Drugs Controller General (India) as its head is the Central regulatory body for enforcing the quality standards of drugs, cosmetics and medical devices in the Central Government."

On August 10, 2009, changes to the Drugs and Cosmetic Act of 1940 to assist whistleblowers became law. According to the Ministry of Health and Family Welfare: "There is no dearth of good intentioned people who may wish to work for the country's interests as the whistleblowers in eradicating the menace."

Monetary and other rewards have been applied in other areas effectively, so the ministry expected success with its approach.

Whistleblowers will be entitled to a reward of up to 20 percent of the total cost of the drugs recovered to a maximum of 25 lakh rupees (approx $62,500) per case. The money will be distributed at different stages: 25

(continued)

Box 5-5 (*continued*)
REWARDING WHISTLEBLOWERS

percent at the time of filing of the charge sheet, 25 percent later on, and the final 50 percent withheld until a successful prosecution, either not appealed or appeal won.

If the whistleblower is a government officer, he may receive up to 30 lakh rupees ($75,000) over his entire career. The eligibility of the informer and the amount of remuneration are decided by a committee made up of members of a wide variety of government departments (the Ministry of Health and Family Welfare, the Central Drugs Standards Control Organisation, state and national drug controller, customs). Finally, the identity of the whistleblower will be known only to the concerned zonal and sub-zonal officers of the Central Drugs Standards Control Organisation and the Drugs Controller General (India). The committee will not know who the informant is.

At first glance these plans look pretty good. It is a shame they still wouldn't apply to my contact at Ranbaxy, but they are useful nonetheless. Withholding some of the payment seems to make sense, in order to have the whistleblower testify where required. And the payments are substantial enough to encourage the possible risk of informing (in the context of the incomes in India). But there are problems with the Indian government's approach. First, legal cases in India can take an absolute age, often many years, sometimes a decade or more, and withholding most of the payment till the end lowers the incentive enormously. Second, the committee can subjectively decide not to make a payment at all (in the case of a government employee) or severely limit it in other cases. And, as of April 2010, an analysis in the journal *Nature Medicine*[1] claimed it wasn't working well.

---

1. "The fight against fake medicines intensifies," *Nature Medicine* (April 2010): 358–66, http://www.nature.com/nm/press_release/nm0410.html.

Drug shipments follow a well-oiled route from Mumbai to Port Louis, Mauritius, where 50 percent of imports are chemical or pharmaceutical goods. From there, bulk ingredients are processed into finished products, and shipments leave by small boats for the coast of Africa. A main destination is a port on the island of Zanzibar, part of Tanzania. Both Port Louis and Zanzibar are known as free ports because of the limited regulation enforced there. While the limited regulations encourage trade and create significant benefit to the port cities' economies, they also make the ports especially favorable for the routes of traffickers in all sorts of dangerous products. From Zanzibar, drugs are typically carried in small amounts by foot passengers or on dhows to Dar es Salaam, the largest port on the mainland in Tanzania. From there, they travel to other ports along the East African coast. Mombasa, Kenya's main port, is a favored destination for direct and onward distribution to the great lakes area of the Democratic Republic of the Congo, Rwanda, Burundi, and Uganda.

Koutouzis's documentary led to a couple of arrests in Mauritius and the seizure of over 185,000 tablets, although the documentary didn't specify what products. However, without better international laws, Mauritius and other locations were unable to prosecute or extradite more of those involved in the counterfeit trade.

International Networks

It is not by chance that the ports of southeastern Africa are the main recipients of drugs (both fake and legitimate) from India. The Indian diaspora in Africa is vast. While local Indian traders may have African partners, Indians are often directly involved in the trade.[19] My research team's samplings found that more drugs in African cities came from India than any other country (see figure 4-5), both those passing quality tests and those failing them (although at least some of the "Indian" drugs failing quality tests may have been made in China, as I will discuss later).

As discussed in the chapter on Africa, Nigeria is one country that has become less than enthusiastic about the quality of many drugs imported from India. Over the past decade, Nigeria placed bans on about twenty Indian exporters after discovering their products to be substandard or counterfeit. NAFDAC now has a presence in several Indian locations where drugs are manufactured and exported and is currently undertaking to physically inspect every shipment bound for Nigeria before it leaves India. Although most of the drugs from India are legitimate and will save thousands of lives, there is a thriving international trade into Africa of fake products from India.

Why India Should Favor More International Cooperation[c]

The trade in fake pharmaceuticals from India to African and other countries highlights the need for more international cooperation for combating counterfeit drugs. India's reputation as a drug producer is on the line, yet the country has long opposed cooperating internationally to combat counterfeit drugs. India currently opposes taking steps against the counterfeit drug trade through the mechanism devised by WHO member states called IMPACT, which stands for International Medical Products Anti-Counterfeiting Taskforce, and India is viewed by other countries as the most significant obstacle to international cooperation. Although India's position is emotionally understandable, given European overreaches against legitimate Indian generics, it also leaves India vulnerable to Chinese-made counterfeits of Indian drugs, which damages the global reputation of the Indian pharmaceutical industry. India should take a more nuanced position on this issue, especially given the international nature of the problem.

Pharmaceutical Threats. India faces pharmaceutical threats from Europe and China; although these threats present themselves in very different ways, both put pressure on India to formulate a thoughtful response to counterfeit drugs.

In the last three years, European officials have: (1) detained and/or confiscated shipments of Indian-made generic drugs while in transit to other countries; (2) lobbied African countries to rewrite their laws such that they would criminalize the importation of Indian-made generic drugs, and; (3) devised a Council of Europe treaty that could be interpreted to criminalize Indian-made generic drugs in the European market. In not one of these cases did Europe demonstrate that the drugs in question contained deliberately falsified ingredients such that they were medically dangerous. Instead, Europe acted in the guise of "fighting counterfeit drugs" to strangle India's burgeoning legitimate pharmaceutical industry. Europe's actions have been criticized in the media and prompted India to file suit with the World Trade Organization (WTO) against the European Union.

---

c. I am indebted to Amir Attaran for originating some and discussing all of these ideas.

India's pharmaceutical industry is also under attack from China. In numerous instances, African authorities intercepted counterfeit medicines labeled "Made in India" that were actually faked in China (see box 5-1, above). Faking Indian products makes sense for the counterfeiters because Indian drugs are the most prevalent in many markets, and hence high fake-drug sales volume is easier to hide. But Indians also think the practice of faking their medicines has been a ploy to deflect responsibility and undermine India's drug industry.[20] The packaging for these compounds is excellent; only experts can tell them apart, and patients often find out only when it is too late. In 2009 India protested and China admitted that its companies were counterfeiting Indian drugs, but because of weak Chinese enforcement, the problem recurred in 2010.[21] China's apparent inaction suggests either a deliberate policy to destroy the reputation of Indian-made generic drugs to grab market share for legitimate Chinese competitors or, more likely, Beijing's inability to rein in the fake-drug trade that benefits some politically powerful players in the country.

Diagnosing Underlying Threats to India. European and Chinese threats to India have one overlooked common thread: in both cases, India is a victim because there is no globally accepted definition of "counterfeit drugs" and no international laws against counterfeit drugs. Some European officials have interpreted "counterfeit drugs" too broadly to block Indian goods on often entirely bogus intellectual-property grounds and to protect European companies. China takes advantage of the lack of rules to export counterfeit drugs and pin the blame on India. Both Europe and China compete against India's pharmaceutical industry and try to undermine it, so each takes the view on counterfeit medicines that most benefits them. They can do this because there are no international rules.

If this diagnosis is correct, it stands to reason that it is in India's interest to *create* global rules on its terms and thereby limit the freedom of Europe and China to engage in abuses.

Global Rules India Could Encourage. In 2004 Indian officials opposed a WHO suggestion for a treaty against counterfeit-drug products. At the time, India feared a counterfeit-drug treaty would be used against it by developed countries and their powerful pharmaceutical industries to marginalize

Indian-made generic drugs. Instead, this has happened perhaps because there is no treaty. Some European officials have filled the vacuum created by the lack of a treaty on counterfeit drugs by interpreting intellectual-property law in a way that pressures Indian drugs out of valuable markets. Europe's actions have also prioritized taking action against medicines that might infringe a trademark or patent over preventing or stopping the trade of dangerous falsified medicines that may kill, partly because doing the latter is much harder under most laws. Without a mandate to address the health dangers of counterfeit drugs, the WHO has remained a peripheral figure in these efforts.

India should reverse course, take the moral high ground—a tactically sensible position—and champion a global treaty against counterfeit medicines. As the proponent of such an initiative, India would be in a strong position to influence the treaty negotiation process, more influence than it will have if another country leads the charge. The Council of Europe has already prepared an intra-Europe treaty, which, in principle, can be signed by non-European states; it is only a matter of time before someone, probably the European Union or an African nation, proposes a global treaty (indeed, Argentina already has done so within another United Nations entity, the Office of Drugs and Crimes). India should propose a WHO treaty ahead of these other countries to maximize its influence on the process and ensure such a treaty will benefit its growing pharmaceutical industry. This idea is discussed in more detail in part IV.

To date, the process has stalled due to infighting, even within the WHO Intergovernmental Working Group on Public Health, Innovation, and Intellectual Property. The United States and Europe have sparred with Brazil and India over control of this group, and its chairmanship ended up in Zambia's hands because no one objected to Zambia. After failing to meet in 2010 because of these differences and an inability to select a chair for the meetings, the participants eventually met for the first time in early March 2011. The level of acrimony continued, with Brazil refusing to acknowledge IMPACT's moderate success and India seemingly wanting to throw all drugs under a catchall phrase of "compromised," which would blur the lines between intentionally and unintentionally bad-quality drugs.

At future meetings of this working group, India should seek exploratory discussions and identify a like-minded group for further development of a proposal to improve access to medicines by providing assistance for developing and strengthening MRAs and agreeing on global criminalization of drug counterfeiting. India and other countries could also table a resolution at the WHO Executive Board and the May 2012 World Health Assembly declaring that counterfeit medicines are a global scourge and mandating that the WHO establish a secretariat to carry out consultations on the modalities for negotiating a Framework Convention against Counterfeit/Falsified Medicines. India or Brazil should offer to host the draft secretariat in New Delhi or Brasilia. India and like-minded countries could then press for a special session of the UN General Assembly (where developed countries are the minority) to discuss and achieve diplomatic consensus on the global problem of counterfeit medicines.

By taking a leadership role in this process, India could avoid ceding vulnerability to Europe on intellectual property and could defend its interests against Chinese infringement. India's ability to conduct treaty negotiations on its terms is assured and is proved by the very favorable outcome India achieved in the 2011 India-EU Free Trade Agreement.

There are other advantages for India of spearheading a treaty on counterfeit drugs. Commercially, India's best generic companies dominate emerging markets, which are also the locations most harmed by fakes. Large Indian producers were second only to Western companies in consistency of products and are a lot cheaper on average.[d] By championing better oversight for drugs, India will enhance the quality reputation of its goods and the market share of its drug companies. Diplomatically, by taking the leadership role at the United Nations for a treaty to stop a worldwide scourge like deadly counterfeit drugs, India would enhance its reputation among a large number of countries, which would also benefit India's long-term campaign for permanent membership in the UN Security Council. India's current attitude at WHO meetings reinforces those who would oppose its holding such a seat.

Furthermore, a treaty proposed by India might pave the way toward overcoming objections made by Brazil and other countries that face the same overall threats. Still, these threats are not entirely similar. India's companies are significantly more advanced, making a wide array of

---

d. This is discussed with the research findings in part III.

bioequivalent products, so their industry will be able to take advantage of any general improvement in standards. The same cannot be said for many of the companies in China and Brazil or Thailand and South Africa, and cannot be said with any certainty for any companies in the rest of Africa. Thus, the commercial benefit India will see from proposing a treaty will not extend to other countries that have often battled with innovator companies over price and quietly stood behind India's opposition.

If India does not take up this challenge, then other countries, perhaps Nigeria because NAFDAC seems most interested in the possibility, could do it. If the EU proposes a treaty instead, it is unlikely to succeed and may entrench opposition from India and other countries.

6

China

China's legitimate pharmaceutical industry is growing extremely rapidly, sometimes too quickly for suppliers to ensure standards. The pace of growth is also augmented by, and sometimes overshadowed by, the trade in substandard and counterfeit drugs. The semilegal and fake-drug industry I investigated there in 2008 is the source of many of the counterfeits I discovered around the world. The Chinese government has made some significant efforts toward reform, but the implementation of quality-control standards has been outpaced by growth in both the legitimate and illegitimate pharmaceutical industries, rendering government efforts insufficient. Domestic problems also plague reform efforts: corruption, willful ignorance on the part of the national government, and complicity with illicit production and distribution on the part of regional governments have further exacerbated the situation. David Kessler, the former head of the FDA, told reporters in 2008 that "China is as close to an unregulated environment as you can get." He went on to imply it was a lot like the United States in 1906. That, he said, was "why we developed an FDA."[1]

Discovering the Source

China's pharmaceutical industry is growing 15 percent per year within an emerging economy that is growing 9 percent per year. The worldwide demand for low-cost drugs is vast, and today China provides at least 40 percent of U.S. drug chemicals (80 percent are from overseas sources, of which China provides roughly half).[2] Potential profits are huge, and production is romping ahead far faster than the government's regulatory capacity can adapt. There is an inevitable mismatch between the quality of drugs produced by the white-knuckle pace of development in China and what is demanded by the culture of extreme risk aversion in mature economies.

Most major cities discussed in the book have centuries, even millennia, of history, but in mid-1980s Shenzhen had a population of a few thousand spread over several villages. Today, Shenzhen is a sprawling city of more than twelve million people. Approaching the city from Hong Kong over the Pearl River, one quickly encounters the market at Yei Wu, which sells everything, and I mean everything, you could ever want, including drugs. They advertise the best DVD copies as genuine fakes, which mean they will work properly, designed to limit competition from worse copies. With no sense of irony or embarrassment one notes, the locals sell all sorts of copies in the heavily policed customs zones.

China has most of the requisite laws to prevent intellectual property (IP) fraud since it joined the WTO in 2001, but there has been little enforcement of these laws for several reasons. Salaries of the police are very low, which means they often want a cut of the fake business. In addition, a major federal offensive against the fake trade would throw many out of work. This is especially true in the provinces, where government officials make money from fakes, and, unlike Beijing, provincial leaders do not worry about offending Western business and political leaders. When I raised the issue of government condoning IP piracy, I was reminded on more than one occasion that the earliest interactions the Chinese had with the English were with my ancestors' piracy on the high seas. As we jointly agreed, English piracy ended, as will Chinese, in time.

Professor Shaohon Jin of Beijing University is director of China's National Institute for the Control of Pharmaceutical and Biological Products. He convinced me that China has made great efforts to raise standards, but regulatory authorities are still playing catch-up and will be for some time: Jin's research found that "14 percent of the many thousands of drug samples tested in 1998 were of low quality." Degraded antibiotics such as amoxicillin were prevalent. In 2002 the Shanghai Drug Administration Bureau found that 12.2 percent (1,833 drugs) of 14,980 drugs inspected were below quality standards.[3] Since then, the situation has improved, and the latest figures Dr. Jin presented at a conference in London in April 2011 showed that under 5 percent of drugs inspected were fake (of 1,060,000 products screened, approximately 50,000 were substandard or counterfeit).[4]

As well as having to contend with the hangover of corrupt and increasingly dispossessed political and military elites, China is loath to lose face in the international arena and tends to brush aside concerns and deploy tactics of blame avoidance when under pressure. African health experts used to tell me that their complaints about fakes from China had little effect; today, responses are at least rhetorically better.

Many sources in China—who will not speak on record for fear of retribution—confirm that a few corrupt military and political leaders participate in the counterfeit trade. Foreign health and counterfeit-drug experts, such as those at NAFDAC, allege that corrupt politicians are paid off to not inspect producers' manufacturing facilities or assess the quality of drugs they produce. Shanghai- and Hong Kong–based insiders tell me that a small fake-drug factory in northern China is even housed inside a military base. According to a 2002 *Washington Post* report, the People's Liberation Army has participated in the drug trade. During an investigation into the producer and distributor of a counterfeit drug used to treat sexually transmitted diseases, an investigator reported that "trucks with military license plates are seen bringing goods in and out of Puning's pharmaceuticals market." The investigator was later threatened and intimidated by thugs, and a rogue element of the People's Liberation Army was identified as having manufactured the drug. Private investigators confirm that military counterfeit pharmaceutical operations are still "tolerated by the Beijing regime."[5]

Alongside the intelligence I gathered on Chinese actors while conducting my investigations in Nigeria, Kenya, and India, I learned from contacts in Shanghai, Hong Kong, and Beijing about dangerous actors in China itself. Several investigators assisted me, and one of them operated in a similar fashion to Suresh Sati. Wen Li grew up on the outskirts of Beijing and has done brand-protection work for much of the past decade. Unlike those in India, private investigators in China were very nervous about publicizing their work; they claim the authorities do not like bad publicity for China as a whole and make life difficult, and sometimes dangerous, for those speaking to foreigners. As a result, I will refer to few real names in this chapter. Illegitimate Chinese producers mirror those in India and range from small-scale garage producers to large-scale manufacturers of products of dubious quality. But China is unique in that it also has many semi-legitimate chemical producers (they are allowed to make the chemicals but are often unlicensed to sell to pharmaceutical companies) that make intermediary compounds for pharmaceuticals in vast quantities. These are very hard to investigate because they sell to other businesses and not members of the public, and hence one must be working for or with a significant business to gain access. Phillipe Andre, professor at the School of Pharmaceutical Science and Technology at Tianjin University, audits many of these companies. His clients are mostly Western pharmaceutical companies sourcing inexpensive chemicals from China. He says there is a "huge difference between the best and the worst" chemical suppliers. Some are "physically dirty" and operate plants that do not live up to GMP at all: more often than not these are owned by the Chinese government. Other plants are as good as those in the West.

Of all the alarming statements he made, perhaps the most remarkable is that while Western firms demand audits of the suppliers of the chemicals they buy, his "own data show that American and European pharmaceutical companies are misinformed about the identity of the manufacturing site of 39 percent of the drug substances they purchase from China." This is a point echoed by Guy Villax, the CEO of Hovione, who told the Pew Trust Conference "Ensuring the U.S. Drug Supply" in Washington, D.C., in March 2011 that the industry "suddenly discovered that to a large degree we do not have control over quality." While he agreed that it was important to combat the fakers of finished products in China, he said that going after those making poor APIs is the most important because substandard APIs can be deadly.[6]

Andre claimed that a plant in Liaoning that had been certified as GMP compliant by the European Agency for Medicines had parts of its factories in a terrible state. He said significant ambient levels of ammonia made it difficult to breathe as he walked around the facilities. Although the ammonia apparently had not reached dangerous levels, he said it was "indicative of toxic solvents," which could be lethal. In other sites in Shanghai, Andre saw rusty equipment, mold, insects, and even a dog that had access to chemicals to be sold to Europe. Almost as worrying as these gross failures is the fact that in his audits, only 6 percent of companies provide impurity profiles of the chemicals in question (see box 13-1 on page 322). In production of some chemicals, "residues of solvents and potentially genotoxic catalysts are rarely controlled" and could be present, he said, because only certain problems are easy to spot in the final chemical. Furthermore, the tests required by the FDA and USP do not find all of the problems.

The Chinese supervisory authorities have not defined the exact starting point where GMP is required; this contributes to the problem (see box 6-1 below). In a worrisome sleight of hand, a process may be certified as upholding GMP even if only the final process in the final location is actually GMP compliant; earlier suppliers often need not demonstrate that they meet these standards. As Andre put it: "Implementing GMP starting from a late intermediate [stage of production] is more economical." Because "U.S./EU customers often neglect to specify their expectations," he said, they may not realize that precursor chemicals were not made in GMP plants. Although Chinese law prohibits the manufacture of drug substances without a pharmaceutical license and GMP certificate, many foreign purchasers do not ask for evidence of these basic qualifications.

All chemicals exported to the United States are supposed to be GMP certified, but many may not be. Most alarming of all, Andre says that "94 percent of my audits of Chinese drug substances bought by Western purchasers are conducted *after* purchase." The U.S. FDA has found problems in Chinese plants before but often has not been able to return to inspect those plants in a timely fashion, which means relying on the word of plant management that changes demanded have been made.[a]

After listening to Andre and seeing a few sites myself, there is little doubt many Chinese companies synthesizing intermediaries for our medicines make inferior products, and U.S. companies often fail to oversee what they are buying, to the extent that they often do not know what they are buying or from whom. Given this cavalier attitude of some U.S. and European pharmaceutical companies, it is not hard to imagine what this means for countries in other parts of the world where oversight is valued even less. Without the resources to buy chemicals in bulk to covertly assess quality, however, my research team could do little in the way of assessing these drug components directly.

---

a. It is often not possible to even know what is being inspected. Inspectors, either private or FDA, are often escorted to a location they are told is, for example, "Wenzhou No.7 pharmaceutical factory," but it is in the middle of nowhere, and there is no street address. At best you'll know which county of which province you are in, and you are unlikely to be able to revisit easily, and you're not sure if the chemicals are actually produced there. None of the normal forms of verification are possible.

Box 6-1

ACETAMINOPHEN

In the synthesis of acetaminophen, only the final reaction would need to be in a GMP plant for the final product to be certified GMP in China. The earlier steps may have been undertaken in unhygienic conditions, causing dangerous impurities. Figure 6-1 demonstrates this very basic process.

Imagine a drug with 70 manufacturing steps with just the final step under GMP. The opportunities for contamination are vast.

FIGURE 6-1

ACETAMINOPHEN SYNTHESIS

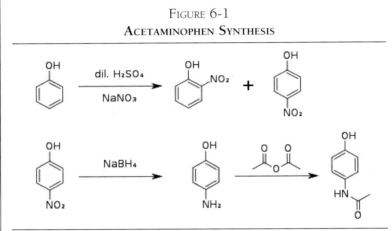

SOURCE: Adapted from Ellis, Frank. *Paracetamol: A curriculum resource.* (2002) Cambridge: Royal Society of Chemistry.

My research team did take random samplings of drugs from Beijing pharmacies, but through these we discovered only a few drug-quality problems. In total, 7 samples out of 113 failed our tests (a failure rate of 6.2 percent), and these were mainly samples of the TB drug isoniazid (see part III for more details). If our sampling and Jin's figures are accurate, Chinese cities appear to have a slightly smaller problem with fake drugs than India (and unlike India, Jin's teams have remarkably covered most of rural China, although Jin did not release the results of rural tests to me). The quality of cleanliness and of the drugs available in Chinese markets was also superior to the quality of markets and medicines in India. Part of the reason for this, I discovered, is the nature of the players in the Chinese market.

Locating the (Legal) Source of Substandard Ingredients

The array of fake products produced may be greater in India, but China almost certainly surpasses India in terms of volume. Legal cases against Chinese counterfeiters have been known to measure volumes of ingredients in the tens of tons. Such large volumes do not exist anywhere else in the world. In terms of producing substandard API, China seems to dominate world trade, but my sense of the market in China is limited by a lack of real exposure to it.

While in China, I witnessed how the lack of transparency and government intimidation of others (mainly locals and certainly not me) made it nearly impossible to conduct thorough investigations. Unlike in India, I could not actually see the inside of fake-drug factories in China, although I did drive past a few production locations. In India, I at least visited problem areas in three distinct parts of the country, but in China I was unable to get any investigative assistance outside of the major eastern and southeastern cities. Most fake drugs are probably made in the northeast, in places such as Harbin City, with a population of five million, and further afield in regions foreigners rarely visit. The chemicals leave mainly from eastern ports, and finished products often travel by air.

Still, research on China was not wasted. Investigator Li introduced me to a former Chinese counterfeiter now providing information for investigators against his criminal colleagues. This thirty-seven-year-old chemist, originally from the city of Guangzhou, made a significant living making intermediary products of the lowest quality. He originally worked for a small Chinese chemical company in Shantou City in Guangdong Province, but he was lured from the legitimate chemical industry by a criminal syndicate with an operation in Shantou that enabled him to treble his former income. His team began by producing chemicals for making about forty thousand painkiller pills per day, assuming clients wanted roughly the correct amount of API. He never saw the downstream product. Li's contacts came upon the small factory by chance. Based on Li's description of the operation, its location—a dingy, poorly lit warehouse basement—matches the picture I have imagined as the setting for nineteenth-century unscrupulous business operations in Europe or the United States. In fact, the way the business had been conducted seemed not unlike the legal but cavalier businesses that operated in the United States a century ago when the DEG catastrophe I described in chapter 1 occurred.

As Li said, "The chemist didn't want to kill people; he just didn't take any care about what he produced. He always put getting the cheap deal above safety." From 2005 until his operation was unearthed toward the end of 2007, the chemist and his team made drugs every day. As Li's investigation continued, he found a criminal network with excellent contacts in East Africa and parts of the Middle East. The chemist in Shantou had provided only a third of the production; two other plants were based in Shenzhen. Each had provided different strengths of active ingredient and finished product to a variety of intermediary businesses; some of these were entirely crooked, others were semilegitimate, and a few may not have broken any laws within their countries. Many of these drugs found their way into small markets across eastern China and, occasionally, to such well-known places as Beijing's Silk Street Market. Generally, the fake drugs appeared away from renowned locations for selling other types of fake products, as these are more likely to be monitored by investigators. Wang Zili, the former manager of this Silk Street Market, likely benefited directly from sales of many fake products, including drugs, at his market. In August 2009, Wang was forced to resign because of the number of traders infringing the trademarks of myriad products. Yang Changjun, now serving three and half years for counterfeiting, claims Wang instigated and funded his counterfeiting operation.

The chemists in this drug ring typically made APIs for painkillers and sildenafil, the active ingredient in Viagra, but these businesses also produced active ingredients of antibiotics and antimalarials (along with diluted versions of the same APIs). Although the downstream firms all insisted on the highest quality packaging, the demands for what went in the packaging varied considerably. Because these businesses were trading as chemical suppliers and not pharmaceutical suppliers, the SFDA had no jurisdiction over their activities, and few final producers demand certificates from apparently legitimate intermediaries. No other legislative body seems to have monitored what this chemical company and possibly many others were actually doing and supplying.

These small companies produced tons of API and finished products every month, and investigators believe most of the businessmen involved did not know where many of the drugs they made might have gone. Significant variation in both API content and processing undermines product quality, and these Chinese businesses were selling myriad APIs. From mid-2007, they sold finished products that contained the correct amount of API, zero API, and almost any amount in between, with varying degrees of quality. Engaging in such a trade is morally reprehensible, but one can almost marvel at how these companies segment their markets, not just by price but also by quality.

Their detailed paperwork shows decisions to undercut dosing for drugs for lethal diseases such as tuberculosis. It reminds me of the detailed records kept by German commanders at World War II concentration camps. Although Chinese counterfeiters do not match death camp guards, they are guilty of gross negligence and, probably, manslaughter of victims they will never know.

The trade itself is obviously odious, but the traders' ability to segment the market is what makes this so dangerous. The prices the counterfeiters charged for their products varied by the amount and quality of API used. API is more expensive than the inert compounds they substituted, such as talcum powder or chalk, and API requires proper processing, which takes more electricity and monitoring effort, and, for fly-by-night firms, proper efforts take time and increase the risk of discovery. By varying the amount of API and segmenting the market, the traders could sell cheaply made products inexpensively to markets with less regulatory oversight while selling more sophisticated products to more developed markets. This gave them access to the largest market possible without cutting into profit margins or dramatically increasing the risk that the operation would be noticed.

A small factory on the outskirts of Beijing is where investigators believe fake drugs are made during a four-hour window in the middle of the night in an otherwise law-abiding firm. For these counterfeiters, speed is essential. Packaging was made at a different location, which investigators still had not found. They would not inform the Chinese police until they could determine the locations of other components of the operation.

From the information I was able to glean, most products this factory created had zero API, perhaps one-quarter had the proper amount of API, and maybe 15 percent had 15–80 percent of the correct amount of API. The products containing 100 percent of API would go to producers making real products that were not necessarily to the highest standards but had the correct ingredients. The zero API and varying quantity API drugs were ordered for manufacture of fake products, which all parties of the deal apparently understood and accepted. The varying amounts of API ordered were determined by the intended market for the finished goods. By understanding the target for these various products, I understood the counterfeiters' view of those markets—what it is worth selling, why, and who to. It is increasingly clear that for counterfeiters there are some markets where there is no need to sell anything better than products with zero API.

The Middle Eastern market is, or perhaps was before recent enforcement actions, one of these markets. By comparison with parts of Southeast Asia and Africa, the Middle East may not be the easiest market to infiltrate, though locals may order products from China for sale in their markets, as was the case with the Dara'a (Syria)-Ramsa (Jordan) racket I discuss in chapter 7. Once products do infiltrate the market, however, chances of detection are minimal, so all efforts are focused on packaging and other nefarious activities, such as bribing officials. The target demographic for these drugs is patients with illnesses they may not recover from, such as cancer; in this way, there is less suspicion if the drug fails and little likelihood the substandard and mislabeled drugs will be assessed.

In addition to Li, Andre, the former chemist counterfeiter, and two other investigators in Hong Kong, I spoke with auditors, pharmaceutical executives, and several professors. Based on these interviews, I have made several conclusions about China's fake-drug industry. First, and most worrying, is that the various legal but shoddy chemical factories and the makers of counterfeit and substandard finished products are producing enormous quantities of chemicals; the sheer size of these operations is alarming. Some produce tons of chemicals every week, much of which finds its way into Western medicines. Other operations make over one million pills, or 100,000 treatments of a variety of medicines, every single day. Some of these may make their way to the West via the Internet. And in these factories, there is no weekend off for the cheap labor.

Some of these factories are owned by companies selling APIs or finished products to the legitimate supply chain. Some are approved chemical producers that operate to poorly enforced standards and are not registered as pharmaceutical companies in China. Others are entirely bogus companies not registered for any trade. Some appear to establish brands they then cannibalize by selling poorer-quality and cheaper versions of them, likely to benefit from the highly segmented illegal markets. Generally, these companies have convoluted company structures and operations, making it nearly impossible to get to the bottom of any supply chain. Steps taken to muddle the chain include separating locations of pill production from packaging, mixing legitimate production with substandard production, and layering cross-ownership structures protected by state authorities.

One thing is certain: these operations are huge. International orders come from various parts of the world, most often from Chinese operators at hubs in India, East Africa, the Middle East, and southern Europe. Cargo containers leave busy Chinese ports full of millions of treatments of varying quality. These containers arrive weekly in busy ports from Alexandria, Egypt, to Dubai to Valetta, Malta, to Rotterdam, Netherlands, to Mombasa, Kenya, to Dar es Salaam, Tanzania, to Chennai and Mumbai, India.

I will discuss Chinese finished products further in chapter 7 because it is easier to follow Chinese counterfeits in markets around the world than it is from China, where private investigators often are not welcome. Also, like much of the Chinese economy, the fake-drug trade thrives on export business. I am convinced China is the largest manufacturer of fake drugs in the world, and nearly every investigator of fake drugs, both inside and outside of China, agrees with me.

The Battle against Counterfeiters in China

Despite government control on Chinese media, reports of counterfeits in China proliferate from other news sources. Many stories are from Hong Kong media outlets, and several discuss Gao Jingde, a local hero who regularly fights counterfeiters. Jingde is a Shanghai-based private investigator and a past victim of counterfeits of medication produced by Zhejiang Jinhuatailai Drug Company for liver disease. The side effects that the drugs caused drove his suspicion, and he subsequently discovered the drugs were fakes. Today, he, more than any other person, is responsible for bringing fake-drug manufacturers to light. Fake drugs have penetrated both the public and the private health sectors in China. In 2007 Jingde reported that twenty-two of thirty-two drugstores investigated in Nanjing and four of fifteen drugstores supported by public medical insurance stocked counterfeit drugs. Jingde says the authorities would like to portray the problem as one of ignorance, but although that may be the case for most patients and some pharmacists, corruption also plays a large role in the prevalence of counterfeits in pharmacies and hospitals. According to Jingde, approximately two-thirds of drugstores in China sold counterfeit medicine in September 2008. From 2004 to 2008, Jingde conducted grassroots investigations of drugstores and hospitals and reported 289 separate incidents involving the sale of counterfeit medicines.

In 2008, after investigating Nanfang University Medical Center hospital, Jingde was attacked by four men he believes were hired by hospital authorities to prevent his exposure of their counterfeit dealings. Jingde has the fortitude and drive of Nigeria's Akunyili and Orhii but none of the protection they are afforded as officers of a government. He may soon find himself in jail because he is surely an embarrassment to Beijing: those who complained most successfully against the melamine contamination of milk and other products in China (see box 6-2 below)—which killed several and harmed hundreds of thousands of babies—spent thirty months in jail for disrespecting the government. Jingde's work is especially important because so few are prepared to speak out against the fake-drug market in China.

As in India, private investigators provide dossiers about criminal activity to the police, at least in the parts of the country where the authorities will be responsive. Even in southeastern China, for most of the past decade, though, it was far from certain whether police would take any action based on such information. When I was in China, investigators told me there are still some problems with enforcement. For example, police in Yiwu City in Zhejiang Province, south of Shanghai, follow up on investigations more often than not, but, as in India, the politically connected always seem to escape. This is not to suggest that Chinese authorities do not want to take action against poor-quality medicines; it is just that their objectives are not entirely clear.

Waking the Dragon: China Begins to Make an Effort

Although the lack of government transparency in China is frustrating, Beijing is slowly responding to calls from its citizens and trading partners to increase transparency and allow greater individual freedom. Despite some encouraging reforms, progress is impeded by erratic implementation and corruption at the highest levels of government. Of course, with China's population of 1.3 billion people, surface area of 3,700 million square miles, 9,000-mile coastline, and land borders with fourteen countries, it is little wonder that even reforms implemented in good faith seem to produce results very slowly.

China has had a modern, comprehensive, and properly functioning MRA for only about a decade. In 1998 Beijing established the State Drug Administration—which later became the SFDA—to consolidate the duties of the Ministry of Health's Drug Administration Bureau, the State Pharmaceutical Administration Bureau, and the State Administration of Traditional Chinese Medicine. The State Drug Administration was to provide unified leadership and oversight to what would become 31 provincial drug agencies, 2,321 county agencies, and 339 municipal departments.

In 2001 China established a national, unified system of pharmaceutical registration and quality standards, and in 2004, more than two hundred monitoring institutions that already existed in thirty-one provinces were coordinated into a national system for reporting and monitoring adverse drug reactions. By 2004 China had also started to make progress curbing illegal pharmaceutical manufacturers through criminal prosecution of large-scale networks. A greatly increased budget for 2006–2007 meant 90 percent of provincial drug-control departments and 60 percent of city ones were capable of conducting at least some full-scale drug tests and could buy more than three hundred near-infrared spectrometers to be used in portable labs in vans that would fan out throughout China to screen for substandard drugs. Professor Jin told me he was pleased that these mobile labs were being deployed and that they were showing distinct benefit.

The most innovative programs involve mobile labs, which rely on simple testing to establish substandard drugs in the marketplace. These labs, housed in small trucks, can test over eight hundred different drug preparations. The Chinese government spent $70 million on 400 mobile labs between March 2006 and September 2007. As of April 2011, 454 labs had been allocated to thirty provinces, covering 88 percent of China's rural areas. In addition, 1,060 technicians have been trained to use the labs.

BOX 6-2

TOO LITTLE, TOO LATE: CHINA'S OFFICIAL RESPONSE TO THE MELAMINE SCANDAL—A REAL HARM FROM CHINA'S COMMUNISM

Many young mothers will remember the contaminated milk scandal that originated in China and came to light in 2008. What many of them do not know is that the Chinese government was aware of the contamination for nearly a year before it took any action.

Concerned Chinese parents first complained about milk sickening their infants in December 2006. The number of complaints from both parents and doctors began to swell over the next few months, and by June 2008, milk-powder producer Sanlu knew it was producing melamine-laced products. Sanlu had ignored warnings from alarmed pediatricians, who then began using blogs and online forums to alert the public to the danger. These doctors also submitted numerous reports to the state regulator, the General Administration of Quality Supervision, Inspection, and Quarantine, detailing infants' reactions to Sanlu's milk and requesting investigations into Sanlu's facilities. On December 3, 2008, the *Washington Post* reported that "the quality watchdog, which had exempted Sanlu and several other well-known dairy companies from government inspection, did nothing."[1]

Milk contaminated with melamine sickened 294,000 babies and killed six, but six months later, the Chinese government still refused to release the name of the company responsible. On September 11, 2008, a Chinese investigative journalist, frustrated by the government's inactions, posted the company's name in a blog and called for increased government accountability. The government still refused to name Sanlu. After nearly 300,000 children became sick and dozens of products were recalled, the Chinese government acknowledged in December 2008 that the problem was more than five times the size originally stated. Efforts to prosecute those responsible, however, remained half-hearted.

When Zhao Lianhai, a former employee of the Chinese Food Safety Board whose son was sickened by the tainted milk, tried to hold a press conference to lobby for more compensation for the victims, Beijing authorities told him negotiation was possible only if he stopped publicizing the scandal.

---

1. Maureen Fan, "6 Chinese Infants Died in Milk Crisis," *Washington Post,* December 3, 2008.

China's Systemic Communist Problem

Western capitalism is often criticized for its short-termism, lack of distributive equality, and occasional ruthlessness. But at its core is a system built on trust and integrity, where breaches of its codes are punished, often severely. Over time, and often in concert with regulations, standards generally improve, including of ethical performance. But while many think that China has adopted some key parts of capitalism, it has never adopted the moral basis of the system, because the individual and his decisions are not central to everything. It is therefore inevitable that without a moral system based on the individual, it is likely to be extraordinarily difficult for China to limit the problems we've been encountering in this chapter.

In late April 2011, China was caught up in another food and drug scandal. Tons of melamine-contaminated milk products were seized from warehouses in Chongqing, a vast municipal area with thirty-five million inhabitants. The tainted milk powder would have made tons of pastry and ice cream; fortunately most of it was caught before any serious damage occurred.

London's *Daily Telegraph* Beijing correspondent says that Chongqing is awash in fraudulent foodstuffs: "Some 917 cases were already under investigation in Chongqing including the use of the textile dye, Rhodamine B, in broad bean paste; the discovery of formalin, an industrial preserving and clotting agent, in the city's famed hotpot restaurants and industrial carbon dioxide to carbonate beer."

The milk problem is the largest concern, however, and it is the tenth serious food scandal in just the past few years. It provides more evidence of the inability of China's officials, corporations, and consumers to prevent lethal production.

Beijing knows it has a problem, and in the last few days of April, 7,900 Chongqing police raided six hundred premises across the city that were suspected of producing illegal or fake food and pharmaceuticals. It was pretty obvious that this action was a bid to restore confidence in the health and other authorities. To coincide with the raids, city officials announced a one-hundred-day crackdown on illicit activity, not unlike the one that preceded the Olympics in 2008.

This was probably the final straw in destroying the already fragile public trust in the government's ability to keep the food and drug supply safe. Even

(continued)

Box 6-2 (*continued*)

Too Little, Too Late: China's Official Response to the Melamine Scandal—A Real Harm from China's Communism

when Beijing is right, it is ignored: government pleas to a nervous population to stop buying useless products that were being touted as remedies for radiation from Japan's stricken Fukushima nuclear power plant following the March 2011 earthquake and subsequent tsunami had no effect.

Even though high-level officials have demanded a robust response to the latest milk problem, few Chinese think much will be done. Part of this is because the rhetoric remains the same as in 2008. Vice-Premier Li Keqiang says his committee on food safety will ensure "a firm attitude, iron hand and more effort" in addressing safety concerns and reiterated that this included the use of capital punishment. But with the threat of death looming over Chinese company directors, contamination continues—the ultimate sanction means little if enforcement is arbitrary or corruptly employed.

At fault is not the occasional bad corporate apple, but the entire Chinese Communist business system. It encourages corner cutting, provides no substantial reward for integrity, and doesn't protect brands (domestic or foreign), so consumers have no meaningful market signals to respond to. After all, if brands are faked, the consumer cannot rely on switching from one brand to another in the search for safety. Even when harmed, consumers have little recourse because China has no real rule of law. And capricious law enforcement means that the very best candidates are not attracted to government roles because they may be subject to the same arbitrary decision making.

Yet over the past decade, while the Chinese people have progressively lost trust in their government's oversight of food and drug production, Westerners have imported more food and vastly more pharmaceutical ingredients from China than before. In 2002 the United States imported $1.9 billion in food and drug products from China; in 2010 it was $6.85 billion.

Since 1998, postmarketing quality surveillance by government officials has been improving, and poor-quality producers are being shut down. According to Jin, of more than forty thousand samples tested in Anhui and Guangxi Provinces in 2009, between 3 percent and 10 percent were substandard.[7] That is an improvement from Jin's earlier finding that 14 percent of medicines sampled were substandard a decade ago.

There are good reasons for this. China's ingredients are cheaper than anywhere else on the planet, and most are perfectly fine. Our drugs would be a lot more expensive if we didn't buy from China.

But there is such a major systemic problem in pharmaceutical production in China, and the SFDA is still reeling from the execution of its previous director for taking bribes from companies to overlook their quality failings. The SFDA is trying to control a system that breeds corruption and has to operate over vast areas with insufficient manpower—partly because the pharmaceutical industry is growing faster than China can train inspectors. So it simply cannot oversee most of the industry, never mind the broader legal and political impediments. And although the U.S FDA has established an office in China and is increasing investigations of the plants that export to the United States, at best it can only assess each site once every thirteen years.

With little realistic oversight and, more important, little ethos of business integrity in China, a major tragedy in the United States from a Chinese export is likely in the near future. And it will probably be far greater than the calamity that killed 149 Americans with contaminated heparin, a blood-thinning drug, imported from China. The heparin was quality checked when it reached the U.S. manufacturer, but the contamination was impossible to detect with the tests that were then recommended. The fraudsters could have been very lucky, but it seems more likely they chose a cunning and sophisticated method deliberately to cheat the system. The problem was only suspected after people started to die.

Yet, even after the heparin disaster, U.S. interests imported $289 million more Chinese pharmaceutical ingredients in 2010 than in 2008. Someday soon, the price of another disaster may be too high for American politicians to ignore.

Official government data suggest that the percentage of substandard drugs circulating in China's market is even smaller than Jin's survey indicated. Between March and August 2006, the SFDA screened 110,426 batches of antimalarial pharmaceutical drugs in mobile labs and found that only 2.8 percent (3,122 batches) contained counterfeit or substandard drugs.[8] Zhong-Yuan Yang, former head of the Guangzhou Municipal

Institute for Drug Control, reports that approximately 0.5 percent of all medicines in China are counterfeit, depending on the sampling venue.[9] These official reports have some problems, though; these figures differ markedly from other independent reports, do not differentiate between counterfeit and substandard drugs, and mask regional and product-specific differences. Regardless, China's efforts to increase testing represent an improvement.

The testing regime China instituted is only part of the solution. China has also made examples of criminals in order to act as a deterrent. In November 2007, in a highly publicized event, the government executed former head of the SFDA Zheng Xiaoyu for taking bribes to falsify drug registrations and arrested 279 manufacturers on criminal charges. The government announced that it would impose stiffer penalties, including heavy fines, life imprisonment, and the death penalty, in counterfeit drug cases.

The 2008 Beijing Summer Olympics prompted Chinese authorities to combat some of the wide-ranging concerns about food and drug quality, especially in light of the melamine milk scandal that became public only months before the games. Numerous concerns about food contamination, drug quality, and hospital safety at the time drew international attention to deep-seated domestic problems. Investigators I interviewed at the time discussed one topic the government wanted to avoid: the military's involvement in the fake-drug market. Numerous unsubstantiated reports claimed fake drugs made by the army were prescribed in military hospitals, which could have been visited by Olympic visitors and even Olympians. Although the government did not want to acknowledge the hospital dangers, it did pressure hospital managers to ensure that only quality products were stocked. This and other concerns about food and drug contamination led authorities to crack down on illegal operators in the months leading up to the games, and observers learned a lot about some of those faking drugs from within the free-trade zone of Shenzhen. As a result, supplies to Middle East gangs (and probably some in West Africa) were curtailed, and I learned more about how fake-drug rings were operating from China.

In 2007 the government announced thirty-four new GMP standards (for a total of 259) and an export licensing and registration system for ten categories of drugs. Beijing also established a network of over 97,000 drug-safety coordinators and over 514,000 information specialists, made qualification examinations and ongoing training for pharmacists mandatory, and issued a set of regulations to standardize nursing practices.[b] Of course, as Andre demonstrated, it is one thing to have these standards and quite another to enforce them.

By December 2007, the SFDA reported stopping 900 counterfeit-drug operations, shutting down 300 drug and medical-instrument manufacturers for making inferior products, and withdrawing 150 GMP certificates. Pharmaceutical companies in the country voluntarily withdrew more than 7,300 drug-registration applications (24 percent of the total). In 2008 the SFDA increased supervision of Internet drug distribution, investigated 300,000 cases of illegal activities related to medicine and medical products; shut down 363 producers of fake drugs, charged ninety-four people with counterfeiting, and shut down twenty-three websites. Still, the scale of some of these operations is shocking; one haul from a ring involving Greek and Chinese nationals included 880 pounds of counterfeit Tamiflu and about forty tons of raw chemical materials.

The SFDA blacklisted twenty-five websites in 2009 for selling fake medicines claiming to cure high blood pressure, skin diseases, diabetes, and other chronic diseases.[10] China's State Administration of Traditional Chinese Medicine blacklisted forty-six websites that same year for selling fake herbal medicines. SFDA director Shao Mingli reported that 36,000 illegal drug advertisements were handed over for investigations, and 231 suspects involved in major cases were arrested in 2009.[11] In January 2010, the SFDA shut down another 558 websites for releasing false drug information.[12] These examples show just a few recent actions the Chinese government has taken to address the massive international trade in counterfeits that originates in China.

---

b. Even with the new guidelines, however, "China still [lagged] behind the United States . . . and even India" in quality standards, Cheng Shuguang, general manager of the drug division at Zhejiang Jingxin Pharmaceutical Company, said (see "SFDA Raises GMP Standards for Chinese Drug Workers," *China Pharmaceuticals and Health Technologies Weekly,* October 31, 2007); Yan Liang, "China Testing Export License System for Drugs," *Xinhua,* January 31, 2008; SFDA, "Status Quo of Drug Supervision in China," ibid.; and "China Issues National Nursing Regulations," *China Pharmaceuticals and Health Technologies Weekly,* February 13, 2008.

Made in India, Faked in China

Indian companies provide vast amounts of generic drugs to middle-income and developing countries. By some estimates, 80 percent of HIV drugs and half of the developing world's supply of antimalarials and antibiotics come from India. It has become increasingly popular for Chinese fakers to copy the common local brands, which often means copying Indian brands. Chinese companies' use of the "Made in India" label on counterfeit drugs reflects Indian companies' dominance in low-to-middle income markets.

Counterfeiters prefer to copy the most popular brands even when they are not the most expensive. Though counterfeiters could make more money faking more expensive products, a familiar product is more easily accepted in the market without suspicion, meaning more fakes may be sold before they are detected. Furthermore, the multinational companies that produce more expensive (name-brand) products are more likely to protect their brands with highly trained security personnel and postmarket surveys and laboratory tests. Because Indian generics dominate many therapeutic categories, it is not surprising that they are the medicines most often faked.

During my research in China, I came to believe that the proliferation of fake drugs in India may be less India's fault than I had expected. In my ongoing research, I have come across Chinese fakes in many countries—including India—that carried a "Made in India" label. After one incident in April 2010, I was informed by sources in both India and China that the New Delhi government had protested to Beijing about this misrepresentation. Indian private investigators of fake drugs and Indian company representatives and consultants also suspect this is a deliberate, Beijing-sanctioned attempt to undermine India's reputation and gain market share, and they are searching for proof. Are Indian investigators correct in thinking Beijing has a hand in this deadly activity?

There is no obvious way to be sure, but countries with greater Chinese government investment probably have more Chinese fakes with "Made in India" labels. Where Chinese government officials and businesses proliferate, such as in helping build power and communications infrastructure, I suspect it would be easier for Chinese entities to infiltrate these markets. The research I have done indicates that this may be true, but my sample sizes are small. Of my total samples, 911 antimalarial and antibiotic products were, according to their packaging, made in India. These were procured from thirteen countries, mainly in Africa but also in Thailand and India. Of these products, seventy-nine (or 8.7 percent) failed basic quality-control tests and were unfit for their intended use. Of these seventy-nine products, we were able to establish that thirty-seven were counterfeits. More products may have been counterfeit, but without responses from the manufacturers or regulatory agencies, it was not always possible to be sure. Of the thirty-seven counterfeits identified, twenty-two were definitely faked in China and delivered to African countries. Thus, from our small sample, over half (59 percent) of the fake Indian drugs were actually made in China. There are other plausible explanations for these findings, however. It just so happens that many places where China enjoys good trade and political connections are also places suffering from widespread corruption and general poverty; these factors alone could generally explain the proliferation of fakes across the African continent and throughout much of Southeast Asia. Although there is no concrete evidence of Chinese government involvement, this is worth monitoring in case any should surface. These allegations also provide more reason for Beijing—if it is indeed innocent of any involvement—to do more to clamp down on the fake-drug industry that flourishes within its borders in order to protect its reputation.

Not all fake drugs from China are copies of Indian products, though. Chinese gangs will copy anything of value, so every major drug company and every country probably has drugs faked by the Chinese. Artesunat, the Vietnamese antimalarial made by the Ho Chi Minh–based company Mekophar Chemical Pharmaceutical, is widely faked by Chinese criminals (see box 4-6). Ongoing research has found fake Artesunat in Nigeria, Ghana, Kenya, Uganda, Tanzania, and Thailand; in each case, the fakes were traced to the handiwork of Chinese counterfeiters.

Within the overall policy of copying popular brands whose trademarks are less likely to be enforced, counterfeiters tend to produce copies of the most expensive drugs that are significant sellers within each category. In the antibiotic category, then, counterfeiters are more likely to fake ciprofloxacin than erythromycin, because the former is twice the price in some markets. The API is more expensive, but counterfeiters who do not include any API can make a white pill in the correct shape for the same price whether it is ciprofloxacin or a cheaper product. My sample sizes are small, but this fits counterfeiting logic.

In addition to monitoring what drugs to fake, counterfeiters adapt what they make and how they make it based on the technologies deployed by anticounterfeiting agencies. For much of the past decade, rapid dye tests have been used to test for the presence of API in medicines surveyed in markets in Africa and parts of Asia (see box 6-3). These simple tests have been deployed by a variety of aid agencies and nongovernmental organizations operating in resource-constrained environments, and the test is a component of the Global Pharma Health Fund Minilab system. Because the test was able to detect fakes only with zero API content, some counterfeiters changed their game and started to add some API to fool it. Partly as a response to this, anticounterfeiting agencies started deploying Global Pharma Health Fund Minilabs, which, as mentioned earlier, provide a semiquantitative assessment of API content. This ensures that drugs without sufficient API are detected. It is possible that counterfeiters are now adapting to this change by adding far more API to drugs. My data are limited, but it makes sense to add far more API for drugs with cheap API, such as many older antimalarial drugs. More surprisingly, it appears fakers might be doing this with artemisinin-based antimalarial drugs, even though artemisinin is relatively expensive and has limited suppliers. However, because most of the artemisinin supply, which comes from the sweet wormwood plant, is in China, perhaps counterfeiters find a ready supply of this key ingredient. That fakers can afford the additional expense and risk of sourcing rare artemisinin indicates how big profit margins must be on fake drugs. Given that counterfeiters can cut processing and GMP costs and still pass these tests, they still make handsome profits in comparison with legitimate producers. They will go to great lengths to tailor their products to target markets. The threat to malaria patients and other potential victims of fake drugs looms large.

The Way Forward for China

Ultimately, Beijing needs to implement and enforce laws to outlaw clever and odious practices. Historically, chemical companies escaped being monitored by the SFDA by claiming to be chemical suppliers and not pharmaceutical suppliers. Although the Chinese government insists it no longer tolerates such

Box 6-3
OLD TESTS, NEW TESTS, AND HARPARKASH KAUR[1]

Most drugs analyzed in this book were tested using the Global Pharma Health Fund e.V. Minilab®, which is a series of tests forming a useful protocol (see box 4-3 on page 80 for more detail). Visual inspection is easy in principle but harder than one would expect, even for those with patience. Thankfully, disintegration and dye tests are straightforward, but although TLC is not very complex, it does require electricity, a fair number of chemicals and laboratory equipment, and some training. A high school graduate could be trained in a week, and someone with laboratory experience from a university, such as myself, could competently use the Minilab in a couple of days. But even those with training will attest that it takes quite a bit longer to truly appreciate this science, which is also something of an art form in interpretation.

So it is possible that in at least some settings in the field, the only tests actually undertaken will be visual inspection and maybe the appropriate dye test. These tests are enough to find the most obvious fakes, but a considerable problem in emerging markets is substandard and degraded products that, like the "better" fakes, might contain enough active ingredients to pass dye tests. So, one has to wonder, how many fakes are missed by just performing the simplest tests?

The Need for a Better Dye Test

In an attempt to answer this question, I went back to a subset of my data on ACTs to see how many of the fake or substandard products identified would have been missed by only undertaking visual inspection, disintegration, and dye tests. Twenty samples that contained some API failed the TLC assay but passed the existing rapid red dye test currently deployed by Minilab. In other words, these products (4.8 percent of the total sample and 37.7 percent of those products that failed the full Minilab protocol) might not have been subject to further testing and would have stayed on the market were TLC not available or not properly undertaken.

(continued)

---

1. Roger Bate, "Improving Assessments of Fake and Substandard Drugs in the Field,"*AFM Working Paper,* January 3, 2011, available at http://www.fightingmalaria.org/pdfs/afmbulletin5_theneedforbetterdyetests.pdf.

Box 6-3 (*continued*)
OLD TESTS, NEW TESTS, AND HARPARKASH KAUR

Given that the Minilab is not a trivial cost (about $5,000 to start, and more if training is required), it is quite likely that there are many places that could afford to deploy stand-alone dye tests (at less than $1/test) but could not deploy TLC and certainly could not afford more sophisticated techniques. In such circumstances, then, at least some poor-quality medicines would remain in circulation.

Improving field assessment methods is important because the counterfeiters watch what regulators are doing and have been able to adapt to changes in packaging and content in the past. In Southeast Asia, sixteen different holograms were copied by counterfeiters to pass off their antimalarial drugs.[2] And prior to the deployment of Minilabs, counterfeiters, some caught on camera by the BBC for the documentary *Bad Medicine,* added a small amount of API to products. They did so in order to pass rapid dye tests, which had been deployed by anticounterfeit agencies to find fakes. So the notion that counterfeiters would adapt again and add much more API while still not ensuring a good-quality product is certainly plausible.

In thinking about this problem, I was alerted to a new dye test developed by scholars at the London School of Hygiene and Tropical Medicine.[3] From speaking with one of the developers of this assay, Dr. Harparkash Kaur, and by assessing the above paper, it appears that this dye test is more sensitive to concentrations of API than current dye tests. Hence, it would have captured most of the twenty samples with nontrivial amounts of API because the result would have been noticeably different from either zero or 100 percent API. Of those twenty samples, seventeen had approximately between 15 percent and 40 percent of API; three had between 50 percent and 75 percent. It is possible that the final three might have passed, and from inspection, appeared to be degraded products, but the remaining

---

2. P. N. Newton et al., "A Collaborative Epidemiological Investigation into the Criminal Fake Artesunate Trade in South East Asia," *PLoS Medicine* 5 (February 2008), available at http://www.plosmedicine.org/article/info:doi/10.1371/journal.pmed.0050032.

3. Jean-Robert Ioset and Harparkash Kaur, "Simple Field Assays to Check Quality of Current Artemisinin-Based Antimalarial Combination Formulations," *PLoS Medicine* 4 (September 30, 2009. available at http://www.plosone.org/article/info%3Adoi%2F10.1371%2Fjournal.pone.0007270.

seventeen probably would have been identified (none of these products can be tested today because they are past expiry and the results would not be reliable). Although full deployment of the Minilab did capture these failures, in the real world, where the Minilab might not be fully deployed, reliance may be placed on rapid and probably inferior dye tests. Having a more informative dye test, like Dr. Kaur's test, might well identify some substandard drugs and lower risks to patients. Hopefully some entrepreneur will operationalize this test for the field. At the very least, and in the short run, it would be beneficial if the Minilab could deploy the Kaur test. Pictures of the dye results for a few samples are shown below.

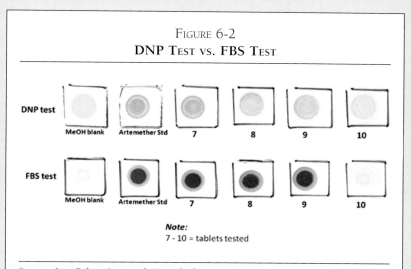

FIGURE 6-2
DNP TEST VS. FBS TEST

Note:
7 - 10 = tablets tested

SOURCE: Jean-Robert Ioset and Harparkash Kaur, "Simple Field Assays to Check Quality of Current Artemisinin-Based Antimalarial Combination Formulations," *PLoS Medicine* 4 (September 30, 2009. available at http://www.plosone.org/article/info%3Adoi%2F10.1371%2Fjournal.pone.0007270.

sleight of hand, Deborah Autor, director of the U.S. FDA's drug compliance program, told me in April 2011 that this "loophole has not been closed."

We should all hope China's drug makers eventually internalize quality-management best practices. Efforts to do this are under way. Article 9 of the 1984 Drug Administration Law already mandates that manufacturers adhere to GMP,[c] but enforcement continues to be a problem. Even where Beijing has issued clear guidelines for how inspectors will measure GMP, there are too few inspectors to examine all suspicious manufacturing sites, and those inspectors rarely demand immediate and significant responses by poor-performing firms. Beijing needs to make a commitment to inspection as well as to laws. As Andre pointed out, although many think China has endless numbers of people, there are not enough qualified staff to perform audits and inspections, to say nothing of higher-level jobs. Indeed, Andre and Hovione CEO Villax say more attention must be paid to GMP in the entire supply chain, not just whether final production facilities are GMP compliant. "Many problems can occur between compliant plants," Andre said.

To help remedy the lack of qualified staff, Zheng Qiang of Peking University started a program to improve manufacturers' understanding of and adherence to best practices. His inaugural class of twenty-five students (twenty-one of whom were on sabbatical from Chinese pharmaceutical companies) started their master's degree program in best practices in March 2007 at Peking University's new Institute for Pharmaceutical Excellence. One hopes that more efforts like this will ensure better-quality Chinese producers and that high-quality products will come to dominate the market and eventually force out most fake drugs.

USP CEO Roger Williams is optimistic about China's future; he says laboratory capacity is expanding due to "huge investment," but he also understands the changes are painful, because imposing GMP may put up to 20 percent of the drug-production workforce out of business. Until such improvements take hold, problems with fake and substandard drugs will

---

c. Drug Administration Law of the People's Republic of China, adopted at the 7th Meeting of the Standing Committee of the Sixth National People's Congress on September 20, 1984, revised at the 20th Meeting of the Standing Committee of the Ninth National People's Congress on February 28, 2001, available at http://former.sfda.gov.cn/cmsweb/webportal/W45649037/A48335975.html.

continue, and inexperienced staff will dominate production and aspects of oversight, particularly in enforcement and the judiciary, such that dangerous products will continue leaving China's shores for other countries. I left China frustrated that my investigations did not bear more fruit, but they did provide information on where Chinese-made drugs were heading. In the next chapter, I will describe how the fake-drug problem is manifested in the Middle East.

7

Middle East

On September 11, 1999, I flew from London to Amman, the capital of Jordan. I sat next to Raza, an Iraqi mother of three who I would guess was about thirty-five. As she lifted her handbag to put it in the overhead bin, several medicine packages fell onto my seat. She apologized and gave me a sheepish look as she gathered up her drugs. We started what was to become an hour-long conversation about the harm Saddam Hussein's regime and subsequent UN sanctions had wrought on Iraq following the (First) Gulf War, and the problems ordinary Iraqis faced in procuring the most basic medicines. She told me her suitcase was full of pharmaceuticals for her extended family because many important supplies were impossible to get at her home in Mosul. She had been worried about getting through security in London because she was not a licensed trader and was carrying too many drugs for what would be deemed personal use. But she was relaxed and chatty now that she was on the plane, saying she knew customs officials in Amman and did not expect to have any trouble there. She was a little concerned she might have to pay bribes on the Jordanian side of the Jordan-Iraq border but was not unduly worried.

As we conversed, it became obvious that this was not the first time she had made such a trip. Raza's actions made it clear that access to legitimate, high-quality medicines was so limited in Iraq that ordinary citizens resorted to smuggling just to keep their families safely supplied with essential drugs. Her willingness to confide in a white, male, British stranger also showed that neither she nor the Iraqi authorities regarded her actions as illegal; after all, she was simply trying to alleviate suffering and had no intention of turning a profit.

Others, however, seized the opportunity afforded by the sanctions to fill the gap in the drug supply by extremely lucrative but immoral or criminal means—and on a commercial scale. Undoubtedly, some were already smuggling goods across borders prior to a series of Iraqi military conflicts, but they stepped up their operation once sanctions were in place. By 2007, the Iraqi markets—as well as those in Palestine, Syria, Jordan, and Lebanon—were replete with dangerous counterfeit or sub-standard products.

Some of these were genuine drugs that had expired; instead of being destroyed as they should, they had been stolen or relabeled and sold with a new date. Expired drugs can lose efficacy rapidly and sometimes break down into dangerous products. Acetaminophen (brand names include Tylenol, Panadol, or paracetamol) is a great pain reliever, but when it degrades, the by-products can be lethal, and expired acetaminophen should always be discarded. Many oncology drugs are even more lethal once expired; ironically, they often become highly carcinogenic.

Fake drugs found in the Middle East have these problems, too. But in addition, fakes are also likely to have fungal, bacterial, and viral contamination because the chemicals are nearly always produced, and finished drugs formulated, in unhygienic conditions. Dangerous ingredients may also be added to make the pills look good. In the fake pills I examined from this region, I have found bleach, road paint, expired drugs, and numerous unidentified organic chemicals. The danger to public health in the Middle East is severe: fake and substandard drugs have killed by being directly poisonous and, more often, simply by not curing the victim's disease or condition.

Because the Middle East is located at the nexus of trade routes connecting Asia to Africa, it is not surprising that it has its share of bogus pharmaceuticals. Much of Africa is awash in them; studies show that up to half of certain drug types in some locations are fake. Lower but similar profiles exist across much of East Asia (which I will discuss in chapter 8). The Middle East is in between, and like both Africa and East Asia, the fake-drug market across the Middle East varies. Some places have major problems, and others do not.

In 2004 Lebanon's National Health Commission estimated that up to 35 percent of pharmaceuticals available in the country were counterfeit. In Iraq in 2008, Sayed Kathem Khawasiya, inspector general for the Ministry of Health, claimed that roughly 20 percent of medicines in the Iraqi market were fakes. His colleague Adil Muhsin, director-general of the Ministry of Health, claimed that 70 percent of the medicines in Iraq in 2008 were expired or had been imported illegally.[1]

Following trends I observed across the globe, reports of counterfeit cases in the wealthier countries in the Middle East—the United Arab Emirates, Oman, Qatar, and Israel—most often involved fake lifestyle drugs, notably diet pills and erectile dysfunction pills. These countries' poorer neighbors faced more widespread problems.

The Vicious Cycle Begins: Iraq

Deteriorating economic conditions, high tariffs and other protectionism, and finally outright conflict in Iraq and subsequent UN sanctions fostered the counterfeit-drug trade in the region over the past two decades. After the allied forces liberated Kuwait in 1991, UN Security Council Resolution 687 placed economic and other sanctions on Saddam Hussein's regime. In addition to the intentional harm these sanctions caused the regime and its elite cronies, the regime passed this pain to much of the population, laying blame on the United States and its allies and rallying support across the Arab world. UNICEF estimates that the sanctions and the Hussein regime's reaction to them caused the deaths of about 500,000 children.[2]

Local Iraqi drug companies do their best to supply the market. Samarra is a state-run company that makes an array of pharmaceutical products. Founded in 1957, it is the principal domestic manufacturer of medicines in Iraq. In my samplings in the region, I came across only one Samarra product: its version of erythromycin, which passed the basic quality-control tests to which my research team submitted it. Samarra received most of its chemical ingredients (API) from wholesalers in Jordan and Syria, especially from the company Shorja, a large and generally well-respected wholesaler. However, Samarra also uses other API suppliers, and the quality of their API is far from certain. Sources tell me it probably originates in China and could be diluted or otherwise dangerous.

There are probably at least a dozen domestic private producers of drugs, and they supply a quarter of the market. The most notable are Asharq Alawasit (probably the most competent), Al Mansour, and Akai (the largest private company, owned by the Arab League). Roughly half of the drugs in the market, including most specialist products to treat cancer and hypertension, are imported. Over 60 percent of Iraqi imports come from European countries, and about 15 percent are from Jordan, 12 percent are from India, and about 5 percent are from Iran, with the remaining 8 percent from many other locations. The value of imported drugs is about $200 million a year.

Infiltration of counterfeit and substandard drugs into this and other Middle Eastern markets clearly presents a serious threat to patients, but bad drugs also drive out good drugs. Law-abiding producers and traders are forced to compete on price with criminal actors who have no regard for the safety of their products and have only contempt for consumers. Under such conditions, honest traders lose heart; they are unable to recoup production costs in such markets because their costs are easily undercut by producers whose drugs are ineffective. Good-quality drug producers that look for ways to compete with fake-drug producers have fewer resources to spend on brand protection, which directly increases the likelihood that fake versions of their products will become dominant. Companies may even give up trying to produce drugs that cannot compete with substandard products purporting to be of equal quality, or they may be targeted by counterfeiters and ultimately abandon doing business in a country entirely.

Dangerous Dealings: Fakes Infiltrate the Markets

The process by which drugs first enter supply chains in the region varies enormously, but Rashid, a thirty-one-year-old Jordanian private investigator, explained one common method to me. A criminal with fakes or expired medicines approaches a pharmacist and asks if he will take a box of an expensive drug at a low price (experts tell me anywhere between 15 and 40 percent of retail face value is possible, usually nearer the lower end).[3] The pharmacist will not be able to sell the drugs to patients (either because they are inappropriate for pharmacy distribution, like vials of oncology drugs that are injected only in sterile hospital conditions, or because he does not have enough customers for the drugs), so he sells them to a distributor. Pharmacists regularly purchase drugs from particular distributors, so the distributor will likely agree to take the drugs from the pharmacist (at a substantial discount, perhaps 50 percent of retail price) to maintain the relationship, though the distributor should wonder how the pharmacist came by the drugs. Rather than cash, the distributor will often exchange products of equivalent value with the pharmacist. The distributor then uses his network to distribute the potentially lethal product—in many instances the products will be sent out of his local area to a market that can absorb the product (especially if it is a drug only administered in hospitals). Each of the parties involved will take a percentage of the normal retail price (allegations abound that hospital administrators pocket 10–20 percent) because of the deep discount given at the beginning of the chain. Only the final patient will pay the retail amount, in addition to the full price of the possibly lethal consequences of the substandard product.

What is interesting and tragic is that once this process starts, fakes can flood the market in a matter of weeks. To my knowledge, this has happened with oncology drugs in Cairo, Egypt, and Beirut, Lebanon. Up to one-third, and in one or two instances as much as half, of products in the market for some drugs are suspect, especially in the less-regulated markets in Syria and Iraq. This means not only that many patients are paying good money for bad products but also that legitimate companies are losing vast amounts of revenue.

I spoke briefly with medical officers of the allied troops in the region in 2004, and they were primarily concerned with leishmaniasis (known by the troops as Baghdad boil), a disgusting disease spread by sand flies which can, in its visceral form, prove fatal. But I also heard conversations about stolen medicines and shortages they had to overcome periodically. It didn't seem like a big deal at the time, but I later remembered these conversations as my research progressed.

The Smuggling Ring Expands: Syria and Jordan

A smuggling operation based in Ramsa, Jordan, and nearby Dara'a, Syria, and run by various local families, took advantage of the chaos after the U.S. invasion of Iraq to branch out. They already were smuggling legitimate medicines across borders; because these drugs were often expired, they were dangerous. The smugglers were producing their own packaging because labels have to be in the local language in most countries so patients can read about the product. The Palestinian territories and most Arab locations insist on packaging in Arabic, so smuggled, often stolen, drugs crossing borders were provided with new packaging. Although such activities had been going on for decades, they intensified after 1991, and in 2003 the smugglers saw an opportunity in chaotic Iraq and got into the business of making drugs themselves. The network made and sold bogus drugs that failed to treat leukemia, breast cancer, and bacterial infections, causing widespread suffering and death.

Jordanian national Wajeh Abu Odeh was a key player in the Middle Eastern smuggling network. He has two Jordanian wives and is also married to Wu Xia, a Chinese national from Shenzhen. In July 2003, Abu Odeh and Xia established Sky Park Co. Ltd, a Shenzhen-based subsidiary of a Hong Kong holding company specializing in "garments, electronics, and economic consultancy." As a report from 2010 by the International Anticounterfeiting Coalition demonstrates, Shenzhen is a location of many companies selling all sorts of fake products.

Drugs from Sky Park Co. Ltd. were flown or sent by ship from China to the various hubs of the organization in Dubai, Amman, Damascus, and, later, Cairo. Initially Amman was the most important hub, particularly for fake lifesaving medicines, and Dubai was the hub for lifestyle drugs. Most of the shipments were carried unwittingly by the Emirates airline, and once alerted to the problem, the airline helped investigators identify the companies or, more accurately, the real people behind the bogus company names suspected of trading illegal products.

The process by which the drugs arrived was remarkably simple. The correct types of documents, such as bills of lading and airway numbers for all imports and exports, were provided to customs. However, the company names and the addresses on these documents were bogus. Because all customs, foreign exchange, or handling fees were always paid, no one looked into the companies, and container after container of fake drugs was distributed to the hubs. Once there, the drugs were traded in the same way narcotics are traded; they were shipped in large amounts (the equivalent to two suitcases) by truck, concealed in fake petrol tanks or false compartments of vehicles, and eventually split up into smaller loads and sent across Middle Eastern borders by human drug-trading "mules." If individuals were searched, they would claim the drugs were for personal or family use, and most customs officials would not know an antibiotic from a cancer drug, though one might sell for $2 a pack and the other for nearly $2,000 a pack. If any of the mules were stopped and the drugs confiscated, these were probably illegally sold by customs agents, because none of the fakes made their way back to any of the companies I spoke with that make the legitimate versions of these products, which is what should have happened.

Sometimes the gangs used more inventive means of moving drugs around. In one instance, drugs were transported inside ping pong balls; in another, drugs were hidden inside cases marked as kitchen cabinets. Drugs have been shipped wrapped in t-shirts, made to look like products in the wholesale clothing trade. Other hiding places include refrigerators, washing machines, and other household appliances.

Over the course of four years, the network profitably sold smuggled, stolen, expired, and, increasingly, fake medicines into at least seven Arab nations: Iraq, Syria, Jordan, Lebanon, Egypt, United Arab Emirates, and the Palestinian territories.

It is well known that distribution of drugs in Iraq is chaotic. The medical supply agency of the Iraqi Ministry of Health, Kimadia, is not known for its transparency, and it is considered by some to be highly inefficient and even corrupt. Privately, sources talk of drugs disappearing after being delivered to Kimadia warehouses in Baghdad. In April 2007, USAID published "Pharmaceutical and Medical Products in Iraq," a detailed report on the situation. The report lambasts Kimadia, at one point saying, "In the current situation the regulatory enforcement regime has failed and drugs are freely available in the marketplace, either having been sold there illegally by Kimadia/MOH [Ministry of Health], sourced from illicit imports, or from goods looted from the Kimadia warehouses."[4] According to the USAID report, preference is given for locally produced goods, and the Iraqi government pays 20 percent more for these products than it would pay for imported products. The USAID report also says, "Because of the nature of the procurement system and inefficiencies within it, there are shortages of some, if not most, products and occasionally drugs are distributed past their expiry date, all of which is blamed on Kimadia."[5]

One private investigator told me that several orders, each for over $5 million worth of cancer and hypertension drugs, simply disappeared after being signed for by Kimadia and before the drugs were logged at bonded warehouses in Baghdad. In at least one instance, Kimadia demanded replacement drugs or a refund even though it had taken possession of the products and simply lost them; whether this happened with or without help from the senior management of Kimadia, knowledgeable insiders could not agree.

Middle Eastern Governments Confront the Counterfeit Trade

The smuggling operation based in Jordan and Syria fed the market in the UAE and likely other Gulf states primarily with erectile-dysfunction and diet drugs and occasionally with painkillers such as Oxycontin. But the other Middle Eastern markets, especially Iraq's, demanded lifesaving medications, so the network started to infiltrate these markets with counterfeit and useless versions of needed drugs.

Death is an inevitable result for at least a small percentage of people suffering from life-threatening conditions or diseases, and in chaotic or degraded environments, the death rate is higher, and clinical statistics are often absent or poorly kept. Those who lose loved ones from such diseases are grieved but not necessarily shocked. As a result, the deaths caused by fake drugs did not raise suspicions and went largely undetected until 2008.

Jordan. In the summer of 2008, a pharmacist in Jordan noted packaging problems with some samples of drugs to treat hypertension and leukemia. The pharmacist told his legitimate suppliers, who contacted the companies concerned as well as the Jordanian anticorruption police. Once the companies determined the products were fake, which was confirmed by Jordanian authorities, the police raided several warehouses and one production center and made several arrests.

The scale of the operation quickly came to light. It requires significant investment to fake a drug and insert it into supply chains. The packaging has to be nearly perfect, and the pills or liquids have to look convincing, too. Even with perfect packaging, it is difficult to insert medicines into supply and distribution chains, especially expensive cancer and hypertension drugs that are closely monitored. Because these drugs have to be administered under strict supervision, they are available only in hospital dispensaries. That the counterfeits in question were for leukemia and hypertension points to corruption or incompetence in the government health care provision system that monitors Jordanian hospitals.

It was therefore obviously with some alarm that drug companies, from Western household names to the larger Indian and Chinese companies to local Middle Eastern producers, found their products being stolen, expired products that should have been destroyed being resold, and faked products being made in large numbers. I spoke with a few, and although most were angered, none wanted to speak about it on the record or really want the issue publicized. At the first raid in Amman, Jordanian security forces found thousands of packs of different types of drugs; all had been made by Sky Park. The most significant haul was of four thousand packs of the hypertension medicines valsartan and hydrochlorothiazide in faked packaging; none of the drugs contained any active ingredient.[6] Reports differ, but at least fifteen people were arrested in conjunction with the raids. As is standard practice in intelligence operations, pressure was applied to those arrested to expose the network. Investigators would threaten long-term jail sentences and possibly violence, while artfully juxtaposing these threats with the possibility of a lighter sentence in exchange for cooperation.

Prosecutors were frustrated by Jordanian law, which, like in many countries, requires proof of harm to a particular individual before a drug will be seen as breaching a major law. This is surprisingly difficult: supplies are introduced secretly somewhere along the supply chain, making them difficult to trace. Prosecutors must prove someone died of a fatal disease because the medicine in question failed to work. Poor record keeping and high demands for scientific cause-and-effect linkage in most instances result in short jail sentences or in no conviction whatsoever. The perpetrators caught in Jordan in the summer of 2007 were all out of jail within two months. They were fined for their crimes; the fines they paid ranged from a few thousand dollars to well over $100,000 for Jordanian national Jamal Abu Afifeh, a key player in the network.[7]

Raed Abu Markieh, one of Afifeh's senior colleagues, had caught wind of the raid in advance. Realizing the network was threatened, he decided to inform on his colleagues to escape arrest. He approached security personnel of Novartis, the company whose products he was selling in the largest amounts, and the Jordanian government, offering to act as an informant. Security experts told me they were skeptical of his intentions from the beginning. As they had feared, Markieh was unreliable, extracted money for helping them, and played the role of a double agent. In an effort to demonstrate his desire to help authorities, he informed on his own brother, Mohammed, who was only a part-time player in the network and previously had been unknown to the police. Mohammed Markieh spent two months in a Jordanian jail and was fined roughly $130,000.[8] The impact on Mohammed of his brother's betrayal and the consequences of it would later be advantageous to the security services.

Within two months of Afifeh and company's release, the same fake leukemia medicine, imatinib mesylate, resurfaced.[a] This time, samples were identified by a worried Jordanian pharmacist who ran a regional trading network from Saudi Arabia. The pharmacist had noticed some inconsistencies in the drug packaging he purchased from Afifeh. Security specialists I spoke with suggest that this pharmacist was operating in the gray areas of legality; he was involved in some small-scale smuggling, but not in the counterfeit trade. He claimed he had purchased ninety treatment packages of imatinib for $100,000, expecting to sell these to Kimadia for a 30 percent markup. After he had bought the drugs, he noticed that the expiration date appeared modified. He contacted Novartis and sent them some samples to ascertain whether the products were legitimate. Novartis told him the drugs were fake. The pharmacist told Novartis the remaining drugs were in an Iraqi warehouse. Because neither Novartis nor the Jordanian authorities have any jurisdiction in Iraq, the drugs were never recovered. They may have been destroyed in Iraq or sold to unsuspecting patients. But the Jordanian security services were intrigued by these fakes, which had batch numbers and imperfect product identification identical to the fakes found in Jordan.

Afifeh had since crossed the border to Syria to set up shop there. Security personnel from Jordan and Novartis alerted Syrian authorities to the significance of this expanding operation.

Syria. Syria's president, Basheer Al-Assad, is a medical doctor (an ophthalmologist), and his father-in-law is a cardiologist based in London. His

---

a. It is difficult to make imatinib mesylate well. It take twenty-four raw materials and seven distinct chemical steps, and you have to control two genotoxic impurities, which shouldn't get over 1.5 micrograms per day. Many legal copies are not able to manage production at a cost affordable to most patients (see "Glivec" in box 2-2 on page 36).

medical family may account for the interest he took in ending the counterfeiting operation. Upon learning of the fake-drug ring doing business within his borders, he installed a close cousin and senior intelligence operative as the main investigator for the issue.

While the Syrian authorities began to monitor the counterfeit network, more of the fake imatinib mesylate surfaced, this time in the Palestinian territories. My investigations there proved the most interesting and distressing part of this whole affair.

Palestine. Al Thulathia is a Palestinian limited-liability company based in the town of Nablus that has marketed and distributed pharmaceuticals across the Palestinian territories for the past decade. It was never an official distributor of products for Western companies and probably distributed drugs from myriad sources. In 2004 the company was investigated by the police on suspicion of marketing and selling illegally imported or expired drugs. None of the directors, including lead actor Baker Abu Hijleh, were charged with any offense.[9]

In 2008 a more substantial complaint was made against the company. Ibrahim Yehia bought leukemia medicine for his sister from Al Thulathia. She had been treated for cancer at an Israeli hospital but had recently been transferred to the Palestinian territories for further treatment. Upon taking the medicine from Al Thulathia, her condition worsened, and she soon died. Yehia suspected the medicine she had taken may have been counterfeit; he noticed that later examples of the packaging were slightly different from previous packs, although the treatments should have been identical. Yehia was a security officer for the Palestinian Authority, and probably because of his status and his training, the police took his complaint seriously. Dr. Rania Ahahin, the general director of the pharmacy department in the Palestinian territories, flew to Amman, where Novartis and the Jordanians confirmed that the fake drug matched the fakes found in Amman.

On March 5, 2008, security services began a weeklong series of raids in which they seized drugs and documents from Al Thulathia. They found fake leukemia medicine—imatinib mesylate—and diverted, expired, substandard, and fake versions of major sellers, including cholesterol-lowering Lipitor and heart medication Plavix (see figures 3-1 and 3-2). Over the following weeks, interrogations of detainees, product examinations, and interviews with twenty-four witnesses led to numerous arrests and criminal charges. Charges included selling counterfeit and expired drugs, trading in stolen goods, smuggling goods (many drugs had Hebrew or Chinese writing; others said they were for sale only in Jordan), tax evasion, document fraud, money laundering, and forgery. One of the unusual pieces of property seized was an ambulance, which the company used to transport products across checkpoints. Traffickers who shrewdly watch for weaknesses at checkpoints had noticed that ambulances traveling on apparently urgent business were understandably rushed through security; they took advantage of this to move drugs across the border quickly.[10]

The case was initially complicated by laboratory analyses undertaken by Al Najah University in Nablus, which declared that seized products passed quality-control tests. Other laboratories—commercial and government—subsequently showed that the medicines contained no active ingredient. Whether the university's declaration was due to an accident or an intentional deception can be speculated. The fake-drug network certainly bribed myriad officials, so it is possible staff at the university had been paid off. Alternatively, the incorrect results could easily reflect the lab's incompetence: several experts doubted that the laboratory contained sufficient equipment and competent staff to conduct the analysis.

The police investigation pointed to the possibility that a local hospital had been complicit in the sale of fake drugs. The Al Arabi Center for Cancer and Blood Diseases was fully owned by Al Thulathia, which also owned 20 percent of the Arab Specialized Hospital of Nablus, where the Al Arabi Center was housed. Suspicion grew after all senior management from the clinic refused to answer basic questions from security personnel.

There was also mixed support from some ministry officials. The Palestinian Ministry of Health must have been embarrassed by the finding, especially because it had bought drugs from Al Thulathia in the past and may have been concerned about the quality of previous purchases. The ministry and Al Thulathia had also infringed on the rights of the approved importer of products for the Palestinian territories, Masrouji Co., a well-known, legal drug distributor for the region. The ministry had bought imatinib mesylate from Al Thulathia for the Al Watani public hospital in Hebron, and fifteen people had died of leukemia. It is uncertain whether any of the deaths were attributable to poor-quality drugs, but Yousef Hourani, Al Watani's director, also declined to speak with security personnel. It became increasingly obvious that the fake-drug network was intimidating and possibly bribing some witnesses, making data collection and building a watertight case increasingly difficult.

The investigation found that Issam Jarrar, one of the defendants, had routinely visited China. He was suspected of having a connection with Sky Park (the Chinese company supplying fake drugs to the criminal gang), because batch numbers on several of the products he had traded matched those previously found in the Jordanian raid. The Palestinian authorities informed the Chinese authorities, and all fifteen Al Thulathia defendants are now prohibited entry into China.

Abu Hijleh, Al Thulathia's leader, is a Palestinian with permanent residency in Canada. He and his colleagues used clever rhetoric in selling the fakes. They insisted they were "low-profit pricing" to provide humanitarian support for the Muslim Brotherhood against their Israeli and Western oppressors. The rhetoric and the marginally lower prices compared with their competitors convinced many pharmacists to buy from them, and most were unaware that the products they were buying were fake. Abu Hijleh was also a pharmacist and adviser for the Al Arabia leukemia clinic, where he perpetrated a clever and odious fraud. He would ensure that patients were initially treated with genuine oncology drugs until a required hematological effect was noted, and then he would switch them to fake drugs for the period for which noticeable improvement is not expected. Al Thulathia's owners would profit handsomely from these drug sales for many months while a patient's condition steadily worsened. After the patient died, Abu Hijleh and his gang walked away.

On being questioned by security officials, Abu Hijleh blamed substandard drugs he may have sold on Raed Abu Markieh, the same Jordanian who had wanted to act as an informant in Jordan. This testimony was seen as conclusive evidence of the Jordanian-Syrian ring's involvement in the Palestinian territories. The fifteen defendants include Abu Hijleh's brother and his brother-in-law. Abu Hiljeh tried several tactics to avoid prosecution, including claiming to have been helping an old lady cross a street when he was kidnapped and driven away in his own car. Forty-eight hours after the incident, police confirmed Abu Hijleh had staged the abduction to avoid appearing in court. In a final attempt to avoid prosecution, the counterfeiter even threatened a former employee of Al Thulathia who was a key witness in the case.

This case is ongoing. While in Israel in the spring of 2010, I tried to investigate these matters in Palestine, but at that time no one would speak to me about it, even off the record. Many witnesses appear to have been threatened. After spending about two months in jail, the fifteen defendants are now in the Palestinian territories. They are not permitted to leave, and Canadian border control has agreed not to allow Abu Hijleh to enter Canada even if he does escape Palestine. Sources tell me that sometimes the prosecutors appear eager to push forward with the case, but at other times there is no action. The chief prosecutor's house was strafed with machine-gun bullets in mid-2009, and his life has been directly threatened on more than one occasion. The drug network is politically well connected: they allegedly bribed the former Arafat regime and may be paying some officials within the current regime led by Mahmoud Abbas to allow business to continue as usual. To permanently stop this ring, it is critical that the Palestinian Authority manages to make hospital records available to the court. At present, this has not happened, meaning they cannot be entered into evidence by the prosecutor. Although some convictions can be made without these data, convictions for manslaughter or murder, which may be warranted at least for the main players, cannot be sought without hospital records to show when a specific patient died and the proximate cause.

China. Once the Chinese connection became evident in Jordan in 2007 and in the Palestinian territories in 2008, the Chinese authorities enacted a domestic clampdown. They raided eleven production centers in four provinces (Guandong, Zhejiang, Jiangsu, and Henan) and arrested people from six independent criminal groups, including Sky Park operatives Abu Odeh and his wife, Xia (see box 7-1 for further information on Chinese fakes in the Middle East and Africa). No one has heard from Abu Odeh since this time; it is unknown whether he is incarcerated or dead, though most of the people I spoke with suspected the latter. Chinese authorities would not comment on this or any other case. Although Chinese authorities likely have not closed down all production for five of the criminal groups, they have certainly prevented production for distribution to the Jordanian group described above, at least for the moment.

Box 7-1

Differences between Fakes in the Middle East and Africa

There is an interesting distinction between the fake drugs found in the Middle East and those in Africa. In the criminal activities described in this chapter, and in other cases in the Middle East of which I am aware, almost none of the fake drugs contained any API. The counterfeiters' main effort is applied to infiltrating the market; by the time products are exposed as fake, the guilty parties either have escaped or will suffer the consequences. In contrast, fake drugs in Africa are more likely to contain active ingredients. Although it is far easier to infiltrate supply systems in Africa, African governments know they have a fake-drug problem, so they randomly test drugs in the market for basic quality. To avoid detection in Africa and continue to ply their trade, counterfeiters find it worthwhile to add some amount of the correct API. This does not mean the drugs will work, though. It is one thing to add the right APIs and another thing entirely to go to the expense and time to formulate a drug so it is bioavailable to humans. Many fake malaria and HIV drugs, for example, do not dissolve properly in the body, rendering them entirely useless even when they have the correct APIs. Fake drugs that contain some API also cause more risk to society overall, as these contribute to drug resistance.

Counterfeiters Adapt. With operations made difficult in Jordan, Palestine, and now in China, the group swiftly moved their production and distribution headquarters to Damascus, where Abu Afifeh fled following his release from prison in connection with the Jordanian crackdown (see figures 7-1 [2007] and 7-2 [2009] to track how drug distribution networks adapted). In Damascus, Abu Afifeh purchased sophisticated printing, pill production, and packaging machinery from China and Austria. The drug ring was again ready to sell fake pharmaceuticals to Iraq and neighboring Arab nations. Because none of the products had any active ingredients beyond acetaminophen and aspirin to give pills that authentic pharmaceutical sheen, it was easy to ramp up production.

Intelligence Triumphs. Security services in Syria began monitoring Abu Afifeh and soon found his production facilities. Within a few months, they had identified all the distribution hubs in the towns of Aleppo, Idlib, Hims,

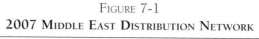

FIGURE 7-1
2007 MIDDLE EAST DISTRIBUTION NETWORK

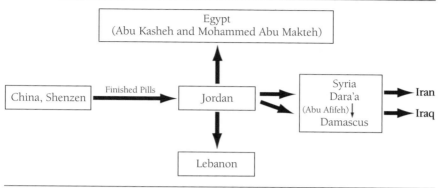

and Hamas and had identified over a dozen people to be arrested. At the same time, Egyptian authorities launched aggressive investigations of their own. Figure 7-1 illustrates the approximate flow of products.

One who had escaped the Jordanian clampdown was Sherif Abdul Kareem Abu Kasheh, later discovered to have owned the raided Jordanian production facility. Abu Kasheh had escaped to Egypt, where he established a new distribution center. The Egyptian operation was more isolated than the rest, as its large domestic market kept Abu Kasheh busy. In comparison, as much as 80 percent of sales from the Syrian and Jordanian operations were in Iraq.

Mohammed Markieh, who had been betrayed by his brother following the Jordanian raids, was approached by security services to give information on Abu Kasheh and, if possible, infiltrate his operation. Security officials hoped he could be turned because he had been betrayed and had not been able to implicate anyone else because of his limited role in the operation. He also had a wife and a life to rebuild, so he agreed to cooperate. He successfully infiltrated Abu Kasheh's operation by explaining his role in the Jordanian operation, his disgust at his brother's betrayal, and his need of a job. After six months, he had Abu Kasheh's confidence and introduced Abu Kasheh to a man, code-named "Monaco," posing as a major drug buyer for the paramilitary FARC (Fuerzas Armadas Revolucionarias de Colombia) in Colombia. Intelligence agents created an entire business cover based in Panama, and Abu Kasheh agreed to sell fake breast cancer and other drugs to Monaco.

Evidence from a concealed camera shows Abu Kasheh explaining to Monaco that the drugs he can provide contain no API. He says he can add API if required, but explains it will increase costs. Mohammed Markieh convinces Abu Kasheh to take two suitcases of fake drugs to Damascus, where Monaco apparently wants to meet. Upon landing, Abu Kasheh is arrested by Syrian security officials. One of the fake drugs he carried is for bone cancer. This is perhaps the most frightening fake drug I have come across: it contained detergent and would have been lethal to an immunocompromised cancer patient, perhaps within a matter of days. In Cairo, investigators found more fake bone-cancer drugs and claimed they had locally verified that several people died from taking them. The packaging was so realistic it took a thorough investigation to show that it was not real. The network had been bribing hospital staff to gather hospital garbage, including the bone-cancer drug vials, which were supposed to be incinerated.[b] The faked medicines have two pinpricks in the rubber stopper at the top: the first is where the drug was taken out with a syringe by the attending doctor, and the second is where someone has refilled the vial with the detergent-laden water that looks like the actual medicine.

In addition to the fake bone-cancer medicines, Egyptian authorities found enough breast cancer medicines to "treat" many thousands of patients in Cairo and other oncology centers in Alexandria and possibly elsewhere. The volume of fakes was more than half the entire annual Egyptian demand for the real versions of these drugs. On realizing how much trade they had lost to the fake-drug network, one Western drug company representative told me that "our number one competitor was the fake [version of our own brand]."

The infiltration action was approved at the highest levels of the Egyptian government. The wife of the ex-president, Mrs. Suzanne Mubarak, who suffered from breast cancer and was active in health charities, was apparently aware of the action against these criminal elements in her country. Given such support from the Egyptian first lady and hence from the president

---

b. Evidence gathered in early 2011 indicated that several Chinese gangs are operating internationally, and especially in the Middle East, to gather all manner of hospital waste.

FIGURE 7-2
2009 MIDDLE EAST DISTRIBUTION NETWORK

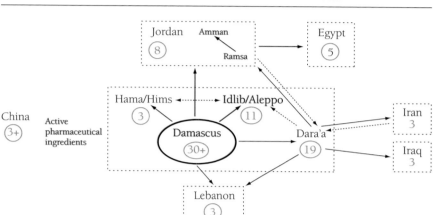

Red numbers = number of known operators/traders
⟶ = definite flow of drugs
┈┈▶ = probable flow of drugs
◯ = major drug production and distribution site

himself, the government appointed General Mostafa Amr, the former head of the narcotics bureau, to increase understanding of the network and learn how to shut it down. Because this was part of a coordinated effort with Syria, Abu Kasheh's Egyptian operation was not closed down entirely until the Syrian authorities were ready to pounce on the entire network.

With the Chinese fake-drug pipeline closed down, Abu Afifeh's Damascus and Dara'a operation was becoming more significant to the network. After gathering sufficient intelligence on this component of the ring, Syrian security personnel conducted multiple raids in May 2009 on the main production facility in Damascus and the smaller distribution outlets in Aleppo. Sixty-five people were arrested in Syria, and a total of ten had already been arrested in Jordan and Egypt and another ten in China (see figure 7-2).

The haul from the warehouses was remarkable. Officials found over four tons of expired, stolen, and predominantly fake drugs. They recovered eighty different medicines in about 120 different formulations (figures 7-5–7-10 show photos taken at Syrian customs, where the drugs from at least seven buildings, including three ware-houses, were taken). Authorities recovered sixty varieties of fake Western-branded drugs, the majority of which were fakes of the largest companies' products; roughly fifteen Indian or Chinese products; and half a dozen domesti-cally produced pharmaceutical brands, includ-ing products made by Nile Pharmaceuticals and Chemical Industries Company (Egypt), Aleppo Pharmaceutical Industries (Syria), and Hikma Pharmaceuticals (Jordan). Many of the pack-ages bore fake stamps attributing ownership to the Iraqi Ministry of Health, indicating that these products were intended for sale in Iraq.

Stopping this operation was a domestic tri-umph for the Syrian government and a major operational success for intelligence cooperation in the region. This may have been the largest counterfeiting ring broken up anywhere in the world. While security sources tell me that per-haps as much as 80 percent of the network has been stopped, there is little doubt that opera-tors in Iraq, Iran, and Lebanon are still at large (I know the names of at least eight suspects the respective authorities are hoping to arrest but who, at the time of writing, had evaded cap-

FIGURE 7-3

Amjad Markieh in jail in Syria

FIGURE 7-4

Raed Abu Markieh in jail in Syria

ture). These people are versatile, and although they will hide for a while, they could soon be back in business if they manage to find other produc-tion sources. For now, Syria is closed to them, and Abu Kasheh, Raed Abu Markieh and his brother Amjad (see figures 7-3 and 7-4), and Abu Afifeh have been arrested and are awaiting trial.

Looking Ahead: More Challenges to Come

Although they have not collaborated with Syria to the same extent as Egypt and Jordan, other neighboring countries are beginning to play their part,

FIGURE 7-5

Syrian customs warehouse: fake products destined for Iraq recovered in Damascus

and Syria, Jordan, and Egypt continue to fight counterfeiting domestically. The results thus far have been mixed.

In Lebanon in 2007, the owner of a hospital and five employees were jailed for just one month for selling water as a $2,000 cancer drug. In January and February 2010, twelve pharmacies and four medical-supply warehouses were closed by the Lebanese Ministry of Health for their involvement in the smuggling and sale of counterfeit drugs. According to local media reports that month, "The head of the Parliamentary Health Committee, Atef Majdalani, warned that counterfeit drugs still posed a danger to hundreds of Lebanese each year, and is attempting to establish the country's first laws dealing with counterfeit medicine, such as banning the advertising of counterfeit or imitation drugs."[11]

The Jordanian Food and Drug Administration has always tackled the matter as effectively as possible within the country's current legal structure. Two major steps have been particularly effective. In 2007 the agency shut down 150 of 1,700 pharmacies for trading in counterfeit products. In 2008 the fines for offenders were doubled from roughly $7,500 to $15,000,

FIGURES 7-6–7-10

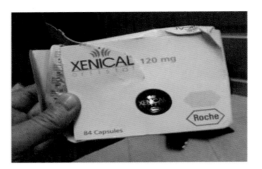

Syrian customs warehouse: fake products destined for Iraq recovered in Damascus

which helps deter the illegal trade. By 2009, the agency needed to close only seventy-five pharmacies.[12]

According to the *Los Angeles Times,* the Iraqi government committed itself in the fall of 2008 to enforcing drug laws. "Under enhanced enforcement measures, a sample of every imported drug is supposed to be tested for efficacy and approved before going on the market. Teams of inspectors perform spot checks of pharmacies and drug warehouses and have stepped up raids on markets where counterfeit dealers operate."[13] *USA Today* reported that the government closed down 120 illegal pharmacies in the fall of 2009. Unfortunately, corrupt soldiers of the Iraqi Army and National Guard, who were supposed to crack down on fraudulent pharmacies, allegedly stole from these businesses "rather than fully shutting down its operations. Even legitimate pharmacists are at risk of this kind of racketeering, often seeing their shops raided and robbed by the very police tasked with regulation."[14]

Before its successful raid took place, Syria did not have a proper law to prevent pharmaceutical crime, and the sixty-five suspects were held under some security provisions. In early April 2010, President Assad's Syrian government passed a law to end the distribution of dangerous medicines within its borders. Legislative Decree 24 is the culmination of three years' work and allows sentencing of up to twenty years of hard labor. Now the sixty-five suspects will be prosecuted under this law. Syrian health minister Saeed Reza told reporters in April 2010 that "the ministry is serious about preventing [drug fraud] . . . through tougher penalties as a deterrent."[15]

Tough penalties are welcome, but holding perpetrators without due process of law is only possible in Assad's dictatorship. And as I write, the regime appears to be losing even some of its regional allies, although it is a long way from entirely crumbling. President Assad's brother Maher, reputedly responsible for the massacres of protestors in early 2011, still has an iron grip on the country. I hear reports that smuggling is once again on the rise, as people try to escape the country and illegal supplies enter it.

Conclusion

One of the advantages of running a dictatorship is that observing Western due process of law is not required; this became evident to those combating fake drugs in parts of the Middle East (and in China). While it is easy to be critical of the political systems and the larger economic malaise that bedevil the Middle East, positive lessons can be learned from the important, lifesaving work undertaken by the security services in the region. The successful breakup of the drug ring described in this chapter also highlights the important role legitimate drug companies, in this case Novartis, play in helping to ensure that those perpetrating gross health and economic frauds are exposed and prosecuted.

That said, all the good could be undermined by changes in governments or their priorities, because none of these countries really have proper systems in place to address fake drugs and continue to rely on intelligence from companies and the observations of members of the medical fraternity. Indeed, Mohamed Al-Kanhal, executive president of the Saudi Food and Drug Authority, told me that he is pushing for harmonization of laws against counterfeiters across the region, and to increase punishments "as harsh for fakes as for narcotics," he forcefully pointed out.

The above example from the Middle East shows how a criminal gang actually operates and how much it depended on China as a country of export for packaging and raw materials. It also shows how versatile these criminals can be: when Chinese help could no longer be counted on, they simply made everything themselves. By that time, they had learned enough and made enough money to buy the machinery required to print high-class packaging with low-quality pharmaceuticals. That these medicines had either zero or incorrect active ingredients, causing untold harm for countless people, is a tragedy that, at least for now, security services have managed to stop.

8

Other Emerging Markets

The previous chapters in this part discussed most of the major types of substandard-drug problems encountered in the middle-income and poorer areas of the world. Of course, the many countries I have not covered have their own unique drug problems and perhaps their own unique solutions. It is with regret that I cannot detail all of their problems, but I do discuss a few more in this chapter. These all have relevance beyond their borders in terms of either the special problems or the unusual solutions they have that people in other countries should contemplate.

Russia

According to the Moscow News, a 2008 survey found that 40 percent of Russians thought they might have taken substandard or counterfeit medicines.[1] That same year, Alexander Chukharev, the deputy chairman of the Committee on Health Care Protection of the State Duma, estimated that between 10 and 12 percent of medicines sold in pharmacies were counterfeit, signaling that counterfeits are not a problem only in the informal markets but have penetrated the official health sector in Russia as well.[2] Many problems with drug quality in Russia stem from local, legitimate manufacturers that make substandard versions of their own drugs to augment profits.

The country's problems with counterfeit drugs can be traced back to events following the great Russian debt default of 1998—when the ruble lost two-thirds of its value—and medicines, already expensive by Western standards, became even more difficult to afford. Until that time, Russia had largely avoided the menace of counterfeit drugs. The Federal Law on Medicines of 1998 did not even mention the issue, and criminal law did not provide clear definitions of what constituted the production, distribution, and sale of counterfeit pharmaceuticals. The government's unpaid wages bill stood at $12.5 billion in August 1998, and the demand for goods that saved even a few rubles created plenty of opportunities for businessmen willing to move into the shadow markets. Meanwhile, ordinary people were left without legal protection.

Vladimir Alekseevich Bryntsalov was already a player in the pharmaceutical business, but in 1998 he took the opportunity to become a major player in the production and sale of substandard drugs in Russia. The grandson of a Cossack general, Bryntsalov is the archetypal rogue capitalist, a billionaire, and one of the richest men in Russia. After graduating as a mining engineer, Bryntsalov was an instructor in a technical college before becoming foreman and manager of a big construction firm. Expelled from the Communist Party for "petty bourgeois trends," he opened a confectionery factory and set up a beehive cooperative that supplied material to the country's largest antibiotics manufacturer, Karpov Pharmaceutical Plant.[3]

In the firesale of Yeltsin's 1990s Russia, Bryntsalov gained control of the newly privatized Karpov. He forged an association with three other plants in the Moscow area, formed a joint-stock company, and started his pharmaceutical empire. The company was called Ferane.

By 1995, Ferane produced 30 percent of pharmaceuticals consumed in Russia, and Bryntsalov controlled 70 percent of the company. Within a few years, he owned 90 percent of it. The company had accounts in sixty countries and business contacts with firms in Hungary, Germany, and India, where Bryntsalov also had other investments. By this time, his empire included a commercial bank, an insurance company, and a law firm, and he produced porcelain, furniture, textiles, and alcoholic beverages, in addition to pharmaceuticals. When Ferane was embroiled in a tax scandal in 1995, Bryntsalov was elected as a deputy to the State Duma, where he sought alliances and switched allegiances with insouciant speed and earned the nickname "Moonshiner," a reference to his vodka fortune.

He launched a presidential campaign in 1996; although unsuccessful (he finished last), the campaign brought him fame for his flamboyant lifestyle and rough, poor-boy-made-good character. From 1996 to 1997, Bryntsalov maintained his notoriety through high-profile scandals in the Duma and by distributing his company's medications for impotence among Duma deputies.

In 1995 Bryntsalov struck a deal with respected pharmaceutical firm Novo Nordisk to purchase their gene-engineered insulin and equipment to process the insulin into finished product in Russia. Now able to supply insulin, Ferane won a $5 million contract to supply the Russian government and the 500,000 Russians with diabetes who require insulin every day. But the partnership with Novo Nordisk turned sour when the company accused Bryntsalov of substituting low-quality animal insulin instead of their insulin into his products and failing to pay $6.5 million in bills. Bryntsalov never denied either accusation, but he did imply that Novo Nordisk had supplied the substandard raw materials as part of a conspiracy to defraud the Russian government.

Ahead of court action that may have seized his assets, Bryntsalov consolidated all his debts in Ferane and withdrew his assets to a new company, Bryntsalov-A. This company is based in a small village in the Caucasus, near his hometown of Cherkessk.

In 2000 the Moscow Court of Arbitration ruled that Bryntsalov alone was guilty. Nonetheless, a year later, some Russian regions were still supplied with Bryntsalov's substandard product, despite bitter protest from the endocrinologists forced to administer the stuff. *Businessweek* magazine reported, "Hospitalized last spring after injections of Bryntsalov-made insulin failed to help him absorb blood sugar, junior army officer Anatoly Lukoshkin, 46, from the Moscow-area town of Domodedovo, now says he would like to ask the tycoon: 'Why are you producing insulin that is causing suffering to people?' The apparent problem: 'It's not concentrated enough,' says Irina Zamotina, a medical consultant for the Mordovia region, who conducted a two-month test of the product last year after patients there said it wasn't working. There have been similar patient complaints in Volgograd, too."[4]

In 2001 the Ministry of Health suspended Bryntsalov's license for Russia's favorite traditional remedy, tincture of hawthorn berry—used variously as heart medication, a sedative, and even to ease labor pains—when it was found to contain 75 percent alcohol. Bryntsalov ignored this setback and continued selling the product to the tune of $4.2 million, or 10 percent of the company's revenue, in the first quarter of the year.

In a 2006 report on fake pharmaceuticals in Russia, *Lancet* described a raid by Roszdravnadzor, the Russian drug regulator, on a crumbling, rat-infested warehouse on the outskirts of Moscow. The building was in use as an illegal distribution depot for fake medicines being sent to hospitals and pharmacies throughout Russia. The owner? None other than Bryntsalov's sister. The raid's haul included $2 million worth of copies of popular, mostly foreign-brand drugs, including brands from Pfizer and Bayer. The counterfeits purported to be antibacterials, a cold remedy, and a treatment for a cerebral disorder.[5] The favored method of producing fakes, said *Lancet*, was for legitimate factories to make copies on the side. A "night shift" would produce extra quantities of a certified drug that would not pass through quality control or sophisticated copies of well-known drugs with reduced levels of expensive active ingredients. (As I discussed before, the same types of activities occur in India and China, too.[6])

Bryntsalov became the subject of a police investigation, but, as ever, he seemed to shrug it off and carry on regardless. Roszdravnadzor rescinded the company's license and started a twenty-month investigation. In April 2009, Tatyana Bryntsalova, Vladimir's sister and a director of Bryntsalov-A, and three other former directors were found guilty of counterfeiting two hundred tons worth of over fifty foreign-branded medicines. They were paroled, given suspended sentences, and fined a paltry $1,500.[7]

Sources allege that Bryntsalov retreated to one of his many residences, probably the exclusive Seaside Plaza in the Fontvieille Marina quarter of Monaco. Monaco's police reported there was evidence of his links with Russian organized crime, but no further action was taken.

In 2008 Bryntsalov was reportedly going into partnership with Belarus's state-owned Belbiopharm to build a new plant to break the dominance of imports, which account for 80 percent of the Belarussian pharmaceuticals market. Plans were shelved during the economic crisis, but in March 2011, they may have been back on the table. The new plant, to be built by 2015, is to be on the base of a state pharmaceutical company called Dialek, and the government of Belarus has promised Bryntsalov all the necessary tax and other benefits for the implementation of the project.[8]

In our small sampling of products from Moscow pharmacies, we did not come across any Bryntsalov-A failures, but a Russia-based investigator showed me a product called "Ciprobrin" (Bryntsalov-A's ciprofloxacin product). This was substandard and almost certainly not a fake version of the real drug, but one the investigator suggests was produced by the company. It seems the approach of diluting or replacing high-quality ingredients with suspect ones continues at Bryntsalov's flagship company. (It is worth noting that one can buy Ciprobrin quite easily over the Internet.) I pushed the investigator for more detail, but he said his investigations are in an early stage and would not tell me more. His caution was understandable, given how often people disappear in Putin's Russia. And it demonstrates that without concerted action, the irrepressible Bryntsalov, who is now sixty-five, shows no sign of reforming or slowing down.

Bryntsalov is far from the only trader in dangerous drugs in Russia, but he epitomizes Russia's substandard-drug problem. He is so powerful no one can stand up to him, at least not for long. Although Russia does not have a massive problem with fake drugs as compared with Africa, the problems it does have are unlikely to improve in the short to medium term. As one investigator told me, the general Russian response is that "this is the way things are done in Russia."

Russia's neighbors act much like Russia. Like Russia, Ukraine's Secret Service, the SBU, has historically been more interested in showing it is tough on fake drugs than actually doing anything substantive about them. As Andrew Jackson, security chief at Novartis, says, the SBU sees "some political mileage in doing a raid and having some nice pictures in the newspaper." And of Russia, Jackson says he'll help out where necessary: "We have paid for the petrol for the police to get out of Moscow to go someplace." Often he has to train his own staff, and this includes sales reps, who may be the first to spot trends of good-selling drugs that suddenly trend downward as a possible indicator that a fake supplier is supplying their market.

Latin America

Generally speaking, drug quality across Latin America is better than in Africa, and at least as far as Brazil is concerned (the only country we tested) it is marginally better than in Asia. But problems remain with substandard drugs, some of which may be "similars" (legal copies of innovator drugs that do not have to prove bioequivalence to the original and hence cannot be called generics), but fakes are also a problem.

Several private investigators I spoke with point to one persistent and widespread problem across the entire region: they claim that several of the local manufacturers making products of inconsistent quality are politically connected. The result of this is pernicious. I heard many stories, but most investigators did not want to reveal the names of the guilty for fear of being sued by the companies in question. Although this is frustrating, it is also understandable, for there is often no proof of wrongdoing, and the companies are litigious. In general, a victim of substandard medicines (or his survivors, if he succumbs) may be offered no recourse, even if someone suspects something. Placing the blame is notoriously difficult in every country across Latin America. Only in Brazil does the government provide some guidance and financial legal help for possible victims of poor-quality drugs, and there is some governmental rhetorical support for Brazilian doctors demanding proven generic drugs instead of similars. Similars are tolerated throughout the region, but one advantage of the openness of Brazil's system is that although drugs may not have to prove bioequivalence, suppliers may be held liable if their medicines cause harm. Brazil's greater transparency is important because no doctor or hospital (yet) would test a drug before administering it. Nor would it probably occur to a doctor that if a patient did not respond to treatment, it may be due to faulty medicines rather than bad luck or perhaps a faulty diagnosis.

In much of Latin America, doctors suspicious of a certain medicine might look up the name and see it listed as a generic drug, when, in actuality, it may be a similar drug. Doctors may be working in public hospitals and administering drugs supplied under a government contract by a public-funded company. They may have to send samples to a government laboratory for analysis, and most doctors likely do not have the authority to do that. Although it is possible that doctors with limited data suggesting a medicine does not work might complain to their bosses, it would be difficult to convince them to spend precious funds to test drugs approved by the government. Complaints are unlikely to be made, and most that are acted on are not likely to result in a positive outcome for the patients or doctors involved. The few doctors I met in my Latin American travels were concerned about the quality of some drugs. They wanted to believe the drugs supplied under government contracts were good, but they could not be certain.

In the worst instances, doctors may even be complicit. The most extreme case I know of involves the Cuban doctors working within

Venezuelan president Hugo Chavez's health system. While at a conference in Miami in 2010, a Venezuelan doctor whose family is in Caracas told me that a few doctors bring drugs with them from Cuba that are suspected of being of uncertain efficacy. There have been stories of patients not responding to treatments, but it is unclear whether medical personnel have made mistakes or—as seems far more likely—if poor-quality drugs are the cause. Patients have no recourse, especially because even an investigation would imply that one of Chavez's key allies might be at fault. When Chavez himself fell ill in June 2011, it was to Cuba he went for treatment, and although the elite in both countries can be sure of the best treatment, that is not the case for the majority.

Substandard drugs in Central America and Mexico often have inferior APIs, which can create drugs that are subpotent or laced with hazardous materials or are "recycled" expired medications, which organized crime rings repackage and redistribute. This is possible because Mexico, in particular, lacks a formal waste-management system for expired pharmaceuticals.

Brazil and Argentina. Brazil provides a fascinating and innovative example of a way emerging markets can respond to imported and locally produced poor-quality drugs from both a public-health and economic development perspective. The drugs we sampled from São Paolo were the most expensive we found in emerging markets and were, with the one exception of four samples of the same product, of high quality. The main pharmacies are also of high quality, but Brazil has a second category of drug shops that legally sell similars. Brazil's drug regulatory agency, Agência Nacional de Vigilância Sanitária (ANVISA), ensures that the plants that make the drugs conform to some reasonable level of GMP, but it does not insist that companies making these products provide bioequivalence data for the drugs. Allowing such products in the market rankles with Western pharmaceutical executives. At one conference, a spokesman from a Western innovator company was almost apoplectic about his company's products having to compete with "unproven quackery." The standard argument is that having double standards for important pharmaceuticals fosters a trade in substandard drugs and endangers people's lives, all with the government's stamp of approval.

This is a valid argument if looked at as a problem in stasis. The government is condoning possibly ineffectual medicines, in effect enabling increased morbidity and even mortality. But I am actually quite impressed by the approach. In many emerging markets, there is a wide variety of drugs on the market; surely it is better to be explicit about what is for sale than to pretend everything is good and perfectly interchangeable. In a strict economic sense, the most obvious of market signals—price—indicates discrepancies in quality.

What is especially encouraging is that as Brazil has become wealthier, ANVISA—recognizing that similars constituted a significant share of substandard medicines in the country—changed the regulations on similars in May 2003. Accordingly, ANVISA now requires that similars manufacturers submit bioavailability data, pharmaceutical equivalence tests, and a copy of an ANVISA-issued GMP certificate during registration.[9] Similars manufacturers registered before 2003 have until 2014 to comply. Although this grace period is not ideal from a public-health standpoint, it is a logical compromise from a development standpoint, and it gives smaller companies time to upgrade practices.

Unlike Brazil, Argentina has not expressed any intent to require bioequivalence testing for its similars manufacturers. Because the two countries are comparably wealthy, Argentina has no economic excuse not to increase regulation on similars as Brazil has done. My ongoing analysis of such medicines leads me to believe similars have far greater variability than proven generics and are a public health threat. Maximilliano Derecho of the Argentinian Anticounterfeit Medicines Program indicated to me in September 2008 that while he considered the quality of all legitimately made Argentinian medicines as good, having many small producers did provide opportunities for increased infiltration of fake products. Indeed, twenty-two thousand Argentineans die each year as a result of consuming counterfeit and adulterated medicines, according to a recent official report of the Argentine Union of Pharmacists and Biochemists.[10]

When regulators such as Derecho talk about similars producers, they have to be very careful in their wording, because many of these legal producers make good-quality products; they just are not as consistent as larger generics producers. The costs of consistently producing high-quality drugs are significant, and some firms choose not to ensure them. Brazil's innovation is to be open about what is happening. Wealthier countries have done what Brazil is doing, but they often did it covertly while increasing the enforcement of regulations over time to ensure more consistently good products.

Perhaps similars provide greater avenues for fakes to enter. Whatever the cause, Brazil does have a problem with fakes. About two hundred unplanned pregnancies occurred in 1998 when a test batch of oral contraceptives made by Schering do Brasil that contained wheat flour in place of active ingredient was stolen, packaged as if it were real, and sold.[11] Schering executives covered up the theft.

Peru. Emerging markets differ considerably in the length of time they take to register drugs. While the average evaluation period ranges from three to six months in poorer countries to twelve to eighteen months in middle-income countries, drug approvals in Peru are determined within just seven days. This is much faster than even the fast-track registration offered by some countries for priority drugs, which still takes at least one month. How is Peru able to achieve this incredible feat? Unfortunately, it is not through an efficient and well-managed regulatory system, but through negligence on the part of a government more concerned with moving drugs through the system than providing thorough oversight. In Peru, if a drug application has not been evaluated within seven days of its receipt, it is registered automatically. There may be many products on the market that regulator DIGIMED cannot be sure work properly.

A tragic case currently under investigation in Peru demonstrates some of the pitfalls of this system. Oncologist Dr. Raul Cordero of the National Institute of Neoplastic Disease administered methotrexate to five children suffering from lymphatic leukemia. The drug caused an adverse effect to the central nervous system and induced a coma in all five cases. Four of the children died. The fathers of three of the children sued the clinic and AC Farma, the company that made the drug, but the health minister declared after a brief government investigation that no negligence could be proven. Cordero had the samples analyzed and found a high percentage of impurities, which likely caused the children's deaths. AC Farma confirmed this finding but emphatically rejected that the drugs were made by the company—in other words, AC Farma argued that the product was a fake.

Elizabeth Carmelino Garcia is a senior official at DIGIMED. I spoke with her briefly in 2008, before I knew of Cordero's case. She impressed me as someone really pushing her organization to aggressively fight fakes. But like every other regulator I have spoken with, she did not want to address local producers that might cut corners.

Although the methotrexate could have been fake, that seems unlikely, given that DIGIMED does not appear to be conducting an investigation into where the "fake" methotrexate originated. In addition, an informed medical source not associated with AC Farma but close to the case indicated this tragedy was the result of a substandard drug problem, not a case of counterfeiting. This source said the suspect product was supplied in the normal way, the packaging is perfect, the batch numbers are correct, and the drug even contains the right amount of API. If it is a fake, it is the best he has ever seen. The more likely explanation is that the suspect samples were made by AC Farma, which either made a one-time mistake in production or systematically cuts corners to turn a bigger profit. Whatever the cause, patients died.

In response to this and many other previously documented cases of adverse drug reactions in cancer patients, cancer sufferers staged a peaceful protest in late 2010 demanding that DIGIMED enact adequate regulations regarding the distribution and sale of certain medicines that are not tested for quality, safety, and efficacy. The cancer patients noted that not only do these drugs present a danger for them but they also contribute to an increasing distrust of the entire health care system. Patients who are not treated effectively may look to bogus remedies or seek "better" treatment overseas, something only the rich can afford.

As if recognizing this parlous state of affairs, the Peruvian Congress passed a law in 2009 that extends the amount of time before immediate registration from the current situation of one week to a far more realistic six months, but at the time of writing, it had not been properly enforced.[12]

Colombia and Its Different Kind of Drug War. For at least four decades Colombia has been synonymous with the costly war against narcotics. But it was a different kind of drug war that brought me to Bogotá in July 2011—the fight against counterfeit and substandard pharmaceuticals.

Cocaine with a street value of over a billion dollars is trafficked from Colombia to West Africa every year, where most of it makes its way into Europe. But less well known is that in the opposite direction goes a small but increasing amount of fake pharmaceuticals. Such bogus medicines harm the lives of Colombians, probably in increasing numbers. Yet shipments coming from West Africa are tiny compared with the tens of thousands of chemicals and treatments that arrive mostly from China. The fake products are then packaged in Colombia or imported after being packaged in neighboring states, especially Venezuela and, to a lesser extent, Ecuador and Peru.

In June 2001, the general director of Colombia's National Institute for the Supervision of Medications and Foods, Dr. Miguel Rueda, estimated that 10 percent of the $1.2 billion worth of Colombia's annual medicine sales were counterfeit. Over the next few years the agency confiscated hundreds of tons of adulterated, relabeled, stolen, contraband, and counterfeit medicines. It discovered counterfeit manufacturing operations in Bogotá, where workers were producing over twenty thousand counterfeit pills of a flu drug, a generic aspirin, and a popular painkiller every day. At least thirty-eight illegal laboratories producing fake drugs were dismantled up to 2005, with the agency finding fake medicines made of flour, sugar, boric acid, and cement lime. Since then hundreds of small-scale processing facilities have been shuttered.

One of the reasons for so much domestic production is that in 1968, the Colombian government established the Institute of Advanced Chemical Research as part of the Universidad Nacional de Colombia in Bogotá. Unfortunately, some of the highly trained chemists who emerged were later attracted to work in the Medellín and Cali cocaine cartels. And some adapted their skills to formulate fake or otherwise illegal medicines.

To make tons of cocaine requires tons of precursor chemicals, so the Cali cartel established a chain of pharmacies in 1990s to cover their chemical purchases. Cali is a very dispersed organization, and according to one foreign investigator of Chinese chemical exports, some of its cells are being supplied with chemicals likely to be made into medicines, not for use in cocaine processing. It is therefore quite likely Cali is selling its own medicines, through pharmacies, and it is unlikely these products are up to the standards required, even if they include the correct ingredients.

In 2003 the U.S. Food and Drug Administration estimated that as much as 40 percent of manufactured drugs in Colombia were counterfeit. The Association of Colombian Pharmaceutical Industries thought this figure was way too high, claiming that only 5 percent were contraband, counterfeit, or substandard, and thanks to the efforts of the National Institute for the Supervision of Medications and Foods, the figure today is probably around or below 5 percent, but no one really knows.

Seizures of medicines grab the media headlines, but just as dangerous to patients are the many drugs past their sell-by date that are bought in neighboring countries such as Peru, Ecuador, and Venezuela and are then repackaged in Colombia with a different expiry date and sold to illegal dealers. Columbia also has an increasing problem with substandard medicines. In 2007, the last year for which full data are available, forty-three lots of medicines, from analgesics to antidepressants, failed to meet quality standards and were destroyed.

Dr. Gustavo Campillo, a physician from Medellín who works with patient advocacy groups, explained to me how poor patients even sell their medicines back into the supply chain to support their families, and these drugs may be sold on under poor conditions, leading to product deterioration. But much worse than this are the blanket reimbursement schemes that have price caps on certain medications, which means that for some diseases, only the cheapest, often inferior, medicines are available.

One of the reasons that fake-medicine trading and substandard medicines are prevalent is because the penalties for trafficking narcotics are far higher than those for counterfeiting medicines. In 2001 the head of corporate security for Novartis, Jim Christian, commented: "If you get caught with a pound of cocaine, you can expect to do serious time. But if you are found with counterfeit medicines, you might do only six months." Since 2001, penalties have increased, and fakers can go to jail for up to eight years now. But as is the problem in most emerging markets, enforcement is uneven, and those able to bribe and threaten are more likely to escape punishment. This makes the highly profitable counterfeit medicine industry attractive to organized Colombian cocaine traffickers.

Even the paramilitary FARC, which has up to twenty thousand combatants, may be making money from fake drugs, according to one local security expert who didn't want to be named. FARC's involvement is apparently widespread, because agents of FARC were, according to Egyptian intelligence in 2009, buying fake breast cancer medicines and other drugs in the Middle East.

Colombian authorities, spearheaded by excellent leadership at the Ministry of Health and the National Institute for the Supervision of Medications and Foods, hope to increase enforcement efforts—opening up a new and winnable war on the traders of lethal products. After all, cocaine can wreck lives, but the people buying cocaine want cocaine. People buying medicine want, often desperately need, what it contains; they do not want a fake or substandard version.

Southeast Asia

Thailand. Oxford professor Paul Newton alerted me to his team's astonishing forensic study documenting the movement of counterfeit medicines from China to nearby Cambodia, Laos, Burma, Thailand, and Vietnam. The products in this study were all fake versions of Artesunate.[13] In the counterfeit samples they collected at the retail level, the tablets or capsules contained no active ingredients or merely derisory, subtherapeutic amounts. Not only do these products cause illness and death—particularly among children, who are most affected by malaria—but they also can promote artesunate resistance in the malaria parasite in the long run, destroying the clinical efficacy of the genuine drug and undermining the confidence of the public and health care workers in drug treatments of all sorts. Both consequences are catastrophic in public-health terms. I have mentioned this before in the book, but it is worth repeating given that it is such a grave problem. Box 8-1 explores additional public health problems Thailand has encountered.

We came across no fake Artesunate in our sampling from Bangkok, though. I spoke with Wimon Suwankaesawong, a senior pharmacist at the Thai FDA, and it seems that Thailand has done a good job of preventing fake antimalarials from entering much of the legitimate supply chain. But from talking to doctors outside the capital, it was easy to see how devastating the few fakes that make it through can be in this part of the world, where drug resistance is already an issue.

Bangkok still has problems (one of which is discussed in box 8-1). While I was there in 2008, a huge amount of fake Viagra was seized from pharmacies and drugstores in the Yaowarat area of Bangkok. News articles alarmed citizens that 93 percent of all purchased Viagra was fake in the capital. Surely this was an exaggeration, but more detailed and believable

---

Box 8-1
THAILAND'S GPO-VIR

Thailand has a state-owned Government Pharmaceutical Organization, or GPO. In 2002 the auditor general, Jaruvan Maintake, said, "The purchase of drugs through GPO . . . gives officials the chance to reap personal benefits. . . . The drug-purchasing process becomes un-transparent, inefficient and wastes money."[1] The GPO facilities manufactured an HIV treatment called GPO-vir, which did not pass the World Health Organization's manufacturing standards and never proved bioequivalence. Lembit Rago, WHO's coordinator of drug quality and safety, put it starkly, "Nobody would buy an airplane without wings. . . . Drugs should be treated the same way. But with drugs it's difficult to understand what makes them up to a certain standard of quality because there are so many elements involved. In certain cases, minor things are wrong, and in some major things. Drugs that are not pre-qualified [WHO approved] may not directly kill people, but they could foster resistance to AIDS drugs."[2]

A 2005 study by Thailand's Mahidol University's faculty of medicine found that GPO-vir had between 39.6 percent and 58 percent resistance in the 300 patients investigated. This result is perhaps the worst case of HIV drug resistance in the world. These patients should already have moved to second-line treatment—the next generation of drugs—which requires expensive hospitalization.

Drug resistance is almost certainly contributing to rising costs, as some patients receive high-quality patented second-line drugs. Yet, when I last looked at the subject, over 100,000 Thai patients were on GPO-vir. Of these, approximately one-fifth have already developed a resistance to the medication encouraged by the substandard product.

---

1. Daniel Ten Kate, "Safe at Any Cost?" *Asia Sentinel*. 24 January 2007.
2. Ibid.

---

stories at the time claimed that the fakes contained less than 50 percent of the genuine active ingredient, while the packaging on most drugs was "near perfect."[14]

I had the impression that drugs in the cities are generally of good quality, but Bangkok reminded me of the general problems Nigeria faces (although Bangkok is a much prettier and wealthier city than Lagos). Thailand has a regulatory authority that seems to be on top of the problem of fakes but able to do little against locally powerful legal manufacturers of suspect medicines. Indeed, no official wanted to discuss any problems with locally made products, including those of the government's own production facilities.

Thai officials do have problems with the area along the Mekong Delta; presumably this is also true of their colleagues in Burma and Cambodia. The delta area boasts so many places selling drugs, and many of them are mobile. Some of my colleagues have described traders in boats selling anything from toiletries to food and drugs. To cut out the fake-drug trade in the delta would require policing an entire river system, and Thai authorities do not have the required manpower to do that. As a result of the river system and other porous parts of the border, experts I spoke with found substandard malaria drugs in ten provinces in Thailand along the Burmese border and in four provinces along the Cambodian border. Samples of tablets taken from the border between Burma and Thailand contained only 3–10 milligrams of Artesunate per tablet; genuine tablets should contain approximately 50 milligrams. In these areas, local pharmacies were the main source of counterfeit and expired drugs.

Malaysia. Mohd Hatta Ahmad, the director of Pharmacy Enforcement at the Ministry of Health, explained to me that in 2005, Malaysia introduced its Meditag program, which required all products registered with the Malaysian Drug Control Authority to bear three layers of holographic security devices. According to Dr. Ahmad, these are difficult to copy. The first layer is fairly obvious and helpful to consumers and pharmacists, the second layer is harder to spot but trained enforcement officers can detect it, and the final layer is only analyzable in the laboratory.

Pharmacies have decoder units designed to be placed on store counters or shelves with instructions on their use. Pharmacists and consumers are encouraged to check the authenticity of a given medicine's Meditag by sliding the medicine pack under the decoder unit. Consumers are also encouraged to verify the registration numbers of the medicines by checking with the pharmacy enforcement branch of the ministry or by visiting its website.[15] In addition to enabling consumers to police their own purchases, Meditag has buttressed local law enforcement. Some of Malaysia's three hundred roving enforcement officers are equipped with portable readers.

According to Deputy Defense Minister Datuk Dr. Abdul Latiff Ahmad, in 2007 the Malaysian government estimated that at least 5 percent of all medicines on the market were fakes. In 2006, $2.2 million worth of fake medicines and beauty products were seized by the Malaysian Health Ministry over the course of 12,362 raids.[16] Commonly counterfeited products include erectile dysfunction and psychotropic medicines.[17] Malaysian customs officials made their largest drug bust ever in March of 2007 when they seized 142 boxes (1.4 million pills), worth $4 million, of fake Viagra. Minister of Health Chua Soi Lek claimed that the medication, deceptively labeled "Miagra," originated in Singapore.[18] In the first half of 2008, law enforcement officials seized $17,000 worth of unregistered pharmaceuticals in fourteen raids.[19]

In September 2008, the Malaysian government also proposed a new bill to combat pharmaceutical counterfeiters, urging the inclusion of heavier fines and mandatory jail sentences to current penalties.[20] The bill came out of roundtable discussions held under the auspices of the Special Taskforce to Combat Counterfeit Products, a unit established that year and overseen by the Ministry of Domestic Trade and Consumer Affairs and by the Pharmaceutical Association of Malaysia.[21]

Though these efforts have had some positive impact on the fake-drug trade, the problem persists. In fact, Meditag shows that even with government-backed tracking systems, if traders want to infiltrate emerging markets they are quite capable of doing so; the tracking system is useful for providing evidence to convict those caught, but doesn't seem to deter the most determined criminals. In 2009 seizures of fake medicine totaled $1.4 million, nearly double the amount in 2008.[22]

Turkey

Other than Internet samples from the European Union and United States, Istanbul, Turkey, was the only place where none of the samples we collected failed quality-control tests. The famed crossroads between the East and West is a huge trading hub, so I expected to find it awash in fake and substandard drugs. There probably are many; we just did not find any. Turkey has a problem with fake drugs, but none of the local security and pharmaceutical experts I spoke with were sure how bad the problem is. Perhaps in keeping with this vibrant city, the drugs that were faked constantly changed, so it was impossible to estimate. Turkey's 77 million people can procure drugs from one of more than 24,000 pharmacies, many of which operate to high standards and are like northern European or U.S. pharmacies, but hundreds are hole-in-the-wall shops with little control over the quality of what they dispense.

Turkish businesses benefit from more than a dozen free-trade zones throughout the country, which allow for a low-tax environment that boosts exports and earns foreign currency. But with the benefits of open trade, particularly light regulation, come the downsides: these zones are easy transit points for fake drugs. According to Cengiz Gumustus, a private investigator working for the pharmaceutical industry and former officer for both the Turkish police and Interpol, these trade zones pose a major threat. Mersin, a free-trade zone in southern Turkey, and two zones near Istanbul have major problems with substandard drugs. He says anything of high value will be faked. Investigators think fakes are coming from all over (notably Russia, India, and especially China) and leave Istanbul for Europe and the Middle East.

The Turkish government has made various attempts to limit the trade, notably by banning Internet drug sales. My own ongoing research shows that Turkish products are widely available via Internet purchase. Local investigators were surprised by this finding because they did not think Turkish drugs would be sold as far afield as the United States. In a sampling of drugs purchased over the Internet in the United States (which I discuss in the next chapter), more packages came from Turkey than any other location. These were Turkish-made products from multinational companies, and they were of obviously high quality. With such vast trade flowing through Istanbul, though, Gumustus says there are plenty of opportunities for unscrupulous suppliers to provide substandard products to the market.

On October 19, 2008, the Istanbul Financial Crimes Department concluded the initial phase of a major operation called Aci Recete (Bitter Prescription) with a series of raids on suspected purveyors of counterfeit drugs. It raided seven dozen targets in Istanbul—including offices, houses, warehouses, and pharmacists—along with sixteen locations in Ankara, Batman, Konya, and Samsun.

Seventy-seven people were arrested in Istanbul alone for threats to public health, various types of fraud, and document forgery. The perpetrators were involved in all aspects of the counterfeit drugs trade and included importers and local manufacturers of counterfeit products, wholesale distributors who were repackaging fake and old medicines (which should have been destroyed), and printers making packaging for the manufacturers. Down the chain, pharmacists, doctors, and nurses were also involved in the scam. It seemed as though no part of the health care system was exempt from corruption. In total, police seized four truckloads of fake or expired pharmaceuticals, large amounts of paperwork, and other printed materials. Over three dozen arrests were made in other parts of Turkey.[23] The Turkish authorities arrested an additional sixty-eight counterfeiters in 2008, which put them fourth on the global list compiled by the Pharmaceutical Security Institute. Only China, South Korea, and Brazil made more arrests.[24]

I was in Istanbul in September 2009 to participate in the launch of the Turkish Ministry of Health's new system (quite similar to Malaysia's Meditag system) to curtail fake drugs: a bar scanner for pharmacists to track drug packages coming from wholesalers (the place where most fakes infiltrate the supply chain). When I arrived at the hotel holding the press conference, I learned that the minister was not coming; the plan was on hold because of cost concerns raised by the pharmacists. The members of the media I talked with at the largely aborted press event in September 2009 were not surprised; previous attempts had also failed.

If Turkish authorities manage to roll out the barcode-tracking system for all pharmaceutical products, it should provide the ability to track products from entry into the country (or production in the country) through the point of sale. At each point along the way the barcode must be scanned with information held on a centralized computer system by legitimate manufacturers. Such a barcode system can be costly, and industry manufacturers and wholesalers I spoke with estimated that it has cost them over $200 million. Some of the smaller pharmacists have balked at the cost of the system, about $150 each to purchase a special barcode scanner. The major pharmacists can easily afford this, but for the smallest companies, $150 may be a week's profit. Small-firm lobbying against the barcode system, which is otherwise ready, has delayed the intended launch of the program; at the time of writing, it still has not been implemented. Nonetheless, government officials remain hopeful it will be implemented eventually. If it is, it will help authorities catch some counterfeiters and make prosecuting them easier. This would send a message that Turkey, a middle-income country, is taking the problem seriously.

Turkey still has much to do even if it enacts this tracking system. Its laws are somewhat confusing in relation to counterfeiting and substandard medicines. For example, trading fake drugs is not a crime unless the legitimate producer files an official complaint. Although most producers will happily complain if their products are faked, the law creates a convoluted system that makes the job of the police less clear and puts the onus of preventing counterfeiters on the corporations. It is encouraging that Turkey is moving forward; it provides an example that should be emulated by some of the countries on trade routes to the south and east.

Conclusion

We have seen that there are many unique problems in the emerging markets of Russia, Latin America, Southeast Asia, and Turkey. Many of them relate to problems with the medical regulatory authorities and their oversight, or lack thereof, of product registration and quality control. But there are also some great suggestions (from Brazil's acknowledgment of quality differences to Malaysia's implementation of a tracking system) from which others can learn. Looking at the differences in the systems in place across countries and the different problems they face reminded me of Anna Karenina's statement that happy families are all alike, but every unhappy family is unhappy in its own way.[25]

Similarly, drug regulatory systems in developed countries are not identical, but they are often very similar and usually do identical things. There is a far greater degree of variability in the MRAs in emerging markets; some do one thing well, others another. But their failings are often significantly different. The result is decidedly unhappy for the millions who live under regimes that allow small percentages of dangerous products to flourish in their environment.

9

The Online Drug Market

In many respects the battle to combat fake drugs sold over the Internet highlights one of the weaknesses of international law, which is impotent for addressing the international criminal gangs we encountered in earlier chapters, particularly in the Middle East. An example is the case of a Canadian Internet pharmacy, RxNorth.com, that did business selling cheaper "Canadian" (or so it claimed) medicines to U.S. and other global consumers. Pharmaceutical company investigators and journalists in Canada and the United States pieced together that RxNorth.com sourced medicines from China. From there, the medicines went to Hong Kong, the United Arab Emirates, and the Bahamas, and then to the United Kingdom, before finally being mailed to consumers from the United Kingdom with UK postage so as to disguise the circuitous route. RxNorth.com told employees to conceal from customers the fact that their medicines were not from Canada. When the U.S. FDA acquired and tested some RxNorth.com medicines, they found counterfeits, including some lifesaving medicines.[1]

RxNorth.com has since closed. Andrew Strempler, its founder, lost his pharmacy license and left Canada—but probably not before becoming a very rich man. The *Winnipeg Free Press* reports that he was in Panama in February 2010, selling medicines from a free-trade zone on a small Caribbean island.[2] In my own investigations of Internet pharmacies, I found that useless faked Viagra pills were being sold through Panama, most of which came from China. The link may not be coincidental. In early March 2011, I spoke with a pharmacist who knew Strempler. He said he had been a real pharmacist who got greedy. To this day the pharmacist I spoke with says he does not think Strempler meant to cause harm, but that he got sloppy and did not check the drugs he was getting from China. If that is the case, Strempler is not the first to have been lured from the path of right into breaking the moral and legal codes he should have upheld.

The Case for Universal Jurisdiction

It is pretty obvious that those dealing in counterfeits, like RxNorth.com and Strempler, should be investigated. And if the allegations are correct, they should be charged, convicted, and severely punished. "I fully believe we are going to be chased around this globe," Strempler once told the *New York Times*.[3] It was not entirely clear from the *Times* story whether Strempler thought he would be chased by the pharmaceutical industry for trademark violations or by the FBI for committing criminal acts, but in reality he has suffered embarrassment and enjoyed impunity and illegally acquired wealth. Canada has not said if it investigated Strempler and took nearly a decade to strip his pharmacy license. The other countries in the supply chain—the United Arab Emirates, United Kingdom, and the Bahamas—did investigate and in some cases prosecuted the intermediaries, but they all lacked jurisdiction to pursue Strempler and RxNorth.com. A frustrated U.S. FDA spokesman told the *New York Times*, "They are not regulated by the United States because we don't have jurisdiction, they're not regulated from Canada because they are shipping to the Bahamas, and they are not regulated by the UK for the same reason."[4]

To solve this problem, medicine counterfeiters should face the same treatment as in, for example, currency counterfeiting, which has a relevant treaty structured to deny impunity to criminal offenders regardless of nationality or where the crime occurs. Article 18 of the 1929 Convention for the Suppression of Counterfeiting Currency reads that the treaty's crimes "should in each country, without ever being allowed impunity, be defined, prosecuted and punished." Article 9 further says, "Foreigners who have committed abroad any offence [under the treaty] and who are in the territory of a country whose internal legislation recognizes as a general rule the principle of the prosecution of offences committed abroad, should be punishable in the same way as if the offence had been committed in the territory of that country."[5]

Combined, Articles 9 and 18 efface the currency counterfeiter's impunity by deeming that in each country, offenses "committed abroad" are tantamount to offenses "committed in the territory," even when committed by a foreigner.

Were this the state of international law for counterfeit medicines—and that is no radical suggestion, because it has been the law for counterfeit currency for over eighty years—then Strempler's impunity in Canada would not have mattered, and he could have been tracked down and punished by the United Arab Emirates, United Kingdom, the Bahamas, or the United States. But he was not, and he is openly carrying on business to this day. (I will return to international law, or the lack thereof, in part IV.)

Internet Pharmacies: Are the Benefits Worth the Costs?

My interest in Internet pharmacies had been piqued long before the Strempler case came to light. By 2006, such pharmacies had become a political football punted between large pharmaceutical interests and those wanting to allow U.S. citizens to import cheap medicines.

The pharmaceutical industry had the best of the economic arguments: having markets tiered by price such that wealthier countries pay more for drugs than poorer ones is both efficient and equitable. As a corollary, preventing wholesale importation of cheaper drugs into the United States, known as parallel trade, is important because the United States is one of the wealthier countries. But of course not everyone is rich; by some counts, forty million Americans do not have medical insurance and pay out-of-pocket for any drugs they buy. Others have insurance that does not cover the full cost of some of their most expensive medicines. This is a key reason for the demand for drugs from overseas. For at least a decade, U.S. seniors have taken bus trips to Canada to buy medicines, for although Canada is almost as rich as the United States on a per-capita basis, its government caps the price of medicines so prices are lower. What started as bus trips morphed over the past decade into Internet sales from foreign pharmacies.[a]

Pharmaceutical company interests in the United States were quick to point out that such sales undermine the tiered-price approach; they were worried because greater quantities of low-cost drugs could be sold over the Internet than would be purchased on bus tours. Pharmaceutical companies probably had not been too worried that not all of the seniors taking the bus

---

a. The array of products for sale on bogus websites is remarkable. I've seen Viagra commercials for "professional," "super active," "soft tab," and even "pink Viagra for women," none of which are reflections of the real product. But then these sellers are not selling a real product, but the appearance of a real product.

tours were the uninsured poor; many could have paid more. They were concerned that the market was expanding to anyone with Internet access, and they also saw that there were potential liability issues related to Internet purchasing. Many of the drugs purchased over the Internet were for consumers who should not have taken them (powerful painkillers or dangerous diet pills from Brazil) or were for conditions patients were too embarrassed to discuss with their doctors (drugs for erectile dysfunction, hair loss, or depression). Fearing a loss of profits on expensive lifestyle medications, and worried that increases in Internet imports might encourage wider changes in policy, the pharmaceutical industry defended its turf.

A Study of Credentials

It is certainly legitimate to worry about the quality of drugs from web drug sellers, especially since it is rarely obvious whether a seller is a pharmacy or something less qualified. As in many instances where an obvious market deficiency exists, an entrepreneur stepped in to provide a solution. Both the U.S. National Association of the Boards of Pharmacy and private entities such as Pharmacy Checker (www.pharmacychecker.com) began credentialing web pharmacies. The difference between the two groups is essentially that the National Association of the Boards of Pharmacy only credentials web pharmacies based in the United States, whereas Pharmacy Checker will credential pharmacies from overseas as long as they are registered pharmacies in their own countries and have been investigated at least once by Pharmacy Checker. Both groups perform random checks through covertly buying from the various sites to check that they are still operating to high standards.

Still, industry interests continued to argue that Internet-sourced drugs from outside the United States were dangerous, so I decided to investigate whether their concerns were valid or whether they were promoting a largely bogus safety argument because it was likely to be more effective at preventing inexpensive imports than a theoretical economic argument.

I expected many of the drugs we procured from web pharmacies would be bogus. Like many people, I had misunderstood the statement made by the WHO that half of all web pharmacies sold suspect products. If that were true, buying from the Internet could be like Russian roulette. When I pulled out the old WHO report to check the facts, I discovered a critical caveat had been dropped from most media reports I had read. The WHO identified the dangerous sites as those that had concealed their identity and address; of these sites, half supplied suspect products.[6]

Even with this new clarification, I suspected we would find a lot of dangerous drugs. To test the various credentialing organizations, my then research assistant Karen Porter and I designed a stratified sampling of web pharmacies. We categorized pharmacies approved by the National Association of the Boards of Pharmacy and Pharmacy Checker, those approved by Pharmacy Checker alone (primarily foreign-listed web pharmacies), those not supported by anyone but without any known concerns, and those thought to be suspect.

Every credentialed web pharmacy should have demanded an original prescription from me because I was the patient (or covert shopper) for the sites. My intent was to act like any other shopper, but I was going to be lazy in the way any patient might be. If I could get away with not sending in a prescription, I would do so. Similarly, if I could use the same prescription more than once, I would. A friendly physician, with approval of his state health board, consulted with me on the project. He gave me numerous prescriptions in varying dosage amounts to make it easier to buy from certain web pharmacies that only sell in large (ninety-day supply) product batches. He also agreed to speak with any pharmacist who might call him to confirm the prescription.

I was afraid some of these pharmacies were fronting illegal operations other than counterfeit pharmaceuticals, so I established a new bank account and debit card and alerted the fraud early warning department at Citibank of my project, requesting that they monitor unusual activity. I also established a new e-mail address to use solely for these purchases in the hope that spam to my regular e-mail accounts would not increase enormously.

Credentialed Sites Are Safe, but Buyer Beware (of Junk Mail)

Armed with the prescriptions, a new e-mail identity, and a new debit card, I started buying medicines online. Most of the credentialed pharmacies did what I expected and demanded original prescriptions. To be able to assess each of the samples procured, we had to establish a baseline standard to compare them against. To do this required high-quality samples of each drug used to establish a spectral profile for each product. Because each spectrum is unique to each specific formulation of the product, I had asked for the prescriptions to demand no generic substitutes. Four of the five drugs are still under patent, so there are no generics for sale in the United States. I assumed the Internet pharmacies would comply with my requests. I was wrong. A few substituted generic sertraline hydrochloride instead of the brand-name Zoloft I had ordered. Because the spectrum is unique, the generic would not pass the spectral comparison even if the drug were bioequivalent (a bioequivalent product can have different dyes and inert compounds, which would throw a slightly different spectrum). Although one can assess whether the active ingredient is present in a copy version of any innovator drug, one cannot be absolutely sure the drug is a perfect copy (a generic), so we were unable to test every sample we received to the standard established for this study.

Some of the uncredentialed sites either did not demand prescriptions or accepted faxed copies, which allowed me to order from numerous sites with the same prescriptions. Indeed, I did this as often as I could and was able to buy from at least eight pharmacies with the same prescription for Viagra. Some of the sites made me fill out questionnaires; I failed to do so accurately in some instances and was gratified to receive a call from one website that told me I should not be buying Viagra if I had an abnormal electrocardiogram. Once I assured them I had just checked the wrong box, they happily sold me the drug (see figure 9-1 below).

FIGURE 9-1

Fake Viagra mailed from China

It should come as no surprise that other than the generic substitutions, every single pill from a U.S. credentialed site passed authentication. In addition, every sample from credentialed sites from overseas also passed (and the drugs were often, but not always, noticeably cheaper). The results for other sites were more interesting. For the most part, even these sites sold good-quality drugs, although they substituted more drugs than the U.S. sites because of where they were selling from: Italy, Germany, Australia, New Zealand, India, Sweden, Turkey, and Canada. Legal copies of the five drugs may exist in these countries. As if to confirm WHO findings, only those sites that did not have a physical address provided me with drugs that failed quality tests, and then, only of Viagra (but that was the only one of the five drugs I was ordering that they sold). Even some of these web sellers without physical addresses provided exactly what I asked for, even though the lack of an address meant I had no chance of following up if they had not delivered the products requested.

In summary, in the free-for-all of uncredentialed, nonlicensed pharmacies, there was danger; some sites did not send products as agreed, and some sent entirely bogus products made with chalk and road paint, among other ingredients. Other products came via highly circuitous routes. I purchased one batch of drugs from a "Canadian" website; given the packaging, the drugs were made in China, but they were sent from Austria, and the money debited from my account was sent to Panama. The Citibank fraud department could not provide me any more information without a court order.

I am not a technically savvy person, and I do not know how complex web entities may operate. I am aware that firms such as Google "know" where your computers are and tailor advertising to match. I am writing this sentence from La Jolla, and when I open Google I see advertisements for local shops in La Jolla and San Diego. So it is of no surprise to me that I now receive far more spam than before, not just to the new e-mail address I established but to all of my e-mail accounts. I probably should have registered the new debit card at a new address, but I thought that was being overcautious, and also that is not a straightforward action, especially to provide a matching phone number. I also had several calls from web pharmacies ensuring that the person receiving drugs at the address was in fact me, the person who had ordered them, and as a result, I now receive far more junk mail. Thus far my identity has not been stolen.[b]

After analyzing the drug data, we published an article in the *Public Library of Science One*, a peer-reviewed journal.[7] See table 9-1 for the

---

b. It is interesting that, with an estimated four million Americans buying drugs online, criminals must have a vast repository of useful information from which they can make not only illegal drug sales but also other gains at the expense of innocent citizens.

Table 9-1

SPECTROMETRY TESTING RESULTS BY DRUG TYPE
AND WEBSITE PHARMACY CLASSIFICATION

	Website classification	Number received	Number in testable form	Percent that failed testing	
Lipitor	NABP Approved	7	7		
	PC Approved	24	24		
	Not Recommended	6	6		
	Combined Total	37	37		
Viagra	NABP Approved	7	7		
	PC Approved	24	24		
	Not Recommended	17	14	8.30%	(2/24)
	Unidentifiable	20	12	25%	(3/12)
	Combined Total	68	57	8.80%	(5/57)
Celebrex	NABP Approved	7	7		
	PC Approved	24	24		
	Not Recommended	6	6		
	Combined Total	37	37		
Nexium	NABP Approved	7	7		
	PC Approved	21	12		
	Not Recommended	7	4		
	Combined Total	35	23		
Zoloft	NABP Approved	7	6		
	PC Approved	24	14		
	Not Recommended	8	6		
	Combined Total	39	26		
Unknown	Unidentifiable	3	0		
TOTAL	NABP Approved	35	34		
	PC Approved	117	98		
	Not Recommended	44	36	6%	(2/36)
	Unidentifiable	23	12	16.70%	(2/12)
	Combined Total	219	180	2.80%	(5/180)

SOURCES: National Association of Boards of Pharmacy (NABP); Pharmcy Checker (PC).

summary results. I was firmly convinced then, and remain so to this day, that buying drugs over the Internet can be dangerous if one is careless, but it does not need to be. Internet purchasers should follow a simple protocol and use sites credentialed in the United States or in a limited selection of other countries.

Technically, it was illegal for me to buy drugs from overseas over the Internet, but it is FDA policy not to enforce the law for individuals buying for personal use for serious medical conditions, as long as the medicine is for a ninety-day supply or less. In other words, they know that enforcing the law could make criminals of hundreds of thousands, possibly millions, of Americans (four million buy online, and a substantial percentage of these buy from overseas). Any law abused this much and ethically dubious in that it denies poor people access to lifesaving medicines should probably be changed; if sustained, the act of limited personal importation at least should be decriminalized.

Several efforts have been made in Congress to address this ongoing problem. Congressmen Byron Dorgan (D-ND) and Ron Paul (R-TX) have both introduced legislation recently to allow U.S. citizens to import pharmaceuticals through Internet purchases. Such a law has not been adopted, and to date the industry has been able to sustain enough votes to block these efforts. But while industry succeeds in preventing legal Internet importation in the short run, it may be harming related efforts in the long run. It is not true that anti-industry advocates are homogenous, but they do talk, and their collective opposition is strengthened when industry acts myopically.

PART III

Drug-Quality Assessments

10

Factors to Consider for Research

As I mentioned at the beginning of this book, I became convinced that drug quality was a major problem when I first came across fake drugs in 2004. At that time I was researching drug quality in southern Africa and parts of Asia and had discovered numerous problems. Doctors in Zimbabwe and South Africa whom I met while writing stories about HIV, medicine use, and court fights over patent rights were concerned that the HIV medications they were giving patients were not working. It was obvious to them that this was not a drug-resistance problem: drugs with no history of treatment failure simply were not performing at all for many patients, while other batches of the same drug were working fine.

At roughly the same time, the brilliant work of two Oxford professors, Paul Newton and Nick White, respectively based in Laos and Thailand, exposed a lethal trade in counterfeit antimalarials along the Mekong River. These scientists documented increasing drug resistance along the Thai, Cambodia, and Burma border areas due to poor-quality antimalarials that were traded in the region in growing volumes. This pioneer work highlighted the threat posed by one particular drug type, but its applicability was regionally limited.[1]

I began to search for comprehensive data detailing the scope of the problem, and I found the data distressingly sparse. WHO first started paying attention to the issue in 1982, when it apparently started collecting data. Interest from Western companies really started in the early 1990s with the formation of the Pharmaceutical Security Initiative, which became the Pharmaceutical Security Institute in 1996. The institute operates a bit like Sherlock Holmes by doing the legwork, finding the guilty party, and then letting law enforcement take the credit. But it is also quite a secret organization that expects us to believe its dire warnings without access to its considerable database.

With these inaccessible exceptions, in most instances data were unreliable, and reporting followed no discernible pattern. Most available data came from press reports and were most concerned with presenting a sensational story about a specific drug bust and not rigorous scientific methodology. Reporting highlighted crowd-pleasing counterfeiting stories, often ignored caveats they should have included, and often failed to acknowledge the more subtle dangers that substandard medications posed. These dangers are rarely understood, but they also were not acknowledged in many cases because the victims are usually very poor and largely voiceless. The counterfeit and the more newsworthy pharmaceutical crime stories are reported in detail in the online materials associated with this book.

Prior to 2009, the most comprehensive data available were published by the WHO's IMPACT initiative.[2] In 2009 these data were withdrawn due to widespread interpretation problems. For example, commentators quoted data on antimalarials in one city as though they were a comprehensive study of a countrywide problem for all drugs. IMPACT, however, never intended people to assume that the data were representative or directly comparable across all drug types or across all countries.

Since 2005, I have explored possible methods to measure drug quality in poorer countries and have become personally involved in assessing the problem. From 2007, my prime concern was identifying drugs that present a public-health threat rather than assessing which drugs are strictly legal. As a result, most of my team's research focused on measuring the quality, rather than the origin, of medications. That does not mean I did not pay attention to trademarks and other labeling on products. Visual inspection (as the various illustrations in this book have demonstrated) is often the fastest and certainly the cheapest method of finding falsified and possibly counterfeit products.

Bringing a Medicine to Market

The following paragraphs briefly outline the complicated process medicines must pass through before they reach the market. Because my concern is primarily with public health, a brief overview of this process is followed by a synopsis of the methods commonly used to ensure the quality of medicines that reach the marketplace.

Bringing a new medicine to market is an extremely long, expensive, and involved process. Pharmaceutical companies undertake research and development on thousands of compounds, and hundreds enter the testing phase. Companies may spend months obtaining proper ethical approvals prior to the beginning of full clinical trials on a specific compound. Clinical trials are extremely expensive and time-consuming. Some patients react adversely even to successful and broadly benign and beneficial medications, so drug regulators have developed detailed parameters defining a "successful" drug.

Once a drug is approved, other manufacturers may be able to produce a similar product using identical API, depending on technical ability and licensing agreements. Before the drug can be marketed legally, generic manufacturers must prove that the drug is bioequivalent and equally bioavailable to humans as the original product. Although nowhere near as expensive or time-consuming as clinical trials, establishing bioequivalence and bioavailability is a detailed process requiring well-trained staff, sophisticated laboratories, and ethical approvals for human testing.

A drug is considered bioequivalent and bioavailable if it can dissolve into the aqueous medium of our bodies (solubility) and be transported between the cells (permeability). Many API are neither readily soluble nor permeable and must be manufactured in a very specific way in order to ensure bioequivalence and bioavailability. Drugs with highly soluble and permeable API may be granted biowaivers that enable their manufacturers to avoid bioequivalence/bioavailability testing.

Once a drug is bioequivalence/bioavailability approved or a biowaiver is granted, manufacturers may still have to demonstrate that their drugs are chemically and physically stable for other authorities in other countries if they seek to market the drug internationally. Assessing this detailed chemical content requires sophisticated equipment and a reasonable level of laboratory skill, but it is cheap enough that even the smallest legitimate pharmaceutical companies of the developing world can undertake to meet these requirements.

Testing Drugs for Quality

Once a drug reaches the market, tests to assess chemical content and physical stability can be undertaken again to assess product quality of suspect products. The majority of these tests are performed in the laboratory of a university science department or a developing country's department of health. In most countries, at least one laboratory in the capital city possesses equipment, such as for HPLC, to assess suspect drugs effectively.

HPLC and other, more complex techniques are required for detailed product assessments, especially when looking for minor quality deviations (products narrowly failing a detailed technical monograph provided by the innovator for each product). Even minor deviations in a drug's chemical makeup, which are difficult to detect, can have devastating effects on patients. To pass quality tests, API concentration must be between 95 and 105 percent of the monograph specification (some countries allow greater variation of between 90 and 110 percent). Experts have established that pills that contain API within a 5 to 10 percent variation of the expected dose will still function effectively. In other words, if a product we test contains only 89.4 percent of API, it will fail the test.

One added benefit of using sophisticated techniques to maintain quality control is that these techniques may provide information that helps intelligence officials arrest criminal producers. In a famous example involving technical assistance from Professors Newton and White, tiny traces of pollen were found in a fake antimalarial drug that helped investigators pinpoint the production location to a specific region in China. This evidence was used to assist in the capture and trial of some of the counterfeiters.

The cost of maintaining quality-control systems is high. Basic equipment can cost more than $100,000 and may require consistent maintenance by technically skilled staff. It is a regular and sad occurrence in many poor countries for expensive equipment to sit idle because local staff were unable to maintain machinery and replace simple parts. Each assay undertaken in these labs is not cheap, and mistakes are easy to make. Testing must be executed by a well-trained laboratory technician or knowledgeable official.

Expensive tests using HPLC equipment are not required to assess whether a product has the right basic materials in roughly the right concentrations, however. Simpler techniques enable staff with minimal training to spot poorly made products or well-made products that have degraded over time (perhaps sold after their expiration date, a classic trick of the counterfeit trade). Many products manufactured using shoddy production systems, impure inputs, or poor equipment can be detected with older and simpler technologies. The following techniques, which provide fast, cheap product screening, have only recently been deployed widely in the fight against faulty drugs.

The Minilab

Patrick Lukulay, a drug-quality expert at U.S. Pharmacopeia, introduced me to the Global Pharma Health Fund Minilab. As described earlier (see box 4-3), the Minilab was developed with the explicit aim of providing cheap and fairly easy assessments of drug quality for developing countries. Minilab protocol includes a variety of tests thoughtfully selected to provide a comprehensive assessment of each pill's authenticity and effectiveness. As we saw, the Minilab has already proven extraordinarily successful in countries such as Nigeria, where it has revolutionized the drug-monitoring system in both rural and urban areas at a relatively low cost.

The first phase of the protocol explains how to visually inspect products and check for irregularities often associated with counterfeit product packaging. Although this sounds simple, it actually requires a lot of patience, product knowledge, and skill to be able to tell well-disguised counterfeit packaging from real versions (see box 5-1, "Ciprotab," on page 136).

The two, sometimes three, second-phase tests attempt to establish product stability. First, a drug is tested for basic product disintegration: to be soluble in the body, it should disintegrate in water of body temperature relatively quickly, so this test begins the process of assessing solubility. Then, technicians assay the drug for API. Some of the products can be tested with a simple dye test for the presence of API. For this, the pill is usually crushed and placed in a test tube; when a solvent is added, a specific color is expected to indicate presence of API. Dye tests do not test for concentration, though, so drugs with a small amount of API can pass these tests (the Kamogra [fake Viagra] in box 5-3 would fall into this category as it contains some sildenafil but not enough). The final step is "semiquantitative" because the interpretation of the results is something of an art form. The Minilab thin-layer chromatography result is a blob on a chromatographic plate that must correspond to the size, color, and position of the reference control sample. Needless to say, this technique allows much greater room for interpretation than HPLC tests. With experience, one can interpret the blob quite accurately, but the test is semiquantitative because it does not yield a percentage or confidence interval. When results are difficult to interpret, the Minilab protocol suggests that the suspect product be tested by HPLC or another, more sophisticated technique.[a] With colleagues based in the United Kingdom and South Africa, I used Africa Fighting Malaria's Minilabs to make such basic assessments from mid-2007 through the summer of 2011 (see figure 10-1).

FIGURE 10-1

Roger Bate learning to use the Minilab in 2007

Handheld Spectrometers

Around the time my research team started experimenting with the Minilab, I also came across two handheld technologies: the Raman spectrometer and the near-infrared spectrometer. These machines rapidly and accurately authenticate a drug by scanning a pill's contents against a known good-quality version of the same product, assuming one exists. One assessment in Nigeria found over 260 antimalarial brands on sale, so finding authentic versions of each one is harder than you might think. Because the products are scanned, one need not break the blister packaging or crush pills to assess products. Rapid, noninvasive testing is encouraging the use of these spectrometers for myriad uses, such as by the Nigerian drug regulator discussed in chapter 4. Like the Minilab, handheld spectrometers have their limitations. In addition to being expensive (around $50,000 for one in 2010), they have other flaws. The details of these flaws will become apparent below (see box 10-1), but for product authentication, the spectrometers are as accurate as HPLC and other detailed laboratory tests, and they are invaluable tools in the public-health arena.

a. But even HPLC cannot do all tests even on API that one might want. For example, one could do the following, given time, budget, skill, and equipment: identity assay, which is easy to do and is done by TLC and HPLC, and impurities, chiral purity, residual solvents, heavy metals, particle size, polymorphs, and microbiology.

In early summer 2007, Richard Tren, Philip Coticelli, Lorraine Mooney, and Kimberly Hess at Africa Fighting Malaria, Amir Attaran at Ottawa University, and I decided to do a small but—we hoped—useful assessment of antimalarial drug quality in selected African cities and towns using a Minilab. From there grew further studies in India using the Minilab; these involved fake-drug investigator Sati and his team, Bibek Debroy and Barun Mitra, respectively, of the Rajiv Ghandi Foundation and Liberty Institute. These were followed by the deployment of the TruScan in studies of the African drugs procured previously; new drugs produced from different African locations; drugs from middle-income cities including São Paolo, Beijing, Bangkok, Moscow, and Istanbul; and drugs procured in the United States over the Internet.[b]

The full methods deployed for these assessments, as well as a more detailed breakdown of the data presented in this chapter, are contained in this part. Much of this research has appeared in peer-reviewed scientific literature; some was first discussed in policy papers at U.S., Indian, African, or EU think tanks, and some has never been published before and is part of ongoing research. The publications are listed in appendix A. Readers interested in the more precise methodologies used in these studies should consult these publications. What follows is an explanation of what we procured and analyzed and the major results and conclusions drawn from this work.

"Substandard drugs" may be nearly identical to the original (for example, a drug with 89.4 percent of the required API would be considered substandard in any developed country), or they may be completely different. Our tests can find only relatively significant failures. The limits of the Minilab are obvious, and if good examples of legitimate products are not available, then the TruScan is of limited use, too. Over time, we tested most of the suspect products with HPLC to establish API concentration.

What We Procured from Where

To conduct our research, we procured samples of medicines for testing from various parts of the world. The following paragraphs indicate the locations of the samples and the number of samples we collected from each city.

---

b. After an initial comparative test using both the TruScan and the Phazir, use of the Phazir was dropped, because it was largely replicating the results of the TruScan.

Box 10-1
RAMAN SPECTROMETRY

As discussed in the main body of the book, over the past four years, 2,512 medicines were procured by covert shoppers from private pharmacies in nineteen cities across seventeen developing and middle-income countries.[1] All medicines were assessed using the Global Pharma Health Fund e.V. Minilab® protocol to identify substandard, degraded, or counterfeit medicines. This includes visual inspection of packaging and pills for correctness, disintegration for basic solubility, and semiquantitative TLC to determine the presence and relative concentration of active ingredients. Each test was run in duplicate, with the generous assumption that the result that was more consistent with the reference was recorded. Quality control of the Minilab was performed daily prior to testing and consisted of performing TLC on Minilab reference samples for the medicine classes being analyzed. In addition, Minilab reagents were quality-control tested using reference samples when a new lot was introduced. The Minilab protocols award medicines a "pass" if they have 80 percent or more of the labeled active ingredient(s). For fixed-dose combinations and sulphadoxine-pyrimethamine, a "pass" was awarded only if both active ingredients met this standard. An aggregate "fail" was assigned to medicines failing at least one of the three quality tests (visual inspection, TLC, or disintegration). Some of these data have been previously published in the literature (see appendix A).

The authors also assessed drug quality using Raman spectrometry. Numerous studies have demonstrated that Raman spectrometry is a quick, reliable,

---

1. An additional forty-seven treatments were procured in error; these were products that could not be tested by the Minilab or were incorrectly purchased. For example, we were unable to test the antimalarial drug Halfan. In addition, 152 samples were collected for the Internet study described in chapter 9.

Africa. Over the past four years, we sampled drugs from ninety pharmacies in nonslum areas in eleven large African cities. Alphabetically, the cities in which research was conducted are Accra, Ghana (nine pharmacies); Addis Ababa, Ethiopia (seven); Cairo, Egypt (eight); Dar es Salaam, Tanzania (eight); Kampala, Uganda (ten); Kigali, Rwanda (two); Lagos, Nigeria (twelve); Luanda, Angola (eight); Lubumbashi, Democratic Republic of the

and cost-effective way for nonspecialists to differentiate between genuine and counterfeit drugs. To ascertain the nature, and not just the spectra, of all compounds in a given drug, including impurities and degradation products as well as the percentage of active ingredients would require using HPLC, which is considered the current gold standard analytical method in drug analysis. HPLC requires sophisticated sample preparation that is expensive and time-consuming and requires trained chemists for analysis and interpretation of results. Given that the aim of this study was to authenticate a finished product (rather than its individual components), comparison with a known HPLC standard was unnecessary (many of the suspect samples were subsequently tested with HPLC). The authors used a handheld Raman spectrometer, the TruScan by Ahura Scientific (Wilmington, MA), on loan for the duration of the study. One necessity, and potential limitation, of spectrometers is that they require exact reference standards, obtained by scanning each separate brand with the same formulation for calibration. This means that a drug substituted for the branded version would record likely as a failure (because the excipients could be different, yielding different spectra, between two equally effective drugs). For this reason, generic substitutes were not sought from websites for this study.

While a pass identifies a good-quality drug, a "failure," as assessed by the authors, does not mean that a given drug is necessarily of low quality. The spectrometer recorded a "failure" if a sampled drug was spectroscopically inconsistent with the reference standard; under this metric, both copy versions and FDA-approved bioequivalent generics of the chosen drugs may fail, because although they must contain the same quantities of active ingredient, they often contain different binding agents (excipients) in different concentrations. The spectrum created by the spectrometer is for the total sample formulation, not only the active ingredient.

Congo (seven); Lusaka, Zambia (seven); and Nairobi, Kenya (twelve). The sampling methods were the same for each assessment; however, a couple of key variations ought to be noted. First, there was some regional variation in the drug samples we were able to procure. Researchers purchased three classes of drugs: antimalarials, antibiotics, and antimycobacterials (to treat tuberculosis). Within drug classes, some brands were found in many places, whereas others were unique to one city. Second, our sampling took place over a three-year period. Six of the cities were sampled in October and November 2007 and six in 2009 (Lagos was sampled a second time in January 2009, and the remaining five were sampled in November and December 2009). In early 2010, Lagos was sampled for a third and fourth time, and Accra was sampled for a second time, giving us limited time-series data.

India. Sampling from India revolved around three separate procurements from seventy pharmacies in three cities, Delhi (twenty-six pharmacies) Chennai (twenty-six), and Kolkata (eighteen) in 2008 and 2009. A portion of the Delhi pharmacies were sampled again in 2010. We used the same methodology as in the African cities, but the malaria drugs we bought were often different, because Indian mosquitoes carry mainly the *vivax* strain of malaria, whereas the *falciparum* strain, which requires newer drugs, dominates in Africa (see the discussion on drug-resistant malaria in Nigeria on page 61).[c] Sampling in India also included an assessment of the same five drugs from four wholesalers in one major location called Bhagirath Palace, in the heart of Delhi.[d]

Other Emerging Markets. The samples from fifty pharmacies in five cities scattered throughout the rest of the developing world are the most inherently unreliable as snapshots even of the cities in question, let alone the rest of their respective countries. However, the exercise gave me some insights into pharmacy operations, problems for drug-quality control, and the myriad ways dubious drugs infiltrate different markets. All samples from

---

c. One failing in this sampling is that we did not consider the time of year for procurement. Because in parts of India malaria is seasonal, it is possible that we would have procured a wider variety of antimalarials, in Delhi in particular, if we had sampled at a different time.

d. Obtaining a representative sample of wholesale drugs is much more difficult than procuring the corresponding drugs from a retailer. A Delhi native can walk into a pharmacy and purchase drugs for personal or family use without suspicion, but most wholesalers do repeat business with drug traders and are more likely to be skeptical of a procurement request from an unknown source. To avoid the wholesaler's suspicion, we contracted a local trader to procure drugs for us. Because the trader we contracted already had an established business relationship with the wholesaler, it is likely that our data from the wholesale evaluation do not reflect the true magnitude of the counterfeit trade.

Bangkok, Beijing, Moscow, Istanbul, and São Paolo were collected between December 2009 and February 2010.

The Internet. Any reasonably priced, small-scale procurement (fewer than several thousand samples) from Western pharmacies, where the drug-supply system is well regulated and quality is consistently high, is not worthwhile. However, drugs purchased over the Internet are often considered dangerous. The WHO has stated that 50 percent of drugs bought over the Internet from sources that hide their location are fake. In order to tentatively test the WHO's statement and assess other types of websites, we procured five commonly purchased brand-name drugs from a total of fifty-five online pharmacies. Each pharmacy was grouped into one of four stratified categories based on an assessment by Western regulatory authorities. All of the products were tested with the TruScan. The results were presented in chapter 9 and are only discussed in this chapter where they form part of a larger analysis.

Overall Procurement. Because the sampling is biased toward Africa, roughly 40 percent of the samples (1,017 of 2,512) were antimalarial drugs, approximately 31 percent were antibiotics (785 of 2,512), and 29 percent were antimycobacterials (710 of 2,512).

11

Results: What We Found

In broad brush strokes, our data paint a picture of a world beset by inconsistent drug quality. As might be expected, the United States has rare and sporadic problems primarily caused by imports of bogus drugs from overseas, middle-income countries have more persistent quality-control problems, and the poorest countries face a massive battle against substandard and falsified medications.

I will discuss Internet-sourced drugs later because they are not directly comparable and not included in the following data assessments. Fewer than 4 percent of samples (96 of 2,512) failed visual inspection. Of these, less than 1 percent (21 of 2,512) of the products themselves were obviously degraded. For roughly 3 percent of samples (75 of 2,512), the nature of the packaging was questionable (incorrect fonts, labels, trademarks, and so forth), and these were almost certainly counterfeits. None of these ninety-six products passed quality-control tests. In other words, none of the obviously falsified products were actually of acceptable quality, which supports Western perceptions that "fake" products are always ineffective and undermines any notion to the contrary.

Overall, 12.2 percent of samples (307 of 2,512) failed one or more quality tests. These failures include all 96 of the degraded and obviously counterfeit products listed above and an additional 211 products, which either did not have enough API or had flawed solubility or spectrum in some way. Figure 11-1 summarizes these results.

Of the 307 total worldwide failures, 141 (46 percent) had no detectable API, which indicates that these products were fakes (see figure 11-1). Of the 75 products that were identified as visual fakes, 50 had no API. This means 25 had some nonnegligible amount of the correct API, supporting the idea that at least some counterfeiters are adding API in order to fool dye tests and other simple quality assessments. It also may indicate failed

FIGURE 11-1
QUALITY TEST-DRUG FAILURES (WORLDWIDE), SUBCATEGORIZED
BY 0-PERCENT API, VISUAL INSPECTION FAILURE, AND DEGRADATION

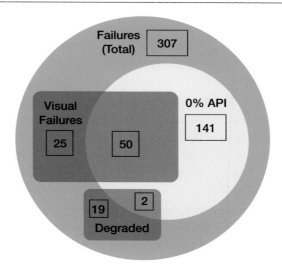

attempts by counterfeiters to make high-quality products in the hopes of winning repeat business. These data support assertions made about some of the China Viagra fakes found in chapter 9.

A higher percentage of malaria drugs failed quality tests (19 percent) than either antibiotics or antimycobacterials (both 8 percent). Fewer of the antimalarial failures had zero content (40 percent) than the other types (55 percent of antibiotics and 53 percent of antimycobacterials). This is probably more indicative of the market location (antimalarials predominate in Africa) than the drug type.

In the poorest continent on earth, an average of 19 percent of products on the market failed quality-control tests. The eleven cities sampled had drug-quality testing failures ranging from 8.9 percent in Cairo, Egypt, to 48.8 percent in Lubumbashi, Democratic Republic of the Congo. Indian cities had an average failure rate of 8.8 percent, ranging from 5 percent in Chennai to 11.5 percent in Delhi. Failures for the cities sampled in the rest of the world averaged 3.7 percent (although sample sizes are too small to draw any strong conclusions). As will become clear in the following sections, the discrepancies between the various countries may highlight profound differences in the markets themselves. African failures include relatively more nonzero API quality-control failures (61 percent) than either Indian (29 percent) or the remaining world (24 percent) markets, which implies that Africa has a far greater problem with substandard drugs (another interpretation is that counterfeiters add more API to the fakes in Africa, which, given the value of the market, appears illogical, although it may not be, given that more random testing is done in Africa than many middle-income nations—a point discussed more in chapter 13[a]).

None of the drugs procured over the Internet from Europe or the United States failed quality tests, but that does not mean there are no fakes in OECD countries. (The evidence from the online supplement to this book, available at phake-meds.org, shows that there are.) Indeed, even if 0.1 percent of the 3.6 billion prescriptions filled every year in the United States contained substandard or fake products, 3.6 million patients would face potential danger.

More Detailed Analysis with More Limited Datasets

Much of the analysis below on registration and variability is based on working with slightly different datasets, all culled from within the main set I have described. Some drugs have been dropped because of a lack of information required for more detailed analysis, and some because of a lack of registration details. Gathering information is costly, and because of the cost, information gathering was not always repeated when new samples were added. In the earliest samplings our attention was focused on drug quality and not wider parameters, so price data were missing. Thus, the price analysis draws from only a subset of the data. For these reasons, drug quality (as measured by failure rates) may vary from one sampling to another. This may appear inconsistent, but these are not errors; they are the results of conducting the analyses on slightly different sample sets.

---

a. According to Andreas Seiter of the World Bank, API for developing nations often goes via brokers who are not cooperative with World Bank or other investigations into the quality of ingredients.

The Role of Registration

One of the critical roles of any MRA, such as the U.S. FDA, is to register medicines available for sale to citizens. The registration process for new chemical entities generally consists of evaluation and assessment of quality data, preclinical studies, clinical trials, and product-information documentation. These tests are expensive and time-consuming, sometimes prohibitively so for smaller agencies.[1]

There are obviously good-quality medicines in the United States that are not registered by the FDA; they can be brought in by individuals without explicit approval from the FDA (for example, some malaria researchers, including myself, had personal supplies of the malaria medicine Coartem before it was registered by the FDA in April 2009).[2] There may also be large amounts of unregistered medicines in any country, possibly smuggled, and these are less likely to be of consistently good quality. In China, for example, the SFDA reported that in 2007 there were 329,613 cases of unlicensed medicines, most of which were manufactured by fly-by-night firms.[3]

In 2007, Nairobi University, Kenya's Ministry of Health, the WHO, and Health Action International assessed medicine availability and quality in Kenya. The study found that 42 percent of malaria medicines on the market in Kenya were not registered and that 16 percent of medicines available failed quality-control tests, but it was not clear from the assessment whether registration was associated with poor quality.[4] As a result of the study, my research team investigated whether registration was a problem in other countries, particularly across Africa, and what impact registration status might have on medicine quality. I attempted to ascertain whether registered medicines perform better in simple quality tests than those that either are not registered or are not known to be registered.

A subset of the total sample discussed in this book is analyzed in depth below. We determined registration status after quality testing to eliminate possible bias. Not all medicines were procured from countries where it was possible to ascertain whether they were registered by the local competent authority.[5] For fifteen of nineteen cities sampled, my research team and I were able to positively identify which medicines were registered in that country and which were unregistered or not known to be registered. In some instances, up-to-date registration lists were not available, so the registration status for some of the medicines could not be confirmed. Many registration websites were incomplete, nonfunctioning, or contained old data. For those with reasonable data, 1,940 medicines of 113 brands were identified, of which 1,589 were registered and 351 were either unregistered or not known to be registered.

Most medicines (81.9 percent, or 1,589 of 1,940) were registered in the countries from which they were procured. Some of the remaining 18.1 percent (351 of 1,940) may have been registered, but incomplete records made it impossible to confirm whether they were. Overall, 5 percent (79 of 1,589) of registered samples failed testing, and 37.3 percent (131 of 351) of unregistered (or not known to be registered) samples failed testing (see table 11-1). African cities had fewer medicines registered (71 percent, or 488 of 687) than middle-income cities: 86.9 percent (610 of 702) of medicines from Indian cities were registered, and 89.1 percent (491 of 551) of medicines from the remaining cities were registered. Samples from African cities also performed far worse in quality tests (18.6 percent failed, or 128 of 687) than samples either from Indian cities (8.7 percent failed, or 61 of 702) or from other middle-income cities (3.8 percent failed, or 21 of 551). The failure rate of registered medicines in African cities (6.6 percent, or 32 of 488) was similar to that of registered medicines in Indian cities (6.7 percent, or 41 of 610), but the failure rate of nonregistered medicines was far worse, at 48.2 percent (96 of 199) for African cities and 21.7 percent (20 of 92) for Indian cities.

Failure rates were highly associated with registration status (see tables 11-1–11-3), although location, medicine type, and time of collection were also weakly associated. The results strongly indicate that medicine registration is highly correlated with better-quality medicines. For every medicine type in every location where both registered and unregistered samples were procured, registered medicines performed better than unregistered medicines, and the result was statistically significant. Across countries, the range of failure rates for registered medicines (0–20 percent) was far smaller than the range for nonregistered medicines (0–100 percent). There was a statistically significant difference in the mean failure rates by city for unregistered medicines (mean is 41.3 percent, standard deviation is 26.7) and registered medicines (mean is 5.7 percent, standard deviation is 5.3).

TABLE 11-1

TESTING RESULTS (FAILURES RECORDED) BY COUNTRY AND CITY OF ORIGIN,
AND REGISTRATION STATUS

Country of origin	City of origin	Registered samples	Unregistered (not known to be registered) samples	Total
Ghana	Accra	(4/61) 6.6%	(21/33) 63.6%	(25/94) 26.6%
Tanzania	Dar es Salaam	(3/31) 9.7%	(9/16) 56.3%	(12/47) 25.5%
Uganda	Kampala	(8/40) 20%	(16/36) 44.4%	(24/76) 31.6%
Nigeria	Lagos	(9/221) 4.1%	(23/52) 44.2%	(32/273) 11.7%
Angola	Luanda	(2/41) 4.9%	(8/21) 38.1%	(10/62) 16.1%
Zambia	Lusaka	(2/59) 3.4%	(6/19) 31.6%	(8/78) 10.3%
Kenya	Nairobi	(4/35) 11.4%	(13/22) 59.1%	(17/57) 29.8%
India	Delhi	(23/229) 10%	(11/52) 21.2%	(34/281) 12.1%
	Chennai	(9/228) 3.9%	(3/32) 9.4%	(12/260) 4.6%
	Kolkata	(9/153) 5.9%	(6/8) 75%	(15/161) 9.3%
Thailand	Bangkok	(2/100) 2%	(5/13) 38.5%	(7/113) 6.2%
China	Beijing	(2/84) 2.4%	(3/26) 11.5%	(5/110) 4.5%
Turkey	Istanbul	(0/97) 0%	(0/6) 0%	(0/103) 0%
Russia	Moscow	(1/99) 1%	(3/11) 27.3%	(4/110) 3.6%
Brazil	São Paolo	(1/111) 0.9%	(4/4) 100%	(5/115) 4.3%
TOTAL		(79/1,589) 5%	(131/351) 37.3%	(210/1,940) 10.8%

NOTES: Istanbul had a 0 percent failure rate in all categories. Percentages are supported by total that failed testing/total samples tested.

Given the expected importance of competent MRAs in registering and overseeing approved medicines, it is of little surprise that registered medicines failed noticeably less often than unregistered or not-known-to-be-registered medicines. This is exemplified most obviously by the performance of medicines procured in African cities. Indeed, we conclude that Africa's poorer performance in medicine quality can at least partly be explained by the fact that African countries have proportionally fewer registered medicines than the other locations.

There was a notable disparity in failure rates by medicine type (see table 11-2): antimalarials performed the worst (14.2 percent, or 101 of

TABLE 11-2

TESTING RESULTS (FAILURES RECORDED) BY LOCATION OF ORIGIN
AND REGISTRATION STATUS AND MEDICINE TYPE[a]

Registration status	Antimalarial		Antimycobacterial		Antibiotic		Total
	Yes	No	Yes	No	Yes	No	
African cities	0.066	0.48	0.032	0.556	0.074	0.477	18.6%
	(25/376)	(60/125)	(1/31)	(5/9)	(6/81)	(31/65)	(128/687)
Indian cities	0.062	0.227	0.075	0.206	0.064	0.222	8.7%
	(10/161)	(5/22)	(15/199)	(7/34)	(16/250)	(8/36)	(61/702)
Cities of remaining countries[b]	0.038		0.0087	0.257	0.013	0.24	3.8%
	(1/26)	(0/0)	(2/229)	(9/35)	(3/236)	(6/25)	(21/551)
Total	0.064	0.442	0.039	0.269	0.044	0.357	10.8%
	(36/563)	(65/147)	(18/459)	(21/78)	(25/567)	(45/126)	(210/1940)
Total for both registered and unregistered[c]	14.2% (101/710)		7.3% (39/537)		10.1% (70/693)		

NOTES: a = Percentages are supported by total that failed testing/total samples tested; b = Countries include Thailand, China, Turkey, Russia, and Brazil; c = Includes samples not known to be registered.

710 failed); followed by antibiotics (10.1 percent, or 70 of 693 failed); and antimycobacterials performed best (7.3 percent, or 39 of 537 failed). In general, African drugs had higher failure rates regardless of medicine type or registration status, with the exception of antimycobacterials from India, which had the highest failure rate for registered antimycobacterials (although the African sample size was small for this subset). The remaining middle-income cities performed best for registered antimycobacterials.

It is not surprising that drugs procured in Africa performed worse than those from middle-income countries in terms of quality-control testing; that they would has been established in the literature.[6] However, a possible testable cause, such as registration status, had not been measured empirically before the study my team conducted in 2010. African cities had far more unregistered medicines than Indian cities, and unregistered medicines from Africa performed worse than those from India. However, medicines registered in African cities performed slightly better than registered medicines from Indian cities.

FIGURE 11-2
FAILURE RATE BY REGISTRATION STATUS

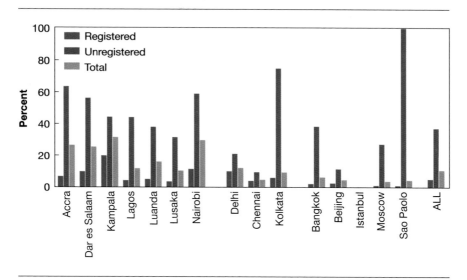

FIGURE 11-3
FAILURE RATE BY REGISTRATION STATUS, TYPE, AND REGION

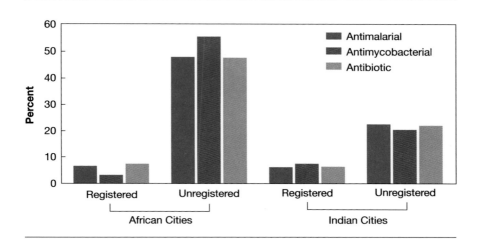

TABLE 11-3
FAILURE RATES BY REGISTRATION TYPE

	Registered	Nonregistered
Total samples	1,589 samples	351 samples
Failing samples	79 of 1,589 samples (5%)	131 of 351 samples (37%)
Zero API	49 of 79 failures (62%)	55 of 131 failures (41%)
Visual failures	34 of 79 failures (43%)	25 of 131 failures (19%)
Quality drugs	1,427	140

Slightly fewer medicines sampled were unregistered in the remaining middle-income cities than in the Indian cities, and registered medicines from these cities performed considerably better than those from India. One possible explanation for this is that more medicines are registered in wealthier nations. In all of these analyses, it is possible that results are affected by medicine types, specific brands, and the locations of manufacturers. I hope to do future research to assess these possible causes.

Table 11-3 compares failure rates and reasons for failure between registered and unregistered samples. As a percentage of total failures, registered products (or, rather, fakes of registered products) are far more likely to fail visual inspection tests or have zero API than nonregistered products (see figures 11-4–11-6). Of course, counterfeiters do not register products, but the data reflect the rational choice by counterfeiters to imitate drugs already registered by legal companies (after all, why risk your fake product being confiscated for being not registered?).

Counterfeiters are copying popular brands more likely to be registered and considered safe by most of the population. The flipside of this is that some, maybe the majority, of the nonregistered failures are likely not fakes but just badly made products. That does not mean they are strictly legal, though. Nonregistered products likely include many locally produced items of lower quality that have not been submitted to any local MRA or inspected by any customs department if imported.

The causes for lack of registration require further investigation. In some countries, it may indicate a problem with the MRA. Regulatory agencies may lack the resources and competent staff required to keep pace with registering new, locally produced, and legally imported medicines. In other

FIGURE 11-4
BREAKDOWN OF REGISTERED AND NONREGISTERED DRUGS

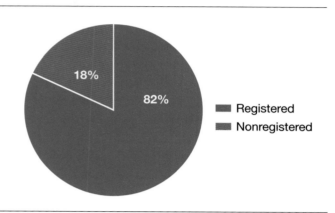

FIGURE 11-5
REGISTERED DRUGS

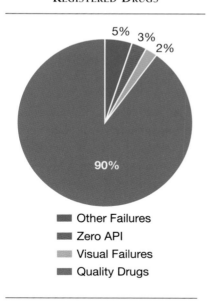

FIGURE 11-6
NONREGISTERED DRUGS

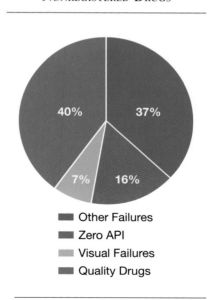

places, poorly regulated borders allow medicines to flow freely in and out of the country, enabling numerous medicines to reach markets without any oversight. In some places, manufacturers may choose not to seek registration for their drugs, either because the costs of properly registering medications can be prohibitively expensive or because they know their drugs would fail to meet strict quality requirements.

Antimalarials failed more often than other medicine types, but more antimalarials were procured in Africa than other medicines. Furthermore, medicines collected in 2007 in Africa performed worse than those collected in 2010;[7] this improved performance could be the result of government efforts to register more medicines. This temporal effect will be analyzed in future research, but because early samplings were not that large, it could be just a statistical anomaly. Another reason antimalarials performed worse than other drug types may be simply because the earlier collections consisted of only antimalarials. It may be hard to disentangle whether location, medicine type, or time of collection is a more important cause of failure, because it is suspected they are often interrelated.

Variability Analysis

Even when we did not have access to perfect copies of legitimate products, we were able to assess consistency within a sample by taking all the drugs that passed all Minilab protocol tests and analyzing the spectrum of each brand against a representative sample spectrum. Any variation greater than 5 percent was considered a failure. The point of this analysis was to assess variability as a reasonable proxy for whether GMP was being enforced in each location and to estimate where we may have overestimated quality.

None of the innovator brands produced in the European Union, Switzerland, or the United States failed spectrometry testing; 4 percent of nondomestically produced generic drugs and 7 percent of drugs manufactured within the countries from which they were procured failed testing. The failure rate of drugs produced by African companies was 9.3 percent (ranging from 0 percent for drugs produced in South Africa and Morocco to 14.3 percent for those produced in Ghana and the Democratic Republic of the Congo); 7.7 percent of Chinese companies' drugs failed; 4.9 percent of Vietnamese companies' drugs failed; 4.4 percent of Indian companies'

TABLE 11-4
FAILURE RATES BY TYPE OF PRODUCER

	Total samples tested	Total samples failing Raman spectrometry	Percent failed
Large Indian Producers[a]	471	6	1.30
Small Indian Producers[b]	327	29	8.90
Chinese Producers	169	13	7.70
Southeast Asian Producers[c]	69	4	5.80
Western Producers[d]	438	1	0.20
African Producers	302	28	9.30
Producers in Mid-income Nations[e]	62	7	11.30
TOTAL	1,838	88	4.80

NOTES: a. More than $300 million in annual revenue; b. Less than $300 million in annual revenue; c. Countries include Thailand and Vietnam; d. Within the European Union, as well as Switzerland and the United States; e. Countries include Brazil, Turkey, and Russia.

drugs failed; and 0.20 percent of Western companies' drugs failed (see table 11-4).[8] One generic drug failed; no innovator brands did.

It was not possible to compare product variability by drug type in a useful way because not all drugs were procured in every location. It is worth noting that there were relatively more failures among antimalarials than among antimycobacterial drugs or antibiotics (see table 11-2). One explanation for this finding is that antimalarials are made and sold in Africa, where drug quality is lower, more often than the other types of drugs sampled.[9] Support for this assumption came from the fact that the one drug sold in all sampled countries, ciprofloxacin, did indeed fail more often in Africa than in other markets (mirroring the overall data), although the samples were small.

Analysis of the Indian drugs procured during this research project and analyzed in this variability dataset showed a marked disparity in product consistency between products of large companies (designated as those with more than $300 million annual revenue) and those of small companies (designated as those with less than $300 million annual revenue) (see table 11-4). Nearly 800 products were made in India; of those, 327 were manufactured by smaller companies, and 471 were manufactured by larger producers. Overall, thirty-five products failed testing, or 4.4 percent of the total, but this conceals a marked difference within the data. When we separated the failure rates by the size of the drug producer, we found that the failure rate of drugs produced by small companies was 8.9 percent, and the failure rate of drugs from large companies was 1.3 percent.

Perhaps the most interesting result was that larger Indian generic-drug producers performed almost identically (1.3 percent failed) to smaller Western (predominantly European) generic-drug producers (1.2 percent failed), although the sample size of the latter was relatively small (one failure out of eighty-two samples).

For fifteen of the nineteen countries sampled, we could positively identify drugs registered in each country, and, for the purposes of our investigation, we considered the rest of the drugs to be unregistered. In some instances, up-to-date national drug-registration lists were not available, so the registration status for some of the drugs could not be confirmed. Many registration websites were incomplete or nonfunctioning, or contained old data. Of the 1,707 products we identified, 1,438 were registered, and 269 were either not registered or probably not registered (see table 11-1). Variability among registered products was 3.3 percent, whereas it was a much higher 13 percent for nonregistered products. Of the 269 unregistered products, 135 were from Indian producers, 26 were from other Asian producers, 104 were from African producers, 2 were from Brazilian producers, and 2 were from European producers.

Overall, the products with the least variability were innovator branded drugs, followed by those produced by large Indian generic-drug companies and European generic-drug manufacturers; these types of products performed noticeably better than products made by other manufacturers.

Survey of Pharmacists

When collecting drugs, our covert buyers also conducted ad hoc surveys of the quality of the pharmacies. On separate occasions, surveys were conducted of the pharmacists to ascertain their willingness to discuss fake drugs. The three graphs below summarize their responses (see figures 11-7–11-9). These data are potentially of significant value, but because the

FIGURE 11-7
PHARMACY SURVEY:
PERCENT SAY FAKES A PROBLEM

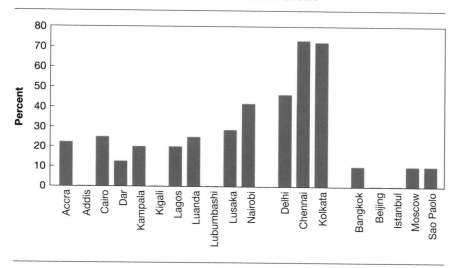

FIGURE 11-8
PHARMACY SURVEY:
PERCENT SAY BEEN OFFERED FAKES

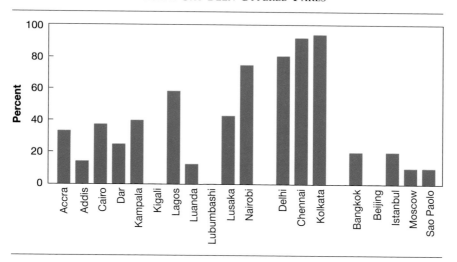

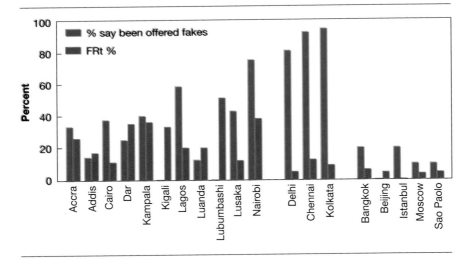

FIGURE 11-9
PHARMACY SURVEY:
PERCENT OFFER FAKES COMPARED WITH FAILURE RATE

surveyors were different and questioning was done on an ad hoc basis and was not a previously designed survey, the results could be highly biased. They are presented because the reader may be interested in the data. Perhaps most interesting is that Indian pharmacists acknowledged being offered fakes and were prepared to discuss it.

12

Results Broken Down for Africa, India, and Other Markets

The previous chapter shows the outline of the data. As the reader will realize, some of the more interesting data are specific to particular regions, and that is what is explored here. There are more data on Africa, followed by India and other markets, and hence they are explored in that order.

Africa

We decided to sample antimalarial drugs in Africa in 2007 because of malaria's high death toll in many countries and the unconventional avenues through which many Africans procure their antimalarial medications. Some antimalarial drugs are administered in hospitals and clinics, but far more are bought privately from pharmacies, kiosks, general stores, and roving traders. In addition, there are an astonishing number of antimalarial drug types and brands across Africa.[a]

In our studies, we collected 121 different antimalarial brands allegedly produced in sixteen countries by forty-seven firms. No single country's products dominated the market in any particular African city. Of rich-country exporters, Switzerland dominated (including diverted products from the public sector), and of middle-income countries, India did. This number of brands and firms involved in such a small-value market is worrisome. Most economic analyses of pharmaceutical markets, including reports from

---

a. The University of Nairobi and the WHO surveyed antimalarial drugs across Kenya and found over 180 different brands of antimalarial drugs. Interestingly, only 42 percent of the drugs procured for this study were definitely registered in the countries in question (16 percent of these failed quality-control tests).

FIGURE 12-1
QUALITY TEST DRUG FAILURES (AFRICA), SUBCATEGORIZED
BY 0-PERCENT API, VISUAL INSPECTION FAILURE, AND DEGRADATION

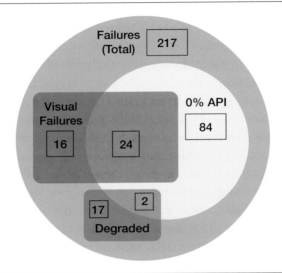

scholars in poorer countries, would consider the value of Africa's antimalarial markets relatively small, probably unable to sustain many firms.[1] The result is often cutthroat competition among the brands in this price-sensitive market, making the temptation to cut corners in production significant for many players. Figure 12-1 summarizes our findings on Africa.

Proliferation of Brands. Where quality is not overseen and access to the market is easy, and where demand is price sensitive, competition may actually drive down quality. The vast number of brands available in some locations is a manifestation of an extremely chaotic market with few controls in place by an MRA and little customs oversight. The presence of so many types of antimalarial drugs is not a sign of an efficient and competitive market, but rather of one that is out of control and where it may be harder for patients to make informed choices.

In our analysis, including drugs that could not be assessed for quality (we had no reference samples) and are therefore not in tables 11-1 through

11-4, we found disparity in the number of antimalarial drugs available in different markets; Kigali (three brands) and Lubumbashi (five) had the fewest; Nairobi (sixty-five brands), Kampala (sixty-two), and Lagos (fifty-nine) had the most. The former are small, poor, or out-of-the-way markets, and the latter are the capitals or largest towns of significant countries by population size. Clearly, these are viewed as viable markets by every trader. While competition in these markets lowers price, I wondered how it affected drug quality.

Where it was possible to assess registration data, we found that only 71 percent of the sampled drugs were registered, which means roughly three in ten products may not have passed any quality-control tests. It is instructive that we could not ascertain drug registration status for Ethiopia, Egypt, Rwanda, or the Democratic Republic of the Congo, because the data either do not exist or were not available. Lack of data is a bad sign, and I expected to find aggregate failure rates higher in countries with poor registration data. While this held true for three of the cities, Cairo, Egypt, seemed to be the exception. Drugs sampled from Cairo performed better than drugs from any other African city. I expect there are registration data; my research team was just unable to locate them.

Of those drugs for which registration information was available, about 18 percent failed quality tests; unregistered drugs failed far more often (over 48 percent failed) than registered drugs (less than 7 percent).[b] This is a startling finding, and perhaps the most significant data finding in the entire book. It also reinforces the widely supported notion that Western aid agencies should help support developing countries' MRAs. MRAs that are poorly resourced have difficulty registering products. In addition, a large number of unregistered products could indicate that importation is the major problem; if most imports are smuggled in, improving customs is also a vital companion policy. At the time, when several billion dollars of drugs are donated by aid agencies every year to Africa, it seems worrisome that many MRAs are not equipped to identify bad copies of these products—and what better place to hide fake drugs than among millions of real ones. As established in chapter 4, donated product theft and diversion are

---

b. While antimalarials failed slightly more often than other drugs, this result was not statistically significant.

a significant headache; perhaps some of those funds would be better spent allocated to MRA development.

The Antimalarial Drug Market. Also worrisome was that 38 percent of the antimalarial drugs sampled were artemisinin monotherapies. At least twelve producers still manufacture and distribute monotherapies, despite advice the WHO gave five years ago that using monotherapies increases the risk of parasitic resistance to artemisinin. In addition, many of the products that failed quality control contained artemisinin, further encouraging resistance.[2]

Older therapies were the most popular group of drugs available and, in total, comprised about 45 percent of total drugs procured. Within that group, cheaper products like sulphadoxine-pyrimethamine were the most popular, followed by mid-priced amodiaquine and then mefloquine, which is comparably priced to artemisinin monotherapies.[c]

Drugs in Africa failed quality-control tests for a variety of reasons. Some of the drugs we procured were obvious counterfeits; packaging errors (misspellings, incorrect fonts, manufacturing dates after expiration dates, and so forth), damaged packs, and pills that crumbled when handled gave away their illegitimate origins. Products that registered no API content when tested with thin-layer chromatography were assumed to be counterfeit, because legitimate but degraded products (years beyond sell-by dates and stored in poor conditions) still register a small amount of API (there were two exceptions to this; these products were so significantly degraded, it is not safe to assume they were definitely counterfeits).[d] Of the remaining

---

c. Given the testing protocols initially available using the Minilab, we were limited to testing only one type of ACT, artemether-lumefantrine in the first sampling. Most of the artemether-lumefantrine samples were Coartem (the best-selling brand), and none of the Coartem pills we tested failed any quality tests, which means all the ACT/artemether-lumefantrine failures came from the sixteen other brands. Later, we added the ACT artesunate-amodiaquine to the protocol, so procured artesunate-amodiaquine became testable.

d. In testing the drugs procured for other studies, we found that one drug in particular, Coartem, seemed to work well after its shelf life had passed. We were not sure of this and so decided to assess stability more fully. Using the TruScan, we did a further study on all of the expired Coartem we had collected from myriad sources: from malaria researchers, from other contacts, and, of course, from those procured publicly. Based on the Coartem assessment and a Kenyan government report showing how few antimalarial drugs were registered in Kenya, we tried our most ambitious work to date: to assess quality of all products by registration status and, where possible, to assess their stability.

failures, some were obviously degraded products, and others were probably more sophisticated counterfeit products that contained some API.[e]

Figure 12-1 breaks out the 217 failures based on whether they failed in terms of API, because they were visual fakes, or because of degradation. Only 39 percent of the failures (eighty-four) had zero API. There were sixteen visual fakes that contained some API. In other words, 100 of the 217 drug failures, or 46 percent, were almost certainly fakes. Seventeen drugs (roughly 8 percent) were obviously degraded, leaving another 100 (46 percent) that were substandard for no immediately apparent reason (that is, it was unclear whether these were fakes, degraded drugs, or just poor-quality, legitimate products).

Lagos and Accra Time Series. Drug quality improved in Accra and Lagos over the time of the procurements, and the finding was statistically significant. Because the initial sample sizes were not large, the resultant conclusions we can draw are limited. If the effect we detected is, in fact, indicative of a real decrease in the counterfeit-drug supply, much of the credit for this improvement should probably go to anticounterfeiting policy in Nigeria, which was discussed at length in chapter 4, and the USAID-sponsored work of USP in Ghana.

From the results from our sample displayed below (in tables 12-1 and 12-2), we could not determine the makeup of the drugs failing tests in Lagos. We know overall quality is improving, but we cannot tell if this is because there are fewer fakes or fewer substandards. In other words, where are the improvements? We do not know if Lagos is running the fakers out of town or ensuring GMP of legal importers and local producers. I suspect there are improvements on all fronts, and I hope future research will be able to explain this more fully.[f]

One possibly worrying interpretation of these results involves the visual inspection failures. While these fell across the board for both cities,

---

e. Our analysis of the drugs surveyed in Africa did not include forensic analysis of all samples, so we cannot make broad conclusions from these investigations, but where possible, explanations are given in the text.

f. Sample sizes are not sufficient to disaggregate and estimate the ratio of zero API failures and other drug failures; both types of failure fall, but we cannot ascertain the statistical significance or whether one is falling faster than the other.

Table 12-1
DRUG SAMPLES FAILING QUALITY TESTS (AS A PERCENTAGE)

Lagos and Accra time series data	Sample size	Number failed	Date sampled	Failure rate
Accra 1	37	13	Oct. 2007	35.14%
Accra 2	57	11	Jan./Feb. 2010	19.30%
Lagos 1	22	7	Nov. 2007	31.82%
Lagos 2	129	21	Jan. 2009	16.28%
Lagos 3	94	12	Jan./Feb. 2010	12.77%
Lagos S4	71	8	Aug. 2010	9.05%
Totals	410	72		18%

they fell only slightly in comparison with quality-test failures. This may indicate that fake-drug makers are improving; they already have good packaging, and more and more are foiling the thin-layer chromatography tests possible with the Minilab. The only evidence I have that this is happening is anecdotal. A few investigators I have interviewed have noticed more fakes with increasing API content. More cannot be said at this stage, but it is certainly worth monitoring whether counterfeiters are changing behavior in this way.

Pharmacy Surveys. African pharmacies, as a whole, performed far worse than any other regional grouping of pharmacies. More than half of sampled pharmacies sold at least one counterfeit drug. The majority of the fakes were confined to a subset of pharmacies, a finding mirrored in other locations, and suggests that the worst offending pharmacies are fully aware of what they are selling. In eleven out of ninety pharmacies, 40 percent or more of the drugs we sampled failed at least one quality-control test. In another fourteen, 30–39 percent of the samples failed.

The most notable exception to this trend occurred in Cairo and, to a lesser extent, in Nairobi and Lagos, where there were several good-quality pharmacies. Of the twenty-one obviously degraded samples in the entire

TABLE 12-2
DRUG SAMPLES FAILING QUALITY TESTS

Sampling	Total Minilab failures	Total visual inspection failures	Total Raman spectrometry failures
Lagos 1	35	10	35
Lagos 2	16.1	9.8	25
Lagos 3	11.3	7.4	19
Lagos 4	9	6.6	15.8
Accra 1	35.4	12.1	41.1
Accra 2	20	10.8	31.1

dataset, nineteen came from Africa. All nineteen products came from five pharmacies: two in Lagos, and one each in Lubumbashi, Kampala, and Lusaka. This problem with grossly degraded products is likely due to the poor storage facilities at these pharmacies.

Assessing Degraded Drugs. To take a closer look at these apparently degraded products, all of which failed our quality-control tests, I asked for assistance from Harparkash Kaur of the London School of Hygiene and Tropical Medicine. Kaur runs one of the few laboratories at the London School and is a key innovator of various assessments of drug quality. Her most notable innovation is a new drug test for the ACT Consortium (a malaria drug group), which, among other things, assesses the quality of the ACT antimalarials from field samplings. Kaur has developed the most sophisticated basic dye test for artemisinin, which allows public-health officials to do basic tests for API concentration at a low cost.[3] With her colleague Albert van Wyk, she agreed to help assess the products we had collected. (See photos of some of the degraded products from pharmacies in Lagos and Delhi on pages 90–91.) As a reminder, degraded products are good-quality products made by legal manufacturers that fail to pass quality-control tests, usually because they have expired or were not stored properly. Products have a shelf life and expiration date because they degrade over time. For example, the main first-line antimalarial, the artemether-lumefantrine fixed-dose combination therapy, has a shelf life of two years. After two years, it may be degrading and is no longer considered of acceptable quality for treating malaria. Using such a degraded medicine may be less effective against malaria as a result, which is dangerous to the patient and may encourage resistance across the patient population. Degrading products may also have potentially dangerous by-products, which could be lethal even to patients who recover from malaria.

In many instances, medicines may be safe to use after their shelf life expires, because product shelf life is inherently conservative (two years is granted by regulators for accelerated drug testing, so it is simpler for companies to achieve). Furthermore, companies may be able to sell more of a product with a shorter shelf life, because expired products that are destroyed have to be replaced through new orders. But although products may be good after their expiration, many products become degraded *before* their expiration dates due to accelerated degradation. This can be caused by poor storage along the distribution chain or poor storage in final user locations.

I asked for Kaur's help in part because I noticed that four artemisinin brands that appeared degraded were identical. They had the same batch numbers and no noticeable differences as compared to those that had passed tests. Furthermore, where we were able to identify the distributor, we found that products from the same batch had been supplied by the same distributor to the different pharmacies where we had collected samples. With reasonable certainty, I concluded that the reason these products failed authentication was either that the product was an excellent counterfeit or that it was legitimate and had degraded due to poor final storage.

Samples of all four compounds, including those that seemed to be degraded versions, were procured from four pharmacies in Lusaka (the products were Artenam, Co-Arinate, and Lonart) and five in Lagos (the product was Artesunat). The failures of each of these products came from one pharmacy in Lusaka and one in Lagos. The samples of these products found in the other pharmacies (three pharmacies in Lusaka and four pharmacies in Lagos) passed authentication tests when first tested in 2009.

The degraded products were transferred in two tranches from Africa Fighting Malaria's office in July and December 2010 to the London School of Hygiene and Tropical Medicine, where they were analyzed in more detail. Most of the degraded products still have a considerable amount of active ingredient in them.[g]

The researchers who bought the drugs noted that neither of the two pharmacies where the degraded artemisinin products were bought had any temperature control in the building. There were no obvious signs of refrigeration, some of the stock was displayed in sunlight, and, from what could be observed in Lagos, adjacent buildings where the drugs were stored were made from corrugated iron, which likely would have exacerbated any heat concerns.

Anyone analyzing a medicine's packaging closely can identify degraded products, and it is easy to see the blister packaging buckling in each one of the examples of the degraded products (see photos on pages 90–91). It is unclear how many customers will pay close enough attention to notice the difference. And for those who do, how many would take the drugs anyway?

Policy efforts to improve storage may improve product stability, especially because the locations most likely to be problematic (kiosks, buses, and traders) were not sampled for this analysis. The storage conditions of these sellers' stocks are not likely any better than the worst pharmacist, so our samplings probably underestimate degradation.

India

As noted earlier, malaria is a killer in India, but the dominant *vivax* strain is far less lethal than the *falciparum* strain dominant in Africa. V. P. Sharma, a founder director of India's National Institute of Malaria Research, says *falciparum* malaria is underreported, and the disease is seasonal; drug stocks are likely to reflect that. Because we did not sample during the high season for malaria, we were probably selecting from a smaller selection of brands.[4] As a result, we selected a different combination of drugs in the three Indian cities

---

g. The Artesunat products have too much artemisinin, which is because some of these products appear to have had far too much active ingredient in them to begin with, perhaps 125 percent of the correct amount. However, the product was degraded, and its solubility was poor. Drug experts I spoke with said some manufacturers may deliberately be producing a formulation without MRA approval with increased "API concentration, knowing that their formulation deteriorates in hot climates." Such practices are certainly breaches of regulations in probably every country and certainly every country I investigated.

we studied to reflect the most important drugs in those areas. During this portion of the study, we sampled chloroquine, an antimalarial still effective against *vivax* malaria; two antibiotics, ciprofloxacin and erythromycin; and two antimycobacterials, rifampicin and isoniazid.

Most medicines in India are domestically produced. More than 98 percent of the samples we procured were made in India. We procured seventy-five brands of the five drug types from seventy pharmacies, ranging from relatively small pharmacies to large organizations with at least seven or eight staff. We collected 782 samples from the seventy pharmacies in the cities of Delhi, Chennai, and Kolkata. The failure rates were generally lower than those found in Africa, with the highest in Delhi (11.5 percent), followed by Kolkata (approximately 9 percent), and the lowest in Chennai (5 percent). Of a total of sixty-nine failures, forty-one had zero API content. In addition, nine of the thirty-one visual failures contained some API, meaning an estimated 6.6 percent of the total sample (50 of 782) should be considered counterfeit.

Compared with Africa (39 percent of failures had zero API), more of the quality failures in India (68 percent) had zero API (see figure 12-2 below for full results). In addition, only two products were obviously degraded. Thus, of substandard drugs in the samples, a greater proportion were counterfeit (as opposed to degraded legitimate products) in India than in Africa.

Failure rates among antimalarials bought in India were roughly the same as among the other drugs purchased, which indicates that the higher failure rate of antimalarials in Africa is caused more by the conditions in particular locations than by the drug type. Admittedly, the drugs purchased in the two continents are of a different type, so our conclusions are not perfectly comparable. However, because it is much easier for counterfeiters to switch the brand of packaging they produce than the distribution network and the location in which they sell a drug, we expect that location is more highly correlated with drug quality than brand name.

Pharmacy Data. Based on a small set of independent surveys, we found that a small but significant proportion of drugs purchased from retailers and traders in Delhi and retailers in Chennai failed at least one quality test. The profile of pharmacies selling substandard drugs was similar across the three cities (and similar to Africa); a few sold a high percentage of fakes, and most

FIGURE 12-2
**DRUGS FAILING QUALITY-CONTROL TESTS (INDIA), SUBCATEGORIZED
BY 0-PERCENT API, VISUAL INSPECTION FAILURE, AND DEGRADATION**

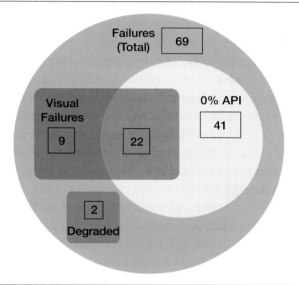

sold none. The worst-performing pharmacies were also responsible for samples with zero API content, which we assume were purposefully faked.

Most of these pharmacies do not meet Western standards, but they outperform most African pharmacies significantly. Most Indian pharmacists acknowledge they have been offered fake drugs, an insight gleaned from detailed surveys of the pharmacies. Far more pharmacists in India than in Africa reported having been approached by drug salesmen and offered counterfeits to sell. Most Indian pharmacists were concerned that government regulators were extracting bribes to allow them to stay in business (and perhaps some for turning a blind eye to illegal activity of the pharmacist, such as selling fake drugs), which led to some pessimism about the helpfulness of enforcement of stricter regulation.

Delhi Wholesalers. Substandard drugs appear to be a more serious problem in Delhi, where drug quality was lower, with samples failing in over

10 percent of cases. We conclude that the problem is largely due to a minority of actors (manufacturers, wholesale traders, and pharmacies) who are intentionally supplying counterfeit and substandard medicines to reap the higher profit margins available from such transactions. The same five drugs were procured from four wholesalers trading out of Delhi's Bhagirath Palace, one of the largest markets for drugs (legitimate and otherwise) in India. The majority of the problems were from one of the wholesalers, and another wholesaler had no fakes (and only a couple of degraded products). As with the pharmacies, the failure rates across drug types were similar. For wholesalers, failure rates ranged from 6 percent for chloroquine to 11 percent for isoniazid; for pharmacies, failure rates ranged from 9 percent for chloroquine to 17 percent for isoniazid. At pharmacies, isoniazid had the highest failure rate (17 percent, or 8 of 48), followed by erythromycin (13 percent, or 8 of 61), rifampicin (12 percent, or 8 of 66), ciprofloxacin (10 percent, or 5 of 50), and chloroquine (9 percent, or 5 of 56). At wholesalers, isoniazid had the highest failure rate (11 percent, or 9 of 79), followed by rifampicin (10 percent, or 8 of 78), erythromycin (7 percent, or 6 of 81), ciprofloxacin (7 percent, or 5 of 75), and chloroquine (6 percent, or 5 of 77). No specific drug type had zero failures, and no specific drug type had all, or nearly all, failures. This suggests that the problem of counterfeiting is not limited to only a few types of pharmaceuticals. Full results are displayed in figure 12-3.

Remaining Cities Tested

We collected only fairly small samples from ten pharmacies in each of the five other cities from the rest of the world. Failure rates averaged just under 4 percent and were isolated to a few pharmacies (mirroring other markets). Istanbul had no failures at all, the others had one or at most two brands (innovator or more likely generic) fail, and there was no discernible pattern.

A higher percentage of failures from the rest of the world had zero API than in the other locations, slightly more than India and many more than Africa. None of the visual failures among this sample (of which there were four) had any API at all. The data are strong enough to indicate that these cities have noticeably lower problems than Africa and a marginally better situation than India (see figure 12-4).

FIGURE 12-3
PERCENT FAILURE BY DRUG TYPE, PHARMACIES VS. WHOLESALERS

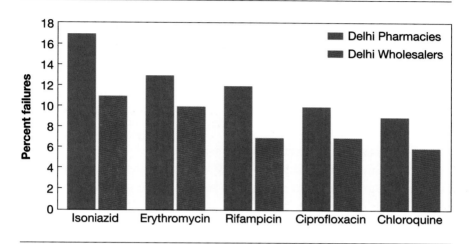

FIGURE 12-4
DRUGS FAILING QUALITY-CONTROL TESTS
(REST OF THE WORLD), SUBCATEGORIZED BY 0-PERCENT API,
VISUAL INSPECTION FAILURE, AND DEGRADATION

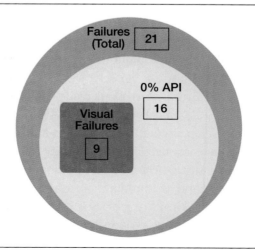

13

Interpreting and Discussing
the Results and Their Relevance

There is considerable product variability across producers by country and by size of company. India is a case in point: the larger Indian generics companies and Western manufacturers, all of which have annual revenues of over $300 million, generally make products with consistent quality, whereas smaller Indian companies, those from other parts of Asia, and most of the companies in Africa have far larger product-quality variability. More consistent production is also associated with (and perhaps caused by) business environments with stricter enforcement of production regulations. Drugs from EU-based or large Indian-based firms, which sell vast quantities of drugs in Africa, performed better than drugs made in markets where regulatory enforcement is weak, such as some countries of East Africa, notably Kenya.[1]

It is not surprising that where we had sufficient details on product registration (in fifteen sampled countries), registered products' quality failed noticeably less often than unregistered or probably unregistered products. This provides support for the importance of the process of product registration. Approval is not just a matter of formality; it is a necessary assessment of product quality and stability.

These results also lend support to efforts made by the international community, such as the USAID-funded PQM project. PQM helps regulators in middle-income and developing countries register products, conduct postmarketing surveillance, form consistent GMP requirements, and assist some companies in achieving GMP status.[2] These efforts appear to be necessary because, as this research project found, the products of many local African and Asian firms are more variable than their Western- or Indian-produced counterparts.

India provides an interesting location for study because its companies make products with differing degrees of variability. My research team has not yet analyzed whether the regulations are the same, or enforced to the same extent, in the various production locations. For example, although it is true that larger Indian companies performed better than smaller ones, it is also true that the best performing companies came from two states, Maharastra and Andra Pradesh, both of which report having better enforcement of laws than other states in India.[3] Perhaps the companies have made high-quality products, won market share, and attained large revenues today as a direct result of the rules enforced in those states. Furthermore, a study of the companies' histories might provide valuable insight as to whether law enforcement has a bearing on how long it takes before product variability is reduced by inculcating GMP and consistent high-quality supply-chain management into the ethos of the company.

Sample sizes of drugs produced in Brazil, Turkey, Russia, and Thailand were small and must not be looked at in isolation. It is interesting to note that these countries had very few products (either domestically produced or imported) that were obviously counterfeit, degraded, expired, or substandard products. This suggests that these countries have generally higher product standards than African countries, but considerable variability in some drugs indicates that quite a few producers do not appear to be up to Western GMP standards.

Analysis of the regulatory structures in each of these countries points to generally high-performing institutions, but each country has unique flaws. As noted earlier, Brazil allows the legal sale of similars, products not established as bioequivalent to innovator brands.[4] Russia's regulatory officials seem to turn a blind eye to a common practice in Russia in which legitimate local companies produce poor-quality versions of medicines to make money on the side.[5] Thailand has had political problems with its government-owned pharmaceutical company, which has produced substandard medicines. One example is GPO-vir, an HIV treatment (see box 8-1 on Thailand's GPO-vir).[6] China has a reputation of producing many of the world's fake drugs,[7] of allowing sloppy production of API for export, and of producing many goods with contaminants that have killed an indeterminate number of people.[8] It is not surprising that some of its legitimate products have some quality problems, given the apparent lack of production oversight. In 2008, prior to the Beijing Olympics, China began tightening its production standards by enforcing more rigorous licensing requirements for drug manufacturers.

TABLE 13-1
TESTING RESULTS BY REGION OF ORIGIN AND DRUG TYPE[a]

	Antimalarials	Antimyco-bacterials	Antibiotics	All drug types
Africa	7.00%	2.90%	7.10%	6.60%
	(34/485)	(1/35)		(42/635)
India	3.90%	5.20%	8.20%	4.40%
	(7/179)	(12/229)		(30/675)
Remaining countries[b]	0%	3.30%	6.10%	3.00%
	(0/21)	(7/212)		(16/528)
Total Failure Rate	6.00%	4.20%	7.40%	4.80%
	(41/685)	(20/476)		(88/1838)

a. Percentages are supported by total that failed testing/total samples tested.
b. Remaining countries include Thailand, China, Turkey, Russia, Brazil.

Like India, however, China still has unevenly enforced quality control, most notably in the poorly regulated Shenzhen free-trade zone.[9]

For now, it is enough to say that based on anecdotal evidence from numerous product seizures and this more systematic research project, it is not safe to assume that products in global demand (ciprofloxacin, for example) are made to the same standards across the globe. Our research demonstrates as much. Table 13-1 and figure 13-1 break down the results of our research by region of origin and drug type. Table 13-2 and figure 13-2 examine the role of manufacturing class. Table 13-3 demonstrates the differences between drugs manufacturered in different countries (taking the packaging of each drug to be accurate and not fake). Table 13-4 examines the result more closely, looking at the size of manufacture (where useful). Finally, table 13-5 looks at how registration effects drug quality.

Comparing Percent API in Various Failures:
Breakdowns of the Data

One of the interesting comparisons that the data yielded was the relationship between the amount of API in a drug and the location that drug was procured. Figures 13-3–13-9 demonstrate some of our key findings.

FIGURE 13-1

TESTING RESULTS BY REGION OF ORIGIN AND DRUG TYPE[a]

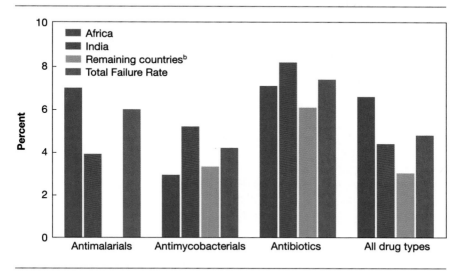

NOTE: None failed which is why these do not appear on the graph.

a. Percentages are supported by total that failed testing/total samples tested.

b. Remaining countries include Thailand, China, Turkey, Russia, Brazil.

What Role Does Price Play in Quality?

Although the initial reason for collecting data was to assess drug quality in emerging markets, information we collected along the way has provided for some interesting analyses. Various records and surveys have provided fascinating insight into pharmacists' opinions, pharmacy cleanliness, and price information for the drugs. I turn now to these.

The price information is not as comprehensive as the quality data. Because our primary aim was to establish quality, not all of our field researchers (residents of each city) kept all the receipts they received; in some instances receipts were illegible, and at some pharmacies, mostly in Africa and India, receipts simply were not given. Nevertheless, we did collect a useful sample of price data for each drug category and city.

Our data may be subject to selection bias. It is likely that pharmacies providing receipts are also the ones that keep better records and sell

TABLE 13-2
TESTING RESULTS BY COUNTRY AND CITY OF ORIGIN
AND MANUFACTURING CLASS

		Originator branded drug*	Non-domestic generic drugs	Locally manu-factured generic drugs	Total
Ghana	Accra	0.00%	2.20%	16.70%	5.20%
Ethiopia	Addis Ababa	0.00%	6.30%	12.50%	5.10%
Egypt	Cairo	0.00%	0.00%	8.30%	1.90%
Tanzania	Dar es Salaam	0.00%	6.70%	16.70%	7.10%
Uganda	Kampala	0.00%	3.80%	18.80%	7.70%
Rwanda	Kigali	0.00%	0.00%	0.00%	0.00%
Nigeria	Lagos	0.00%	9.70%	14.40%	10.90%
Angola	Luanda	0.00%	0.00%	0.00%	0.00%
D.R. Congo	Lubumbashi	0.00%	5.60%	14.30%	6.30%
Zambia	Lusaka	0.00%	4.20%	8.00%	4.70%
Kenya	Nairobi	0.00%	7.10%	12.50%	5.60%
India	Delhi	0.00%	0.00%	6.10%	5.80%
	Chennai	0.00%	0.00%	3.90%	3.70%
	Kolkata	0.00%	0.00%	3.90%	3.70%
Thailand	Bangkok	0.00%	4.90%	12.50%	3.70%
China	Beijing	0.00%	3.30%	8.90%	4.90%
Turkey	Istanbul	0.00%	0.00%	16.70%	1.00%
Russia	Moscow	0.00%	0.00%	11.50%	2.80%
Brazil	São Paulo	0.00%	2.40%	7.10%	2.70%
TOTAL	TOTAL	0.00%	4.00%	7.00%	4.80%

legitimate products. If there is a bias in the quality of the drugs for which we have some price data, it is probably in favor of higher-quality products (and probably more expensive ones, assuming that more organized pharmacies charge more than kiosks).

I am indebted to Ginger Zhe Jin of the University of Maryland and Aparna Mathur, my colleague at AEI. Both are excellent economists, and they designed the economic model from which the following is taken.[10]

FIGURE 13-2
**FAILURE RATE BY COUNTRY AND CITY OF ORIGIN
AND MANUFACTURING CLASS**

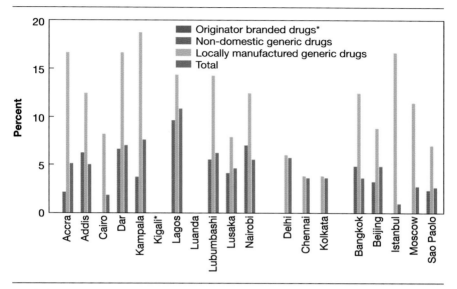

*No failures, which is why these do not appear on the graph.

The price analysis is not done by region or drug type, except where explicitly stated, because sample sizes for each drug type by location were not large enough to break out results and maintain any statistical significance. From an economic perspective, the harm of substandard or counterfeit drugs depends on whether consumers can tell drug quality from direct or indirect information. If poor-quality drugs can always pretend to be of high quality, consumers are deceived and manufacturers are discouraged from producing high-quality drugs in the long run. Regulatory enforcement of trademarks and quality standards could curb the proliferation of poor-quality drugs and reduce consumer fraud.[a] In contrast, a poor consumer may suspect low quality from the package or market cues, but still choose to purchase

_____

a. It is important to remember that not all counterfeits breach a trademark. A drug that claims to be ciprofloxacin on the package but contains chalk is "falsified," even if it does not infringe a competitor's trademark.

TABLE 13-3
TESTING RESULTS BY APPARENT COUNTRY OF MANUFACTURE

	Total samples tested	Total samples failing Raman spectrometry	Percent failed
India	798	35	4.40
China	169	13	7.70
Vietnam	61	3	4.90
European Union[a]	168	1	0.60
Switzerland	151	0	0.00
United States	119	0	0.00
Nigeria	121	13	10.70
Kenya	30	2	6.70
Tanzania	30	2	6.70
Uganda	22	3	13.60
Ghana	21	3	14.30
Zambia	24	2	8.30
Brazil	30	3	10.00
Russia	26	3	11.50
12 samples or fewer collected per country of manufacture[b]	68	5[c]	7.40
TOTAL	1,838	88	4.80

a. Countries include United Kingdom, Belgium, Denmark, France, Germany, and Italy.

b. Countries include Egypt, Democratic Republic of the Congo, Ethiopia, South Africa, Morocco, Thailand, and Turkey.

c. One sample from each of the following cities failed: Cairo, Addis Ababa, Lubumbashi, Bangkok, and Istanbul.

low-quality drugs in the hope that low-quality drugs will work sometimes and are better than no treatment. In this case, the economic consequence of a ban on low-quality products is not so clear: on one hand, it may deprive the extremely poor of a treatment that sometimes works; on the other hand, consumer belief in the efficacy of substandard or counterfeit drugs is likely wrong, and a misinformed choice could be worse than no purchase.

More important, the issue of poor-quality drugs is not independent of drug affordability. According to the WHO, over fifty surveys have shown

TABLE 13-4

TESTING RESULTS BY REGION (AND SIZE WHERE APPROPRIATE) OF APPARENT MANUFACTURER

	Total samples tested	Total samples failing Raman spectrometry	Percent failed
Large Indian Producers[a]	471	6	1.30%
Small Indian Producers[b]	327	29	8.90%
Chinese Producers	169	13	7.70%
Southeast Asian Producers[c]	69	4	5.80%
Western Producers[d]	438	1	0.20%
African Producers	302	28	9.30%
Producers in Mid-income Nations[e]	62	7	11.30%
TOTAL	1,838	88	4.80%

a. More than $300 million in annual revenue.
b. Less than $300 million in annual revenue.
c. Countries include Thailand and Vietnam.
d. Countries include those within the European Union, as well as Switzerland and the United States.
e. Countries include Brazil, Turkey, and Russia.

that drug prices are prohibitively high for many blue-collar workers in low- and middle-income countries, with some treatments requiring over fifteen days' wages to purchase a thirty-day supply.[11] Public policies such as tariff reductions, price ceilings, and compulsory licensing for patented drugs have tried to lower drug prices, but these have been insufficient. For many of the poor, buying potentially low-quality drugs is the only way to fight against unaffordability. And as Wiltshire Johnson, registrar at the Pharmacy Board of Sierra Leone, told me, in his country "fakes are just a little bit cheaper" than real products. The price differential is enough to encourage some people to buy them.

When my colleagues and I undertook this analysis in late 2010, it was the first empirical study on the economics of poor-quality drugs with an emphasis on the prevalence of poor-quality drugs in association with local regulation, income, literacy rates, and the extent to which consumers can infer the likelihood of poor quality from market price and pharmacy

TABLE 13-5

**TESTING RESULTS BY COUNTRY AND CITY OF ORIGIN
AND NATIONAL DRUG REGISTRATION LIST STATUS**

Country	City	Registered samples	Unregistered (or probably not registered) samples
Ghana	Accra	(2/57) 3.5%	(2/20) 10%
Ethiopia	Addis Ababa	Registration list unavailable	
Egypt	Cairo	Registration list unavailable	
Tanzania	Dar es Salaam	(1/22) 4.5%	(1/6) 16.7%
Uganda	Kampala	(2/37) 5.4%	(2/15) 13.3%
Rwanda	Kigali	Registration list unavailable	
Nigeria	Lagos	(13/167) 7.8%	(9/35) 25.7%
Angola	Luanda	(0/35) 0%	(0/10) 0%
D.R. Congo	Lubumbashi	Registration list unavailable	
Zambia	Lusaka	(2/50) 4.0%	(1/14) 7.1%
Kenya	Nairobi	(1/28) 3.6%	(1/8) 12.5%
India	Delhi	(8/202) 4.0%	(6/41) 14.6%
	Chennai	(5/211) 2.4%	(4/30) 13.3%
	Kolkata	(4/144) 2.8%	(3/47) 6.4%
Thailand	Bangkok	(3/98) 3.1%	(1/11) 9.1%
China	Beijing	(1/82) 1.2%	(4/20) 20.0%
Turkey	Istanbul	(1/97) 1.0%	(0/2) 0%
Russia	Moscow	(3/98) 3.1%	(0/8) 0%
Brazil	São Paolo	(2/110) 1.8%	(1/2) 50%
TOTAL		(48/1438) 3.3%	(35/269) 13.0%

appearance. Drawing insights from economic theories, we show that price and quality are fundamentally linked and that the fight against poor-quality drugs cannot be isolated from drug affordability.[12]

One reason for the limited literature on this topic is the lack of systematic data on poor-quality medicines. Our dataset, including only samples for which we have full price information, consisted of 899 drug samples across seventeen developing and middle-income countries. We ended up with drugs from 185 pharmacies. We find that 15 percent of the drug

FIGURE 13-3
FAILURES WITH X PERCENT API

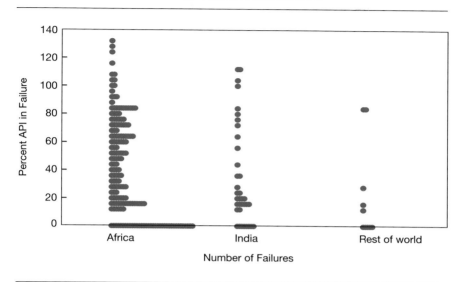

FIGURE 13-4
BOX AND WHISKER PLOT, FAILURES WITH X PERCENT API

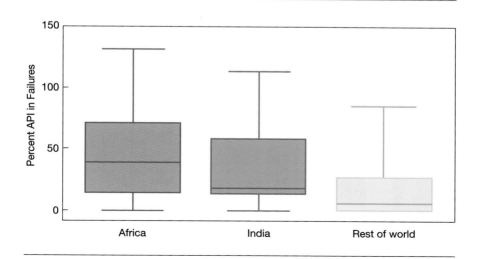

FIGURE 13-5
NUMBER OF FAILURES WITH X-PERCENT API: AFRICA

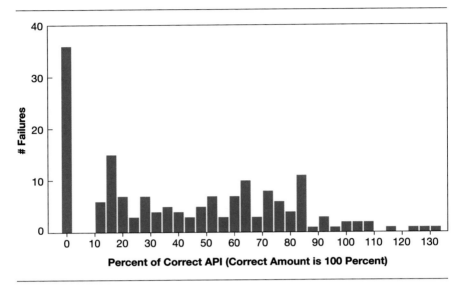

FIGURE 13-6
NUMBER OF FAILURES WITH X-PERCENT API: INDIA

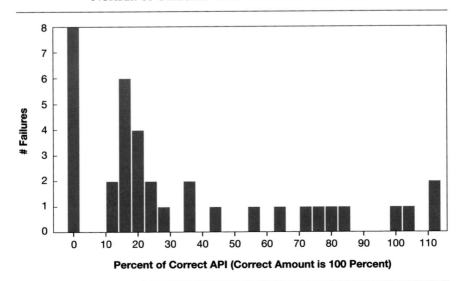

FIGURE 13-7
**FAILURES GROUPED BY API CONCENTRATION,
AS A PERCENTAGE OF TOTAL FAILURES: AFRICA**

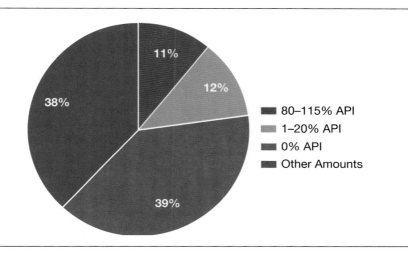

FIGURE 13-8
**FAILURES GROUPED BY API CONCENTRATION,
AS A PERCENTAGE OF TOTAL FAILURES: INDIA**

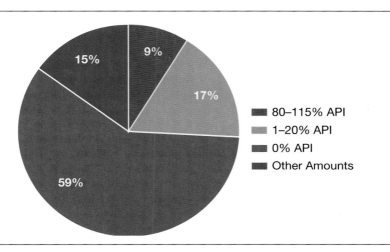

Figure 13-9
Failures Grouped by API Concentration,
as a Percentage of Total Failures: Rest of World

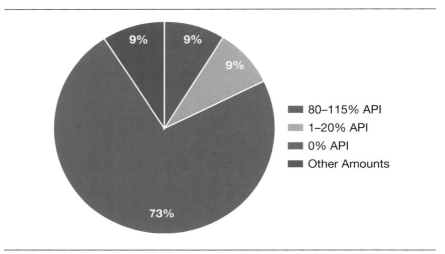

samples fail at least one of the tests, indicating that this subset of the larger data (where the overall failure rate was 12.2 percent) is likely to be fairly proportional and not hindered by any positive bias.

While quality is relatively easy to establish, it is far more difficult to determine how much consumers recognize about drug quality. As we have seen already, many pharmaceutical companies and governments are reluctant to publicize the problem of substandard and counterfeit drugs, fearing that the publicity will prevent patients from taking genuine medicines. Under such secrecy, consumer knowledge of drug quality is limited to self-inspection, word of mouth, and market cues. It is often difficult, if not impossible, to tell poor-quality drugs from packaging. In this subset, 3 percent of drug samples fail the visual test (this compares exactly with the large total sample). Full information may not be available after consumption either, because drug effectiveness varies from person to person, and even authentic drugs may not work well if the patient does not follow a doctor's instruction. Still, consumers may not be completely in the dark either: some quality information may be inferred from personal anecdotal experience tied to observable attributes such as price and the expected quality of certain distribution channels, such as pharmacies.

We asked our team of covert shoppers to report their subjective assessments of whether each pharmacy looked "good" or "poor." This assessment turns out to be correlated with our objective test results, but the correlation is low (correlation coefficients ranged from 0.14 to 0.27, all with p-values < 0.001). Another way to reveal drug quality is drug price. After controlling for drug type, local regulations, income, and literacy rate, we find that drugs that fail three quality tests are priced 13–18 percent lower than drugs of good quality. The absolute price differential, on average $0.59 to $0.82, could mean a big difference in local currencies. This suggests that at least some buyers might suspect that a drug is low quality because it costs less.

Why is there a demand for likely inferior medicines? One possibility is that patients derive benefit from them because some inferior drugs work, or give the impression of working due to placebo effect, without being harmful. Ignorance of pharmacology is another reason: less-educated patients might buy cheap medicines because they incorrectly believe that if expensive medicines treat one quickly, cheap, low-quality medicines just take longer to work. Alternatively, a family living in extreme poverty may decide that buying cheap medicines is a risk worth taking rather than not taking any medicine at all.

Although poor-quality drugs are, on average, sold at cheaper prices, price is not a foolproof indicator of medicinal quality. Drugs priced 30 percent lower than the average are only 8.62 percentage points more likely to fail any test (24.54 percent versus 13.92 percent), while drugs priced 30 percent higher than the average are only 4.13 percentage points less likely to fail any quality test (9.79 percent versus 13.92 percent). This suggests that the signaling effect of price is not as clear as economic theory suggests: high price does not guarantee high quality, and the existing price dispersion reflects market frictions as well as imperfect drug-quality information.

I suspect the explanation is as follows, although there are not enough price data to be entirely sure. While innovator products pass, the few fake versions often fail and are sold at the same price. For these products, there is little doubt that the customer is deceived and that price is no indicator of quality. The same is true of the best generics. However, other failing products (nonfake substandards) are generally cheaper, and hence for these products, price does provide some indication of quality (in this sense the customer is not deceived by these products). But because many patients, especially those who are poor and desperate, are unable to distinguish substandards from fakes, they may get the incorrect impression that all cheap drugs will probably work. The economics of counterfeiting literature supports the idea that such incorrect impressions on the part of consumers will invite counterfeiters into the market, further blurring the signaling effect of price on quality.[13] This raises a concern that isolated efforts to lower drug price (for example, by encouraging generics) could worsen the fight against counterfeit and substandard drugs because they undermine the role of price in signaling. I suspect this may be happening with the vast number of brands in the antimalarial market, but we have too few data to properly identify this effect.

Further Price Analysis

In the autumn of 2011 I kept analyzing the products and received feedback from manufacturers about batch numbers and other facets of production. There were 42 samples which I identified as definitely being counterfeit, most with very high quality packaging, which only an expert might be able to identify as fake. For each of these 42 samples we had procured at least one authentic version of the same drug, sold in the same part of the same city and bought at the same time.[b] Figure 13-10 maps out the deviation in price between the fake and a good quality sample.

In the above research (originally published in the *Journal of Health Economics*) I concluded that price signaling was mixed, and I asserted that was because we have substandards and fakes, where the former are likely to be cheaper, but the latter probably less likely since they are being passed off as the real thing (by definition, and since no one buys fake drugs for image reason—unlike watches, bags, etc.—there is no advantage to the retailer in discounting the price, assuming the retailer is aware the product is fake).

---

b. If the reference was not bought at the same pharmacy and there were multiple reference samples from other pharmacies in the same city, I took a simple average of those real product prices as my reference, so we'd expect very minor price deviations anyway.

FIGURE 13-10
FAKE PRICE DEVIATION FROM QUALITY DRUG PRICE

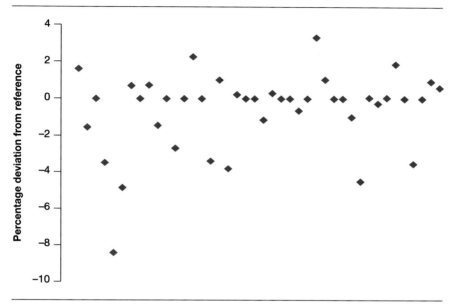

As you can see from the graph above, the variation in price among the known fakes is remarkably small. The average discrepancy is only 0.6 percent, the largest discrepancy in one sample is 8 percent, and overall the discrepancy is statistically not significantly different from zero. In other words fakes are priced at the same price as authentics (at least within the same location of a city for the same drug; it is quite possible the fakes are sold at lower prices in other locations where the real versions are not available).

In the above section the price discrepancy of poor-quality drugs from good quality was about 14 percent. Implicit in this large set and the smaller specific counterfeit price set discussed immediately above (and graphed below) is support for the notion that fakes are priced the same as authentics, and substandards (or not well-packaged fakes) are sold at a discount to authentics of that drug type.

It is impossible to perfectly isolate fakes from substandards because not all manufacturers respond to requests for information, and no manufacturer will admit to substandard manufacture. However, fifteen samples were

FIGURE 13-11
SUBSTANDARD PRICE DEVIATION FROM GENERIC DRUG PRICE

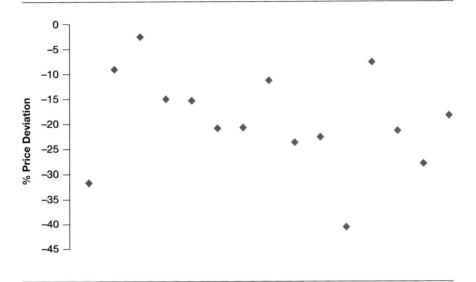

almost certainly substandard since they either contained the right amount of API but were poorly formulated or contained an incorrect amount, but over 60 percent, of the required amount of API. In some cases, drugs contained over 120 percent of the required API amount. Given that most fake products are fakes of well known market dominant products, it is instructive that these likely substandards are not well known products and have no known fake versions, supporting the assertion that they are substandards. These fifteen poor-quality drugs were on average 19.3 percent cheaper than the generics they copied, ranging from 2.5 percent to 41 percent cheaper (see figure 13-11). The difference in price is statistically significant; in other words, poorly produced drugs are, statistically speaking, cheaper than high-quality generic drugs.

If the limited analysis holds up, it might influence policy, for while it doesn't affect the general policies to improve quality and combat fakes, it might reveal interesting information about sources of substandard drugs and how some companies and wholesalers vary their pricing based on quality, which could be a red flag to a buyer or regulator.

African Price Data

Because experts agree that the high price of drugs is a key problem in limiting access to medicines for the poor, I analyzed the prices of the drugs we bought in Africa. By speaking to a few manufacturers and comparing the price of the same drugs sent to different countries, I saw that it was obvious that prices are marked up substantially by importers and wholesalers as well as by various tariffs and taxes. Markups are greatest in the private sector; presumably the rationale is that the relatively richer Africans who buy drugs out of pocket can afford to pay these markups, while the very poor cannot afford the nonmarkup price anyway. At worst, three months' wages would be required for an innovator treatment, compared with roughly two weeks for a generic version.

The price a patient in a private pharmacy pays varies by drug type and country, but in the aggregate, the price is proportionally made up by the percentages approximated in figure 13-12.

There are no tariffs on locally made products, and in many instances no taxes either, local producers being given an extra advantage so they can compete with more efficient international manufacturers. Distribution chains vary; some are short, and others are convoluted and have many intermediaries. Generics often have higher-percentage markups (although usually smaller absolute amounts), because they start with a lower manufacturer price. Some countries (such as Ethiopia) have higher registration fees for imports (after importation charges for both generic and innovator drugs) than for locally made drugs.

Regulation, Income, and Literacy Rate: An Analysis of Possible Confounding Variables

The main data described above are supplemented with data on local drug regulations, income, and literacy rate. Because local regulations are related to the price and cost of substandard and counterfeit drugs, income and literacy rates are likely to affect both demand and cost of supply. The aim is to see if other variables are heavily associated, perhaps even causally so, with drug quality. I took male and female adult literacy rates for ages fifteen and over from the United Nations Development Programme's 2009

FIGURE 13-12
RATIO OF INPUT COSTS IN RETAIL PRICE

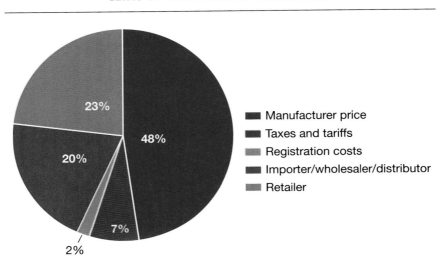

human development report. They are country specific and were compiled from censuses and surveys conducted by the UN Educational, Scientific, and Cultural Organization between 1999 and 2007.[14] We took the average of female and male literacy rates, as they are highly correlated (their correlation coefficient is 0.89), and the literacy rate available for all countries except Ethiopia and Turkey.

The year- and city-specific GDP-per-capita data are denominated in U.S. dollars in purchasing power parity. They were constructed using 2008 city GDP estimates by PricewaterhouseCoopers and the 2009 and 2010 city population estimates from the 2009 revision of the UN's *World Urbanization Prospects* report. We extended the 2008 GDP estimates to 2009 and 2010 using country-level GDP growth rates from the International Monetary Fund. We extended the city population estimates backward to 2008 using the UN report's 2005–2010 average population growth figure. For Istanbul, Lubumbashi, Kigali, Kampala, and Lusaka, city-level data were not available, so we used country-level GDP per capita from the International Monetary Fund's World Economic Outlook database as of October 2010.[15]

After these procedures, GDP-per-capita data are available for all countries except for Ethiopia.

Regulation

We included four variables to capture local drug regulations: drug registration, country-specific taxes and duties, maximum prison sentences for counterfeiting, and direct price regulations set by the government. As already established, drug registration is the most basic regulation on legitimate drugs, and its availability and implementation vary greatly across countries. Using drug registration data, we created a dummy variable equal to one if a drug has been registered in the purchase country at the purchase time and equal to zero if not registered. Some countries impose import tariffs, sales taxes, and other duties on ethical medicines.[16] They are the average taxes and duties applied to chapter 29 (the customs category of active pharmaceutical ingredients) and chapter 30 (the customs category of finished pharmaceutical products) in 2006, by country. This variable is available for ten countries and accounts for 735 of the 899 drug samples.[17]

The third regulatory variable we measured is the maximum prison sentence for drug counterfeiters. We hand-collected minimum and maximum penalties from the latest legal documents we found from each country. For example, Egyptian intellectual property law sets down a number of penalties, including prison terms, for persons making or selling counterfeit goods. Monetary penalties range from $90 to $9,000, and terms of imprisonment range from two months to three years. Prison terms are mandatory only for repeat offenders.[18] In July 2008, the Indian cabinet approved a bill that increases fines for convicted counterfeiters from $250 to a minimum of $22,550 or three times the value of the drugs confiscated, whichever is the larger amount. They also increased the jail sentences for those convicted of counterfeiting from five years to a minimum of ten years and up to life in prison.[19] To accommodate diverse sentencing guidelines, we coded monetary fines as "zero months" and the death penalty as "360 months" (thirty years)—the same as a life sentence. We used the maximum penalty in the data. This variable is available for twelve countries, accounting for 691 of the 899 drug samples.

The last regulatory variable we analyzed was the presence of direct price regulations, such as price ceilings, mandatory retail prices, and price guidance. We hand-collected these regulations from each country's most recent government documents. Given the variety of price regulations, we defined a dummy variable equal to one if a country adopted any price regulation on pharmaceuticals in the data-collection year, and zero if otherwise. This variable is available for ten of the nineteen cities, accounting for 554 of the 899 observations.

Even when price is able to signal quality, the difficulty of differentiating poor-quality products from genuine drugs (from nonprice information) will push up the price of genuine drugs, because the expected price premium from high quality must exceed the temptation to cut corners. To support this argument, we find that the price discount for failing drugs is greater in countries with a lower-than-median literacy rate (24.1 percent) than in those with higher literacy rates (14.3 percent), after controlling for local factors. These findings highlight the fundamental links between price and quality, suggesting that public policies on price and quality must be coordinated.

In theory, stricter regulations on drug quality should raise the cost of substandard or counterfeit production, thus increasing the probability that more expensive drug samples pass the quality tests. High import tariffs, no price regulation, and the status of innovator brands may imply higher drug prices, thus inviting counterfeits, but it is also likely that innovator brand holders devote more efforts to brand protection in such circumstances by hiring investigators, pursuing counterfeiters, and making the packaging harder to imitate. It is also possible that price regulations limit the range of markups (that is, price minus cost), thus reducing the potential reward for high-quality drugs, which likely leads to more drug failures.

These data suggest that registered drugs are more likely to pass quality-control tests, and this is confirmed in more rigorous modeling. Moreover, patented medications are more likely to pass quality tests, and drugs we procured in countries that have higher taxes and duties are more likely to fail these two tests. The correlations between test results and price regulations are less clear: the presence of price regulations tends to be associated with a lower passing rate for visual appearance but higher passing rates for the other tests. The maximum penalty for counterfeiting drugs is not significantly correlated with any test result except for the spectrometry test, which had a counterintuitive negative sign. This reflects the possibility that countries with severe counterfeit problems may adopt harsher penalties. Richer and more literate countries have higher-quality drugs.

Macrolevel Analysis

The previous section described probably the most significant economic analysis performed on any drug data involving substandard products. Nevertheless, this study is severely limited. When we look at the economic data as a whole, we see that there appears to be little difference whether one uses income (GDP) or literacy as a proxy for the development of a country.

By calculating an aggregated single drug quality failure rate for each city and using the income figures measured above, it is possible to ascertain a basic relationship between income and drug failure. A priori and in the literature, richer countries have less of a problem with substandard drugs than poorer ones. Thus, the existence (or lack thereof) of an association in my data between income and drug quality is a key test of the quality of the drug research.

By regressing income on the estimated historic failure rates provided by IMPACT (see Figure 13-13, these figures were withdrawn), we found an inverse relationship, as expected. The linear relationship is statistically significant, although statistical significance is lost when the more correct logarithmic conversion is applied. In any event, the linear relationship is weak at best.

I wanted to test whether this was due to the known problems with the data, or if there really is no strong relationship. After all, the IMPACT estimates were withdrawn because they were—by their own admission—established from small samples. Furthermore, they had used different methodologies across drugs types, making the data unsuitable for econometric analysis.

In the sampling my research team undertook, our sample size was still small, but we sampled consistent, if not identical, drug types across countries and we used identical methods. I hypothesized that, using these data, we would find a more significant result. Indeed, the results confirmed my hypothesis that lower-income cities have a worse problem with substandard and counterfeit drugs than wealthier cities.

FIGURE 13-13
MODELING POOR QUALITY DRUGS (IMPACT) ON COUNTRY WEALTH

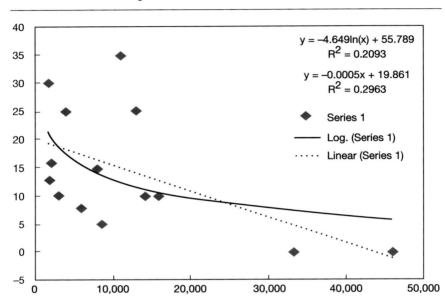

When data from the Internet study are added to the African and Indian data, as well as studies in the other five middle-income cities, we observe a very strong relationship; 72 percent of drug quality is explained by income (68 percent of drug quality is explained by income if we excludes the Internet data that includes results from the EU and United States).

Figure 13-17 (page 321) shows this relationship, but note that income (or literacy) does not determine the quality of the drugs in any specific place. As we saw in Nigeria, quality can be improved significantly over a short period of time even while income barely changes. Indeed, if all countries improved in the way Nigeria has, the curve would be lower, showing higher-quality drugs at each income level.

Counterfeit or Substandard?

We did not undertake detailed forensic analysis to establish the cause of any drug-quality failings in a systematic way across all data. Some drug samples were obvious visual fakes, and my research team and I were able to conduct some basic forensic analysis for a few other groups, such as the drugs we procured from the Internet studies and some of the antimalarials from Nigeria and a few of the other cities. Although we lacked a detailed forensic analysis across all of the data, one way to differentiate between products that are almost certainly counterfeit and those that may be just substandard or degraded is by the content of API. A reasonable number of products either had zero API or were obvious fakes because of packaging errors. The samples were split; we considered all zero API or bad-packaged goods as counterfeit and all other failures substandard.

We find that there is a statistically significant relationship between income and quality for both counterfeit and substandard drugs (see figures 13-14 and 13-15). In both categories, income, or another proxy such as literacy, explains roughly half the variability in the data. The explanatory power of the association between substandard drugs and income is interestingly higher (the correlation coefficient is 0.71) than between income and fakes (0.41); 71 percent of the cause of substandard drugs is related to income.

This effect is further revealed in the gradients of the curves (interpolated regression equations) and their intercepts. As expected a priori, the problem of substandard medicines disappears above a certain income level. This is borne out by the regression; when a city's income per capita reaches roughly $22,500, the substandard problem vanishes. The curve for substandard drugs (see figure 13-15) is steeper than the counterfeits curve (see figure 13-14), implying that substandard medicines are a far greater problem at low incomes than counterfeits. Until per-capita city income reaches about $10,000 (where curve 1 crosses curve 2 in figure 13-17), the more dominant effect is from substandard drugs. The curve for counterfeits is shallower, and problems with counterfeit drugs are more ubiquitous because they occur at all income levels.

In absolute terms, fakes are more of a problem at lower incomes than at higher incomes. These regression equations support the notion that at the lowest incomes, combating substandard drugs should be the higher priority, while combating fake drugs is important for every country. Figure 13-14 shows the regression for counterfeits, and figure 13-15 shows the regression for substandard drugs. Figure 13-16 shows the combination of the two. Figure 13-17 shows all three curves.

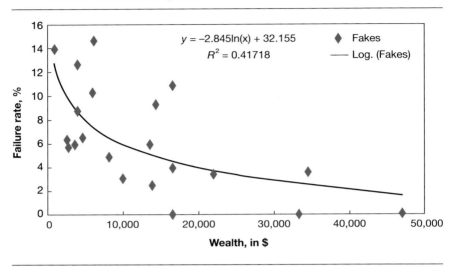

FIGURE 13-14

FAKES—MODELING QUALITY BASED ON COUNTRY/CITY WEALTH

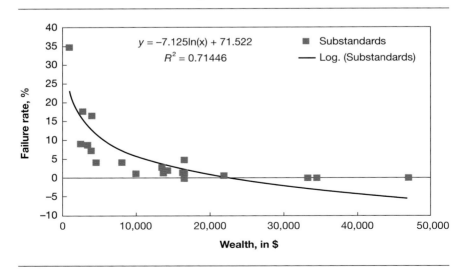

FIGURE 13-15

SUBSTANDARDS—MODELING QUALITY BASED ON COUNTRY/CITY WEALTH

FIGURE 13-16
BOTH—MODELING QUALITY BASED ON COUNTRY/CITY WEALTH

FIGURE 13-16
BOTH—MODELING QUALITY BASED ON COUNTRY/CITY WEALTH

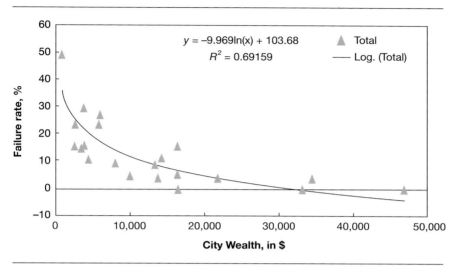

FIGURE 13-17
ALL TOGETHER—MODELING QUALITY BASED ON COUNTRY/CITY WEALTH

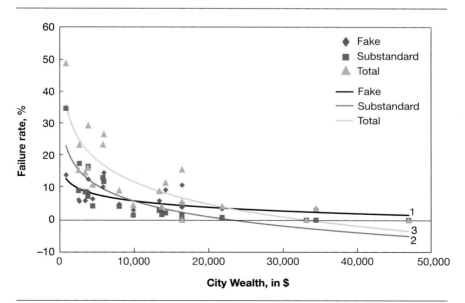

Box 13-1

WHAT DO COUNTERFEITERS PUT IN THE FAKES?

We identified 141 counterfeit products that were definitely fakes, and conducted a more detailed content analysis with the TruScan Raman spectrometer and with the help of Ahura spectroscopist Bob Brush. Fourteen products contained unidentifiable contents, and a wide variety of compounds were identified in the remaining 127.

The most regularly occurring compounds were acetaminophen (46/127, 36 percent), talcum (baby) powder (32/127, 25 percent), and flour (29/127, 23 percent). Chalk, sodium hypochlorite, aspirin, caffeine, lactic acid, a variety of vitamins, titanium oxide, and borosilicate were also identified in a few samplings.

The spectra of the most common compounds found in fake drugs are shown below. One of the reasons for analyzing these compounds is to try to identify the fake drugs' origin and distribution networks. If two batches of fakes for different products contain the same compounds in the same ratios, they are likely to come from the same fake-drug ring.

In the fake samples from Delhi, for example, we found the same incorrect compounds in roughly the same ratios in both chloroquine and rifampicin.

FIGURE 13-18

FAKE ARTESUNAT SPECTRA VS. REAL ARTESTUNAT SPECTRA

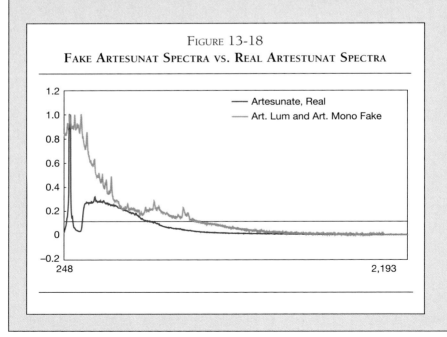

Fake antimalarials in Kenya and Tanzania also had the same compounds in similar ratios. These samplings identified a plausible link in a criminal trading enterprise; the same ratio of wrong ingredients (mainly acetaminophen and talcum powder) were found in four different fake "brands," one cipro and three artesunate, in Nairobi and Dar es Salaam. What is certain is that drugs made from acetaminophen and talcum powder cost far less than those made from cipro and artesunate. The "API" in these fakes probably cost less than 10 percent of the price of the original product.

These examples support anecdotal evidence that gangs produce numerous fake products with the same ingredients, differentiating the packaging, product shape, and, to a lesser extent, color. Accurately identifying the trace elements (such as pollen) that might shed more light on the drug's manufacturing location would require far more detailed analysis, beyond my research team's technical abilities. Paul Newton's research team did indeed unearth such detail to help nail Chinese counterfeiters of artesunate products in Thailand, Laos, and Cambodia.

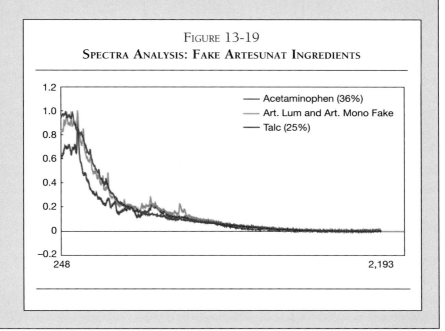

FIGURE 13-19
SPECTRA ANALYSIS: FAKE ARTESUNAT INGREDIENTS

PART IV

The Way Forward

14

Developing Medical Regulatory Authorities: The U.S. FDA as a Case Study

I have discussed the problem of dangerous drugs as they affect poor and middle-income areas, but the robust regulatory system that protects American patients is relatively new in historical terms. As recently as 1951, patients were not required to have a prescription from a certified doctor in order to obtain medication. A decade before that, there were virtually no rules in the United States governing drug manufacture or production. Only in the last few decades has the United States developed a regulatory system capable of effectively monitoring the drug supply. The relevant question today is, how did the United States develop such a regulatory body?

There is no simple answer. Indeed, in some ways this entire book is about answering that question. If you ask the experts—drug-company executives, doctors, and pharmacists—they will say the best MRAs, such as the U.S. FDA, do a good job of protecting patients by enforcing drug-quality regulations, directly monitoring supply-chain activities, and working with enforcement agents to bring criminals to justice. These opinions are correct, as far as they go. Experts within hierarchical systems, such as health care, often overemphasize the importance of regulations and undervalue concepts of market competition, branding, and the liability structures of modern commercial systems. Nevertheless, the FDA is vital and central to U.S. success in drug quality. But the United States did not transition from not having an MRA to having the modern-day FDA overnight. Many painful lessons were learned along the way. Because other countries might be able to learn from these lessons, it is worth briefly investigating how the U.S. FDA came about and how long it took before it (and other actors) could ensure good-quality products for Americans.

Improvements in drug quality have been brought about by an interaction between competitive businesses, the medical fraternity, regulators (supported where appropriate by police agencies), and, in the past thirty years, pressure groups. Philip Hilts's informative history of the FDA explains that it was founded to "protect consumers from cheats" yet "has evolved into the body that sets the scientific marks against which progress is measured."[1]

That evolution has taken a century. Although a poor country today can aspire to its own MRA, demanding that it emulate the modern FDA without being aware of the FDA's path may be bad advice. Some of the examples of dangerous products in Europe and America in the nineteenth and twentieth centuries are echoed in modern-day Asia and Africa. This chapter will be more historic than any of the others and naturally less personal because of that.

Why an FDA? It Is All about Economics

Economic theory argues that for most goods, competition will lower price and improve quality. There is no doubt that in nineteenth-century Europe and the United States, significant competition among purveyors of all sorts of goods raised quality standards across the board for foods and consumer goods and medicines alike. While consumers can easily spot a shoddy piece of craftsmanship, it is not as easy to pick out a dangerous food or medication. Indeed, much of the problem for such products in the nineteenth century was adulteration, a problem so widespread the FDA developed an acronym for it that is still used today: EMA (economically motivated adulteration).

Adding impure or inferior ingredients or diluting good ones has been a trick of unethical players for centuries. Virginia and Massachusetts outlawed such practices in the 1600s, but it became widespread in the nineteenth century, particularly adding chalk to bread and diluting wine and milk with water. Such asymmetry of information, wherein producers have far more knowledge of the product than consumers and use that knowledge to abuse consumers, is the main economic justification for regulation of such products. The eminent economist George Akerlof ably demonstrated that when such asymmetries exist, more expensive high-quality products may be driven out of the market by poorly produced but cheap alternatives.[2] Regulators can draft legislation to assess quality and restrict such activities to drive many bad products from the market. The costs of this are less competition and generally higher prices, but most people accept that as a price worth paying for increased safety. Regulation alone does not cure the problem; markets can also self-correct over time if it becomes obvious that certain brands are better than others. I discuss the positive brand examples of Crosse and Blackwell in Britain and H. J. Heinz in the United States later in this chapter.

Even when a great brand displaces bad products, the need for regulation likely remains, especially if those brands are vulnerable to fakery. Early government inspectors were concerned for what consumers were ingesting and provided an impetus for expanding inspection. Copper sulfate made faded vegetables appear green again, and sodium benzoate prevented decaying tomatoes from rotting altogether. Red oxide of mercury can restore the dark color of chocolate when it has faded through age. Additives were often used to deceive consumers.

The case for regulation appears obvious, but regulation creates winners, and not all of them are worthy. Incumbent producers may lobby for regulations to make it more costly for newer producers, which might have less expensive and better products, to enter the market. According to renowned economists George Joseph Stigler and Sam Peltzman, this enables established companies to maintain high prices without improving quality, in which case regulation can harm consumers.[3] Ultimately, though, when well-educated and wealthy consumers are unable to differentiate good from bad, the case for regulation becomes overwhelming.

The Creation of the FDA

The first step toward establishing drug-quality standards was taken in 1820, when eleven doctors founded the United States Pharmacopeia.[a] Over time,

---

a. "The United States Pharmacopeia (USP) is a non-governmental, official public standards–setting authority for prescription and over-the-counter medicines and other healthcare products manufactured or sold in the United States. USP also sets widely recognized standards for food ingredients and dietary supplements. USP sets standards for the quality, purity, strength, and consistency of these products critical to the public health. USP's standards are recognized and used in more than 130 countries around the globe. These standards have helped to ensure public health throughout the world for close to 200 years," "About USP," it developed into a group of pharmacists and doctors who present and revise formulations of drugs and tests for purity. Leading members and others founded the American Medical Association in 1848 and the American Pharmaceutical Association in 1852.

The first federal drug law in the United States was the Drug Importation Act of 1848. This law required the U.S. Customs Service to inspect for low-quality imports, although "the law became moribund" due to lack of proficiency of the customs agents.[4] In the early nineteenth century British politician Jacob Bell quipped that foods not fit for the Brits were "good enough for America!"[5] because of the lower standards and lack of control in the United States at the time (medical treatments at the time were essentially tonics and supplements, most food based). In 1883 the innovative Harvey Wiley was appointed chief chemist at the Department of Agriculture's Bureau of Chemistry, the precursor of the FDA, and he undertook significant food adulteration studies. According to Hilts, Massachusetts reported that 37 percent of drug samples taken between 1882 and 1900 in the state were adulterated. In New York, of the 343 samples of one drug purchased, phenacetin, 315 were diluted with acetanilide, a hazardous painkiller. In sum, drug supply was "unreliable, the purity suspect, the price high and variable, and the corrupted substances sometimes fatal."[6]

Wiley established a "poison squad," men who agreed to eat food with different preservatives, whose concentrations were increased over time, to determine the safety of the newfangled chemical treatments. In many respects, this was the first systematic, organized human testing of food products. Many of the results were frightening, including permanent impairments to the brave volunteers who acted as guinea pigs. Wiley pushed for legislation to improve standards and increase testing as well as for the establishment of a federal agency. In 1906 Congress passed the Food and Drug Act, and President Theodore Roosevelt signed it. This increased the responsibilities of the Bureau of Chemistry (which in 1927 became an independent agency, the Food, Drug, and Insecticide Agency). This Food and Drug Act incorporated the standards established by the USP, requiring manufacturers of any drugs listed by the USP in its National Formulary to

---

www.usp.org/aboutUSP (accessed May 30, 2011). Today USP is at the forefront of promoting good drug-quality standards in the developing world.

conform to the standards USP had laid down. The act also made it unlawful for states to buy or sell food and drugs that were mislabeled or tainted. In 1912 the Sherley Amendment made it unlawful for sellers to make fraudulent medical claims about their products, but because deliberate intention to mislead had to be proven to get a conviction even under this amendment, prosecutions were rare, and the amendment did little to change behavior.

"Insecticide" was dropped from the name in 1930 because at that time insecticide regulation was the responsibility of the Department of Agriculture. The Environmental Protection Agency took over insecticide evaluations when it was formed in 1970, and it still tracks insecticide production and use today. Insecticides are less important to public health in the United States now than they were in the beginning of the 1900s, because insect-borne disease declined in the United States over the past century. Developing countries still have terrible problems with insect-borne diseases; it may be wise to consider insecticides a public-health issue to be influenced by a health regulatory agency instead of an agricultural or environmental one.

Drug Regulation and the Market's Decisions

Some analysts assert that the 1906 law suited the interests of existing manufacturers and that later laws proposed by the FDA reflected "regulatory capture" by large national food manufacturers who wanted federal regulation to act as a barrier to smaller local firms. Clayton Coppin and Jack High specifically claim that Wiley was a "bureaucratic entrepreneur" who saw the law as a way to preserve and expand his agency.[7] Investigations by journalists such as Upton Sinclair, whose book *The Jungle,* about the disgusting state of the meat industry, appalled readers, aroused public opinion, and made political action inevitable. *The Jungle* is so well known in U.S. regulatory circles that it has become a term of reference for poorly regulated conditions. Roger Williams, CEO of USP, says that parts of the developing world, notably India and China, are so poorly regulated that they were living through their own "Upton Sinclair period . . . maybe we can sort it out faster than the next 100 years."[8]

Corporations have always lobbied for legislation to preserve or expand their market share, and sometimes this benefits the public. The Heinz Company found that when ketchup was made with very fresh fruit under sterile conditions with secure bottling, they did not need to add sodium benzoate, a dangerous preservative used by Heinz's competitors. Heinz's competitors claimed it was safe, and the disagreement went all the way to the president's office. Though Roosevelt came to believe Heinz was correct, legislative changes took a long time to occur. Still, the publicity around the debate led the more-educated public to patronize Heinz's products. In the United Kingdom in the late nineteenth century, the better brand won a similar argument despite similarly slow legislative action. Crosse and Blackwell's pickles won the public-opinion battle, changing preferences from bright green pickles, which were toxic in large enough doses, to less exciting-looking brown pickles, which were equally tasty and not dangerous. Both Heinz and Crosse and Blackwell are still selling products, whereas none of their competitors are.

Another product that survives today is Listerine. As Hilts explains, this is a rare "example of a product that succeeded under both lax and, later, tougher law, the difference being that dangerous and dishonest marketing was dropped."[9] In the 1930s, Listerine was sold as a preventative for tuberculosis and the common cold, and although it does kill many bacteria it has no impact on TB or viruses. While the company was lying about what the product could do, the product was robust and did a valuable job. As advertising standards were enforced, the marketing department simply changed tack. It was not a fundamental product problem, just one of marketing overreach. Similar marketing overreach is prevalent in the developing world today: advertisers tout quack cures for malaria, HIV, and other terrible afflictions. Many of these products are bogus and will disappear over time, but others may be useful over-the-counter local products and herbal remedies. Like Listerine eighty years ago, these companies need to be exposed for their fraudulent claims today.

By the 1930s, a tipping point had been reached when feedback loops among consumers were improving and good-quality products were more identifiable. From then on, federal regulation enforced what the most advanced businesses were already doing.

The Massengill Massacre

The early laws and powers of the FDA were limited, and even when terrible incidents occurred, changes were not inevitable. As Hilts explains,

"What seems required to make a new law is the presence of two circumstances when a crisis occurs—a bill must *already be present* in Congress, and legislators and significant elements of the public must already be *educated and paying attention* when the crisis hits. Some say the crisis must also involve children."[10]

In 1937 two such circumstances coincided when one of the earliest useful antibiotics, sulfanilamide, was mixed with DEG to make it easy to ingest. As discussed in chapter 1, DEG is toxic and can be lethal at fairly low doses. The Massengill Company's elixir sulfanilimde with DEG had not been tested before its release and killed at least 105 people, including many children. People may have demanded that drugs be tested in advance at some point anyway, but the behavior of the company ensured it. Massengill had kept poor records of where the lethal concoction had been sent, was too slow to issue a recall, and gave doctors no explanation for the recall when it was issued. Public outcry over the incident broke congressional deadlock, and on June 15, 1938, the provision requiring safety tests before marketing a product, which had been debated by Congress but had achieved no agreement earlier in the 1930s, was signed into law.

This was a significant shift from poorly enforced ex post liability for companies to ex ante regulation. Previously, the only deterrent for manufacturers of dangerous products was the threat of being sued after harm was caused, but now they had to prove in advance that their products were safe. In principle, abuse of the approved product could lead to jail time for directors of companies. Most defend this decision, although Krauss claims that ex post liability did work at least to a certain extent because Massengill was successfully sued for gross negligence by an array of plaintiffs.[11] The increased power emboldened the FDA. Within a decade, it had identified many drugs it believed too dangerous to continue being sold over the counter and began enforcing the prescription system.

And with the Durham-Humphrey Amendment of 1951, certain drugs are only legally obtained with a prescription certifying the approval of a qualified physician. It is worth highlighting this change because my research team and I were able to procure prescription medications without any prior doctor's approval in all seventeen countries where we sampled drugs over the past three years. After 1951, the U.S. government ensured that many drugs were limited to prescription only, which indirectly increased the power of doctors to control the market. Doctors cannot always be trusted, and some were known to turn a blind eye to dangerous and failing products, usually to protect their reputations and sometimes for financial gain.[12] Still, doctors are one of the most trusted groups in every society around the world. So it is right and relevant that in most countries, doctors play a role as gatekeepers for drugs. Although this is true of the poorest countries as well, and one would like to say that drugs to cure malaria and TB, where drug resistance is a concern, should only be provided with a prescription, in reality there are so few doctors and so little access to them that the result would mean the majority not getting such products. But over time, as wealth increases, greater reliance on doctor recommendations would be a boon to low- and middle-income countries fighting these diseases.

The easiest way to determine the impact of demanding prescriptions is to note how advertisers changed their focus. As Hilts points out, "In 1930, about 95 percent of drug company advertising was aimed at the public. By 1972, perhaps as much as 90 percent was aimed at doctors."[13] The amendment driving this advertising change made some sense; if a pill is missing a key ingredient or simply does nothing, a patient may never find out. An alert doctor talking to his colleagues, on the other hand, can analyze patterns among his patients and provide scientific, evidence-based proof. Totally bogus claims made by producers about their antimalarial drugs are common today in Nigeria, as chapter 4 illustrates, and most Nigerians buy their drugs directly with little input from doctors.

During the 1940s and 1950s, after considerable political bickering, Congress introduced additional amendments establishing basic GMP. Other new laws ensured that drug labels explain a drug's purpose and that firms include informational inserts describing benefits and hazards of drugs with each pharmaceutical product.

The FDA's Expanding Authority

The most significant expansion of the FDA's authority over drugs came after another disaster. Thalidomide was marketed from 1957 by German manufacturer Chemie Grünenthal as a safe sedative to combat morning sickness in pregnant women, but it resulted in about eight thousand birth defects in Europe. Frances Kelsey of the FDA did not approve the drug for widespread use in the United States because she was not satisfied with the safety reports from the manufacturer. Richardson-Merrill wanted to market the drug in the United States, but due to reports of Thalidomide's harm in the *British Medical Journal,* this did not occur. Not all Americans escaped unscathed, however; seventeen American babies whose mothers had taken pills with thalidomide were affected because some U.S. doctors had been persuaded to put the drug on trial in the United States. The media avidly reported the largely averted disaster in the United States, and this, according to the FDA, led to a clamor for "stronger drug laws," which provided the public support necessary to push the Kafauver-Harris amendment to the Food, Drugs, and Cosmetics Act into law.[14] This amendment established that drugs had to be both safe and effective prior to FDA approval (the 1938 law only required proof of safety). The major change this amendment made would have made no difference to the Thalidomide case, because the drug's safety was at issue. Nevertheless, post-Thalidomide, the FDA required stricter controls for advanced testing of new drugs. Though these likely were not too oner-ous for the best companies at the time, the testing requirements led to the demise of many firms.

From 1973 on, many economists, led by Sam Peltzman, have argued that these amendments reduced the flow of new drugs entering the mar-ket.[15] Gieringer is probably one of the more outspoken researchers, claim-ing that the drug lag induced by the 1962 amendments has caused more deaths than the FDA's extra caution has saved.[16] Hilts denies this categori-cally; he provides data to show that the fault lies with the companies them-selves, which often did not fill out forms properly and lazily used the FDA as a sounding board or a cheap expert external reviewer.[17]

Both sides have good arguments, but I am marginally more persuaded by the economists. The incentive for the FDA is quite simple; officials may be criticized for delays, but to allow a second Thalidomide incident would be terminal to a career, so the bias toward caution certainly exists. The Orphan Drug Act of 1983 sped up and simplified approval for drugs with small markets: awareness of patients in dire need of treatment ultimately drove reform. In addition, multinational companies can benefit from delays and high approval costs, because smaller firms cannot afford them. Small firms often partner with large firms and are occasionally bought out, so large firms can generally control market entry. Companies can be cavalier, though, as the fraud at GSK shows (see the "GSK Whistleblower" box in chapter 5), so it is hard to know exactly where the equilibrium is and how stringent regulations should be. Within the context of this book, I would say it is a wonderful dilemma to have. Most countries would love to be worrying about whether drug systems are slightly overregulated instead of dealing with hopelessly enforced regulations and firms that regularly make lethal products.

The 1980s saw the largest corruption case involving the FDA, and it highlights the opportunities for graft that flourish in cultures that have yet to tackle corruption. Charles Chang and David Brancato, officers in the generics approval division of the FDA, accepted bribes to approve some companies' generic drugs faster than others. This led to investigations, hearings, and other federal actions. Hilts writes, "More than two hundred generic drugs were pulled from the market, at least temporarily. Fifty-five employees of fifteen generic drug companies were convicted of felonies along with five FDA officials."[18] If this is happened in the United States, one can imagine the problems facing Nigeria, India, and China.

The Prescription Drug User Fee of 1992 increased fees from companies and earmarked that revenue to directly pay for reviews. Prior to 1992, companies did not pay directly for any reviews (although their corporate taxes contributed to government revenue). Now, a fee of approximately $200,000 must be submitted with applications for new-drug approval. According to Philipson and his coauthors, this increase in funding for the FDA reduced review times and did not undermine safety.[19]

The FDA and China

Perhaps the most important and relevant change over the past few years has been for the role of the FDA in monitoring drug quality coming into the United States directly in the country of manufacture. Much manufacturing moved overseas over the past two decades, and drug production was part of that move; Indian and Chinese companies produce a lot of the chemical ingredients for American companies' drugs. Michael Miller, senior adviser in the office of the Secretary of Health and Human Services during the second term of the Bush administration, spoke with me about his concerns over this shift. He told me both the FDA and Health and Human Services were increasingly concerned that some of the products from China were suspect. He said they all "recognized the need for action before any tragedies occurred." Before the United States acted, though, tragedies caused by contaminated Chinese products had led to mass outrage and extensive media coverage, both in China and internationally. The melamine milk contamination harmed hundreds of thousands of Chinese children and was found to have contaminated pet food and toothpaste that had made it to U.S. markets. In 2006–2007, a counterfeit of the blood-thinning drug heparin contaminated U.S. supplies and probably killed 149 Americans, as described in chapter 1. Miller says that these tragedies "clarifie[d] everybody's thinking, we had to address offshore production."

Within weeks, the FDA changed oversight of products from China, and new tests for heparin were devised by scientists at universities working with USP and the FDA. Companies employed these tests.

Health and Human Services secretary Michael Leavitt and his opposite number, Chinese health minister Gao Qiang, both agreed that improving Chinese API required action from both countries. The solution to the problem lay in a symbiotic relationship between officials in the two countries. Around that time, Leavitt had told me that "we cannot inspect our way to safety." This was not to say U.S. inspections were not important, but that with a country of over a billion people and thousands of manufacturers and traders, only the Chinese could oversee production in China, and then only in principle, given the lack of expertise in China. U.S. expertise could assist, especially in designing programs, but the United States could not do it alone.

Because of the vast volume of Chinese imports to the United States, U.S. inspections of everything from China would mean "commerce would grind to a halt; we had to seek to ensure safety is built in along the way," Leavitt said.

The U.S. FDA, the SFDA, and the Chinese Administration on Quality Supervision, Inspection, and Quarantine created an agreement, and programs began in earnest. The U.S. FDA opened an office in Beijing in November 2008. Andrew von Eschenbach, then commissioner of the FDA, testified before Congress that the FDA now demands that all glycerin entering the United States be tested to ensure it is not contaminated with DEG.[20] The FDA is also working with the drugs industry to guarantee the provenance of API throughout the supply chain and to improve the traceability of excipients, because these currently are not traced throughout the supply chain. Eschenbach said, "We have limited knowledge of the quality of ingredients and products manufactured in China as this fast growing source is just beginning to put in place a national regulatory infrastructure. In the past four years, the number of FDA-registered drug manufacturers in China has at least doubled. The Chinese government is in the process of rewriting its GMP for drugs. Drug manufacturers in China, and some other developing countries, comply with GMP inconsistently and to varying degrees. Provincial authorities who conduct inspections of drug manufacturing sites in China are not always equipped with the expertise needed for this complex undertaking."[21]

The move was welcomed, at least by firms U.S. reporters could interview. "It is definitely good news, helping Chinese active pharmaceutical ingredients (API) exporters to achieve better recognition by the U.S." said Li Kechun, general manager of Chiral Quest, a process-development company based in Zhejiang Province.[22]

Miller was generally positive about the Chinese and U.S. responses. The most negative thing he said was that if the United States had cultivated a better relationship with Chinese officials prior to the heparin problem, the "reaction time would have been faster." Other American experts I spoke with were far less supportive of the Chinese, but none wanted to speak on the record for fear of upsetting their Chinese counterparts. In general, they agreed that the two governments' relationship was positive and that Chinese federal officials genuinely wanted a productive agreement to resolve problems, but the Chinese may have been more concerned with preserving "brand China" than with solving public-health problems. In China, this problem had two different levels. At the national level, Chinese officials needed to save face. At the more local level, though, some of the regions were not as committed as Beijing to the reform package.

All government officials like to speak highly of their countries, so bad news is often ignored or brushed under the carpet. In China, where there is little practical distinction between the Chinese government and Chinese companies, this can be a particularly acute problem. It is one of the key reasons food and drug scandals are hidden. As one commentator put it, there is little "recognition of problems" because they "hate to be seen as sloppy and third world."

One U.S. official said even some Beijing officials who spoke positively about the relationship with the United States could never accept that Secretary Leavitt could not simply overrule an FDA decision. In China, a potentially embarrassing decision could be averted if desired, at least temporarily, whereas the FDA's findings cannot be struck down arbitrarily by an immediate political superior. Along with the power Chinese officials have to change results on a whim, though, comes great responsibility; officials have been executed for making poor decisions.

Still, some of the old ways appear to be changing. Premier Hu Jintao visited hospitalized victims of the melamine milk tragedy, exactly as a U.S. politician would have, to show that those in the political system acknowledged their suffering and would act.

In China, the regions control oversight. In the United States, the states control food and drug inspections, too, but although occasionally fraught with difficulties, the relationship between Washington and the states is functional. In many parts of China (and India, too), the federal government has little real influence. That some of the regions were not fully committed to China's reform package is problematic, especially as it applies to the People's Liberation Army, which another U.S. official characterized as a "state within a state." He told me the army owns "hospitals and hotels and may even make some of the tainted API."

Change is occurring slowly in China, and there is little the FDA can do. U.S. companies may actually have more leverage because they buy so much from China. But because they cannot afford to stop buying from China, one wonders how much leverage they could actually exercise.

According to Ilisa Bernstein of the FDA, the FDA's foreign inspections are risk based, targeting the most likely problem sites. But inspections appear to be driven by other criteria. It is stressful and tiring to inspect plants in time zones halfway around the world, where inspectors do not speak the language, nor do they have unrestricted access, and where extending an inspection may be impossible due to visa denials. Marcia Crosse, director of health care reporting at the Government Accountability Office, told me that whereas the FDA inspected 40 percent of U.S. production facilities in 2009, it inspected only 12 percent of Indian sites and only 6 percent of Chinese sites. If the FDA really implemented a risk-based approach, it should inspect far more sites in China and India, where only restricted access is granted and more problems have been seen in recent years. But because each of these foreign inspection costs over $60,000, the FDA budget may not allow so many inspections. Crosse also explained that most inspections are of plants that want to be inspected because they are trying to introduce a new drug entity.

There have been attempts to encourage third-party inspections, where trusted inspectors working for auditors or other corporate entities undertake the task, but these have been done sparingly, partly because of design flaws. Crosse told me there are "disincentives that may prevent establishments from opting for third-party inspection": third-party inspectors assigned to a business will always show up, and the business being inspected pays for the inspection; compare that to FDA inspectors who do not show up this year or the next, and they do the inspection for free.

Crosse suggests that the FDA should establish foreign rotations within its staffing so it becomes a requirement of the job for employees to have, for example, a two-year foreign tour of duty every decade. This would bring the FDA into line with the U.S. State Department, and because over 25 percent of all imports into the United States are overseen by the FDA, it is arguably worth the expense. Establishing overseas offices would also make inspectors feel more supported; the FDA already has offices in China, India, Europe, Latin America, and the Middle East. Currently all jobs and postings are voluntary, though, so it is not surprising the FDA has more volunteers to inspect plants in Italy than in China.

Challenges to MRA Development

It is important to keep in mind what is possible in middle-income and emerging economies. It is important that they have competent MRAs staffed by experts in various relevant disciplines. MRAs are the linchpin of improved drug quality, whether registering products and ensuring legal production or assisting criminal detection, but only if they are honest and efficient and have the support and cooperation of customs, police, and the courts.

But what should be funded, and what metrics should donors demand? Learning from the U.S. experience, including the history of the FDA set out by Philip Hilts, I suggest that the following questions need to be considered and resolved: Does a country have the requisite factors in place that made the FDA the respected entity it is today? Is there a free press, private legal recourse, wealth to pay for education, publicly responsive legislators (far more likely in a democracy)? Will an MRA have any authority in countries where there is little understanding of the dangers of bad products? Might it not take a domestic disaster, such as the Thalidomide tragedy that galvanized American popular demand for safety, to actually force action? What would be the response if an MRA is corrupt, or the government behind the MRA is corrupt? The incremental increases in the power of the U.S. FDA were possible only because people looked to the government to solve a problem. If people only expect self-serving corruption from their government or authorities, they will hardly want more of it.

So while establishing an MRA in, say, Malawi, is important, if Malawi does not have other factors in place, the MRA may not be successful. Take Kenya: it has a weak but fairly free press, the legal system is corrupt and unresponsive, and the political system may be responsive but is very corrupt. Education levels are low because wealth is low, and the staff at the Kenyan MRA are few in number and underresourced. Although Nigeria has historically been even worse off in these regards than Kenya, it has raised quality standards, so the situation even in Kenya is far from hopeless.

What parts of U.S. history can an emerging economy bypass? Any government can use foreign disasters to demonstrate that action is required, even if it refuses to acknowledge domestic disasters.

What of the other, more costly, and time-consuming requirements?

Nigeria's NAFDAC is an example where additional funding, including from donors, has worked well. Although a few allegations have been made, no evidence of corruption has been found. NAFDAC is a shining beacon, even an anomaly. It was driven by the conviction of one woman who fortuitously gained the trust of a president not normally known for his impartiality, and he allowed her autonomy. NAFDAC had gained enough momentum and status that it was able to attract a superb successor, and the agency continues to improve.

Concerted efforts by NAFDAC have increased drug quality in Lagos dramatically (my own data confirm this finding), perhaps most obviously by ensuring criminals are punished and working with global bodies, notably Interpol. NAFDAC has developed such a good relationship with its Chinese counterpart that six Chinese nationals were tried and convicted in China for smuggling fake antimalarials into Nigeria. The punishment handed down was far heavier than Nigeria could have imposed, showing that the legal obstacles to international criminal cooperation can be resolved. In short, much of NAFDAC's deserved success is due to its criminal-enforcement work and diplomacy; yet this is not something many supporters of MRA action emphasize.

When I was investigating the diversion of antimalarial drugs in East Africa, it became clear that corruption was a significant problem in the region. Impoverished developing-country governments rarely turn down donor offers, but such funding can easily be abused, and donors must be prepared to pull funding if this happens. Of course pulling funding rarely occurs, because donor staff also benefit from their grants; in fact, their jobs may depend on giving away funds. MRAs are often unable to prevent substandard drugs from local producers, because their staff are powerless against politically powerful businessmen. In 2007 China executed the head of its drug regulator for allegedly accepting bribes from counterfeiters. Also in 2007, drug inspectors in Orissa, India, were accused of working in cahoots with counterfeiters, as was the case in Argentina in 2009 when a drug counterfeiting scandal went up to the ministerial level. Drug theft in Togo was run out of the very government department charged with drug distribution. Many smaller cases go unreported every year.

Even assuming MRAs work well, they still suffer from the same problem as the U.S. FDA: they cannot inspect all packages of drugs even if they inspect all factories for GMP. High-quality medicine supplies are also a product of the successful interplay of civil law and trademark protection. This allows consumers to obtain redress against negligent manufacturers through the courts on the one hand, while allowing manufacturers of quality medicines to defend their brands on the other.

Although legal and regulatory systems are unreliable, new technologies may allow consumers to verify the quality of medicines, for example, text message-based authentication of the kind pioneered by Ghana's mPedigree, expanded by Sproxil in Nigeria, and enhanced by PharmaSecure[b] in

---

b. PharmaSecure has benefited from a law in India, January 21, 2011, mandating that all export pharmaceutical products have unique coding on primary, secondary, and tertiary packaging.

India.[c] In the longer term, a high-quality drug supply can be achieved only from the bottom up, as companies seek to maintain a competitive advantage through maintaining the integrity of their brands.

Limits to International Assistance

Despite the long and dismal experience of well-intended development programs that have withered on the vine as soon as the international money stops flowing, donors are ever ready to keep trying. So, how can the WHO or the U.S. FDA or others help?

The WHO can provide a list of suppliers of essential drugs so that African MRAs do not have to research and credential suppliers. Education of pharmacists, wholesalers, and other traders about storage conditions is important. But membership in the WHO is a voluntary affair, and the WHO has no power to monitor the drugs actually on sale in an African country, such as Kenya, and can do nothing about the quality of locally produced drugs on sale.

The WHO, USP/USAID, and others can train the local MRA officials and even establish bachelor's and master's courses in the country's universities for training the next generation, but they cannot ensure that these courses are funded indefinitely. USP/USAID/World Bank personnel can train customs officers and even potentially give them technology (Minilabs and TruScans) to find fake drugs, but if the customs officers' pay is low, they may readily accept bribes from smugglers or traders of fakes, which no amount of training or technology can make up for.

Donors can buy drugs for the public sector, but most drugs (in the poorest nations) are bought in the private sector, where donors have little reach. The AMFm, as discussed in box 4-10 on page 114 is a rare exception. But even the AMFm cannot really influence local conditions for drug purchasing over a long time period. The urge of international aid organizations

---

c. While such serialization schemes are useful, criminals always find their way around them. According to one security source based in the United States, on at least one occasion, counterfeiters have bribed security personnel at code location storage depots and have been given back-up data disks as a reward. This enables them to copy codes and hence fake the serialization.

to donate the highest quality medicines to the public sector with the intention of distributing them free to the poorest and needy is a commendable one. However, the people of a recipient country may quite reasonably view the act differently: there are many people in the country who can afford to pay for their own medicines but have no access to anything decent. Yet donors are selectively giving away top-quality medicines for next to nothing. The few good local companies have very good reasons to be alarmed by Western largesse because it can totally undermine a market they were hoping to supply. Western generosity seems like product dumping to an African drug producer. Of course, it is a long way from appreciating all the anomalies between Western markets and those problems described above to actually justify stealing from government stores and gaining financially from the fraud.

I suspect that until the poorer across society become wealthier and more literate, we will be plagued with significant quality failings (and, as established, even the rich world is subject to fakes). So what are we to do while standards vary?

This is arguably the most intractable issue, and it is still to be resolved, for it is largely one of perception. It is obvious that drug quality in Lusaka and Lagos is not as good as in London or Los Angeles, but is assuming emerging markets should operate at rich-country levels holding back progress?

Priorities for MRAs in Developing Countries

The history of the FDA shows a dynamic give and take—often a fight between business and regulators, heavily informed by the public mood. Some profit-seeking firms cut corners, leading to harm, a free press exposes wrongdoing, and responsive regulators (many no doubt acting in their own self-interest) establish laws to prevent such actions occurring again. Over time, the regulations become stricter and business practices improve, sometimes as a direct consequence of regulation and sometimes as a result of punishing litigation, but also because GMP and social responsibility and brand reputations become standard practice. Social responsibility for U.S. firms developed over time: the carrot of increased profit and market share for good behavior and the stick of FDA oversight and sanction for bad behavior made firms change policies. It took decades, one could argue most of a century, for this to occur, and along the way there were a few major disasters.

Will it take emerging markets decades to change, too? The quality of drugs in developing countries may not be as good as in the West, but should these countries' officials tacitly accept that trying to match the West is counterproductive? Ignoring the difference between poor and rich countries and arguing that poor people should never have poor-quality drugs may actually worsen outcomes.

The good news for developing countries is that they can get help if they want it. China is using the expertise of independent agents and the U.S. FDA to conduct inspections. Such collaborations usually encompass technology transfers through training programs and advice on designing university courses that will gradually create local capacity to manage improvements themselves.

USP has long been involved in helping developing countries improve the quality of their medicines (see box 4-3, "Basic Testing Using the Mini-lab"), and its work has made a discernible difference to countries that embraced its advice. The USP technique involves breaking down all the features of a given function into component parts and explaining precisely what should be done and how to do it. If fledgling MRAs attempted to become fully functional copies of the U.S. FDA overnight, they would be overwhelmed; USP helps them take manageable steps toward building quality systems instead of trying to do everything at once.

Although all the identified functions of the FDA may be desirable, some improve safety and quality much more effectively than others. For example, as part III demonstrated, drug registration is a vital function of MRAs; it is perhaps the single most important function for safeguarding quality. Here, I set out the priorities for developing countries' MRAs. These suggestions are based on the USP recommendations.

MRAs are extremely complex organizations and require staff with high levels of expertise across many disciplines. MRAs are also expensive, so scarce resources must be prioritized according to the functions with the greatest impact on quality and safety.

Research by myself and others has documented that drugs not registered by a national MRA are more likely than registered drugs to be substandard. This is because registration does not mean merely keeping a record of medicines for sale; registered products should have undergone rigorous assessments before being allowed onto the market. Any local manufacturers or importers applying for licenses to market products must submit comprehensive dossiers, and the MRA must thoroughly evaluate these.

Dossiers should contain documentation demonstrating the following: an applicant's qualifications; the factory and equipment used (which must be inspected to assess compliance with GMP); that effectual quality controls were applied to active and inert ingredients before and during production to eliminate impurities and contamination; that the product has the correct characteristics (that is, that ingredients conform to pharmacopeial standards for the drug and the drug works correctly); and that labeling and packaging conform to technical and regulatory requirements, such as accuracy and ease of understanding (and is the language spoken locally). Packaging must also contain the correct physical address of the manufacturer, information on exactly what active and inactive ingredients were used, manufacture and expiration dates, batch numbers, and storage conditions. Generic products must submit test results showing that the drug is interchangeable for quality, safety, and efficacy with the innovator product. (For more details, see box 5-2, "The Biopharmaceutics Classification System.") The registration protocol is demanding on both the manufacturer (or importer) and the MRA, but it is clear why higher quality exists when this process is followed.

Another important and demanding part of an MRA's job is to set standards covering manufacturing, procurement, distribution, and storage processes and practices maintained in laboratory and pharmacy premises. It must enforce these standards by making inspections (preferably unannounced) that can be followed by meaningful punishment for companies that fail to meet standards. Postmarketing surveys provide a useful method for getting a snapshot view of what is offered for sale. To conduct these, an MRA sends covert buyers into retail pharmacies to buy a sample of medicines that can then be tested for quality. This provides a cross-check that correct storage conditions and stock-management systems are maintained throughout the production, distribution, and retail chain, and that drugs that patients take have not degraded because of bad handling or because they have been on the shelf too long. Postmarket surveys can also pick up samples of drugs that slipped past the registration and inspection processes.

Sometimes a problem is not discovered until people become ill or die, and the first warning is raised through an adverse drug reaction (ADR) reporting system, which the MRA should maintain. ADR systems are not always in place, and without them, it may take significant and expensive investigations to solve problems. This was the case for many of the examples of DEG poisonings described in chapter 1. Ideally, nationwide product-recall procedures and enforcements support an ADR reporting system.

To help patients protect themselves, information on which medicines are approved for sale by the MRA should be readily available, reliable, and up to date. MRAs should be ready to respond to new developments or conditions that may require regulation and then to implement such regulation and disseminate new rules to all concerned parties. The national MRA is responsible for approving and monitoring clinical trials. This is an underdeveloped function in many low-income countries, and is a setback to research into cures for the diseases of poverty. These functions are far from all a fully developed MRA does, but embryonic MRAs should develop these functions in the given order for the greatest impact on raising quality.

Even while developing and transitional countries are catching up with all the functions carried out by the U.S. FDA, the FDA keeps growing because new threats to public health keep emerging.

The MRA Role in Protection through Registration

The registration process is perhaps the most important, as well as the simplest, part of product regulation. In the West, we take for granted that our food and drugs come from registered, well-monitored environments. The U.S. FDA is respected and trusted to oversee product quality, but most MRAs are not like the FDA; they are underfunded, poorly administered, and often corrupt. Product registration and high-quality products are not always the norm in much of the developing world where pharmaceutical products are not monitored. In economic jargon, product registration is a necessary but not sufficient condition for good-quality medicines. High-quality medicines can exist in a country that has not registered them, but these are usually brought in by visitors for personal use or smuggled illegally across borders.

The lack of drug registration is a serious and well-documented problem. By some estimates, as many as 30 percent of drugs in Brazil are not registered, and 19 percent of drugs for sale in Nigeria were not registered as of 2006.[23] In Vietnam, a 2006 study on antimalarial drugs found that 60 percent of antimalarial samples were not registered.[24] A 2007 study in Kenya found that 42 percent of antimalarials were not registered.[25] Unregistered pharmaceuticals are easy to find in informal markets, and they can also be found in hospitals, pharmacies, wholesalers, and medicine stores in the formal health sector. Some pharmacists sell them unknowingly, whereas others buy unregulated products from traders to save money. Unless a competent authority oversees drug registration for pharmaceuticals produced domestically and imported from abroad, product quality varies significantly.

Without standardized oversight, unregistered medicines may come from a variety of sources. Some are produced in laboratories with a GMP license that are registered to produce that particular medicine, others are made in reputable manufacturing plants that choose to avoid registration to cut costs, and still others are mixed in crude cement mixers in backyard shacks. In 2007 the SFDA reported 329,613 cases of unlicensed drugs in China, most of which were manufactured by fly-by-night firms.[26] In Russia, legitimate drug companies are known to produce unregistered medicines on the side for extra profit; from 2002 to 2005, Russian officials estimated seizures of over one thousand tons of illicitly manufactured pharmaceuticals.[27] In countries that do not have significant domestic drug-manufacturing plants, such as Thailand, most unregistered products are imported or smuggled across the border, especially when regulatory presence at the borders is weak. Product registration is not sufficient to ensure drug safety and quality, not least because the relevant authority could register products without conducting proper analysis, as is the case in Peru, but it is generally necessary for a start.

Registration Is a Means, Not the End

Companies may cheat the registration process by sending well-made products as the samples to pass tests and selling products produced under less stringent and less costly conditions. This is one reason the production processes of domestically manufactured drugs must be inspected before product registration is granted. GMP certification of production facilities, postmarketing surveillance (random sampling and testing of products on the market), and ADR reporting are also important, but proper product registration is the first and arguably most important role an MRA plays.

Table 14-1 highlights the different registration timelines in twelve emerging countries, which I investigated separately from the drug sampling, and hence the overlap is significant but not exact. The registration process is discussed in more detail in the book's online component, available at www.phake-meds.org. While many of the application requirements are the same, specific tasks companies have to do to register their products vary. We found differences in the costs of registration, quality-analysis requirements, the length of the evaluation processes, the duration of registration certificates, renewal policies, and GMP compliance. The cost of registering a product varies from a few hundred dollars in countries such as Uganda to many thousands of dollars in places such as Russia and Brazil. Fees often differ depending on whether a drug is locally produced or imported and whether it is a generic or innovator product.

Some countries require companies to submit clinical trial or bioequivalence data with their registration applications; other countries do not specify if any such data are required. Still others, such as Brazil and Argentina, do not require bioequivalence data to register similars. Most countries we studied require companies to submit two or three drug samples with applications for analysis.

Similar variations exist within the twelve countries' registration-renewal policies. In most of these countries, registration certificates are valid for five years, after which time the drug must be reregistered. In India, reregistration is required every three years, but it is never required in Thailand.[28] Because drugs are not required to go through renewal processes after achieving initial registration in Thailand, many unsuitable or inappropriate drug formulas registered decades ago may still be available for sale. According to the Thai FDA, 230 drug formulas registered in 1983 remain on the market today; these have not been reviewed in nearly twenty-six years.[29] Thailand has also been slow to recall medicines with probable adverse effects; from 2002 to 2008, only seventeen registered drugs were withdrawn in Thailand,[30] whereas in Nigeria, at least ten drugs were recalled from the market in 2009 alone.[31] In Russia, if a drug is granted reregistration, it is given an open-ended certificate. In comparison, an imported drug

FIGURE 14-1
REGISTRATION TIMELINES BY COUNTRY

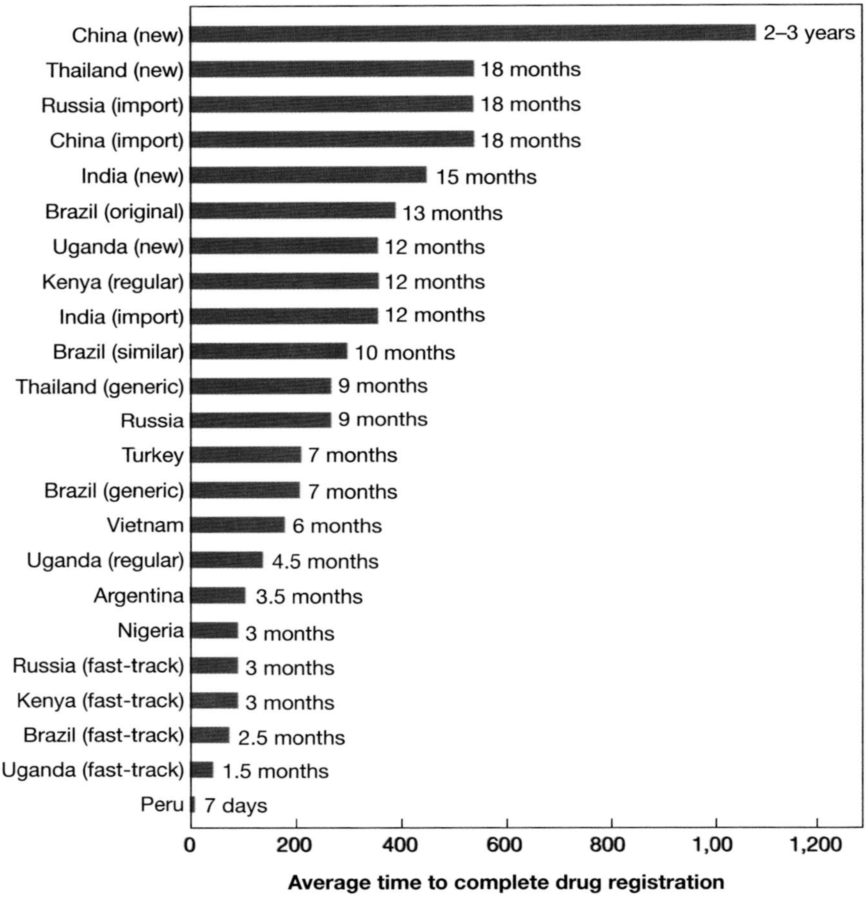

Country	Time
China (new)	2–3 years
Thailand (new)	18 months
Russia (import)	18 months
China (import)	18 months
India (new)	15 months
Brazil (original)	13 months
Uganda (new)	12 months
Kenya (regular)	12 months
India (import)	12 months
Brazil (similar)	10 months
Thailand (generic)	9 months
Russia	9 months
Turkey	7 months
Brazil (generic)	7 months
Vietnam	6 months
Uganda (regular)	4.5 months
Argentina	3.5 months
Nigeria	3 months
Russia (fast-track)	3 months
Kenya (fast-track)	3 months
Brazil (fast-track)	2.5 months
Uganda (fast-track)	1.5 months
Peru	7 days

Average time to complete drug registration
(x-axis: 0, 200, 400, 600, 800, 1,00, 1,200)

SOURCE: Various media and online sources.

can be reregistered only once in Nigeria (for an additional five years) before it has to start being produced locally. Many governments desire local drug production, but Nigeria mandates it.

Although some countries have MRA websites detailing registration procedures, the quality and accessibility of these sites vary significantly; some are so difficult to navigate they prolong the registration process. For instance, despite claims that registration for foreign manufacturers has been made simpler, Russia's MRA (Roszdravnadzor) website is available only in Russian, and it recommends that companies hire an authorized agent to undertake registration.[32] Registration for importing pharmaceuticals into Russia takes an estimated twelve to eighteen months.[33]

We found similar problems in accessing online registered-drug lists intended to help local consumers. Brazil's list of registered medicines seems to be constantly "under construction," and the link to Peru's registered drug list was broken repeatedly whenever I tried to access it. India's online registered-drug list was organized by year of registration and broken down by state totals, but it had no cross-referenced index or figures for the country as a whole. Finding any information on Vietnam was difficult because its site is in Vietnamese only, and although in China the registration process is available in English, the list of approved drugs is in Chinese only. Thailand's registration website was relatively complete and easy to navigate, but it also required translation. Kenya, Uganda, and Nigeria had accessible, up-to-date, and navigable drug registration databases and websites. It is interesting that African countries have a greater level of transparency and organization. This may be the direct result of demands made by donors that require such information to be readily available and accessible, especially on the Internet.

Coordination and inter-country cooperation have been another major challenge. This is displayed in box 14-1, and discussed more fully online at www.phake-meds.org.

Challenges to Implementation

India is unusual in not having a central drug regulatory authority to control both drug product registration and manufacturing quality. Individual states in India control manufacturing, laboratory, and sales standards, which means product quality varies greatly across regions within the country. Maharastra and Andra Pradesh have good reputations for enforcing GMP; Haryana and Uttar Pradesh do not live up to the same standards (and my own data support these assertions, because companies in the reputedly better-performing states had better-quality medicines).[34] The Mashelkar report found that of thirty-one states, only seven possessed properly equipped laboratories capable of fulfilling the functions of

---

Box 14-1
MEDICINES TRANSPARENCY ALLIANCE (MeTA)

The Medicines Transparency Alliance was a pilot project that ran from 2008 to 2010. It was funded by the UK's Department for International Development (DFID), and in-country staff of the World Bank and World Health Organization provided technical assistance. Its intention was to create an international alliance that would provide a forum for all interested parties where there could be frank and confident discussions about all the factors affecting the availability of medicines in developing and transitional countries.

Seven countries joined the alliance (Ghana, Jordan, Kyrgyzstan, Peru, Philippines, Uganda, and Zambia), and each set up an office and formulated a work plan. For example, the Ugandan plan talked about "findings from the reports/surveys [that] will be disseminated to the public, in efforts to improve transparency and accountability in the way drugs are procured, regulated, distributed and supplied."[1] The aim was to obtain from all participants high-quality information on price, quality, and the availability and promotion of medicines with a view to increasing access. The participants—representatives from government, the private sector, and nongovernmental organizations—met at a conference in London's Regents Park in the summer of 2010 and enthusiastically stated their support for the aims of MeTA.

This may have proved a valuable exercise to all involved, but despite this, little progress can be attributed to the project. An independent review for the Department for International Development expressed reservations

---

1. *MeTA Zambia Country Workplan.* Edited by Chama Nshindano. http://www.medicines transparency.org/fileadmin/uploads/Documents/Zambia-MeTA-workplan.pdf.

---

regulating manufacture and sales of medicines.[35] This causes problems, as a drug licensed by India's CDSCO and approved for manufacture in one state may be sold in other states without further interference, unless the drug can be shown to be harmful.[36] Furthermore, CDSCO is responsible for monitoring adverse drug reactions, but individual states are responsible for the recall procedure. In addition, individual states inspect and approve manufacturing sites, but CDSCO is responsible for obtaining

about the scope, design, and focus of the project, questioned the expertise of the department in operating in many countries at once, and even questioned whether MeTA itself fulfilled the department's Paris principles for aid effectiveness, including country ownership, alignment to government systems, and donor harmonization.

The reviewer went on to state that "for a project which has transparency at its core, there does not seem to be widespread knowledge of the total allocations (including those to the World Bank and WHO) and the proportion controlled by country multi-stakeholder fora is small. . . . It is equally important to ensure greater transparency about the totality, allocation and source of resources, how these may be accessed and who makes the decisions at which levels."[2]

Compared with USP's PQM project, which has a far more defined project aim and more sustained funding, there is little evidence that MeTA was much of a success.

The Zambian report says that "on August 19, 2009 an orientation workshop was organized for MeTA Council members to build their capacity on pharmaceutical issues. Unfortunately the department of procurement at MOH failed to show up for this important learning workshop for MeTA council members." This may be indicative that the organization wasn't focused enough to succeed.

---

2. Elizabeth Ollier. *Evaluation of the Medicines Transparency Alliance Phase 1 2008-2010.* http://www.medicinestransparency.org/fileadmin/uploads/Documents/Evaluation/MeTA_Evaluation_Summary_Report.pdf.

WHO GMP certification. In 2008 the regulatory authority of Maharastra State detected 547 samples of substandard drugs; 421 of which were manufactured in Himachal Pradesh, Karnataka, and Andhra Pradesh.[37] Haryana State has established a zero-tolerance policy under which producers of substandard medicines can be blacklisted, but there is little evidence this is working because neither Haryana nor CDSCO have any authority to enforce manufacturing standards in other states. Part of the general problem is that drug inspections are severely understaffed and inspectors are underpaid; some have been caught taking bribes, even as little as $100, to overlook discrepancies.[38]

China has a central authority, but the states have de facto control of production. Local drug inspectors have accepted bribes; some of these inspectors have been punished severely, and there are cases where inspectors received the death penalty, but control is inconsistent.[39] Enforcement of the removal of dubious products from the market is uneven. Products that are not registered or are registered with fake GMP certificates cause a considerable problem in the Chinese market. In June 2010, China's drug regulator banned the export of raw materials from ten Chinese drug companies because they were supplying products without proper GMP certificates. These drugs were exported to India, so the drugs controller general of India canceled registration for products from approximately six Chinese companies, and a few other companies surrendered their licenses because they did not comply with GMP.[40]

In Uganda, when high-ranking officials were found guilty of accepting bribes in exchange for registering substandard medicines, the National Drug Authority reinstated the ministers in their positions within the Ministry of Health almost immediately after they posted bail.[41] Worse, the whistleblower, a subordinate, lost his job. When the government advertised to fill his position, the post requested qualifications much lower than his.[42]

In other countries, corruption occurs more quietly, often among the members of registration-approval committees. In both Nigeria and Thailand, transparency is lacking not only in regard to the members of these committees and their necessary qualifications but also in the decision-making process for approvals.[43] In Russia and Uganda, similar problems exist: affluent political figures have been directly tied to local production ventures of questionable quality, abusing their power and influence behind the scenes for profit.[44]

It is vital that emerging markets sort out the problems they have with their MRAs and prioritize their actions. Proper product registration should be at the top of their list. If emerging market regulators follow sensible policies, they can put a significant dent in drug-quality problems (see box 14-2 on MRA overreach).

Box 14-2
Dangers of MRA Overreach

Problems can occur if an MRA overreaches or is otherwise overzealous, undermining access to medicines in the country. In a 2010 industry-backed survey[1] roughly 90 percent of companies said that some countries' "specific labeling requirements are problematic to implement," which increases the costs of medicines. As one company representative said: "The volume purchased by some of these countries does not justify the cost of implementing a country specific label." This same survey found that over a quarter of African countries took over three years to register drugs, another major detriment to access to medicine.

Perhaps as important to lack of access to medicines is the lack of registration harmonization across countries with low-value markets, which increases costs. This is especially so given the lack of acceptance by many of these domestic agencies of international standards set by stringent agencies such as the FDA, meaning GMP inspections are demanded by and undertaken by poorly resourced local agencies. As the report suggests: "Costs are in many instances exorbitant and not always one off. In some instances the costs of GMP inspections do not warrant sale of the product in the country. . . . [GMP costs] could be a deciding factor in whether companies pursue registration in a country." Six companies indicated they would not supply medicines to certain African nations because of the costs. And even companies that did supply often had to interrupt their drug supply to address changes in registration demands.

Harmonizing registration across regions in Africa would be a good idea, and there is a website and project dedicated to this (www.amrh.org), but when I went to it repeatedly for information, the site was down for lack of payment of a bill—an inauspicious situation.

I suspect that if counterfeiters know which companies are selling in each country, they may well supply fake versions of famous medicines into countries where the real suppliers have decided not to enter.

---

1. "Impact of Regulatory Requirements on Medicines Access in African Countries," Pharmaceutical Industry Association of South Africa, 2010.

15

International Cooperation against Criminals and the Lethal Trade in Fake Medicines

International cooperation against counterfeits should relieve the current acute pressure on domestic law enforcement created by criminal activity. An obvious and more important benefit may arise by generally raising standards on drug quality.

There may be differences of opinion about appropriate sentencing for those intentionally making, smuggling, and selling counterfeit drugs that can be lethal, but there is agreement that such people are criminals and should be heavily sanctioned. Because of political realities and histories, however, there still is no global consensus on how to combat this crime.

The WHO and WTO (along with Interpol's anticounterfeit-drug office) have driven hardest toward removing dangerous products from the market and hence improving patients' access to good-quality drugs over the past twenty years. I do not intend to spend pages rehashing old political battles that have led to major policy disagreements, but it is important to understand that the battles themselves color everything for some participants, even when the battles have little relevance to the specific issue of improving drug quality. The main battle that continues to cause problems when the subject of drug counterfeiting is raised is over intellectual property rights. This topic can impede progress on international cooperation against drug counterfeiters even when steps could be taken to address the problem without addressing IP. Generally speaking, Western industry has pushed for strengthening IP rights over the past several decades. Proponents of strong IP rights claim that increased protection would improve drug quality in emerging markets and is necessary to underpin increased investment by innovator companies through partnerships in developing countries. Many health groups have opposed strengthening IP rights, arguing that doing so would drive up prices and limit access while doing little to improve investment.

Both sides have some good arguments, and both push them for all they are worth—often too far. I have sided with industry more than activists because activist positions are often based on visceral, knee-jerk opposition to all forms of IP rights. When activists claimed patents were causing high drug prices across Africa, my occasional coauthor, Amir Attaran of the University of Ottawa, exposed the fact that only about 1 percent of drugs sold in Africa were on patent. This did not change many of the activists' arguments. Health activists do get some things correct, though, and often when industry has things wrong.

I have joined them in criticizing industry's reluctance to tier-price HIV medicines in Africa until the drugs industry was shamed into doing so, for incorrectly scaring U.S. seniors in order to limit personal drug importation from web-based drug sellers, and for blindly pushing for IP legislation without thinking through local circumstances. These incidents harm patients and damage companies' reputations enough to hurt the companies in the long run as well.

It is not necessary to know the myriad and extensive details of these fights to appreciate the level of antagonism that exists. India, Brazil, Thailand, South Africa (and their respective drug industries), and health activists have battled with OECD countries and Western industry. If U.S. industry supports something, there is a pretty good chance health activists will oppose it. This is not a universal truth, but it is a useful guide as a starting point. Efforts by Western countries and industry to extend and deepen IP rights through the WTO enjoyed great success during the 1980s and 1990s, but IP opponents have had the upper hand in the last decade. The WHO has always been more favorable ground for health activists, but it has sometimes been criticized for siding and cooperating extensively with industry. Yet the notion that WHO has spent too much on anticounterfeit activities is not borne out by the evidence. The budget of Hans Hogerzeil, who oversees drug quality for the WHO, is $60 million, of which only $2 million is spent on counterfeit drug work. The WHO has always emphasized the importance of quality, though; over the last decade it has helped developing countries' industries establish quality assurance for products intended for donor purchase. In any event, I introduced the ongoing IP debate briefly to provide some context on the world of global health politics and why the ability to combat fake drugs globally is often compromised.

There is no international agreement on how to combat fake drugs. Some experts are less concerned about combating fake drugs than they are about generally improving quality control in emerging markets. Indeed, they have argued that for many poor countries, effective criminal action would resolve only a small part of the substandard-drug problem. They claim, with some justification, that some efforts against counterfeit drugs are a smokescreen for anticompetitive efforts. Bluntly put, Western industry efforts against counterfeits are seen as a means to limit sales of competitor products, particularly Indian generic drugs, around the world. International trade rules, governed by the WTO, are the only rules that have been universally adopted, so they are used to punish counterfeiters in cross-border operations in the absence of anything better. This chapter explores these often contrary positions and suggests possible ways to break the current impasse.

Counterfeit Medicines and International Law

Officials combat counterfeit and adulterated drugs through domestic law enforcement, but probably more than half the countries in the world do not have adequate laws against dangerous medical products. The WHO's IMPACT has done a good job of designing model legislation for countries that have not yet enacted effective laws. At a WHO-sponsored meeting to discuss counterfeit-drug definitions in March 2011 in Geneva, well over half of the ninety-three countries present acknowledged having received significant help in this area from IMPACT. While these efforts have been useful, however, it would be more helpful if countries could sign a global convention against dangerous medicines and draw legislation from this common understanding. This would help motivate countries lacking adequate legislation to enact much-needed local laws, and it would also assist with harmonization of existing laws across countries. Such a convention is urgently required; this chapter provides arguments for why this is the case and recommendations for how such a convention could be drafted.[a]

_____

a. Language for a convention already exists, as designed by the Council of Europe for its Medicrime convention, which should be ratified in 2012. Medicrime has blazed a trail in

The Problem. Currently, a key barrier to combating fake drugs is a lack of transnational jurisdiction to pin down the highly mobile players of international syndicates involved in this most odious of trades.[b] If a counterfeiter from country A produces and exports fake drugs to country B, normally only country A has the authority to prosecute the criminal because that criminal act occurred on its territory. Country B, despite being the home of the victims, usually has little criminal jurisdiction over the matter. Country B might have criminal jurisdiction over acts ancillary to the counterfeiting, such as fraud or smuggling, but these are not the same crime, probably were not committed by the same person, and likely do not carry an appropriate penalty. With no international agreement to treat medicine counterfeiting as a serious crime, judicial and police cooperation between countries A and B cannot be taken for granted. As a result, medicine counterfeiters have practical impunity.

Knowingly making fake medicines that do not help people, or that harm or kill them, ought to be a more serious transnational crime. Other evil acts that deliberately endanger life on a transnational, widespread, and systematic basis, such as terrorism or hijacking, receive far stronger legal treatment internationally. So does currency counterfeiting, which, as noted earlier, though an age-old scourge, became an international crime in 1929. The international legal community declared that those who faked money should, "without ever being allowed impunity," be placed under universal jurisdiction and made liable to prosecution in any country, not just the country where the counterfeiting took place.[1] Eighty-two years after this development, our basic humanity and the defense of public health require that we likewise create global legislation to punish those who trade in

---

developing the concept of a pharmaceutical crime. In principle this treaty can be signed by others, but it has no chance of being adopted globally because of the emphasis on IP rights in the document. The EU has been the most aggressive enforcer of IP rules, and India and Brazil do not trust the EU to enforce IP rules fairly. For that reason alone, the Medicrime convention can be viewed as a useful document for research purposes but not as a treaty that would dispense with the following analysis.

b. I am enormously indebted to the work of Amir Attaran and Megan Kendall of the University of Ottawa, who did all the heavy lifting of what appears in the following pages. Our paper in the *Journal of International Criminal Justice* was informed by my knowledge of the problem, but nearly all the legal work was theirs and well beyond my legal competence.

counterfeit medicines. Criminalizing medicine counterfeiting on an international scale would present no insurmountable legal barriers and would offer significant advantages over the current national-scale approaches.

The Unsatisfactory Medical and Legal Realities of Medicine Counterfeiting. A critical part of counterfeiting is organized crime. Although small-scale faking occurs, as we saw in India in particular, most counterfeiters rarely act alone, selling fake drugs from their individual workshops. To infiltrate markets for legitimate medicines, highly sophisticated criminal enterprises mimic at least part of the business model of the genuine pharmaceutical industry. A manufacturing branch of a criminal enterprise making the fake medicines might, for example, press ersatz ingredients into pills and print plausible packaging with forged trademarks. A marketing branch might coordinate the covert distribution of counterfeit outputs in a way designed to trick inspectors and wholesale customers and the separate retail branch that exists downstream of them. Finally, a financial branch might launder the revenues of these illegal sales.

A criminal enterprise of that sort is no small undertaking. It cannot be haphazard, or it would fail. At the extreme, the nature of the crime is widespread and systematic and assumes the dimensions and overall control consistent with a crime against humanity. There may even be links between medicine counterfeiting and other crimes: Interpol believes some of the revenues from medicine counterfeiting flow to terrorist organizations, including al Qaeda.

The Complexities of National Enforcement of a Transnational Crime. The WHO has highlighted a variety of factors that contribute to the proliferation of counterfeit drugs. These include the following:

- insufficient national regulation of drug manufacturing and distribution;
- poor enforcement of existing legislation;
- weak penal sanctions for violations of drugs legislation;
- poor regulation by exporting countries and within free-trade zones;

- complex transactions involving many intermediaries;

- high demand and prices for (genuine) curative and preventive drugs and vaccines;

- inefficient cooperation among stakeholders.[2]

Current efforts to mitigate these obstacles are aimed at the WHO's first two points, which entail addressing the problem at the country level only. While these steps are necessary and welcome, they are also inadequate.

As established throughout this book, the trade in counterfeit medicine is often transnational. Taking a country-level approach to criminalization and enforcement is problematic. Because definitions and standards vary, the lack of supranational regulation means enforcement and penalties for counterfeiting also vary. In some countries, medicine counterfeiting is not a crime, though governments may enact laws after the problem manifests itself, as Syria did. Other countries, such as China, have draconian penalties, including the death penalty, but these measures are often a façade for selective and inconsistent enforcement. Too few countries have a flexible approach with judicial discretion as to terms of imprisonment and monetary fines. Some positive examples of countries that do are the Philippines (up to life imprisonment and $25,000 fines) and (at least in principle) India (up to ten years' imprisonment and $32,000 fines).

Such sharp differences in the criminal-law treatment between countries create difficulties in transnational enforcement. Extradition laws often contain a requirement of double (or dual) criminality, meaning people can be extradited from country A only at the request of country B, and only if the act for which they are accused is criminalized in very similar terms and with comparable penalties in both countries. A country that does not recognize counterfeiting as a crime affords criminals the basis to resist or avoid extradition.

The WHO has tried to harmonize national legal approaches by convening numerous anticounterfeiting conferences and launching IMPACT in 2006. IMPACT is made up of international organizations, nongovernmental organizations, enforcement agencies, pharmaceutical manufacturers associations, and drug and regulatory authorities. To date, it has done much to raise awareness, but as IMPACT has no legal powers, it cannot impose harmony by moral suasion alone. As Margaret Chan, director general of the WHO, put it, "The role of the WHO should be concentrating on public health, not on law enforcement."[3]

Within the sphere of public health, law is sometimes a theoretical concept. According to the WHO, only a few countries (20 percent) have well-developed drug regulation; most (50 percent) have limited regulation, and many (30 percent) have practically no regulation. Corruption and poor governance thrive in countries in the latter category. The poorest developing countries, such as the Democratic Republic of the Congo, do not have sufficient resources to evaluate the quality of drugs on the market. Many drugs in such countries are unregistered, with already overstretched MRAs. Corruption can also be a problem in poor countries; Cambodia, for example, is dogged by cozy relationships between underhanded dealers and government officials.

The Extent and Effects of Medicine Counterfeiting

It is difficult to measure the scale of the problem with counterfeit drugs. I have discussed TB and malaria a lot to this point, and a comparably unhappy state of affairs is emerging in the field of HIV treatments. Although there is no cure for HIV, daily and lifelong use of a combination of anti-retroviral therapy can stabilize the infection and, in many instances, halt the onset of AIDS illness or death. In the past decade, a 90 percent drop in prices for antiretroviral therapy ensured that many more patients in the developing world have access to these treatments. The last official count proclaims that three million patients now receive these drugs. While this is encouraging, the widespread use of antiretroviral therapies, which cost several hundred dollars per patient per year in developing countries, offers an especially attractive target for counterfeiters in places that lack sufficient regulatory controls or have corruption problems. Counterfeits of antiretroviral therapy have already been discovered in at least eleven countries, including Zimbabwe, where my investigation started.

Counterfeit medicines are not confined to epidemic zones or the world's poorest regions, however. The U.S. FDA, arguably the most sophisticated drug regulator in the world, saw an 800 percent increase in reported instances of counterfeit drugs between 2000 and 2006. The significant difference here is that these cases are detected and investigated, and the offenders are often punished appropriately.

The vast number of incidents runs the gamut from one-off opportunistic crimes, such as the theft of Schering do Brasil's test batches of birth control pills, to widespread and systematic crimes, as with the transcontinental Middle East operation. The counterfeit trade attracts criminals of all stripes because, as the OECD writes, "pharmaceutical counterfeiting has been described as the 'perfect crime' since if the patient's condition improves, there is no investigation, and if the patient's condition deteriorates, it will be attributed principally to the medical condition or disease."[4]

Counterfeiting is a deliberate crime. The most advanced counterfeiters use sophisticated techniques to deceive both consumers and regulators in the mimicry of product appearance, trademark, labeling, and packaging. With the help of digital technology, virtually identical packaging is easily reproduced. Counterfeiters have copied trademarks embedded in security holograms, and they have prepared their products using cheaper or lower concentrations of the best ingredients that mimic the chemical characteristics of the proper ingredients. These high-tech fakes are indistinguishable from the real product except by chemical analysis, and sometimes not even then, as the heparin case demonstrated.[c]

Most consumers are likely fooled by these criminals' arsenal of tricks without once thinking they might be at risk of taking a counterfeit medicine. Even if consumers know the risks—and probably few do—they may choose to run them anyway. In poor economies with weak regulation, small price differences between legitimate and counterfeit medicines can be enough to persuade price-sensitive pharmacists or consumers. In rich countries with strong regulation, foreign Internet pharmacies of questionable provenance tempt consumers with counterfeit medicines through the mail, which is exceptionally hard to control.

When patients take counterfeit medicines containing little or no active ingredients for an infectious disease such as malaria, HIV/AIDS, or tuberculosis, or for noncommunicable conditions such as hypertension or hypercholesterolemia—all of which can be deadly if untreated—morbidity and

---

c. Recall that a new test had to be developed to determine the cause of the deaths of patients taking heparin; see chapter 1.

mortality rates will increase. When counterfeits contain toxins, allergenic ingredients, or pathogens (bacteria, fungi, viruses, or parasites), patients' conditions may worsen, and in some cases patients may die. Substituting one active ingredient for another can be dangerous, too, as patients taking the wrong medicine may experience adverse effects without realizing any clinical benefit.

With time, the increasing prevalence of drug-resistant pathogens brought about by subtherapeutic counterfeits destroys the efficacy of a genuine drug; this phenomenon was observed with malaria drug resistance in Southeast Asia. This can happen to drugs for any other infectious disease. Drugs lost to resistance in this way are not lost to the patient alone; they are lost to the world, possibly forever.[d]

Counterfeit medicines strike at the essential core of trust that makes a health care system possible. A patient whose treatment proves ineffective because it was counterfeit has little reason to trust medicines or anyone prescribing them in the future. The loss of confidence is especially devastating in prescientific societies, where belief in the healing power of pharmaceuticals and clinical medicine is tenuous and in constant competition with unproven therapies offered by traditional or alternative healers. While belief remains in unproven remedies, or in the fear that occult forces and the "evil eye" cause illness, perhaps the most insidious and wicked consequence of counterfeit medicines is that those who need proper treatments look elsewhere for cures.

Goals, Doctrines, and Proposals for a Counterfeit Medicines Treaty

Country-level responses to medicine counterfeiting that prevail today leave much to be desired, and criminalizing the trade at an international level would improve the current situation. According to legal experts, crimes should be elevated to "international crimes" if they amount to an offense against an entire international community, if international cooperation is necessary for effective control over the transgression, or both. By this rubric,

---

d. Because retaining resistance can have a "cost" to pathogens in genetic terms, if the resistance is not tested for multiple generations, it may be lost, which means old drugs can occasionally make a comeback.

medicine counterfeiting should be an international crime. Counterfeit medicines are often traded internationally. Successful prosecution in such circumstances is beyond the ability of any country acting alone: it depends on cooperation of two or more countries that agree upon the severity of the crime, especially in cases involving extradition. Public-health harms, such as drug resistance, may arise in a single country, but they inevitably spread and endanger all people. The case for international criminalization could hardly be more persuasive.

Many have recognized the need for international cooperation on this issue. Lembit Rago, the head of the drug prequalification program at the WHO, suggested in 2004 that a treaty against such products may be required.[5] The Declaration of Rome, arising from the February 2006 WHO International Conference on Combating Counterfeit Medicines, holds that counterfeiting medicines is "widespread and has escalated to such an extent that effective coordination and cooperation at the international level are necessary for regional and national strategies to be more effective."[6] In 2007 a task force of legal experts convened by WHO-IMPACT reached consensus on a proposal that counterfeiting should be an offense subject to universal jurisdiction and prosecutable by all countries, but the task force fell short of recommending a treaty to bring that about. Delegates from the innovator pharmaceutical industry blocked agreement on the need for a treaty, despite the fact that their firms probably bear the greatest financial loss and reputational risk when products are faked. Mike Muller, then head of anticounterfeiting efforts at Eli Lilly, explained that he and other industry representatives were afraid such a treaty would alarm the public and damage valuable brands.[7] Brands and patients have been damaged by alarmism, especially when patients stop taking medication for fear it may be contaminated, but the status quo provides too much impunity to counterfeiters. Furthermore, Western media are unlikely to avidly report drug conventions when the language becomes tedious and technical, so this argument is weak. Industry's attitude seems to be changing, though; more company anticounterfeit-drug experts I have spoken with are in favor of an international agreement now in 2011 than was the case in 2006.

For several years, progress stalled at a strange halfway point, with agreement on the need for an international crime of universal jurisdiction, but disagreement over whether a treaty was needed to achieve it. Some progress emerged from the Council of Europe and its Medicrime Convention. More valuable than the details of the treaty was the fact that countries wanted to negotiate one in the first place.

During the past few decades there has been widespread international consensus on the importance of international crime; multilateral treaties have established that aircraft hijacking, hostage taking, and narcotics trafficking are all international crimes. With similar endangerment to life and similar international criminal networks at play, medicine counterfeiting should be made the subject of a similar treaty. To a large extent, established legal doctrines of these forerunner treaties provide precedent. Beginning with a clean slate or inventing new legal doctrines would be wasteful and needlessly controversial. Obvious differences aside, treaties on currency counterfeiting, hijacking, and narcotics trafficking share the following features:

- They define the basic "evil" at which the treaty is directed precisely.

- They set out several wrongful acts on which there is an international consensus to achieve criminalization, and they require states to enact legislation to forbid and punish the specified criminal acts when committed within their territorial jurisdiction or by their nationals.

- They require states to arrest alleged offenders within their territory, whether the criminal acts were committed inside or outside their territorial jurisdiction and whether they were committed by nationals or foreigners.

- They require states either to prosecute alleged offenders in their custody or to extradite them for prosecution in another state, with no option of impunity.

- They commit the states to mutual assistance in matters of prevention or enforcement, such as through information and evidence sharing or cooperation with agreed international organizations.

- They provide mechanisms for states to enter or leave the treaty regime.

Goal One: Identifying Wrongful Acts. An international treaty requires a consensus on the spectrum of wrongful acts it means to prohibit and requires that most states party to the treaty enact national laws making those wrongful acts criminal offenses. After that, each country is free to define offenses as broadly or narrowly as suits its particular legal requirements.

The supply chains for counterfeit medicines can be long, and those responsible can belong to sophisticated criminal enterprises with specialized divisions of labor. To be thoroughly effective, the treaty must impose a criminal prohibition at each step of that chain and on each participant. Taking inspiration from the 1929 International Convention for the Suppression of Counterfeiting Currency, the following are some acts which, when carried out intentionally, appear appropriate to punish as ordinary crimes within national jurisdiction, in accordance with a treaty:

- the manufacturing or preparation of counterfeit medicine;

- the provision or possession of equipment, instruments, or ingredients used in the manufacturing or preparation of counterfeit medicine;[e]

- the sale, offering for sale, dispatch, transportation, and import or export of counterfeit medicine or of the equipment or ingredients used in the manufacturing or preparation of counterfeit medicine;

- the falsification of documents in relation to a counterfeit medicine or its ingredients; and

- entering into a conspiracy to commit, or attempting to commit, or aiding, abetting, facilitating, or counseling another to commit any of the aforementioned offenses.

None of these proposed offenses relates to intellectual property. There are already countless multilateral and bilateral treaties stipulating that countries punish IP offenses in their jurisdiction, so reiterating these offenses in

---

e. This would, of course, include legitimate businesses whose staff moonlight to make suspect products.

a new treaty for counterfeit medicines would be redundant and could be counterproductive because of the controversy inherent in IP discussions.

Although a case can be made for strict liability in domestic laws, to reach agreement at an international level and ensure procedural fairness for the accused, proposed crimes should be strictly limited to cases in which the accused has acted with intention (*mens rea*). One would not wish, for example, to make a criminal of a person who unwittingly offers a counterfeit medicine for sale. Equally, one would not want to make a criminal of a person who supplies ingredients or equipment used to make counterfeit medicines if the supplier had no knowledge of their intended use. The Austrian manufacturer of the packaging and printing machines sold to the Middle Eastern counterfeiters we encountered had no knowledge or suspicion that its machinery would be used for illegal acts and, thus, should not be held liable for selling these machines.

There are two possible ways to introduce this necessary element of intentionality, each with equivalent legal effect. The familiar approach, and the one used in the Council of Europe's Medicrime Convention adopted in December 2010 and due to be signed by participants in 2011 or 2012, is to incorporate the requirement of intention within the definition of the criminal activities themselves: for example, to write that the "intentional" manufacturing of a counterfeit is criminalized. This approach allows a medicine to fit within the legal definition of "counterfeit" and be treated as such, even if no one has acted intentionally to engage in criminal wrongdoing. The less familiar approach, but one that deserves consideration because it is used by the WHO, is to embed the element of intentionality into the definition of a counterfeit. A medicine does not cross the counterfeit threshold without some evidence of intentional deception. The difference is subtle, but there are convincing political reasons to prefer the WHO's treatment.

Goal Two: Defining Counterfeit Medicines. Any treaty against counterfeit medicines requires a standardized definition of the term. Currently, there is no consensus among countries. Codifying a definition of counterfeit medicines would be beneficial in establishing a common understanding of the associated crimes while empowering country-level regulators, law enforcement, and judiciary.

The WHO has used the following definition of counterfeit medicines since the 1990s: "A counterfeit medicine is one which is deliberately and fraudulently mislabelled with respect to identity and/or source. Counterfeiting can apply to both branded and generic products and counterfeit products may include products with the correct ingredients or with the wrong ingredients, without active ingredients, with insufficient active ingredients or with fake packaging."[8] The WHO definition is not internationally accepted. Some countries bedeviled by counterfeits, such as the Philippines, have national laws conforming very nearly to the WHO definition, whereas others, such as Nigeria, deviate almost entirely from it. Other countries, such as the United States, demonstrate that success at interdicting counterfeits is possible even without conforming to the WHO's definition. It is not necessary to know all of the differences in these countries' rules, but the WHO is correct to write that "the definitions used in . . . different countries differ enough to create problems in the . . . implementation of measures to combat counterfeit drugs."[9] Among those measures is the development of a treaty.

A great virtue of the WHO definition is that its use of the phrase "deliberately and fraudulently mislabelled" captures only instances where a counterfeiter intentionally misrepresented a product. Under the WHO's definition, there can be no such thing as an accidental counterfeit: a substandard or degraded medicine that results from a manufacturing or storage error—a medicine produced with good intent but that has a bad outcome—will never be a counterfeit medicine under the WHO definition because no deliberate fraud is involved. Nor will legitimate generic medicines be captured by the WHO definition, for they are important health interventions. Instead, the WHO definition captures only medicines made to deceive, whether because they intentionally have wrong ingredients or because they intentionally misrepresent their identity or source.

These distinctions are clear when the criterion of intentionality is embedded in the definition of "counterfeit," but become confusing and murky when intentionality is written into specific offenses. In choosing the alternative approach, the Medicrime Convention defines "counterfeit" in relation to a medical product to "mean a false representation as regards identity and/or source."[10] This overbroad definition could be interpreted to mean that medicines that have accidentally or unintentionally become substandard are counterfeit. Not only is this definition illogical, but it will be opposed by legitimate generic-medicine manufacturers.

Despite its superiority, the WHO definition has become eclipsed by controversy following the organization's attempt to revise the definition in 2009. The WHO's intention was to extend the definition beyond counterfeit medicines and apply it to counterfeit medical products of all sorts, such as medical devices, but the revisions fueled an already seething debate brought about by poor interpretations of the definition of counterfeit products. European Union countries seized legitimate generic products entering their territory. Kenya, advised by European actors, passed an unreasonable law that branded any medicine counterfeit if it was made without the authorization of intellectual-property holders anywhere in the world. Brazil, India, and other countries regarded these mistakes as proof that anticounterfeiting efforts are primarily about enforcing IP rules instead of protecting public health, when they can be both. Nongovernmental organizations, such as Third World Network, stoked the polarization by presenting the baseless argument that because counterfeit is defined in trade law with reference to trademarks, the WHO's campaign against counterfeit medicines "undermines public health."[f]

Brazil and India are correct to insist that anticounterfeiting measures not impede the trade in legitimate generic medicines, but by opposing anticounterfeiting measures too broadly, the same countries risk undermining efforts to exclude life-destroying counterfeits from commerce, including where such drugs affect their own citizens or industries. To move the debate in the right direction and partly solve this conundrum, a treaty on counterfeit medicines must aim to reduce the conflation of public health and IP or trade concerns. Such a treaty should not follow any preexisting definition of counterfeit found in IP or trade treaties and would be redundant if it did. The treaty should define "counterfeit

---

f. I have far more sympathy for the arguments raised by Oxfam and Médecins Sans Frontières that the main problem facing poor countries is not criminal counterfeiting but substandard drugs. While I agree with their assessment, I do not agree with the inevitable conclusion of their publications: that we should pay little attention to counterfeiting. All countries face threats from criminal counterfeiters, and efforts to combat them do not prevent or undermine efforts against substandard products.

medicine"—or perhaps "falsified medicine," if using a different word helps avoid confusion with existing IP language.[g]

By emphasizing the criminal wrongdoing of those who act against public health with intention to deceive vulnerable patients about a treatment, the word "counterfeit" takes on a wholly different complexion from how it is used in IP treaties, where the crime is infringement. If it is framed in these terms, those who worry that IP concerns could trump public-health concerns have no reason to be opponents of a WHO definition of counterfeits. Such opposition is self-defeating for two reasons. First, opposition makes a treaty to criminalize those who carry out offenses against public health impossible, while leaving intact the many treaties that today criminalize IP offenses. Second, without a public-health treaty, those who counterfeit medicines that are not protected under IP rights, but that harm or kill nonetheless, enjoy total impunity in international criminal law. Neither of these establishes a formula for making public-health considerations paramount.

Goal Three: Addressing Jurisdictional Gaps. Jurisdiction to prosecute crimes is usually accorded to the state where the criminal act was committed. National criminal laws for fraud, homicide, or even medicine counterfeiting are commonplace, and making use of those laws to prosecute an offender in a country's territory is uncontroversial. But the rapidly globalizing counterfeit trade allows actual counterfeiting to take place in a country where it may not be a crime, even though victims may be in a country where counterfeiting is a crime.

International law allows universal jurisdiction for problems that are pressing or egregious enough that it does not matter where the crime was committed, where the victims were, or where the accused lived or operated. In such cases, states may criminalize and punish acts occurring outside their territory, they may seek the prosecution of offenders acting and dwelling extraterritorially, and they may request the assistance of other countries to arrest and extradite those persons. Decisions to broaden the state's

---

g. I understand that in the Portuguese Brazilian law, "counterfeiting" applies only to trademark violations, whereas public-health concerns involve the broader term "product falsification." Subtleties of language obviously need to be addressed, but these should not cause a stumbling block to agreement on how to act.

jurisdiction thus are politically difficult and are never taken lightly, out of respect for state sovereignty, but as far as international law is concerned, they are allowed. I argue that a treaty can help make this hard political choice justifiable and, therefore, easier. Specifically, treaties can pressure countries not to be havens for counterfeiting, can ease the difficulties of extradition, and can lend credibility to the otherwise fraught imposition of universal jurisdiction.

Extradite or Prosecute? International criminal law is worthless if unenforceable. Treaties concerned with international crimes must spell out the forms of cooperation necessary if states are to prosecute offenders within their territory or extradite offenders to face trial elsewhere. The preference to extradite or prosecute has changed with time, but the mere presence of a currency counterfeiter or aircraft hijacker in a particular state's territory implicates that state's duty to prosecute or, if it is unable or unwilling, to extradite.

Extradition is not straightforward. Because a criminal offense must exist in similar terms in both the requesting and the requested state, it is crucial for a treaty to achieve international agreement both on a single definition of counterfeiting and on the specific offenses arising from that definition. Extradition also entails a distinct legal process, an extradition hearing, quite apart from the trial of the offense, and that is governed by its own legal regime. Any counterfeit-drug treaty would have to address such hearings to obtain agreement for how they should be handled. The prosecution option is easier to put into place. Assuming that a state enacts domestic criminal law to prohibit wrongful acts, the state can extend those domestic prohibitions to acts occurring outside its territory. This is the case in Canada and Germany.

Whether a state chooses extradition or prosecution to deal with an offender, intergovernmental cooperation, such as the exchange of police investigations and evidence, is necessary. It is of extreme importance when, as is often the case, the country where a counterfeit drug is manufactured is unaware of any crime until the counterfeit is exported. This is illustrated by the 1995 meningitis epidemic in Niger mentioned earlier in which Nigeria donated 80,000 vaccines that contained no active ingredient at all. By the time doctors realized the vaccines were fakes, 60,000 people had been inoculated with them; thousands died (for more details, see chapter 4).

Unless police and prosecutors cooperate across borders in a case like this by granting judicial assistance and marrying evidence of the counterfeiter's intent in the source country with evidence of the misrepresented medicine in the recipient country, the most either can prove are economic crimes, such as fraud or trademark infringement. Niger almost certainly would not have criminal jurisdiction over medicine counterfeiters or traffickers from Nigeria—so no possibility to extradite—and at the time, Nigeria maintained penalties for counterfeiting medicine of as little as $70, hardly a meaningful punishment. On every level, this episode shows the importance of having an international treaty in effective practice.[h]

Universal Jurisdiction. Although the above describes that countries must either extradite or prosecute any offender in its territory, it says nothing about the threshold at which a country has met the preconditions to seek extradition or prosecution. That has a related but different set of jurisdictional considerations.

Countries may decide when to apply their laws extraterritorially. Normally, that discretion is muted within politically and diplomatically reasonable limits by insisting on some tangible link between the state seeking extradition and the accused. Where such a link is missing, a state's request to another jurisdiction to extradite the accused would be met coolly unless it was understood by prior agreement that a specific link was not needed.

Universal jurisdiction is found in numerous international criminal treaties. It means no link between the accused and the state desiring to extradite or prosecute the accused has to be demonstrated. Any state party to the treaty can exercise jurisdiction in prosecuting a perpetrator, irrespective of where the crime was committed. Equally important, universal jurisdiction is accepted only as a last resort, to avoid giving offenders impunity when a country is unable or unwilling to act despite obvious legal standing.

With regard to the counterfeiting of medicines, universal jurisdiction enables third-party states that are neither the source nor the destination of the counterfeit but are a trans-shipment point to act. Currently, if a

---

h. This is not to say that successful cooperation cannot occur between countries without a treaty, just that it is rare and not systematic. Nigeria is cooperating with both the Chinese and Indian governments to attempt to bring counterfeiters to justice (see chapter 4).

third-party state detects a shipment of counterfeits, it may impound the shipment and notify the source and destination states, but it is unlikely to criminalize offenses that occurred outside its territory.

Universal jurisdiction is an important aspect of any international criminal treaty, but it can easily be abused. European authorities detained nineteen separate shipments of Indian drugs en route to emerging markets, claiming they violated IP rules. Given this, universal jurisdiction is sure to be a sensitive topic for debate. Sensitive or not, it needs to be discussed, and a protocol should be established; the consequences otherwise are dire. The middle of the counterfeit-medicine supply chain is effectively without law-enforcement options because the link between such states and the crime is often insufficient to enable the state to exert ordinary criminal jurisdiction. The link reappears only as the counterfeit medicine nears its destination, where it can be distributed to patients to their detriment. Too narrow a jurisdictional view heightens the risk of criminal injury; thus, universal jurisdiction is required.

The bogus Canadian Internet pharmacy RxNorth.com could not be prosecuted because Canada decided to drop investigations and the other countries in the supply chain lacked the jurisdiction to pursue Strempler and RxNorth.com. To solve this problem, a medicine-counterfeiting treaty structured to deny impunity to criminal offenders, regardless of nationality or where the crime occurs, must create universal jurisdiction.

Article 18 of the 1929 Convention for the Suppression of Counterfeiting Currency reads that the treaty's crimes "should in each country, without ever being allowed impunity, be defined, prosecuted and punished."[11]

Combined, Articles 9 and 18 prevent the currency counterfeiter's defense so that in each country, offenses "committed abroad" are tantamount to offenses "committed in the territory," even when committed by a foreigner.[12]

Were this the state of international law for counterfeit medicines, Strempler's impunity in Canada would not have mattered; he could have been prosecuted by any country his products passed through. But he was not, which is proof of how ineffectual the current law is.[i]

---

i. For the discussion of the Strempler case, see chapter 9.

Counterfeiting Crimes Are Widespread and Systematic

As the RxNorth.com example shows, medicine counterfeiting is a strange business. While normal companies work tirelessly to make their supply chains relatively short and more efficient, RxNorth.com deliberately made its supply chains long and convoluted to provide fake provenance to consumers and confuse the authorities. Walt Bogdanich, the *New York Times* journalist who won a Pulitzer Prize for his investigation, discovered "a complex supply chain of fake drugs that ran from China through Hong Kong, the United Arab Emirates, Britain and the Bahamas, ultimately leading to an Internet pharmacy whose American customers believed they were buying medicine from Canada."[13]

My own research in the Middle East found a fake-drug and smuggling ring operating across the borders of Jordan and Syria. Pharmaceutical ingredients and finished pills were sent from China to Jordan to Damascus, after which pills and packaging were sent to Lebanon, Iran, Iraq, Egypt, and the Palestinian territories. When this operation was finally closed down, four tons of pills were found in one single warehouse in Damascus.

Supply chains such as these suggest an intention to carry out a crime on a widespread, systematic basis. The words "widespread" and "systematic" have special importance in international criminal law because they are central to the definition of some crimes as being crimes against humanity. "Crimes against humanity" is a relatively new concept. These are often defined by social expedience—genocide and apartheid are examples—but they may be long-established crimes—murder, enslavement, torture, and rape, for instance—when orchestrated as repeat attacks on a civilian population in a fashion that can be described as widespread or systematic. All crimes against humanity so deeply shock the conscience that their perpetrators are enemies of all humankind.

The most egregious cases of medicine counterfeiting certainly do shock the conscience. Deceptive drugs that sicken or kill thousands are tantamount to an attack on a civilian population. The only pertinent question is whether a person who criminally participates in the counterfeiting has knowledge that his or her isolated acts are organized or orchestrated in such a way as to achieve larger significance, thus amounting to a widespread or systematic attack on a civilian population. If so, that criminal's acts ought to be viewed and punished, without hyperbole, as a crime against humanity. It is not a stretch to suggest that causing widespread death or injury by fake medicine ought to be made a crime against humanity, by means of a future treaty.

The largest and most organized forms of medicine counterfeiting surpass the legal requirement that a crime against humanity be widespread or systematic, as they often are widespread *and* systematic (box 15-1 discusses the legal issues in more depth). RxNorth.com sold counterfeit medicines on wide scale to Americans and had systematic plans by which it acquired Chinese counterfeits and made them appear to be Canadian medicines. Where the counterfeiting of medicines is linked to organized crime, where a particular counterfeit recipe is found throughout a geographic area, or where 100,000 counterfeit tablets are possessed by a single pharmacy, it cannot be said that the perpetrators are acting as petty criminals enmeshed in random or contained occurrences.

The crime against humanity known as extermination comes closest to a condemnation that those who interfere with proper medical treatment are *hostis humani generis*. Extermination is defined in international law as "the intentional infliction of conditions of life, *inter alia* the deprivation of access to food and *medicine,* calculated to bring about the destruction of part of a population."[14] Although the calculated destruction of a population has, so far, never been established as a feature of medicine counterfeiting, international law already recognizes that improperly manipulating medicines can form part of a widespread and systematic attack on a civilian population.[j] In essence, this is what medicine counterfeiters do by supplying

---

j. Nazis were prosecuted under the crime of extermination for performing cruel and unethical medical experiments on people and for providing the concentration camps with "medicines" (actually poison gas). Although neither situation makes a perfect analogy to medicine counterfeiting, both show that those who commercialize a product with willful disregard to the fact that it will kill or harm on a large scale can be viewed in the law as *hostis humani generis*. See "The Farben Case," in *Trials of War Criminals before the Nuremberg Military Tribunals under Control Council Law No. 10* (Washington, DC: Government Printing Office, 1953); "Trial of Bruno Tesch and Two Others (The Zyklon B Case; British Military Court, Hamburg)," in *Law Reports of Trials of War Criminals,* UN War Crimes Commission (London: HMSO, 1947); and K. R. Jacobson, "Doing Business with the Devil: The Challenges of Prosecuting Corporate Officials Whose Business Transactions Facilitate War Crimes and Crimes against Humanity," *Air Force Law Review* 56 (2005): 168–231.

nontherapeutic fake drugs—the regular use of which can lead to therapeutic failure, toxicity, and drug resistance—instead of the real medicine.

Not all those involved in medicine counterfeiting do so with the knowledge they are participating in an organized criminal enterprise that sickens or kills people, but those who do know the dark nature of their enterprise and carry on regardless for profit are an exceptionally deplorable sort of criminal. A future treaty on medicine counterfeiting offers a mechanism for defining such crimes as crimes against humanity.

WHO Authority to Negotiate a Treaty against Medicine Counterfeiting

Treaties need a forum in which to be negotiated, and there really is one obvious choice for counterfeit drugs: the WHO. It is the primary global health body; it also has the power to negotiate a treaty and has done so before. Using the WHO as a negotiating forum requires a diplomatic understanding of the WHO's discourses and processes. The right to health, which is enshrined in most of the internationally ratified human-rights treaties and agreements and which is always evocative when trying to drive an agenda at the WHO, forms a basis for a treaty against medicine counterfeiting. Counterfeit medicines are self-evident anathema to the right to health. The WHO also places great store in its constitution of 1948, which establishes the organization's raison d'être as "the attainment by all peoples of the highest possible level of health."[15] The WHO constitution grants the organization a number of competencies, the most important of which for present purposes is the power "to develop, establish and promote international standards with respect to . . . pharmaceutical . . . products."[16] The constitution also accords the WHO discretion "to propose conventions, agreements, and regulations, and make recommendations with respect to international health matters."[17]

Thus, the WHO is a permanent platform upon which new international law for health can be proposed, negotiated, and constructed. Others have noted that it is held back by a bureaucratic culture of conservatism and a historical lack of attention to the possibilities of international law. It also is handicapped by its own constitution, which requires the support of two-thirds of the WHO member states to adopt a treaty. Depending

---

Box 15-1

STRICT LIABILITY AND THE ISSUE OF INTENT

There are significant disagreements about the best way to deal with purvey-ors of dangerous products where intent is less obvious. It is possible to make drug quality a strict liability offense, where guilt is determined by poor drug quality rather than intent to make the product badly; of course, it would be necessary to allow for differences in sentencing such that proven intent mer-its a tougher sentence. The advantage is that more products that endanger public health would be brought under the convention, and any subsequent protocols the convention spawns may address such products, too.

The disadvantage is that any manufacturer, from Pfizer and GSK to the lowliest approved producers in China and Nigeria, can make a bad batch of a product at times. Given this reality, lack of intent must really only apply to companies that routinely infringe quality-control rules; because interpreta-tions of this will leave corporations uneasy, it is unlikely that strict liability is a viable option within a criminal legal treaty. There is no reason the treaty has to just address criminal matters, though, and even if it does, guidelines could be produced around what constitutes the most basic GMP rules that have to be followed everywhere.

It may be bad law to discuss negligence and intent in a treaty also address-ing criminal acts; it is above my legal competence to know for sure. If the aim is to improve public health, it is inconsistent not to focus to some degree on all dangerous drugs in a drug convention, especially when serial gross

---

on the divisiveness of the subject, that supermajority vote may be more or less onerous than convening an ad hoc conference of the parties to negotiate a treaty.

The WHO has been moved to exercise its treaty-making power only once, for the Framework Convention on Tobacco Control (FCTC). The preamble to the FCTC acknowledges issues relevant to counterfeiting. For instance, it recognizes "a global problem with serious consequences for public health that calls for the widest possible international cooperation and the participation of all countries in an effective, appropriate and com-prehensive international response."[18] It also recognizes "that cooperative action is necessary to eliminate all forms of illicit trade in cigarettes and

negligence occurs in so many places. This is partly because it is the offense most likely to be ignored by regulators, especially against politically powerful local firms.

Perhaps a convention, and definitely national drug-quality regulations, should discuss GMP standards that need to be maintained for firms to avoid being accused of negligence, even if GMP standards are not mentioned in any treaty on counterfeit medicines as part of a crime. Strict liability could be limited in scope by allowing that if firms are honest about the source of products and hold GMP certificates, then the onus is on investigators to prove negligence. Even if a convention never includes a clause on strict liability, simply discussing it in the negotiations will draw attention to substandard products and counterfeits (and hence include the harms of nearly all deadly medicines).

Subject to minor changes, the Medicrime Convention of the Council of Europe could play much the same role as the convention proposed above, although it would have fewer members. In addition, ongoing bilateral and regional solutions will lessen the problem and could be harmonized over time into a system with a similar effect to a convention. I suspect that a treaty will help move things along faster; without one, the way forward will be slow, spasmodic, and riddled with holes, providing opportunities to counterfeiters, who react faster than regulators, to adapt and continue their work.

other tobacco products, including . . . smuggling, illicit manufacturing and counterfeiting."[19]

If it is possible to mobilize WHO's treaty power against the scourge of counterfeit cigarettes, one hopes the same can be true for counterfeit medicines. As with the FCTC, the process would begin with a resolution of the World Health Assembly, which is the annual congress of WHO member states. In 1996, World Health Assembly resolution WHA 49.17 requested that the director general of the WHO initiate the development of the FCTC in the most general terms: the entire resolution was only one page. The WHO struggled for a time to know what to do with this porous mandate. Two years later, the incoming WHO director general, Gro Harlem Brundtland, declared global tobacco control a priority for the WHO and began a work program that returned the issue to the World Health Assembly in 1999, where the member states passed resolution WHA 52.18 and established both an FCTC working group and an intergovernmental negotiating body. The working group began meeting shortly thereafter and delivered a report to the World Health Assembly, which adopted a third resolution as a basis for negotiations of the FCTC. In three years, the idea of a treaty against tobacco transformed from a skeletal notion into an unstoppable movement with a secretariat and a mandate for treaty negotiations. From that moment, the creation of the FCTC became inevitable; it was unanimously adopted by the World Health Assembly in May 2003.

There is a salutary lesson in this experience: the decision to embark on a public-health treaty does not need to be taken with a fully formed version of the treaty already in hand, an error made by the Council of Europe with its draft Medicrime treaty, and it ought not be strangled in the crib by objections over what the final treaty might say. This error is illustrated by the hasty opposition of Brazil and India to the WHO's efforts to curb the counterfeit medicine scourge. The decision of the World Health Assembly to proceed with a treaty should be based on little more than a notion, and countries should bring their concerns and objections to the intergovernmental negotiating body, where they are guaranteed to enliven negotiations. No credence can be given to the thought that countries as sophisticated as Brazil and India could not hold their own in negotiations.

By proceeding this way, incrementally and from the most rudimentary agreement imaginable, it was possible in due course to create a full-fledged treaty. The same outcome probably would have been unreachable had countries instead sought to wage their battles about tobacco up front rather than showing the restraint that made it possible to reflect and safeguard their interests in the detailed process of negotiating the treaty.

A Call to Action

To protect the global community from counterfeit medicines, states have to arrest, prosecute, and punish the counterfeiters; that is obvious. But this is not happening because not enough countries take the crime seriously, and there is no treaty to underscore the gravity of the crime or mandate international cooperation. A treaty against counterfeit medicines is a legally feasible aspiration and not overly ambitious; more than twenty international criminal conventions providing for universal jurisdiction have emerged since the Hijacking Convention in 1971.

When asked why no international treaty against medicine counterfeiting exists, a WHO representative pointed the finger at a lack of political will. That is a somewhat mistaken assessment, however, because some countries—notably Brazil and India—are deploying considerable political will, albeit in a misguided direction, toward reducing the WHO's efforts to stop counterfeit medicines. Their resistance arises from the understandable worry that other countries may use anticounterfeit-medicine rhetoric to hinder the legitimate trade in quality generic medicines as part of a hidden pro-IP agenda. Competing resolutions put forward at the 2010 World Health Assembly underscore that countries are not lacking the will to address counterfeit medicines, but they are using that will against one another rather than against the problem.

The sickest and often the poorest are harmed by this narrow calculus of fear. Imagine the world in 1929, as unstable markets, beggar-thy-neighbor policies, and competitive currency depreciations eventually produced the Great Depression and a decade of turmoil. Fear was certainly a defining emotion, yet that was the year countries reached agreement on a treaty against the counterfeiting of currencies. The public interest prevailed because countries found the wisdom to make an enemy of the problem at hand rather than of one another. As a commentator of that period writes, the treaty

> was the natural outgrowth of a conviction, held by the majority of states, that the counterfeiting of currency was an international crime, and moreover, that it was one of a decidedly virulent and insidious character. Had this belief not been widely prevalent, the proposal of the French Government that the League of Nations should undertake the drafting of a convention for the suppression of this crime would have fallen on barren ground. As it was, the existence of the conviction that the whole community of states had an interest in the repression of this form of criminality was what made the agreement at all possible. Repeatedly, especially during the years

immediately preceding the drafting of this convention, the states had had occasion to observe that purely national action against counterfeiters was often insufficient, and that international action was in many cases extremely difficult, if not impossible. Thus, in the face of this common menace, with which separately the states were unable to cope, they came in time to realize that international cooperation was necessary, and what is more, that it was imperative, if they were to make any headway in the prevention and punishment of such crime.[20]

Almost a century later, the same could be said about the counterfeit-medicine problem, with the single exception that countries lack the rationality and cohesiveness they once possessed to let the public interest prevail. Individual countries surely have this conviction, but collectively they are failing to harness it into constructive work to negotiate a treaty, and never more so than at the 2010 World Health Assembly. A more dismal commentary on the contemporary state of public-health diplomacy is scarcely imaginable.

Medicine counterfeiting is a public-health catastrophe. In other fields, experts propose creating new international crimes against a variety of wrongful acts, such as corruption, organized crime, the trafficking of human beings, forced labor, and man-made famine. An opportunity exists to address the growing criminality and impunity of medicine counterfeiters. Justice for the sick or dead victims of counterfeit medicines requires action.[k]

---

k. In the above I have primarily referred to deliberately false medicines as "counterfeit" medicines. That was the WHO-approved term for about two decades, but it is becoming obsolete, after a decision in March 2011 by a WHO working group to reject it (see WHO. Working Group of Member States on Substandard/Spurious/Falsely-Labelled/Falsified/Counterfeit Medical Products, Report A/SSFFC/WG/5 of March 11, 2011, available at http://apps.who.int/gb/ssffc/pdf_files/A_SSFFC_WG5-en.pdf (accessed July 5, 2011). The Working Group acted because the word "counterfeit" is confusing to some: it denotes both affronts to human health (which is how I used it) and affronts to patent or trademark rights (which is how it is used in international intellectual property law, particularly the TRIPS Agreement). Several WHO member states protested that this ambiguity could be exploited to turn a treaty against "counterfeit" medicines into an implement to heighten intellectual property rights, rather than to protect human health. Because WHO member states have largely rejected the use of the word "counterfeit," it makes sense in legal discussions, if not elsewhere, to henceforth call them "falsified" medicines.

Final Thoughts and Recent Developments

Is WHO the only choice for a convention? Could such a treaty be situated under the auspices of the UNODC? Some member states of the WHO have spoken in favor of a treaty.[21] So too did the editorial board of *Lancet,* arguably the world's leading medical journal.[22] The WHO will continue deliberating into 2012.

But the government of Argentina on April 11, 2011, presented a resolution to UNODC's Commission on Crime Prevention and Criminal Justice concerning the international criminalization of "fraudulent medicines."[23] As passed, Argentina's resolution does not separate or distinguish intentionally falsified medicines, which are the deliberate result of criminal activity, from accidentally substandard medicines, which are the result of noncriminal negligence—and this is a very serious problem.[1] Nevertheless, Argentina's approach easily could be adjusted, and it would then be a serious proposal for a UNODC-led process.

Argentina's resolution mentions the "potential utility of the United Nations Convention against Transnational Organized Crime" (CATOC). The CATOC is in essence a framework convention for various international criminal offenses in which there is a structured criminal conspiracy of several persons. There are currently three protocols under CATOC, which criminalize: (1) the trafficking of persons; (2) the smuggling of persons; and (3) the smuggling of firearms. The first two protocols were adopted by the UN General Assembly as a package and at the same time as CATOC in 2000, and the third protocol followed separately soon thereafter, in 2001. All of the protocols specify that their secretariat is the UN Secretary General, who has assigned the day-to-day responsibility to the UNODC in Vienna.

So how about engaging UNODC to create a new CATOC protocol for medicines? History teaches that there would be advantages and

---

1. Argentina's resolution reads that "the term 'fraudulent medicines' includes medicines whose contents are inert, are less than, more than or different from what is indicated, are misbranded or have expired." That wording does not distinguish between intentional and accidental causes. It treats identically those medicines that are inert because they were falsified by organized criminals and those medicines that are inert because of a manufacturing error by honest pharmaceutical manufacturers. The lack of such a distinction is so serious that it should be considered fatal to the proposal as it now stands.

disadvantages, compared with a WHO-led treaty. Although the UNODC route is diplomatically less demanding, the WHO route is practically more effective.

The UNODC option is comparatively fast and easy. Creating a new protocol under CATOC requires nothing more than a decision of the UN General Assembly, which could be passed in a single sitting. In contrast, a WHO-led treaty probably would take years of hard negotiations at intergovernmental negotiating conferences. The complexity and cost could hardly be more different.

But the same ease that makes CATOC attractive is arguably also its worst disadvantage. Treaty negotiations are not just an arduous and expensive waste to be avoided. On the contrary, the iterative process of negotiations helps countries refine their interests and objectives and cements their political will. A protocol that shortcuts that process is likely to be ignored by countries and to have no actual effect.

Consider, for example, the Protocol on Firearms, to date the only freestanding CATOC protocol to be enacted (i.e., it was not enacted together with CATOC itself).[24] The protocol has been a disappointment precisely because most countries hardly noticed or cared when it came into being. In the decade since it was opened for signatures, under half of UN member states, and only seven of the G-20 countries, have ratified or otherwise accepted it.[25] Thus the Protocol on Firearms, while technically in force, is practically weak.

This history augurs poorly for Argentina's efforts to create a new CATOC protocol against "fraudulent" medicines. Even if successfully enacted, it probably would be unnoticed and ignored by most countries, just as the Protocol on Firearms was.

CATOC also suffers from serious limitations in what can be criminalized. As its name suggests, CATOC is a framework convention for the development of international criminal law against organized crime, involving several criminals acting concertedly. The definition of an "organized criminal group" requires that there be "a structured group of three or more persons, existing for a period of time and acting in concert with the aim of committing one or more serious crimes or offences." Not all criminals would be caught by this formulation. For example, if a manufacturer in Country X, a middleman in Country Y, and a smuggler in Country Z informally form a supply chain for falsified medicine, only the middleman in Country Y is obviously in a conspiracy involving three persons, because he did business with persons before and after him in the chain. The smuggler in Country Z, who is the closest to the patient and the most likely to be caught by police, could escape punishment altogether, unless prosecutors proved that he knowingly entered into a conspiracy with the others. A CATOC protocol is therefore more suited to prosecuting the biggest criminals who orchestrate the falsified medicine trade—for example, those who internationally trade fake drugs in large quantities—but it would let escape lesser criminals.

CATOC is also purely a criminal law treaty. Thus it can do an excellent job on issues such as cooperation in investigations, extradition, witness protection, and so forth, but it cannot embrace the other actions needed to better the global medicine supply.

Here we must remember that the legal challenge is twofold: criminal law is needed to stop criminally falsified medicines, but regulatory law is also needed to avoid negligently substandard medicines. It is an error to apply criminal law to both, as Argentina's resolution so far does. Because the quality of drug regulation is weak or even nonexistent, and is seen this way by influential countries, a treaty therefore must both internationally criminalize falsified medicines and fortify drug regulatory agencies in poorer countries to block substandard medicines. A WHO-led treaty could do both these things, but a UNODC-led treaty could not.

But medicine regulatory agencies in impoverished countries cannot be strengthened by words alone, and so while ideally these MRAs should be funded by domestic taxes, for the treaty to succeed it will probably have to raise foreign aid money for poor MRAs. Here again the evidence shows that a WHO-led treaty is a more effective option. Following the WHO Framework Convention on Tobacco Control, development assistance for tobacco control rose to about $240 million annually.[26] That sum far outstrips CATOC's Crime Prevention and Criminal Justice Fund, which raised $50 million annually, to be shared among all three CATOC protocols.[27]

Because there is emerging support within WHO member states for a treaty, this should probably be nurtured, in preference to a UNODC-led treaty. However, it should not be forgotten that CATOC contains some superb language in the international criminal law domain, and that UNODC knows that treaty best. Thus the optimal outcome would be to negotiate a new WHO-led treaty, but to do so with UNODC as a major partner, including perhaps even sharing the secretariat function.[m] Medicine falsification is quintessentially a multidisciplinary problem, and if the UN is flexible enough, a multiagency solution would be best.

---

m. There is one further reason for involving UNODC, and that is one of political courage. The following is quoted from a UNODC paper on West Africa and trafficking. It shows a level of robustness of writing when dealing with corrupt member states of the UN one never sees from the WHO. And a treaty that does not acknowledge, and have any provision for combating, corruption in member states has no chance of working: "Fear that law enforcement counterparts cannot be trusted limits the amount of assistance the international community can give to afflicted states. There is no use giving tip-offs to local authorities if the contraband subsequently disappears, as it often does in West Africa. It is counterproductive to supply equipment and training to putative civil servants who will only use it to commit further crime. But as a result, it becomes very difficult in any given instance to discern whether the failure to stop trafficking is due to collusion or incapacity or (as is often the case) a combination of the two." United Nations Office of Drugs and Crime (UNODC), "The Globalization of Crime," 2010. Available at: http://www.unodc.org/documents/data-and-analysis/tocta/TOCTA_Report_2010_low_res.pdf (accessed Oct 12, 2011).

16

A Market for Products of Varying Quality and the Intellectual Property Debate

Most health activists have argued for the past decade that Indian generic drugs are safe, cheap, and more readily available than generics produced outside of India. Médecins Sans Frontières says, "Because generics are in general a lot cheaper than patented products, they have played a huge role in making sure people actually have access to essential medicines in the developing world. MSF relies overwhelmingly on quality Indian generics for its antiretrovirals to treat HIV/AIDS, for example."[1] Although the best Indian copy drugs are bioequivalent products and can and do significantly increase access to drugs, many producers in developing countries, including India, do not make consistently high-quality products. My own analysis of product quality and variability shows that the best Indian firms make products on a par for quality with Western generics firms and second in performance only to Western innovator firms, but many other producers in India, Southeast Asia, and particularly Africa make inferior products, at least some of the time. But producing decent products most of the time is not acceptable. GMP must be inculcated in people and systems so mistakes are found before products reach the market.

As a child, I dreamt of being a professional trumpeter, and I was promising enough to be able to meet the principal trumpeter of the London Symphony Orchestra, who in 1979 was Bill Howarth. Howarth told me "an amateur practices till he gets it right, a professional practices till he doesn't get it wrong." He was trying to see how serious I was. Even at thirteen, I think I realized I liked playing the trumpet but was essentially an amateur trumpeter, then and always; I did not want to practice enough to be a professional. Howarth's words came to mind as I studied the demands of GMP. Companies producing medicines should practice GMP like the professional trumpeter practices: never (or very rarely) accepting a mistake. Instead, too many companies are more like the amateur (happy a decent product has been made most of the time).

Approaches to GMP

Western-style GMP is about preventing bad products from reaching the market. This hyperprecautionary approach is accepted and admired because Western society considers it, rhetorically at least, unacceptable for a single person to be harmed by a product regardless of the cost increases that occur as a result.[a] But is such a precautionary approach the one that Westerners themselves took fifty years ago or that, say, Africans should take today? As I have traveled in Africa and other poor locations and worked on drug projects, I have noticed that it is often the Indian and Chinese companies—and not always the largest and best Indian firms—whose drugs penetrate private markets where most Africans buy medicines. The products of Western companies such as GSK, Merck, and Pfizer are often absent, presumably because these markets are relatively insignificant for their companies. Innovator companies supply large orders of treatments (often heavily discounted or donated) for high-profile diseases to donor agencies such as the Global Fund or directly to African health ministries, but their products typically are not sold in private markets (except where they are stolen and diverted). Novartis's antimalarial Coartem is one of the more available products, but it is still found in far fewer private pharmacies than a variety of Indian drugs. The choice for an African consumer is often between Indian, Chinese, or African products and no medicine at all. These products are cheaper, but they carry a higher risk of having been made in plants that would fail GMP. In such circumstances, is taking nothing the best option?

This is obviously not the case for products from top Indian companies—including Ranbaxy, Cipla, Piramal, Dr. Reddy, and others—that consistently

---

a. I say "rhetorically" not to be argumentative. Inevitably mistakes are made; bad products slip through, occasionally with devastating consequences. From most mistakes we learn and improve systems so that type of mistake is less likely in the future. The idea that there must never be a death from a fake drug is rhetorically fine but practically impossible. To stop all fakes would be to stop all trade, which would have far more devastating consequences for health.

make high-quality products (as supported by my team's own quality and variability research). Yet, I have seen at least forty Indian antimalarial brands from ten or more other companies during my quality-assessment research; some of these failed basic quality tests. (A few products from the top companies failed as well, but this was likely due to poor storage.) The U.S. FDA and the European Medicines Agency would be correct to refuse entry of products like these, because Americans and Europeans demand the best products possible with the lowest risk that is economically sensible. Then again, there is little U.S. demand for antimalarials, and export-motivated companies can make different-quality products for different markets.

It is natural for companies in the developed world, and indeed any company that can comply with GMP, to want the very best standards adopted globally; it is to their advantage that this be done. Heinz lobbied for stricter regulation on food production; this made food safer, but the reason Heinz lobbied so hard was because it was the only company able to do it. It had huge market share to gain if its approach was adopted as a requirement of law.

In the long run, it makes sense for standards to improve. As consumer wealth increases and industrial technology improves, today's standards will one day seem too low, just as Western standards and approaches thirty years ago look slack today. Thus, the notion that there is one global standard is almost certainly flawed.

Perhaps the best standards should be adopted globally in some circumstances. For example, to prevent the emergence of dangerous drug resistance where there are few chemical entities available, it is defensible to ensure that only the best products are sold. This is especially true for diseases that require consistent treatment for many months or years (TB and HIV/AIDS in particular), because substandard products are far more likely to lead to resistance. There may be other examples of drugs that are toxic if produced badly (some oncology products probably fall into this category, as in the problem in Peru with bad methotrexate drugs that were substandard, probably due to trace by-products of an impure process and not gross negligence). Undoubtedly, every innovator can make some similar case for its favorite products and claim that only its product is good enough. Undoubtedly, a lost product can be costly, financially as well as in human life: artemisinin is an example of a product at risk of becoming compromised. But it is impossible to calculate the likelihood that a product will be lost due to poor-quality production and even harder to assess the impact of such an eventuality.

Even so, it is arguable, and perhaps even testable, that poor countries benefit from having more relaxed standards, both for imported products and those locally produced, if this means generally good drugs are more widely available. After all, for many products, solubility and permeability are not problematic and, where a biowaiver is given, only stability testing is essential.

However, not holding products to the strictest possible standards in order to assure availability of generally good medicines does not mean countries should allow all drug producers, regardless of quality, access to the market. Unfortunately, that appears to be the situation in many African countries. Nigeria's markets boasted an astonishing 260-plus brands of artemisinin-based antimalarials. Countries that are able to should at least guard against the lowest-quality products, perhaps by using basic thin-layer chromatography, dissolution testing, and product authentication with handheld spectrometers, which combined assess basic product stability, variability, and availability (although not bioavailability).[b] As mentioned earlier, Dora Akunyili, Nigeria's minister of information and communications and former director general of NAFDAC, told me it is better to have access to no drugs than access to counterfeit drugs. But she also has studiously avoided discussing Nigeria's own producers, some of which make products that are legal in Nigeria but on quality grounds should be avoided.[2]

Other governments in Africa indirectly condone even lower-quality drugs. Kenya's *Daily Nation* reported in January 2009 that an unpublished

---

b. It is not entirely certain what might be the impact of partnerships of local producers with more experienced firms—one hopes better quality. According to the UN Conference on Trade and Development, Indian firm Cipla has partnered with Quality Chemicals of Uganda, Chinese firms are partnering with firms in Ethiopia, and Rwanda will have a drug factory financed by Cadila of India and the Hozman group of the United States. A Jordanian firm is partnering with an Eritrean producer, and Brazilian firms are targeting Lusophone African countries. As the UN agency says: "These examples point to increasing importance of South-South investment for countries seeking to attract investors in the pharmaceutical sector." United Nations Conference on Trade and Development, 2011. "Investment in Pharmaceutical Production in the Least Developed Countries." Available at: http://www.unctad.org/en/docs/diaepcb2011d5_en.pdf (accessed Oct 12, 2011).

Ministry of Health report confirmed "what had always been known to be the biggest obstacle to a successful anti-malaria campaign—well-entrenched cartels of drug manufacturers and distributors working in cahoots with corrupt health ministry officials to supply their own drugs."[3] The *Daily Nation* shared a copy of the report with me, and it was alarming: more than half of all 187 malaria drugs the report evaluated in the country were not registered, and 16 percent of the drugs, many of which were produced locally, failed quality tests.[4]

Still, these countries may be right to tacitly condone mixed drug quality. As people become wealthier, they will demand better products, and the worst drugs will be driven from the market by improved consumer knowledge, competition, and increasingly stringent regulation. There is some danger that substandard suppliers, which can often sell at lower prices, may corner the drug markets and dominate political decision making, making subsequent improvement less likely. At worst, condoning such behavior could even encourage firms currently making good products to cut corners, possibly lowering overall quality.

Evidence from countries such as India and Brazil, however, suggests that markets with mixed-quality products tend to improve over time. Brazil retains its dual-category system, which permits the sale of innovator products and their bioequivalent generics, as well as similars.[5] Soon, however, similar manufacturers will have to submit bioavailability data, pharmaceutical equivalence tests, and a copy of an ANVISA-issued GMP certificate during registration.[6] While this grace period is not ideal from a public-health standpoint, it works from a developmental perspective. This is surely a possible solution for other countries.

Even if the Brazilian authority had not taken such action, industry watchers believe that growth in the generics market—fueled by growing profit prospects, the changing consumer preferences of a more affluent public, and government support—would have driven similars from the market.[7]

Brazil could still back away from enforcing the law, and it could be many decades before Africa's poorest countries are in the position Brazil is in today. Until that time a messy world of mixed-quality drugs is what we will have, even if no one wants to admit it.

I think we should admit it. Nearly everything is of lower standard in Africa than in the West, but as the history of the FDA and drug quality in the United States demonstrates, it took a long time and a push and pull between industry and regulators for the West to get where it is today.

India chose to protect its domestic industry from overseas competition with tariffs and quotas on imports and explicitly decided not to enforce product patents for decades, which made India a poor location for innovators to sell products. Today, it is the only country with producers that can match the West. Protectionism is divisive and costly to the population at large—it is a blunt instrument by which to allow infant companies to survive—but it will be copied by other emerging countries because it worked for India, unless other countries have better options (such as technology transfers or partnerships with Western industry).

On their own, perhaps emerging markets should do what Brazil did rather than India, segmenting the market by product quality approval ratings and ruling out all but the best products by improving standards over time. Another advantage of such an approach is that it focuses poor countries' MRAs on the basics: registering products, conducting basic postmarketing surveillance on product stability, and working with customs to help identify any products that should not be imported. Allocating resources on overseeing bioequivalence testing or clinical trials should not be a high priority of a less-developed country's MRA.

In the End, It Is All about Endogenous Growth

Oxfam and its fellow travelers set up something of a straw man in their one-eyed preoccupation with improved regulation. If the alternative to strengthening MRAs were solely expansion of IP provisions, as they imply, they would have a much stronger case, but that is not the only way forward. Combating lethal drugs with a treaty, as described earlier, and implementing domestic laws based on public health, and not IP, is undeniably a part of the solution.

Most of the improvements required in a country will be undertaken by various entities working in cooperation, so it seems to make sense to attack the problem from all angles, from agreeing upon criminal sanctions globally to encouraging development. Development takes time, and many countries will probably go through pain and suffering similar to what the United States experienced before it developed effective regulatory bodies. That does not mean emerging countries will be unprotected in the meantime; there are ways to work around many of these problems.

Drug Quality and Income. Our research demonstrates that, as one might suspect, wealthier cities have a smaller problem with drug quality than poorer ones. Both substandard and counterfeit drugs are a greater problem in poorer cities, something borne out by the analysis in part III. This relationship is strong, statistically significant, and implies that the major problems can be overcome only by economic development.

That does not doom poor countries to terrible problems, though. If my team's data are accurate, in less than four years, Lagos improved drug quality by lowering the rate of drugs that failed tests from roughly 32 percent to 9 percent (even if this exaggerates the fall because the initial sample was small, there is no doubt, given the data and sources I have seen, that the rate has fallen substantially). During this time, the city's GDP per capita has remained fairly steadily around an annual level of $2,600 per person. This implies that by concerted action, drug quality can be improved.

Corporate Responsibility. One thing activists get wrong and business gets right is that private enforcement of IP rules, and notably trademark protections, can lead to significant improvements in quality in the market. Private interest is a powerful agent in ensuring quality, and ignoring this, or denying it, is counterproductive.

From Heinz to Merck, the best U.S. companies have sustained trust in their brands because of good practices, and they did this independently before the U.S. FDA became a reliable watchdog. Even when Merck had trouble with its painkiller Vioxx, it was not because the product was badly made but because dangers not spotted during rigorous clinical trials became apparent only after it was used by tens of thousands of patients.

Far from being an antipatient, pro-corporate tool, trademark protection is a necessary precondition for a market filled with quality products. Trademarks protect all producers of quality products, big and small, as well as their customers. The need to cultivate brand identity based on reputation should also preclude the emergence of the primarily Indian and Chinese manufacturers of low-quality copy drugs. Pro-consumer advocates should welcome the inclusion of trademark protection in local legal regimes and international agreements such as the Agreement on Trade-Related Aspects of Intellectual Property Rights (better known as TRIPS, the WTO's 1994 agreement that requires that trademark laws of member jurisdictions be compatible with each other).

The main mechanism for companies to protect their brands is the registration and enforcement of trademarks, something easy to do in the United States and EU, but difficult in countries such as Kenya or Uganda. The inability to protect trademarks affects not just well-known U.S. companies but also generic drug makers from India. The good reputation of generic manufacturers, such as Piramal and Ranbaxy, has not arisen spontaneously, but rather through consistent investment in the factories and standards necessary to manufacture high-quality generic medicines. As we saw in India, these companies suffer from counterfeiters imitating their brands, which poses a risk not only to their bottom line but also to unwitting patients. This problem can also affect smaller, legitimate, local manufacturers in countries such as Kenya.

That said, trademark laws are useless without proper enforcement, which can be slow and inconsistent in countries with corrupt, inefficient courts. For trademarks to signal quality effectively, drug manufacturers need to be able to defend their brands; this requires strong, independent courts; the rule of law; and efficient legal systems. Unfortunately, many legal systems are beset with corruption and judges who are bought too easily.

Although in principle there can be nontrademark-infringing falsified products, these generally are rare. The only one I have directly encountered was the totally bogus Salaxin product in Nigeria made by the nonexistent company Saphire Lifesciences. Because the counterfeiters of this product were not copying a real product's logo or packaging, this drug did not infringe IP rights. I have heard of other non-IP infringing products—brandless ciprofloxacin for example—but not seen them. I have seen many generic brands that have been faked. In many cases, the real manufacturer may not have the margins to protect its trademark. But it is rare that a trademark is not infringed in a fake medicine. While brand protection is beneficial to the company that owns the brand, it is also useful to society. In many of the locations I visited, notably India, Nigeria, and China, the larger companies (Western and occasionally local) often provided the information to combat counterfeiters because the medical authorities were not competent enough to do the job and the police were totally uninterested. In some instances, MRAs may not have sufficient funding; in others, they were corrupt (in which case, increasing funding may have made problems worse).

IP enforcement can be a problem if it conflates generics with counterfeits, but it can also be a benefit. In the United States, the quality of drugs is due to not just the regulations enforced by the FDA but also the systems in drug companies that inculcate a general ethos of maintaining or improving quality. Medicine quality in the United States is high because companies defend their reputations for manufacturing products of consistently high quality. No bureaucracies can possibly have the capacity to check every new consignment of medicines, whether imported or produced domestically. Unlike flaws in some products, it is difficult for consumers to spot problems with drugs. This is why postmarketing surveillance by regulators is warranted, but over time, consumers will change buying decisions if a company's good reputation becomes unjustified.

There is no simple solution. Every problem has its challenges, every solution has costs. But most of the solutions are worth the effort, and the costs can be minimized. It is up to each country's regulators, businesses, and consumers to decide what is worth doing and by whom, and they must act; lives are lost daily due to inaction.

17

Conclusion

Truly evil people are rarely encountered in public-health circles, but a few of the counterfeiters described in this book certainly fall into that category. It is debatable whether bad actors have committed crimes against humanity, but I think some qualify for that unique and truly odious determination.

As a society we should be making greater efforts to hound these people until they are stopped and brought to justice. But much of the debate over improving drug quality is a long way from such black-and-white categorization. Diverging opinions abound on issues ranging from IP enforcement and strengthening the police to subsidizing local production and MRAs; there are even huge disagreements about what constitutes a bad product. I have tried to walk a fair line through these debates and to explain why various positions have been held, but that does not mean I have refrained from choosing a side in some instances where I think certain arguments, no matter how eloquently stated or passionately felt, are simply wrong.

The Indian government has painted far too rosy a picture of the state of drug quality in its country, while Western industry has erroneously alarmed the public about the state of Internet-sourced drugs from foreign-registered pharmacies. IP is not the panacea some friends of industry portray it as, but IP enforcement also has great uses for public safety, a fact health groups completely ignore. Given these strongly held divergent views, compromise is obviously the way forward, but is equally obviously hard to achieve.

The everyday tragedy of poor-quality drugs should lead to urgent and major efforts to improve quality; this has not happened because of extreme positions from both industry and health activists and similarly extreme positions of antagonistic countries. That may be changing. There are enough benefits to all legitimate players that action should and may happen soon.

I am at a loss as to why novelists and Hollywood have not used fake-drug trading as the backdrop to thrillers or even horror movies.

I mentioned the 1949 movie *The Third Man* in the preface, for it reflected a major problem with penicillin dilution by European criminals. The Belgian pharmacy association APB (Association Pharmacéutique Belge) was actually formed three years later to "combat post-war fraud of penicillin-containing pharmaceuticals," Filip Babylon of the APB told me. Yet, although small parts of the international community have been quite vocal about the problem for a decade, there are no movies or novels about the subject. Serious policymakers may scoff at the importance of this type of attention, but outrage plays an important role in combating problems such as fake drugs. And with fake drugs there is plenty of odious material for the writer to create outrage.

Part of the reason the pharmaceutical industry is disliked almost as much as the tobacco and oil industries is because of the way movies portray it. Such Hollywood blockbusters as *The Fugitive* (1993) and *The Constant Gardener* (2005), while entertaining, ludicrously portray the pharmaceutical industry as condoning the production of drugs known to kill a sizable minority of those using them. Although it is quite possible that bad apples exist in all companies (and we've encountered a few in this book, such as those exposed by whistleblowers at Ranbaxy and GSK), for the board of directors of companies with revenues of billions of dollars a year to promote a drug that harms or kills hundreds of users in trials of thousands would not only leave them open to charges of manslaughter but also destroy the company and their wealth. One could write a more nuanced case, quite similar to the story lines chosen, that would be fairly realistic, but the writers of these movies didn't bother.

Ironically, it is not impossible, in fact in some instances it is quite likely, that real-life fake-drug traders do kill the kind of percentages of these mythical celluloid evil pharma firms. Surely, the backstreets of Lagos, Delhi, Nairobi, Shanghai, and Moscow would make a great location for a movie—with the most lethal products going to some poor senior in Omaha, Nebraska, buying them from a bogus "Canadian" web pharmacy. One could even suggest a terrorist link behind the attempt to harm Americans via the web. Until such a time, it is likely that fake drugs will not really make their way into the public consciousness and hence may only receive marginal efforts to combat them globally.

As this book demonstrates, drug quality varies across the planet, and quality is correlated with wealth and literacy. If my empirical research is correct, substandard drugs dominate poorer countries but are rarely found in wealthy ones. In absolute terms, counterfeits are more of a problem in poor countries, too, but they constitute nearly all of the examples of bad drugs for the wealthy. Somewhere around $10,000 GDP per capita, substandard drugs become less significant than counterfeits.

This leads to an important conclusion: while it is important to fight counterfeit drugs everywhere, the highest priority for the poorest countries must be to limit substandard medicines. The methods to combat the two are often considerably different. The link between the two types of dangerous medicines is often the MRA. Combating substandards requires MRAs to be better informed and to educate producers and ensure that postmarketing surveillance occurs. Combating fakes requires MRAs to work with customs, drug companies, and criminal law enforcement to ensure criminal counterfeiters are caught. Even in poor countries, it does not require that much work to ensure that laws against counterfeiting are in place. Are poor countries capable of tackling only one issue at a time? Prioritizing the fight against substandards does not mean these countries should do nothing to stop fakes. It does not take much for a government to ensure that its laws are logical. IMPACT offers template legislation, and countries that do not trust IMPACT can look to the laws of India and Brazil and copy those; both offer good points. NAFDAC seems to benefit from its staff's awareness of both types of problems, and sometimes it can combat even the gray areas of semilegitimate firms operating with negligence. Yet, arguably the largest single problem for substandard drugs in the poorest countries is drugs made by well-connected local companies. In such cases it does not matter how much an organization such as NAFDAC wants to act; politics intervene. That being the case, it may be politically easier to tackle the counterfeit problem first. Countries can focus on the international trade of the truly odious. Politicians from poor countries can go to Geneva to discuss options with their developed-country counterparts and be part of a global network that is doing good. Although it may be less immediately important to them, a convention against the most dangerous faked goods may be the quickest win in the short term.

Having jointly proposed an anticounterfeit medicine treaty in the law literature, I obviously think it would be beneficial. But it would not be sufficient. We need more overt solutions to the substandard problem in developing countries, and for that I think we have to look at the progress and process Brazil has followed. The first step is to acknowledge that in many countries, drugs are of differing standards. These countries should establish that anyone wanting to be called a generic producer must follow innovator or generic GMP standards. We must not fudge this. At the same time, emerging countries should allow the sale of other products, give local companies time to improve standards (not more than a dozen years), and explain the risks of these products to consumers and let them decide what to buy.

MRAs must negotiate this process, conduct postmarketing surveillance, and demand all companies, local and foreign, inform them of any problems and pull anything from the market if it fails basic physical and chemical stability tests and take away anything else where evidence of clinical failure is established. Many, especially within the Western drug industry, will argue that we should demand more than this, even in poor locations, but in the short-to-medium term, this is the practical solution. If we demand more, we will probably get less.

If we aim for reasonable but varied approval standards, then we can be overt about them and move forward to improve standards over time. If not, we will be left with a poorer world of obfuscation and, in some places, lowering standards. MRAs will have to defend leaving obviously inferior products on the market without providing better corporations an advertising benefit of saying they are GMP approved and bioequivalent. The poorest and most vulnerable deserve better.

To get better outcomes we have to look to policymakers. In many ways the most intransigent are those who would like to see IP dominate discussions. I suggest they look at the trade in fake airline parts, a fake market likely to appall jetset policymakers; do they really think IP law is enough to protect them? Do we need another DEG or similar tragic event where a terrible outcome from poor-quality products kills thousands of people across continents, to drive action? Sadly the answer is yes. Until that time, it is likely there will be piecemeal policy changes, useful but not substantial enough to make a difference.

I hope this book provides useful information to policymakers to help drive policy in the right direction. I have endeavored to be transparent throughout, but on a few occasions I have been intentionally opaque. An investigator showed me files taken from a Chinese counterfeiter's computer, which contained two photos from one of my public presentations. The counterfeiter was literally learning from my exposition. From that moment on, I have tried not to assist counterfeiters in this way. If there is anything in this book that is useful to them, I apologize to those people who fight counterfeiters on a day-to-day basis. I hope the good in the book outweighs any advantage the bad guys may gather.

If this book focuses more attention on the problem of drug quality and especially the concern about fake drugs, I will be happy.

Relevant Publications by Roger Bate

Peer-Reviewed Publications

Roger Bate, Paul Newton et. al "The primacy of public health considerations in defining poor quality medicines." *PLoS Medicine* December 7, 2011. http://www.aei.org/files/2011/12/07/-the-primacy-of-public-health-considerations-in-defining-poor-quality-medicines_094342491251.pdf.

Roger Bate, Aparna Mathur, and Ginger Zhe Jin. "Does Price Reveal Poor-Quality Drugs? Evidence from 17 Countries." *Journal of Health Economics* (August 18, 2011), available at http://www.aei.org/docLib/Does-Price-Reveal-Poor-Quality-Drugs.pdf.

Roger Bate, Lorraine Mooney, and Julissa Milligan. "The Danger of Substandard Drugs in Emerging Markets: An Assessment of Basic Product Quality." *Pharmacologia* 3 (2012): 46–51, available at http://docsdrive.com/pdfs/pharmacologia/2012/46-51.pdf.

Amir Attaran, Roger Bate, and Megan Kendall. "Why and How to Make an International Crime of Medicine Counterfeiting." *Journal of International Criminal Justice* (February 10, 2011), available at http://www.aei.org/docLib/Why-and-How-to-Make-an-International-Crime-of-Medicine-Counterfeiting.pdf.

Roger Bate, Lorraine Mooney, and Kimberly Hess. "Medicine Registration and Medicine Quality: A Preliminary Analysis of Key Cities in Emerging Markets." *Research and Reports in Tropical Medicine* (December 13, 2010), available at http://www.aei.org/docLib/medicine-registration-and-medicine-quality-Roger-Bate.pdf.

Roger Bate and Amir Attaran. "A Counterfeit Drug Treaty: Great Idea, Wrong Implementation." *Lancet* (October 29, 2010), available at http://www.aei.org/article/102712.

Roger Bate, Lorraine Mooney, and Kimberly Hess. "Antimalarial Medicine Diversion: Stock-Outs and Other Public Health Problems." *Research and Reports in Tropical Medicine* (September 2, 2010), available at http://www.aei.org/docLib/Antimalarial-drug-diversion-stock-outs-and-other-public-health-090210.pdf.

Roger Bate and Kimberly Hess. "Assessing Website Pharmacy Drug Quality: Safer Than You Think?" *PLoS One* (August 13, 2010), available at http://www.aei.org/docLib/Bate-Assessing-Website-Pharmacy-Drug-Quality.pdf.

Roger Bate and Kimberly Hess. "Anti-Malarial Drug Quality in Lagos and Accra: A Comparison of Various Quality Assessments." *Malaria Journal* (June 11, 2010), available at http://www.aei.org/docLib/BateAntiMalarialDrugQuality.pdf.

Roger Bate, Kimberly Hess, and Richard Tren. "Drug Procurement, the Global Fund, and Misguided Competition Policies." *Malaria Journal* (December 22, 2009), available at http://www.aei.org/docLib/Drug%20Procurement%20Global%20Fund%20Competitiion.pdf.

Roger Bate, Richard Tren, Lorraine Mooney, Kimberly Hess, Barun Mitra, Bibek Debroy, and Amir Attaran. "Pilot Study of Essential Drug Quality in Two Major Cities in India." *PLoS One* (June 23, 2009), available at http://www.aei.org/article/100667.

Roger Bate and Kimberly Hess. "Affordable Medicines Facility for Malaria." *Lancet Infectious Diseases* (June 23, 2009), available at http://www.aei.org/article/100671.

Roger Bate, Richard Tren, Kimberly Hess, Lorraine Mooney, and Karen Porter. "Pilot Study Comparing Technologies to Test for Substandard Drugs in Field Settings." *African Journal of Pharmacy and Pharmacology* (April 1, 2009), available at http://www.aei.org/docLib/Bateetal.pdf.

Roger Bate, Richard Tren, Kimberly Hess, and Amir Attaran. "Physical and Chemical Stability of Expired Fixed Dose Combination Artemether-Lumefantrine in Uncontrolled Tropical Conditions." *Malaria Journal* (February 25, 2009), available at http://www.aei.org/docLib/Bate%20Malaria.pdf.

Roger Bate, Philip Coticelli, Richard Tren, and Amir Attaran. "Antimalarial Drug Quality in the Most Severely Malarious Parts of Africa: A Six Country Study." *PLoS One* (May 7, 2008), available at http://www.aei.org/article/27954.

Roger Bate, Richard Tren, Philip Coticelli, and Kimberly Hess. "Malaria Treatment in Africa." *Africa Fighting Malaria,* Policy Paper (May 1, 2008), available at http://www.aei.org/docLib/20080508_AFMTreatmentPolicyPaper.pdf.

Working Papers

Roger Bate "The market for inferior quality medicines." AEI Economic Policy Studies Working Paper 2011-05, December 14, 2011.

Roger Bate, Thompson Ayodele, Franklin Cudjoe, Kimberly Hess, and Richard Tren. "The Global Fund's Malaria Medicine Subsidy: A nice idea with nasty implications." *Africa Fighting Malaria,* Working Paper (September 8, 2011), available at http://www.aei.org/paper/100246.

Roger Bate, Ginger Zhe Jin, and Aparna Mathur. "Does Price Reveal Poor Quality Drugs? Evidence from 17 Countries." National Bureau of Economic Research, Working Paper 16854 (March 2011), available at http://www.nber.org/papers/w16854.pdf.

Roger Bate. "Improving Assessments of Fake and Substandard Drugs in the Field." *Africa Fighting Malaria,* Working Paper (January 3, 2011), available at http://www.fightingmalaria.org/pdfs/afmbulletin5_theneedforbetterdyetests.pdf.

Roger Bate. "Are Drugs Made in Emerging Markets Good Quality?" *AEI Online* (December 22, 2010), available at http://www.aei.org/docLib/20101222-Bate-WP.pdf.

Roger Bate and Aparna Mathur. "The Impact of Improved Detection Technology on Drug Quality: A Case Study of Lagos, Nigeria." *AEI Online* (February 14, 2011), available at http://www.aei.org/docLib/Nigeria-Working-Paper-v1.pdf.

Roger Bate, Emily Putze, Alexandra McPherson, Sarah Naoshy, and Lorraine Mooney. "Drug Registration: A Necessary but Not Sufficient Condition for Good Quality Drugs." *Africa Fighting Malaria* (October 1, 2010), available at http://www.aei.org/docLib/bate-putze-productregistration-101001.pdf.

Roger Bate, James Taylor, Emily Putze, and Richard Tren. "The Push for Local Production, Costs and Benefits—A Case Study of Uganda's Quality Chemicals." *Africa Fighting Malaria* (September 2, 2009), available at http://www.aei.org/docLib/Bate-workingpaper-localproduction.pdf.

Roger Bate, Kimberly Hess, and Robert Brush. "Pilot Study of Internet Drug Availability, Pricing, and Quality." *Africa Fighting Malaria* (August 20, 2009), available at http://www.aei.org/docLib/20090820-BateHessBrush.pdf.

Roger Bate, Thompson Ayodele, Richard Tren, Kimberly Hess, and Olusegun Sotola. "Drug Use in Nigeria." *Africa Fighting Malaria* (August 1, 2009), available at http://www.aei.org/docLib/nigeria-drug-project-august2009.pdf.

Roger Bate, Richard Tren, Kimberly Hess, Jasson Urbach, and Donald Roberts. "Bias and Neglect—Public Health Insecticides and Disease Control." *Africa Fighting Malaria* (December 17, 2008), available at http://www.aei.org/docLib/20081218_AFMBate.pdf.

Roger Bate, Richard Tren, and Philip Coticelli. "MA Field Report of Uganda's Efforts to Build a Comprehensive Malaria Control Program." *Africa Fighting Malaria* (September 1, 2007), available at http://www.fightingmalaria.org/pdfs/AFM_Uganda_Report_9.04.07.pdf.

Roger Bate and Kathryn Boateng. "Africa Malaria Day 2007—Time for a Checkup." *Africa Fighting Malaria* (April 23, 2007), available at http://www.aei.org/docLib/20070423_MDG.pdf.

Roger Bate and Lorraine Mooney. "WHO's Comprehensive HIV Treatment Failure—Will We Learn the Real Lessons from 3 by 5?" *AEI Online* (November 30, 2006), available at http://www.aei.org/docLib/20061130_AEIWP133.pdf.

Roger Bate. "Poor Countries Need Relief from the World Bank's 'Help' on Malaria." *AEI Online* (October 18, 2006), available at http://www.aei.org/docLib/20061018_bate.pdf.

Roger Bate, Richard Tren, Lorraine Mooney, and Kathryn Boateng. "Tariffs, Corruption and Other Impediments to Medicinal Access in Developing Countries." *AEI Online* (August 4, 2006), available at http://www.aei.org/docLib/20060804_Tariffs Corruption.pdf.

Notes

Chapter 1: Historical Examples of Dangerous Medicines

1. Philip J. Hilts, *Protecting America's Health: The FDA, Business, and One Hundred Years of Regulation* (New York: Knopf, 2003). The book provides a fascinating history of the FDA and drug regulation. Quote available online at "The FDA at Work—Cutting-Edge Science Promoting Public Health," *FDA Consumer Magazine,* January–February 2006, http://www.fda.gov/aboutfda/whatwedo/history/overviews/ucm109801.htm.

2. "Internet 'Viagra' Turns out to Be Bird Droppings | Stuff.co.nz," *Stuff.co.nz—Latest New Zealand News and World News, Sports News and NZ Weather Forecasts,* June 3, 2010, http://www.stuff.co.nz/national/health/3411519/Internet-Viagra-turns-out-to-be-bird-droppings.

3. Carol Ballentine, "Sulfanilamide Disaster," *FDA Consumer Magazine,* June 1981, http://www.fda.gov/AboutFDA/WhatWeDo/History/ProductRegulation/SulfanilamideDisaster/default.htm.

4. Luis Ferrari and Leda Giannuzzi, "Clinical Parameters, Postmortem Analysis and Estimation of Lethal Dose in Victims of a Massive Intoxication with Diethylene Glycol," *Forensic Science International* 153 (2005), http://www.sciencedirect.com/science/article/pii/S0379073805002070.

5. J. Marraffa, M. Holland, C. Stork, C. Hoy, and M. Hodgman. "Diethylene Glycol: Widely Used Solvent Presents Serious Poisoning Potential," *Journal of Emergency Medicine* 35 (2008): 401–6.

6. Leo J. Schep, Robin J. Slaughter, Wayne A. Temple, and D. Michael G. Beasley, "Diethylene Glycol Poisoning," *Clinical Toxicology* 47 (2009): 525–35; 1998: J. Singh, A. K. Dutta, S. Khare, N. K. Dubey, A. K. Harit, N. K. Jain, et al., "Diethylene Glycol Poisoning in Gurgaon, India, 1998," *Bulletin of the World Health Organization* 79 (2001): 88–95.

7. "World Briefing-Africa-Nigeria-12 Held over Tainted Syrup-NYTimes.com," *New York Times, Breaking News, World News and Multimedia, New York Times,* Feb.–Mar. 2009; web, July 11, 2011, http://www.nytimes.com/2009/02/12/world/africa/12briefs-12HELDOVERTA_BRF.html?ref=africa.

8. M. Hanif, M. R. Mobarak, A. Ronan, D. Rahman, J. J. Donovan Jr., and M. L. Bennish, "Fatal Renal Failure Caused by Diethylene Glycol in Paracetamol Elixir: The Bangladesh Epidemic," *British Medical Journal* (1995): 88–91.

9. Ferrari and Giannuzzi, "Clinical Parameters."

10. Walt Bogdanich, "F.D.A. Tracked Poisoned Drugs, but Trail Went Cold in China," *New York Times,* June 17, 2007; web, July 11, 2011, http://www.nytimes.com/2007/06/17/health/17poison.html?_r=1.

11. Walt Bogdanich and Jake Hooker, "From China to Panama, a Trail of Poisoned Medicine," *New York Times,* May 6, 2007, available at http://www.nytimes.com/2007/05/06/world/06poison.html (accessed February 24, 2010).

12. "U.S. Checking All Toothpaste Imports from China," CNN.com, May 23, 2007, http://web.archive.org/web/20070526145153/http:/www.cnn.com/2007/HEALTH/05/23/china.toothpaste.reut/index.html; U.S. Department of Health and Human Services, Food and Drug Administration, Center for Drug Evaluation and Research (CDER), May 2007, http://www.fda.gov/downloads/Drugs/GuidanceCompliance-RegulatoryInformation/Guidances/ucm070347.pdf.

13. Margaret Chan, "Tuberculosis," World Health Organization. Last modified November-December 2010. http://www.who.int/mediacentre/factsheets/fs104/en/.

14. "Campaign for Access to Essential Medicines," Médecins Sans Frontières, March 22, 2011, http://www.msfaccess.org/media-room/press-releases/press-release-detail/?tx_ttnews[tt_news]=1675&cHash=15c0880adb&no_cache=1&print=1; "A 24-Month DR-TB Treatment Regimen Can Cost as Much as US$9,000 for One Patient–470 Times More Than the $19 per Patient It Costs to Cure Standard, Drug-Sensitive TB."

15. Some South African data can be found here: Jerome Amir Singh, Ross Upshur, and Nesri Padayatchi, "XDR-TB in South Africa: No Time for Denial or Complacency," *PLoS Medicine* 4 (2007): E50.

16. Richard Coker, "Lessons from New York's Tuberculosis Epidemic," *British Medical Journal* 317 (1998): 616–20.

Chapter 2: Understanding the Problem

1. Julian Harris, "Fake Drugs Kill over 700,000 People Every Year–New Report | International Policy Network," *Home | International Policy Network,* July 11, 2011, http://www.policynetwork.net/health/media/fake-drugs-kill-over-700000-people-every-year-new-report.

2. Peter Pitts, "Counterfeit Drugs and China," Center for Medicine in the Public Interest, http://www.cmpi.org/in-the-news/testimony/counterfeit-drugs-and-china-new/.

3. Some data can be found here: "IMS Health Lowers 2009 Global Pharmaceutical Market Forecast to 2.5–3.5 Percent Growth," Imshealth.com, April 22, 2009, http://www.imshealth.com/portal/site/imshealth/menuitem.a46c6d4df3db

4b3d88f611019418c22a/?vgnextoid=1e61fa8adbec0210VgnVCM100000ed152 ca2RCRD.

4. IMS Health Services; calculation is based on their published data online, available at http://www.imshealth.com/portal/site/imshealth/menuitem.a953aef4d73 d1ecd88f611019418c22a/?vgnextoid=bb967900b55a5110VgnVCM10000071812c a2RCRD&vgnextfmt=default.

5. "Drug Counterfeiting," http://ec.europa.eu/internal_market/indprop/docs/ conf2008/wilfried_roge_en.pdf.

6. "FDA Opened 72 New Counterfeit Cases in 2010—A New Record," *Pharmaceutical Commerce,* March 22, 2011, http://www.pharmaceuticalcommerce.com/ frontEnd/1618-FDA_OCI_Bernstein_counterfeit_Pew.html.

Chapter 3: Overview of Research Findings and Possible Solutions

1. Misha Glenny. *McMafia: A Journey Through the Global Criminal Underworld.* London: Alfred A. Knopf, 2008.

2. "Transnational Trafficking and the Rule of Law in West Africa: A Threat Assessment July 2009," http://www.pharmaceuticalcommerce.com/frontEnd/1618- FDA_OCI_Bernstein_counterfeit_Pew.html.

3. Kirsty Barnes, "GSK to Strip Down through Outsourcing and Offshoring," In-pharmatechnologist.com, October 2007.

4. U.S. Department of Commerce, International Trade Administration, "Data and Statistics, US Imports of Pharmaceuticals and Medicines," http://tse.export.gove/ TSE/MapDisplay.aspx.

Chapter 4: Africa

1. Barnes, "GSK to Strip Down through Outsourcing."

2. Andreas Seiter, *A Practical Approach to Pharmaceutical Policy* (Washington, D.C.: World Bank, 2010).

3. Drug distribution and fake drugs in Nigeria. D Pole - Basel: Institute for Medical Information, 1989; NAFDAC page referencing the study is "NAFDAC: Global Trends, 2009," http://www.nafdacnigeria.org/globaltrends.htm.

4. "Nigeria Reaffirms Efforts to Eliminate Fake Drugs," Xinhua General News Service, February 13, 2003, reporting on survey by the Nigerian government's Institute of Pharmaceutical Research.

5. UNODC, "Transnational Trafficking and the Rule of Law in West Africa: A Threat Assessment," July 2009, available at http://www.unodc.org/documents/data- and-analysis/Studies/West_Africa_Report_2009.pdf.

6. See box 4-1 for more on the case and its relation to the reemergence of polio in Nigeria.

7. Chinua Achebe. *The Trouble with Nigeria.* N.p.: Heinemann, 1984.

8. Foundation Chirac, "The Cotonou Declaration," October 12, 2009, available at www.fondationchirac.eu/en/programs/access-to-medicine/international-mobilization-against-the-traffic-of-falsified-medicines (accessed July 27, 2010).

9. "Acute Drug Shortage in Public Hospitals Condemns the Sick to Misery," *Daily Nation* (Kenya), http://www.nation.co.ke/News/-/1056/857262/-/vq13j4/-/index.html (accessed July 12, 2011).

10. "Coartem Stocks Run Out, 300 Die Daily," *Independent,* March 9, 2010, available at http://www.independent.co.ug/features/features/2581-coartem-stocks-run-out-300-die-daily (accessed July 8, 2011).

11. "Uganda: Patients Stranded at Mbarara Hospital without Drugs," *Monitor,* May 2, 2010, available at http://allafrica.com/stories/201005040510.html (accessed July 8, 2011).

12. "Uganda Health News: NDA to Fight Counterfeit Drugs," *UG Pulse,* November 19, 2008, available at http://www.ugpulse.com/uganda-news/health/nda-to-fight-counterfeit-drugs/7176.aspx (accessed July 8, 2011).

13. USAID Audit Report, Office of the Inspector General, "Audit of USAID/Angola's Procurement and Distribution of Commodities under the President's Malaria Initiative," Audit Report No. 4-654-10-001-P, December 21, 2009, available at http://www.usaid.gov/oig/public/fy10rpts/4-654-10-001-p.pdf.

14. Ibid.

15. "AIDS Drugs Being Sold Illegally on Market Stalls in Kenya," *Lancet* (January 31, 2004), available at http://www.thelancet.com/journals/lancet/article/PIIS0140-6736(04)15479-2/fulltext (accessed July 8, 2011).

16. American Enterprise Institute, "Africa's Stolen-Drug Problem," September 1, 2010, available at http://www.aei.org/article/102484 (accessed July 8, 2011).

17. "Witness Pins Officials on Drug Diversion," *New Vision,* April 27, 2010, available at http://www.newvision.co.ug/PA/8/13/717754 (accessed July 8, 2011).

18. R. Bate, "Shell shouldn't bow to environmentalists," *Wall Street Journal Europe,* June 5, 1996.

Chapter 5: India

1. Informants indicated that some of the API for the fake injections came from Agra. See "Nursing India's Drug Market Back to Health," *American,* April 16, 2009, available at http://www.american.com/archive/2009/april-2009/nursing-india2019s-drug-market-back-to-health/article_print (accessed July 11, 2011).

2. "Shady Parties, Donors Use Flawed System to Get Rich," *Daily News and Analysis,* April 14, 2009, available at http://www.dnaindia.com/india/report_shady-parties-donors-use-flawed-system-to-get-rich_1247557 (accessed July 11, 2011).

3. "The Deadly World of Fake Drugs," *Foreign Policy* (September/October 2008), available at http://www.foreignpolicy.com/story/cms.php? story_id=220 (accessed July 11, 2011).

4. Central Drugs Standard Control Organization, "Report on Countrywide Survey for Spurious Drugs," 2009, available at http://cdsco.nic.in/REPORT_BOOK_13-7-10.pdf (accessed July 11, 2011).

5. Ibid.

6. Roger Bate, "Delhi's Fake Drug Whitewash," *Wall Street Journal India,* last modified September 2, 2010, http://online.wsj.com/article/SB100014240527487038 82304575465170785077144.html.

7. Ibid.

8. Pew Charitable Trusts, "The Prescription Project: Advancing Medical Practice and Policy," August 2010, available at http://www.pewtrusts.org/news_room_detail.aspx?id=34192 (accessed July 11, 2011).

9. Roger Bate and Lorraine Mooney, "WHO's Comprehensive HIV Treatment Failure—Will We Learn the Real Lessons from 3 by 5?" *AEI Online* (November 30, 2006), available at http://www.aei.org/docLib/20061130_AEIWP133.pdf.

10. European Parliament and Council, "Directive on the Community Code Relating to Medicinal Products for Human Use," 2001/83/EC, November 6, 2001 (amended), available at www.emea.europa.eu/pdfs/human/pmf/2001-83-EC.pdf (accessed June 12, 2009); and *Code of Federal Regulations* 21, § 320.23.

11. International Policy Network, "Good Move on Bad Drugs," October 3, 2008, available at http://www.policynetwork.net/es/health/media/good-move-bad-drugs (accessed July 11, 2011).

12. U.S. District Court for the District of Maryland (Southern Division), July 2008, available at http://www.pharmalot.com/wp-content/uploads/2008/07/ranbaxy-response.pdf (accessed July 11, 2011).

13. Response of Ranbaxy, Inc. to Motion to Enforce Subpoenas, *U.S. v. Ranbaxy, Inc., and Parexel Consulting* (D. Md. filed July 14, 2008), 2, available at www.fdalaw blog.net/fda_law_blog_hyman_phelps/files/response_of_ranbaxy.pdf (accessed June 18, 2009).

14. "Daiichi Sankyo and Ranbaxy Announce Reconstitution of Ranbaxy Executive Leadership," news release, May 24, 2009, available at www.ranbaxy.com/news/newsdisp.aspx?cp=924&flag=ARC (accessed June 18, 2009).

15. WHO, Public Inspection Report for Ranbaxy Laboratories Ltd., Paonta Sahib, India (SOP-IN01.1-App1, May 8–10, 2007), available at http://apps.who.int/prequal/WHOPIR/WHOPIR_RanbaxyLabs8-10May07.pdf (accessed June 11, 2009).

16. WHO, Public Inspection Report for Ranbaxy Laboratories Ltd., Paonta Sahib, India (Annex A, November 18–21, 2008), available at http://apps.who.int/prequal/WHOPIR/WHOPIR_Ranbaxy18-21Nov08.pdf (accessed July 11, 2011).

17. "Life-Saving or Life-Threatening?" American Enterprise Institute Outlook Series, June 2009, available at http://www.aei.org/outlook/100049 (accessed July 11, 2011).

18. *Trafic Mortel,* available through *Daily Motion* at http://www.dailymotion.com/video/xjkmd_trafic-mortel_news (accessed July 12, 2011).

19. This is evident in *Trafic Mortel.*

20. Rema Nagarajan, "Chinese Passing Off Fake Drugs as 'Made in India,'" *Times of India,* June 9, 2009, http://timesofindia.indiatimes.com/business/india-business/Chinese-passing-off-fake-drugs-as-Made-in-India/articleshow/4633377.cms (accessed May 25, 2011).

21. PTI, "Fake 'Made in India' Drugs: China Admits Its Cos' Involvement," *Times of India,* August 11, 2009, http://timesofindia.indiatimes.com/india/Fake-Made-In-India-drugs-China-admits-its-cos-involvement/articleshow/4881726.cms (accessed May 25, 2011); and P. T. Jyothi Datta, "Chinese-Origin 'Made in India' Fake Medicines Seized in Nigeria," *Hindu Business Line,* July 23, 2010, http://www.thehindubusiness line.com/2010/07/23/stories/2010072352600200.htm (accessed May 25, 2011).

Chapter 6: Middle East

1. U.S. Congress, House of Representatives, Subcommittee on Oversight and Investigations of the Committee on Energy and Commerce, *FDA's Foreign Drug Inspection Program: Weaknesses Place Americans at Risk,* 110th Congress, 2nd Session, April 22, 2008, 5, available at http://www.gpo.gov/fdsys/pkg/CHRG-110hhrg52415/pdf/CHRG-110hhrg52415.pdf.

2. "Statement by Joshua M. Sharfstein, M.D., Principal Deputy Commissioner, Food and Drug Administration (FDA), U.S. Department of Health and Human Services (HHS) on Drug Safety–An Update from the FDA," U.S. Department of Health and Human Services, http://www.hhs.gov/asl/testify/2010/03/t20100310a.html.

3. "Counterfeit Drugs in China: Shanghai Steps Up Drug Monitoring Systems," *PBI Asian Medical eNewsletter* 2 (March 4, 2003), available at www.osdir.com/ml/filesystems.reiserfs.general/2003-03/msg00269.html.

4. "Statement by Shaohong Jin in Optimizing Capabilities to Combat Counterfeiters, the Sixth Global Forum on Pharmaceutical AntiCounterfeiting," London, May 4–6, 2011, Reconnaisance International Conference speech http://www.google.com/#hl=en&xhr=t&q=Shaohon%20Jin%20London%20in%20April%202011%20showed%20that%20under%205%25%20were%20fake&cp=12&pq=shaohon%20jinlondon%20in%20april%202011%20showed%20that%20under%205%25%20were%20fake&pf=p&sclient=psy&source=hp&aq=f&aqi=&aql=&oq=Shaohon+Jin+London+in+April+2011+showed+that+under+5%25+were+fake&pbx=1&bav=on.2,or.r_gc.r_pw.&fp=c488823cce0a6f39&biw=926&bih=517.

5. Peter S. Goodman, "China's Killer Headache: Fake Pharmaceuticals," *Washington Post,* August 30, 2002; Tim Browning and Carol Wang, "China IP Focus 2004: Enforcement," *Managing Intellectual Property* (January 2004), available at www.managingip.com/Article.aspx?ArticleID=1321688 (accessed April 16, 2009); unnamed sources, personal communication with author, April–July 2008. These investigators declined to be named for fear of government reprisal.

6. "Statement by Guy Villax, CEO Hovione: After Heparin: A Roundtable on Ensuring the Safety of the US Drug Supply," March 2011, 4, available at http://www.prescriptionproject.org/assets/pdfs/Villax.pdf.

7. Jin Shaohong, personal communication with author, April 1, 2008.

8. Jin Shaohong, "Mobile Labs for Detection of Counterfeit Drugs in China" (presentation, Third Global Forum on Pharmaceutical Anticounterfeiting, Prague, March 14, 2007), cited in U.S. Pharmacopeia, "Matrix of Drug Quality Reports Affecting USAID-Assisted Countries," February 3, 2009, available at www.usp.org/pdf/EN/dqi/ghcDrugQualityMatrix.pdf (accessed April 16, 2009).

9. Zhong-Yuan Yang (presentation, Pharmaceutical Sciences World Congress, March 25, 2007), cited in ibid.

10. Lu Hui, "China Launches National Campaign against On-line Sales of Illegal Drugs," *Xinhua,* January 31, 2008; "SFDA Clarifies Drug Inspection Priorities for 2008," *China Pharmaceuticals and Health Technologies Weekly,* March 26, 2008.

11. SFDA, "SFDA Issues 2009 First Safety Warning Announcement regarding Buying Medicines Online," news release, February 26, 2009; "China Blacklists 46 Websites for Selling Fake TCM," *Xinhua,* March 23, 2009.

12. "China Shuts Down 558 Websites." *New Straits Times* (January 19, 2010), available at http://www.nst.com.my/articles/20100119104313/Article/index_html (accessed January 28, 2010).

Chapter 7: Middle East

1. Milissa McGinniss, "Media Reports on Medicine Quality: Focusing on USAID-Assisted Countries by Promoting the Quality of Medicines Program," *United States Pharmacopeia,* January 3, 2011, http://www.usp.org/pdf/EN/dqi/Media_Reports-01_2011-final.pdf.

2. Mohamed M. Ali and Iqbal H. Shah, "Sanctions and Childhood Mortality in Iraq," *Lancet* 355 (May 2000): 1851–57.

3. Major criminals with established networks just go to wholesalers under their influence, but there are few such players, and most illegal traders prefer to run the lower risk of first trying to interest a pharmacist, who is unlikely to be politically connected.

4. USAID, "Pharmaceutical and Medical Products in Iraq," April 17, 2007, 9, http://www.izdihar-iraq.com/resources/papers_pdfs/pharmaceutical_and_medical_products_in_Iraq_0appx_rev_web2.pdf.

5. Ibid., 59.

6. Figures supplied by security personnel. The author attempted to assess their veracity and believes them to be true, but was unable to find corroborative evidence from media or other sources.

7. Ibid.

8. Ibid.

9. Ibid.

10. Ibid.

11. Nadine Elali, "Fake Drugs Are a Real Threat," *New Lebanon,* March 29, 2010, http://www.nowlebanon.com/NewsArchiveDetails.aspx?ID=157136.

12. A. Halteh, "Unified Efforts Needed to Combat Counterfeited Medicines in Jordan, Experts Say," *AG-IP News,* April 15, 2008, available at: www.ag-ip-news.com (accessed April 16, 2008); see also http://www.usp.org/pdf/EN/dqi/ghcDrugQuality-Matrix.pdf, 38.

13. Tina Susman and Caesar Ahmad, "Iraq Takes on Fake Drugs," *Los Angeles Times,* August 30, 2008, http://articles.latimes.com/2008/aug/30/world/fg-iraqdrugs30.

14. Charles Levinson, "Iraq Returns to Its Alternative Medicine Roots," *USA Today,* November 3, 2008, http://www.usatoday.com/news/world/iraq/2008-11-02-herbalmeds_N.htm.

15. Figures supplied by security personnel. The author attempted to assess their veracity and believes them to be true, but was unable to find corroborative evidence from media or other sources.

Chapter 8: Other Emerging Markets

1. "Counterfeit Drugs: A Threat to Russia's Security," *Moscow News,* June 10, 2008, available at www.mnweekly.rian.ru; see also http://www.usp.org/pdf/EN/dqi/ghcDrugQualityMatrix.pdf, 54.

2. Ibid.

3. Vladimir Pribylovsky, "Russian Political Parties and Their Leaders: Russian Presidential Candidates 1996," *Panorama,* http://www.panorama.ru/works/oe/brynt-sae.html.

4. Paul Starobin, "The Trials of a Russian Drug Czar," *Businessweek,* January 29, 2001, http://www.businessweek.com/archives/2001/b3717150.arc.htm.

5. Tom Parfitt, "Russia Cracks Down on Counterfeit Drugs," *Lancet* 368 (2006): 1481–82.

6. Ibid.

7. Ibid.

8. "Russian Billionaire May Construct Largest Pharma Plant in Belarus," *PharmaLetter,* March 9, 2011, http://www.thepharmaletter.com/file/102642/russian-billionaire-may-construct-largest-pharma-plant-in-belarus.html.

9. "Resolution-RDC 133 of 20 May 2003," ANVISA website, www.anvisa.gov.br/eng/legis/resol/133_03_rdc_e.htm (accessed September 10, 2010).

10. "Un Negocio Millonario que Mata a Miles al Personas al Año en al País," *El Día,* September 26, 2010, http://www.eldia.com.ar/edis/20100926/informacion general0.htm (accessed February 7, 2011).

11. Claudio Csillag, "Epidemic of Counterfeit Drugs Causes Concern in Brazil," *Lancet* 352 (1998): 553.

12. "Multisource Drug Policies in Latin America: Survey of 10 Countries," *World Health Organization* (January 2005), available at http://www.who.int/bulletin/volumes/83/1/en/64.pdf (accessed July 2, 2010).

13. P. N. Newton et al., "A Collaborative Epidemiological Investigation into the Criminal Fake Artesunate Trade in South East Asia," *PLoS Medicine* 5 (2008): e32, http://www.plosmedicine.org/article/info%3Adoi%2F10.1371%2Fjournal.pmed.0050032.

14. "The Scourge of Fake Medicine" (editorial), *Bangkok Post,* February 9, 2008, available at http://www.aegis.org/news/bp/2008/BP080204.html (accessed March 9, 2010).

15. Milissa McGinnis, "Matrix of Drug Quality Reports Affecting USAID-Assisted Countries," U.S. Pharmacopeia Drug Quality and Information Program, report, August 3, 2010, available at http://www.usp.org/pdf/EN/dqi/ghcDrugQualityMatrix.pdf (accessed February 19, 2010).

16. "Fake Medicines Worth RM7.8 Million Seized Last Year," *Materia Medica Malaysiana* (April 5, 2007), available at http://malaysianmedicine.wordpress.com/2007/04/05/fake-medicines-worth-rm78-million-seized-last-year/ (accessed Jan 28 2010).

17. "Malaysia Pharmaceuticals and Healthcare Report Q3 2007," *Business Monitor International* (October 2007), available through ProQuest Research Library (accessed March 26, 2010).

18. "Malaysia Seizes Fake Sex Drug 'Miagra,'" *Channel News Asia* (March 22, 2007), available at http://www.channelnewsasia.com/stories/afp_asiapacific/view/265625/1/.html (accessed March 9, 2010).

19. Brenda Lim, "Sex Stimulants Top Counterfeit Drugs Seized," New Straits Times Online (May 14, 2008), available at http://findarticles.com/p/news-articles/new-straits-times/mi_8016/is_20080514/stimulants-counterfeit-drugs-seized/ai_n44401233/ (accessed January 28, 2010).

20. "New Bill to Help Curb Counterfeit Medicines." *Malaysian Bar,* September 22, 2008, available at http://www.malaysianbar.org.my/legal/general_news/new_bill_to_help_curb_counterfeit_medicines.html?date=2010-08-01 (accessed February 15, 2011).

21. Ibid.

22. "Spotlight/Fake Medicines: Listen Up, There's No Easy Cure," *New Straits Times,* February 1, 2010, available at http://fakemed.ph/news.php?newsId=252 (accessed March 9, 2010).

23. Roger Bate, "Fighting a Bitter Prescription," *American* (July 30, 2009), available at http://www.american.com/archive/2009/july/fighting-a-bitter-prescription/ (accessed March 10, 2010).

24. Pharmaceutical Security Institute, http://www.psi-inc.org/geographic Distributions.cfm.

25. Leo Tolstoy, *Anna Karenina,* trans. R. Peaver and L. Volokhonsky (New York: Penguin Publishing, 2000), 1.

Chapter 9: The Online Drug Market

1. W. Bogdanovich, "Counterfeit Drugs' Path Eased by Free Trade Zones," *New York Times,* December 17, 2007, available at http://www.nytimes.com/2007/12/17/world/middleeast/17freezone.html (accessed November 26, 2010); Roger Bate, Amir Attaran, and Meghan Kendall, "Why and How to Make an International Crime of Medicine Counterfeiting," *Journal of International Criminal Justice* (February 2011), available at http://jicj.oxfordjournals.org/content/early/2011/02/10/jicj.mqr005.full.

2. J. Skerritt, "Online Pharmacist Eludes Ban: Strempler Moves Business to Caribbean, Manitoba Regulators Can't Stop Him Now," *Winnipeg Free Press,* February 26, 2010, available at http://www.winnipegfreepress.com/local/online-pharmacist-eludes-ban-85460077.html (accessed November 26, 2010). See also the website of PharmaCheck: http://www.pharmacheck.com/contact.cfm.

3. C. Krauss, "Going Global at a Small-Town Canadian Drugstore," *New York Times,* March 5, 2005, available at http://www.nytimes.com/2005/03/05/international/americas/05strempler.html (accessed November 25, 2010).

4. Ibid.

5. International Convention for the Suppression of Counterfeiting Currency, Geneva, April 20, 1929, http://treaties.un.org/pages/LONViewDetails.aspx?src=LON&id=551&lang=en.

6. "Growing Threat from Counterfeit Medicines," *Bulletin of the World Health Organization* 88 (2010): 247–48, available at http://www.who.int/bulletin/volumes/88/4/10-020410.pdf.

7. Roger Bate and Kimberly Hess, "Assessing Website Pharmacy Drug Quality: Safer Than You Think?" *PLoS One* 5 (August 13, 2010), http://www.plosone.org/article/info%3Adoi%2F10.1371%2Fjournal.pone.0012199; see part III for updated tables and results; read the PLoS paper for a full methodology of how each site was selected and tested.

Chapter 10: Factors to Consider for Research

1. Newton et al., "A Collaborative Epidemiological Investigation," e32.

2. IMPACT, *The Handbook,* January 2011, http://www.who.int/impact/resources/handobook/en/index.html.

Chapter 11: Results: What We Found

1. Suzanne Hill and Kent Johnson, "Emerging Challenges and Opportunities in Drug Registration and Regulation in Developing Countries," DFID Health Systems Resource Centre, May 2004, http://www.hlsp.org/LinkClick.aspx?fileticket=0TXMdaAk5KA%3D&tabid=1643.

2. U.S. Food and Drug Administration, "FDA Approves Coartem Tablets to Treat Malaria," FDA news release, April 8, 2009, http://www.fda.gov/NewsEvents/Newsroom/PressAnnouncements/ucm149559.htm (accessed November 13, 2010).

3. "Regulators Struggle to Tame Fake Medicine Market," *China Daily,* May 25, 2009, http://www.chinadaily.com.cn/bw/2009-05/25/content_7937588.htm (accessed November 13, 2010).

4. Republic of Kenya, Ministry of Health Pharmacy and Poisons Board and Division of Malaria Control, "Antimalarial Medicines in Kenya: Availability, Quality and Registration Status," December 2007, http://apps.who.int/medicinedocs/documents/s16424e/s16424e.pdf (accessed November 13, 2010).

5. For more detailed information on medicine registration, see R. Bate, E. Putze, A. McPherson, S. Naoshy, and L. Mooney, "Drug Registration: A Necessary but Not Sufficient Condition for Good Quality Drugs—A Preliminary Analysis of 12 Countries," *Africa Fighting Malaria,* October 1, 2010, http://www.fightingmalaria.org/pdfs/productregistration.pdf (accessed November 13, 2010).

6. U.S. Pharmacopeia, "Matrix of Drug Quality Reports Affecting USAID-Assisted Countries," February 3, 2009, available at www.usp.org/pdf/EN/dqi/ghcDrugQualityMatrix.pdf (accessed April 16, 2009).

7. R. Bate and K. Hess, "Anti-Malarial Drug Quality in Lagos and Accra: A Comparison of Various Quality Assessments," *Malaria Journal* 9 (2010): 157

8. "Western" companies were those located in the EU, Switzerland, and the United States.

9. Roger Bate, Philip Coticelli, Richard Tren, and Amir Attaran, "Antimalarial Drug Quality in the Most Severely Malarious Parts of Africa: A Six Country Study," *PLoS One,* May 7, 2008.

Chapter 12: Results Broken Out
for Africa, India, and Other Markets

1. Roger Bate, James Taylor, Emily Putze, and Richard Tren, "The Push for Local Production, Costs and Benefits: A Case Study of Uganda's Quality Chemicals," *Africa Fighting Malaria,* September 2009.

2. World Health Organization, "60th World Health Assembly: WHA 60.18; Malaria, Including Proposal for Establishment of World Malaria Day," May 23, 2007, http://apps.who.int/gb/ebwha/pdf_files/WHA60/A60_R18-en.pdf (accessed February 9, 2011).

3. Roger Bate, "New Test Finds More Fake Medicines," AEI Enterprise Blog, January 13, 2011, http://blog.american.com/?p=24886.

4. V. P. Sharma, "Current Scenario of Malaria in India," *Parassitologia* 41 (September 1999): 349–53; and V. P. Sharma, "Re-emergence of Malaria in India," *Indian Journal of Medical Research* 103 (January 1996): 26–45.

Chapter 13: Interpreting and Discussing
the Results and Their Relevance

1. See Bate et al., "Drug Registration: A Necessary but Not Sufficient Condition."

2. USAID, "Growing Threat of Substandard and Counterfeit Medicines in Developing Countries Addressed by New USAID-USP Cooperative Agreement," news release, October 26, 2009, www.usaid.gov/press/releases/2009/pr091026_1.html (accessed May 30, 2011).

3. Roger Bate, Lorraine Mooney, Julian Harris, and Barun Mitra, *A Safe Medicines Chest for the World: Preventing Substandard Products from Tainting India's Pharmaceuticals,* International Policy Network (May 2010), www.policynetwork.net/sites/default/files/Safe_Medicines_Chest_2010.pdf (accessed May 30, 2011).

4. ANVISA, "Frequently Asked Questions," ANVISA official website, www.anvisa.gov.br/eng/generic/faq.htm#02 (accessed August 15, 2010).

5. IHS, "New Russian Pharmaceutical Bill Passed on Final Reading," Global Insight Perspective, March 26, 2010, www.ihsglobalinsight.com/SDA/SDADetail18459.htm (accessed August 2, 2010).

6. Daniel Ten Kate, "Safe at Any Cost?" *Asia Sentinel,* January 24, 2007, www.asiasentinel.com/index.php?option=com_content&task=view&id=351&Itemid=392 (accessed August 17, 2010).

7. Katie Lewis, "China's Counterfeit Medicine Trade Is Booming," *Canadian Medical Association Journal* 181 (October 5, 2009), www.cmaj.ca/cgi/content/full/181/10/E237 (accessed May 30, 2011).

8. One example is the fatal melamine contamination of milk; see BBC News, "Chinese Milk Scam Duo Face Death," January 22, 2009, http://news.bbc.co.uk/2/hi/asia-pacific/7843972.stm (accessed May 30, 2011).

9. Office of the U.S. Trade Representative, "2007 Special 301 Report," www.ustr.gov/sites/default/files/asset_upload_file230_11122.pdf (accessed August 15, 2010).

10. Roger Bate, Ginger Zhe Jin, and Aparna Mathur, "Does Price Reveal Poor-Quality Drugs? Evidence from 17 Countries," National Bureau of Economic Research, Working Paper 16854, http://www.nber.org/papers/w16854.pdf.

11. Alexandra Cameron, et al. "The World Medicines Situation 2011: Medicines Prices, Availability and Affordability," World Health Organization, Geneva, 2011, available at http://www.who.int/medicines/areas/policy/world_medicines_situation/WMS_ch6_wPricing_v6.pdf.

12. For more details, see Bate, Jin, and Mathur, "Does Price Reveal Poor Quality Drugs?"

13. Yi Qian, "Impacts of Entry by Counterfeiters," *Quarterly Journal of Economics* 123 (2008): 1577–1609, doi:10.1162/qjec.2008.123.4.1577.

14. United Nations Development Programme, International Human Development Indicators, "Adult Literacy Rate (Both Sexes)," http://hdrstats.undp.org/en/indicators (accessed May 30, 2011).

15. For the data used, see PricewaterhouseCoopers, "Which Are the Largest City Economies in the World and How Might This Change by 2025?" *UK Economic Outlook,* November 2009, https://www.ukmediacentre.pwc.com/imagelibrary/down loadMedia.ashx?MediaDetailsID=1562 (accessed May 30, 2011); and United Nations, Department of Economic and Social Affairs, *World Urbanization Prospects: The 2009 Revision,* http://esa.un.org/unpd/wup/index.htm (accessed May 30, 2011).

16. For the country-specific taxes and duties we used, see R. Bate, R. Tren, and J. Urbach, "Still Taxed to Death: The Role That Taxes, Tariffs and Regulations Play in Denying Access to Essential Medicines to Patients in the Developing World," AEI-Brookings Joint Center, Washington, D.C. (2006), http://www.aei-brookings.org/publications/abstract.php?pid=930.

17. Please refer to ibid. for detailed data description, as different types of tax duties come from different data sources.

18. "Egypt: No to Fakes," www.notofakes.com/Resources/TravelAdvisory/Africa/Egypt/tabid/495/Default.aspx (accessed May 30, 2011).

19. Central Drugs Standard Control Organization, "Guidelines for Taking Action on Samples of Drugs Declared Spurious or Not of Standard Quality in the Light of Enhanced Penalties under the Drugs and Cosmetics (Amendment) Act, 2008," http://cdsco.nic.in/Guidelines%20under%20new%20penal%20provisions.pdf (accessed May 30, 2011).

Chapter 14: Developing Medical Regulatory Authorities: The U.S. FDA as a Case Study

1. Hilts, *Protecting America's Health.*

2. George Akerlof, "The Market for 'Lemons': Quality Uncertainty and the Market Mechanism," *Quarterly Journal of Economics* 84 (1970): 488–500.

3. George J. Stigler, "The Theory of Economic Regulation," *Bell Journal of Economics and Management Science* 2 (1971); Sam Peltzman, "Toward a More General Theory of Regulation," *Journal of Law and Economics* 19 (1976).

4. U.S. Food and Drug Administration, "The History of Drug Regulation in the United States."

5. U.S. Food and Drug Administration, "The History of Drug Regulation in the United States" (2006), http://www.fda.gov/AboutFDA/WhatWeDo/History/FOrgsHistory/CDER/CenterforDrugEvaluationandResearchBrochureandChronology/ucm114470.htm.

6. Hilts, *Protecting America's Health,* 27.

7. Clayton Coppin and Jack High,*The Politics of Purity: Harvey Washington Wiley and the Origins of Federal Food Policy* (Ann Arbor: University of Michigan Press, 1999).

8. Williams's statement at the 2011 Pew Health Group Roundtable. A paraphrase of the quote is available here: "Supply Line Safety under Scrutiny" March

17, 2011. *The People's Pharmacy Online*. Available at: http://www.peoplespharmacy. com/2011/03/17/supply-line-safety-under-scrutiny/.

9. Hilts, *Protecting America's Health*, 83.

10. Ibid., 89 (emphasis in the original).

11. Michael Krauss, "Loosening the FDA's Drug Certification Monopoly: Implications for Tort Law and Consumer Welfare, *George Mason Law Review* (1996).

12. This is documented throughout Hilts's book; see Hilts, *Protecting America's Health*.

13. Ibid., 121.

14. U.S. Food and Drug Administration, "The History of Drug Regulation in the United States: 1962: Drug Efficacy," June 18, 2009, available at http://www.fda.gov/ AboutFDA/WhatWeDo/History/FOrgsHistory/CDER/CenterforDrugEvaluationand ResearchBrochureandChronology/ucm114470.htm#1962 (accessed 7/15/2011).

15. Peltzman, "Toward a More General Theory of Regulation."

16. D. H. Gieringer, "The Safety and Efficacy of New Drug Approval," *Cato Journal* 5 (Spring–Summer, 1985): 177–201.

17. Hilts, *Protecting America's Health*, 315.

18. Ibid., 253.

19. Tomas Philipson and Anupam Jena, "Who Benefits from New Medical Technologies? Estimates of Consumer and Producer Surpluses for HIV/AIDS Drugs," *Forum for Health Economics and Policy* 1 (2006).

20. Statement of Andrew C. von Eschenbach, M.D. to U.S. Congress, House of Representatives, Subcommittee on Oversight and Investigations of the Committee on Energy and Commerce, *FDA's Foreign Drug Inspection Program*, November 1, 2007.

21. Ibid.

22. Hepeng Jia and Dan Chen, "FDA Opens Foreign Office," *Chemistry World* 6 (January 2009), http://www.rsc.org/chemistryworld/Issues/2009/January/FDA OpensForeignOffice.asp.

23. United Nations Office on Drugs and Crime, *Transnational Trafficking and the Rule of Law in West Africa: A Threat Assessment*, July 2009, www.unodc.org/documents/ data-and-analysis/Studies/West_Africa_Report_2009.pdf (accessed September 17, 2010).

24. Krystyn Alter Hall, Paul N. Newton, Michael D. Green, et al., "Characterization of Counterfeit Artesunate Antimalarial Tablets from Southeast Asia," *American Journal of Tropical Medicine and Hygiene* 75 (November 2006): 804–11, www.ajtmh. org/cgi/content/full/75/5/804 (accessed September 17, 2010).

25. Republic of Kenya, Ministry of Health, *Antimalarial Medicines in Kenya: Availability, Quality, and Registration Status*, WHO and Health Action International Africa, December 2007, 8, http://apps.who.int/medicinedocs/documents/s16424e/s16424e. pdf (accessed June 24, 2010).

26. "Regulators Struggle to Tame Fake Medicine Market," *China Daily*, May 25, 2009, www.chinadaily.com.cn/bw/2009-05/25/content_7937588.htm (accessed September 10, 2010).

27. FDA News, "Russia in New Crackdown on Counterfeits," *Daily International Pharma Alert* 2 (December 27, 2005), www.fdanews.com/newsletter/article?articleId=83366&issueId=8849 (accessed September 16, 2010).

28. Tunya Sukpanich, "Drug Registration Needs Overhaul," *Bangkok Post,* January 24, 2010, www.bangkokpost.com/news/investigation/31670/drug-registration-needs-overhaul (accessed September 7, 2010).

29. Ibid.

30. Ibid.

31. "Pharmacovigilance: FDIC News," *NAFDAC Newsletter* 3 (2009), www.nafdac.gov.ng/nafdac-newsletter (accessed September 14, 2010).

32. "Drug Regulatory Requirements in Russia," Pharmabiz.com, June 24, 2004, www.pharmabiz.com/article/detnews.asp?articleid=22502&sectionid=50 (accessed August 3, 2010).

33. DRW Research and Information Services, "Navigating Pharmaceutical Product Registration in the Russian Federation," *DRW Monthly,* November 2009, www.drw-research.com/newsletter/Nov%2009.htm (accessed August 1, 2010).

34. "FDA Review Reveals Sale of Inferior Drugs," *Times of India,* January 28, 2009, http://timesofindia.indiatimes.com//city/mumbai/FDA-review-reveals-sale-of-inferior-drugs/articleshow/4039057.cms (accessed May 31, 2011).

35. Government of India, Ministry of Health and Family Welfare, "Report of the Expert Committee on a Comprehensive Examination of Drug Regulatory Issues, Including the Problem of Spurious Drugs," November 2003.

36. Meir Pugatch and David Torstensson, *Keeping Medicines Safe: A Study of the Regulations Guiding the Approval of Medicines in Emerging Markets,* Stockholm Network, 2010, 52, www.stockholmnetwork.org/downloads/publications/Keeping_Medicines_Safe_Final_Draft_2010.pdf (accessed June 15, 2010).

37. "FDA Review Reveals Sale of Inferior Drugs."

38. Bate et al., "Drug Registration: A Necessary but Not Sufficient Condition."

39. Ariana Eunjung Cha, "China Executes Former Head of Food, Drug Safety," *Washington Post,* July 11, 2007, www.washingtonpost.com/wp-dyn/content/article/2007/07/10/AR2007071000165.html (accessed September 8, 2010).

40. Khomba Singh, "Drug Regulator Bans Raw Material Import from 10 Chinese Firms," *Economic Times,* June 15, 2010, http://economictimes.indiatimes.com/news/news-by-industry/healthcare/biotech/pharmaceuticals/Drug-regulator-bans-raw-material-import-from-10-Chinese-firms/articleshow/6048536.cms (accessed June 22, 2010).

41. Folusho De-grata Shado, "The Torn Veil: Access to Information as a Tool for Combating Corruption with Reference to Uganda" (master's thesis, University of Pretoria, October 2004), www.up.ac.za/dspace/bitstream/2263/1101/1/shado_fd_1.pdf (accessed September 10, 2010).

42. Ibid.

43. World Health Organization, *Measuring Transparency in Medicines Registration, Selection and Procurement: Four Country Assessment Studies,* 2006, www.who.int/

medicines/areas/policy/goodgovernance/Transparency4CountryStudy.pdf (accessed September 17, 2010); and Inge Amundsen and Harald Mathisen, "Corruption, Lack of Political Will, and the Role of Donors (in Uganda), Working Paper, Chr. Michelsen Institute, Bergen, Norway (December 2005).

44. "Pharmaceuticals Executives Given Suspended Sentences for Counterfeit Medicines," MosNews.com, April 3, 2009, www.mosnews.com/money/2009/04/03/751/ (accessed July 13, 2010); "RosZdravNadZor Chief Slams Justice System," *Russian Pharmaceutical Review* 1 (March 2009): 3, www.ssees.ucl.ac.uk/RPR.pdf (accessed August 3, 2010); and "Uganda Health Ministry Diverts ARV Money," *Plus News,* August 10, 2009, www.plusnews.org/Report.aspx?ReportId=85658 (accessed September 10, 2010).

Chapter 15: International Cooperation against Criminals and the Lethal Trade in Fake Medicines

1. International Convention for the Suppression of Counterfeiting Currency, Geneva, April 20, 1929, http://treaties.un.org/pages/LONViewDetails.aspx?src=LON&id=551&lang=en.

2. *Counterfeit Drugs: Guidelines for the Development of Measures to Combat Counterfeit Drugs,* UN Doc. WHO/EDM/QSM/99.1, 1999.

3. Stephanie Nabehey, "Counterfeit Drugs on Rise, Pose Global Threat—WHO," *Reuters,* May 21, 2011, http://in.mobile.reuters.com/article/businessNews/idINIndia-48676720100521.

4. OECD, "The Economic Impact of Counterfeiting and Piracy," 2007, 102, http://www.oecd.org/dataoecd/36/34/39543417.pdf.

5. Liza Gibson, "Drug Regulators Study Global Treaty to Tackle Counterfeit Drugs," *British Medical Journal* 328 (February 28, 2004), http://www.bmj.com/content/328/7438/486.4.

6. "'Declaration of Rome': Conclusions and Recommendations of the WHO International Conference on Combating Counterfeit Medicines," World Health Organization, February 18, 2006, 1, http://www.who.int/medicines/services/counterfeit/RomeDeclaration.pdf.

7. Roger Bate, Amir Attaran, and Megan Kendall, "Why and How to Make an International Crime of Medicine Counterfeiting," *Journal of International Criminal Justice* (February 10, 2011), available at http://www.aei.org/docLib/Why-and-How-to-Make-an-International-Crime-of-Medicine-Counterfeiting.pdf, 268.

8. "General Information on Counterfeit Medicines," World Health Organization, http://www.who.int/medicines/services/counterfeit/overview/en/.

9. Ibid.

10. "Convention on the Counterfeiting of Medical Products and Similar Crimes Involving Threats to Public Health," Council of Europe, October 28, 2011, 5.

11. International Convention for the Suppression of Counterfeiting Currency, Geneva, April 20, 1929, at Article 18, http://treaties.un.org/pages/LONViewDetails.aspx?src=LON&id=551&lang=en.

12. Ibid.

13. Walt Bogdanich, "Chinese Chemicals Flow Unchecked onto World Drug Market," New York Times, October 31, 2007, http://www.nytimes.com/2007/10/31/world/asia/31chemical.html.

14. Rome Statute of the International Criminal Court, "Crimes against Humanity," July 17, 1988, at Article 7, http://www.icrc.org/ihl.nsf/WebART/585-07?OpenDocument.

15. Constitution of the World Health Organization, April 7, 1948, http://www.who.int/governance/eb/who_constitution_en.pdf, 1.

16. Ibid., Article 2, Section U, 3.

17. Ibid., Article 2, Section K, 3.

18. World Health Organization, preamble to the Framework Convention on Tobacco Control, February 27, 2005, 1, http://whqlibdoc.who.int/publications/2003/9241591013.pdf.

19. Ibid., 2.

20. Ernestine Fitz-Maurice, "Convention for the Suppression of Counterfeiting Currency: An Analysis," American Journal of International Law 26 (July 1932): 533.

21. Ibid.

22. "Fighting Fake Drugs: The Role of WHO and Pharma" (editorial), Lancet, doi:10.1016/S0140-6736(08)61345-8 (2011).

23. See ECOSOC Document E/CN.15/2011/L.12 of April 11, 2011. available at http://daccess-dds-ny.un.org/doc/UNDOC/LTD/V11/820/84/PDF/V1182084.pdf?OpenElement (accessed Oct 13, 2011).

24. UN General Assembly, Protocol against the Illicit Manufacturing of and Trafficking in Firearms, Their Parts and Components and Ammunition, Supplementing the United Nations Convention against Transnational Organized Crime, May 31, 2001, A/RES/55/255, available at http://www.unhcr.org/refworld/docid/3dec85104.html (accessed July 5, 2011).

25. As of April 2011; see the status of ratifications at http://www.unodc.org/unodc/en/treaties/CTOC/countrylist-firearmsprotocol.html.

26. Cynthia Callard, "Follow the Money: How the Billions of Dollars That Flow from Smokers in Poor Nations to Companies in Rich Nations Greatly Exceed Funding for Global Tobacco Control and What Might Be Done about It," Tobacco Control, doi:10.1136/tc.2009.035071 (2010).

27. The total was $176 million from January 2005 to June 2008, or about $50 million annually on average. See United Nations General Assembly, Strengthening the United Nations Crime Prevention and Criminal Justice Programme, in particular its technical cooperation capacity (document A/63/99 of July 4, 2008), available at http://daccess-ods.un.org/access.nsf/Get?OpenAgent&DS=A/63/99&Lang=E (accessed July 5, 2011).

Chapter 16: A Market for Products of Varying Quality and the Intellectual Property Debate

1. Médecins Sans Frontières, "Counterfeit, Substandard and Generic Drugs," April 2009, available at www.msfaccess.org/main/access-patents/counterfeit-substandard-and-generic-drugs (accessed June 18, 2009).

2. Dora Akunyili, personal communication with the author, Washington, D.C., April 14, 2008; see also R. B. Taylor et al., "Pharmacopoeial Quality of Drugs Supplied by Nigerian Pharmacies," *Lancet* 357 (June 16, 2001): 1933–36.

3. Gatonye Gathura, "Alert over Low Grade Malaria Drugs," *Daily Nation* (Kenya), January 4, 2009.

4. Kenyan Ministry of Health, "Antimalarial Medicines in Kenya: Availability, Quality, and Registration Status," November 2007. A copy of this unpublished report is on file with the author.

5. "Registration of Medicines," ANVISA website, 2010, www.anvisa.gov.br/eng/drugs/registration.htm (accessed September 8, 2010).

6. "Resolution—RDC no. 133 of 29 May 2003," ANVISA website, 2010, www.anvisa.gov.br/eng/legis/resol/133_03_rdc_e.htm (accessed September 10, 2010).

7. Denise Claux, "Brazilian Consumer Defence Agency in Public Audience to Discuss 'Similares' Fate in Brazil," *Global Insight,* June 3, 2009; and Teva Pharmaceutical Industries, "Teva Strategy Overview," February 21, 2008, www.teva.co.il/pdf/Presentation21.02.08.pdf (accessed June 11, 2009).

Index

Abdul Latiff, Ahmad, 242
Absorption variance in generics, 38b
Abu Hijleh, Baker, 214, 216–17
Abu Kasheh, Sherif Abdul Kareem, 219–20
Abu Odeh, Wajeh, 209, 217
AC Farma (company), 235–36
Accra, Ghana, 32f, 114b, 116b, 117b, 119b, 287–88
    See also Results, research
Acetaminophen
    as component of fakes, 109, 218, 322–23b
    DEG contamination of, 19, 20
    expired, dangers of, 26, 205
    synthesis of and Chinese GMP policy, 182b
Acetanilide (painkiller), 330
Achebe, Chinua, 99
Aci Recete (Bitter Prescription) operation, 243–44
ACT (artemisinin-based combination therapy) (antimalarial)
    AMFm program of Global Fund, 114–17b
    diversions of, 119–20b, 122–24
    efficacy of, 62
    new dye test for, 199–201b
    See also Antimalarial drugs

Active pharmaceutical ingredient (API), *See* APIs (active pharmaceutical ingredients)
Addis Ababa, Ethiopia, 32f, 119b
    See also Results, research
Additives, food, 329, 330, 332
Address of company, fake or hidden, 64, 152–53, 209, 250, 252
Adulteration of food/drugs, 328, 330
    See also Contaminated drugs/products; Diluted foods/drugs
Advanced testing requirements, U.S., 333
Adverse drug reaction (ADR) reporting systems, 43, 347
Advertising
    illegal, China, 195
    illegal, Lebanon, 223
    prescription requirement, impact of, 334
    regulation of by MRAs, 44
    targeted, 83b, 252
    See also Claims, fraudulent; Packaging
Afifeh, Jamal Abu, 212, 213, 218–19, 221, 222
Africa
    Angola, 32f, 117, 118
    Benin, 101
    Botswana, 99
    Congo, Democratic Republic of the, 32f, 171

Africa (*continued*)
    drug pricing in, 313
    Egypt, 32f, 53f, 208, 219–22,
        220, 288
    Ethiopia, 32f, 92b, 111b, 119b
    local production, barriers to,
        88–89, 94–96b
    Niger, Republic of, 15b, 19–20,
        65–66, 114b
    Niger delta, 125–31
    sampling breakdown by city,
        264–66
    sampling research methodology,
        52–53
    South Africa, 19, 23
    Togo, 114b, 115b, 122–24
    Zambia, 32f, 352b, 353b
    Zimbabwe, xxi–xxii
    See also Ghana; Nigeria; Results
"After Heparin," 12
Agra, India, 149–51, 152
Agriculture, U.S. Department of, 17,
    330, 331
Ahahin, Rania, 214
Ahmad, Mohd Hatta, 241
Ahura Scientific, 265b
    See also TruScan spectrometer
AIDS, 108, 150–51, 161, 240
    See also HIV
Airlines' role in dangerous drug trade,
    72–73, 99, 209
Ajanta Pharma Limited, 2, 107
Akai (company), 206
Akerlof, George, 328
Akintayo, Olumiyiwa, 89
Akunyili, Dora, 65–67, 101, 390
Akwhale, Willis, 121
Al Arabi Center for Cancer and Blood
    Diseases, 215
Al Mansour (company), 206
Al Najah University, Nablus, 215
Al Thulathia (company), 214–15

Al Watani public hospital, 215
Aligarh market, 149
Al-Kanhal, Mohamed, 226
American Medical Association, 330
American Pharmaceutical Association,
    330
American Society of Health-System
    Pharmacists, 14, 16
AMFm (Affordable Medicines Facility-
    malaria) program, 114–17b, 124
Amman, Jordan, 209
Amr, Mostafa, 221
Analgesics, *See* Painkillers
Andre, Phillipe, 180, 181, 186, 202
Anesthetics, fake, 150
Angola, 32f, 117, 118
Anti-American sentiments, 50, 70–71b,
    216, 357
Antibacterials, *See* Antibiotics
Antibiotics
    ciprofloxacin, 136–38b, 143b,
        166, 230–31
    in drug classification rating, 143b
    erythromycin, 135, 143b
    failure rates, overview, 269
    fake, India, 135
    and Massengill elixir incident, 17,
        333
    penicillin, xxiii, 397
    Pfizer/Trovan controversy, 69,
        70–71b
    in TB treatments, 21–23
Anticlotting drugs, *See* Blood thinning
    drugs
Antidepressants, 41b, 150, 251
Antiepileptic drugs, 40–41b
Antimalarial drugs
    artemether, 2–3, 45f, 107
    Artesunat/e, 86–87b, 90–91b,
        109, 197, 239–41, 322–23b
    chloroquine, 62
    Cotexcin, 129

Antimalarial drugs (*continued*)
    diversion of, 45–46
    in drug classification rating, 143b
    failure rates, results, 269, 286–87
    Lonart, 73–74, 81
    LuMether, 44, 45f
    monotherapies, 114–15b, 129-30,
       143b, 286
    packaging, fake, 2–3
    Salaxin (spurious), 64, 394
    See also ACT (artemisinin-based
       combination therapy) (antima-
       larial); Coartem (antimalarial)
Antimycobacterials, *See* AntiTB drugs
Antirejection drugs, 40b
Antiretrovirals (ARVs), xxi, 95, 143b,
    362
AntiTB drugs, 21–23, 143b, 154, 182,
    269
Anti-Western sentiment, 50, 70–71b,
    216, 357
ANVISA (Agência Nacional de Vigilância
    Sanitária), 233, 234
APB (Association Pharmacéutique
    Belge), 397
APIs (active pharmaceutical ingredients)
    in China, substandard, 12, 180,
       183–87, 206
    quality testing for, 260, 261
    results of concentration testing,
       263, 298, 305–8f
    threshold for "substandard," 263
    See also Underdosed drugs
Approval process, timing of, 335, 349,
    350f
Arab Specialized Hospital of Nablus,
    215
Argentina, 20, 234–35, 383
Arrests
    China, 15b, 194, 195
    Egypt, 15b
    Jordan, 15b, 211, 212, 213
    Mauritius, 15b
    Nigeria, 85
    Palestine, 215
    Syria, 15b, 221
    Turkey, 244
    Uganda, 122
Arsenic contamination, 17
Artefan (antimalarial), 2–3, 107
Artemether (antimalarial), 2–3, 45f, 107
Artemisinin-based combination therapy
    (ACT) (antimalarial), *See* ACT
    (artemisinin-based combination ther-
    apy) (antimalarial); Monotherapies
    (antimalarial)
Artesunat/e (antimalarial), 86–87b,
    90–91b, 109, 197, 239–41, 322–23b
Asharq Alawasit (company), 206
Assad, basheer al-, 213–14, 225
Assih, Mamessile, 123
Atorvastatin, 162
Attacks, *See* Danger to investigators/
    officials; Violence
Attaran, Amir, 263, 357
Austria, 19
Authentication strategies, 83–84b, 241,
    342–43
    See also Track and trace technology
Automated tracking systems, *See* Track
    and trace technology
Autor, Deborah, 202
Avian influenza, 81b
Awagu, Elizabeth, 85
Ayodele, Thompson, 73
Azikiwe, Andrew, 61, 62, 104, 105

Babangida, George, 130–31
Babylon, Filip, 397
Bad Medicine (documentary), 200b
Baghdad boil, 208
Balzac, Honoré de, 59
Bangkok, Thailand, 32f, 239
Bangladesh, 20

Bans, import, 13, 21, 162–63
Bar code scanning, 78, 82–83b, 244–45
Barnett, Randy, 76b
Basheer al-Assad, 213–14, 225
Basu, Prabir, 143b
Bat droppings in drugs, 17
Bate, Roger, 69f, 149f, 150f, 262f
Baxter International Inc., 12
Bed nets, 117, 121
Beijing, China, 32f, 73, 173
Belarus, 230
Belbiopharm, 230
Belgian pharmacy association, 397
Belgium, 64
Bell, Jacob, 330
Benin, 101
Bernstein, Ilisa, 339
Bhagirath Palace market, 157
Bhati, Minhu, 166
Bioavailability, 29, 41b, 234, 259
Bioequivalence
    definition, 37
    in drug rating systems, 142–43
    in generics, 37, 38b, 259
    and GMP debate, 37, 40
    lack of in WHO program, 159–60
    and "similars," 233
Biological availability, 29, 41b, 234, 259
Biopharmaceutics Classification System
    (BCS), 142–43b
Biowaivers, 259
Bird droppings in drugs, 17
Birth control pills, fake, 15b, 235
Birth defects, 334–35
Bitter Prescription (Aci Recete) operation, 243–44
Black market operations, 26, 63, 121,
    132
    See also Organized crime
Blame avoidance by Chinese, 179
Blood pressure drugs, contamination
    incidents, 20, 212

Blood thinning drugs
    heparin scandal, 11–14, 16–17,
        193b, 337
    Plavix, 50–51b, 214
    substandard, 41b
Boats, markets from, 241
Bogdanich, Walt, 375
Bogotá, Colombia, 49, 237
Bogus drugs, 64, 156, 394
    See also Fake drugs
Bonny Island, Nigeria, 128
Botswana, 99
Brancato, David, 336
Brand protection, 192b, 338, 365
    See also Intellectual property (IP)
        rights, protecting
Brand trust, building, 393–94
Brazil, 15b, 32f, 174, 232, 233–35, 297,
    348
Breast cancer drug fakes, 220
Bribes, 60, 65, 66, 99, 153, 217, 336
    See also Customs services
BRIC countries (Brazil, Russia, India,
    China) failure rates in, 31–32
British Medical Journal, 335
Brundtland, Gro Harlem, 379–80
Bryntsalov, Vladimir Alekseevich,
    228–31
Bryntsalov-A (company), 229
Bryntsalova, Tatyana, 230
"Bunkering," 127-28
Bureau of Chemistry (U.S.), 17, 330
Burma, 241
Burn ointment, contamination incidents,
    19
Burundi, 110b, 171
Businessweek, 229
Busts, criminal networks/operations, See
    Shut-downs of operations
Buying behavior
    confidence in modern medicine,
        lack of, 102, 239, 364

Buying behavior (*continued*)
consumer knowledge, 141–42, 308–9, 347, 351
lack of choice/affordability issues, 166, 301–4, 363, 388
and mixed-quality markets, 233–35, 389, 391, 392, 398–99
persistence of, 105–6
smuggling by citizens, 204, 205

Cairo, Egypt, 32f, 53f, 208, 220, 288
Cali drug cartel, 49–50, 237
Cambodia, 114b, 241, 362
CAMEG (Centrale d'Achat des Médicaments Essentiels Génériques) (Togo), 122–24
Campillo, Gustavo, 238
Canada, 246, 248, 252, 375
Cancer drugs, 50b, 150, 205, 208, 216, 220
Capital Insurance Brokers Pvt. Ltd., 152–53
Capital punishments, 74–75, 192b, 193b, 194
See also Executions
Carmelino Garcia, Elizabeth, 235–36
Casodex (hormone), 50b
Category rating systems for drugs, 142–43b
CATOC (Convention against Transnational Organized Crime, United Nations), 383–86
CDSCO (Central Drugs Standard Control Organization) (India), 156–59, 169–70b, 351–54
Centers for Disease Control, U.S. (CDC), 20
Central America, 20, 246, 252
Central *vs.* state control, and barriers to reform, 339, 351–54
Centrifuge mixing, skimping on, 141
Certificate of free sale, 68

Chalk as component of fakes, 322b
Chamberlain, Gethin, 153
Chan, Margaret, 362
Chang, Charles, 336
Changzhou Scientific Protein Laboratories (CZSPL), 12–13
Chavez, Hugo, 233
Chemical manufacture in China, 13, 20–21, 179–80, 198, 202
Chemie Grüenthal (company), 334
Chennai, India, 32f
China
APIs, substandard, 12, 180, 183–87, 206
authorities, reticence of, 5–6
capital punishments in, 74–75, 192b, 193b, 194
chemical manufacture in, 13, 20–21, 179–80, 198, 202
Colombia, involvement in, 237
donated drugs from, 132
drug industry overview, 5–6, 177
enforcement/regulatory efforts, 188–89, 192–95, 217, 354
fake "Indian-made" drug production, 49, 73–74, 169, 196–98
FDA oversight of production in, 336–40, 345
heparin scandal, 11–14, 16–17, 193b, 337
investigations of, hindrances to, 181, 183
jurisdictional issues, internal, 339, 354
Middle East, involvement in, 209–10, 212–13, 216, 217
Nigeria, relations with, 72, 73–74
online drugs from, 246, 251f, 252
organized crime in, 49, 73
pharmaceutical industry, growth of, 177–78

China (*continued*)
    policy recommendations, 198,
        202–3
    problems, identifying, 177–83
    regulatory issues, 184
    as source of contaminated ingredi-
        ents, 13, 20–21
    trust in food and drug supply, lack
        of, 191–92b
    unregistered drugs in, 348
    volume of drug market, 186–87
    whistleblowing in, 187–88, 190b
    See also Results, research
Chinese Administration on Quality
    Supervision, Inspection and Quaran-
    tine, 337
Chips, electronic, 82–83b
Chirac, Jacques, 101, 104
Chirac Foundation, 101, 104
Chiral Quest (company), 338
Chloroquine (antimalarial), 62, 114b,
    143b
Cholesterol drugs, 162, 214
Chongqing, China, 191b
Chromatography
    HPLC (high-performance liquid
        chromatography), 13–14, 260,
        262
    TLC (thin-layer chromatography),
        81b, 199b, 261–62
Chua Soi Lek, 242
Chukharev, Alexander, 227
Cifran (antibiotic), 166
Cipla (company), 38b
Ciprobrin (antibiotic), 230–31
Ciprofloxacin (antibiotic), 136–38b,
    143b, 166, 230–31
Ciprotab (antibiotic), 136–38b
Civil actions as solution, 55–56, 341,
    342
Claims, fraudulent, 44, 45f, 64, 195,
    331, 332, 394

Classification system for rating drugs,
    142–43b
Clinical trials, 44, 69–70, 259
Clozapine, 41b
CNSC Fortune Way, 20
Coartem (antimalarial), 63, 125, 129
    diversion of, 45–46, 117, 120b,
        122–24
    expired, efficacy of, 26
    fake, Ghana, 102–3b
    mismanagement of, Uganda, 113
    See also ACT (artemisinin-
        based combination therapy)
        (antimalarial)
Cocaine, 49–50, 237
Collaborative programs
    Interpol and East Africa,
        110–12b, 130
    PQM program in Ghana,
        102–3b
    U.S. FDA and China, 337–38,
        345
    WADRAN, 100–101
College market for fakes, 151
Colombia, 49–50, 236–39, 237
Combination therapies, malaria, *See*
    ACT (artemisinin-based combination
    therapy) (antimalarial)
Combitic Global (company), 152–54
"Commercial" amounts, definition, 34
Communist business system, 193b,
    338–39
Compensation to victims, 56, 74, 341
    See also Civil actions as solution
Competition
    concept of, 36
    with Indian pharmaceutical
        industry, 172–73, 196
    and local production, barriers to,
        93b, 207
    and quality improvement,
        328–29

Confidence/trust in health care system
 anti-Western/anti-American sentiments, 50, 70–71b, 216, 357
 China, 191–92b
 Indian products in U.S. drug supply, 158–59
 loss of, impact, 102, 239, 364
 and reliance on doctors as gatekeepers, 334
Confiscation of assets, 74, 76
 See also Seizures of drugs
Congo, Democratic Republic of the, 32f,
 171
The Constant Gardener (film), 397
Consumer education, 141–42, 308–9,
 347, 351
Contaminated drugs/products
 adulteration of food/drugs, 328,
  330
 arsenic contamination, 17
 China, incidents in, 190–93b, 337
 definitions, 29
 DEG (diethylene glycol) incidents,
  17–18, 19–21, 333, 337–38
 detergent in cancer drugs, Middle
  East, 220
 GSK incident, 164–65b
 heparin scandal, 11–14, 16–17,
  193b, 337
 in Middle East, 205
 Peru, 235
Contraceptives, fake, 15b, 235
Controls (samples), availability of, 263,
 265b, 278
Convention against Transnational
 Organized Crime, United Nations
 (CATOC), 383–86
Convention for the Suppression of
 Counterfeiting Currency, 367, 374
Convictions
 China, 341–42
 deterrent power of, 76–77b

Nigeria, 66, 341
progressive legislation for, 315
U.S., 336
See also Arrests; Sentencing of
 criminals
Cooperation, international, See International cooperation, importance of
Cooperation, regional, 218–22, 226,
 355b
Coppin, Clayton, 331
Copyrights, See Intellectual property (IP)
 rights, protecting
Cordero, Raul, 235
Corruption
 East Africa, 5, 121–22
 in FDA, 336
 India, 155
 Kenya, 390–91
 in military, 179, 194, 225, 339
 and MRAs, 56
 in Nigeria, 60, 65, 98–99, 127–28
 Uganda, 108–9, 354
 See also Organized crime; Political
  corruption
Costs
 drug diversions, 123
 expired drugs, mismanagement
  of, 63
 fake packaging, 145–46
 foreign site inspections, FDA, 340
 inputs, 314f
 malaria drugs, comparison, 115b,
  116b
 malaria treatments, 63
 production vs. profits, 139
 quality control systems, 260
 registration, 349
 regulatory controls, 68, 72
 TB treatments, 23
 testing equipment, 79, 189, 262
 track and trace technology, 83b,
  244–45

Cotexcin (antimalarial), 129

Coticelli, Philip, 263

Cough syrup, contamination incidents, 19

Council of Europe, 358, 365–66, 368, 379b

Counterfeit currency, international treaty structure for, 247, 359–60, 367, 374, 381

Counterfeit drugs
adaptability of perpetrators, 1–3, 86–88, 218
choice of product to fake, 197–98
deceptive counterfeiting, definition, 135, 138
definitions, issues with, 27–28b, 28–29, 368–71, 382
enterprise profile, 139–41
and intellectual property rights, 28–29, 301
by legitimate companies, 141, 142–43, 227, 230
spurious drugs, 64, 156, 394
See also Contaminated drugs/ products; Fake drugs; Fake/ substandard drug market; Organized crime; Underdosed drugs

Country-specific labeling, 208–9, 355b

Coverups, government, 156–59, 164–65b, 235

Credentialing of web pharmacies, 249–50, 250–54

Crimes against humanity, 360, 375–77

Criminal intent, establishing, 145, 368, 378–79b, 383

Criminal networks, See Organized crime

Criminalization of counterfeiting, international, 359–60, 364

Criminalization of Indian-made generics by Europe, 172

Crosse, Marcia, 339–40

Crosse and Blackwell (company), 332

Crown Agents (British), 60

Cuban involvement, 232–33

Culture-specific labeling, 208–9, 355b

Currency counterfeiting, international treaty structure for, 247, 359–60, 367, 374, 381

Curse of the Black Gold (Kashi), 128

Custom made fakes, 152–55, 168, 185–86, 220

Customs services
bribing of, 60, 73, 77, 204, 343
infiltrations of, 73, 98, 99
theft in, 209–10
time lag, Nigeria, 72
training of, 343
U.S., 77, 330
See also Raids; Seizures of drugs

Cyclosporine (antirejection), 40b

Dahiya, Rakesh, 153

Daily Nation (Kenya), 390–91

Daily News and Anaysis (Mumbai), 152

Daily Telegraph (London), 191b

Damascus, Syria, 218

Dan Rather Reports, 85

Danger to investigators/officials
to author's group, 104–5, 106, 130–31
Niger delta, 129–30
Nigeria, 69, 100, 106
Palestine, 217
Russia, 231

Danger to whistleblowers/witnesses, 160–61, 179, 188, 216–17

Dangerous drugs, definitions and overview, 26–30, 34–35
See also Counterfeit drugs; Fake drugs; Fake/substandard drug market; Substandard drugs

Dar es Salaam, Tanzania, 32f, 124–25, 171

Dara'a, Syria, 208
Databanks
    and automated tracking systems,
        82b, 85
    dearth of, 257–58
    online consumer information,
        problems with, 351
    of registered drugs, Nigeria, 71
    and research results, 270
Death rates from disease
    malaria, 62, 122
    tuberculosis, 21–22
Death sentence punishments, 74–75
    See also Executions
Deaths due to UN sanctions in Iraq, 206
Deaths from contaminated products
    DEG, 17–18, 19, 20, 21
    detergent in cancer drugs, Middle
        East, 220
    heparin scandal, 11–12, 15b,
        193b, 337
    melamine in milk, China,
        190–93b
    Peru, 235
Deaths from dangerous drugs
    Argentina, 234
    meningitis drugs, Niger, 15b,
        65–66
    Middle East, 211
    Palestine, 214, 216
    worldwide numbers, 30
Deaths of investigators/officials, 69, 100,
    127–28
Debroy, Bibek, 263
Deceptive counterfeiting, definition,
    135, 138
Declaration of Rome, 365
Decoder units, Meditag, 241
Decriminalizing online purchase, 254
DEG (diethylene glycol) and contamina-
    tion incidents, 17–18, 19–21, 333,
    337–38

Degraded drugs
    definitions, 26, 27–28b
    and drug resistance, 115, 123,
        290
    examples, 90–91b
    results, Africa, 286–87, 289–91
    in street markets, 123
    See also Expired/expiring drugs
Delays in approval process (U.S.), 333
Delhi, India, failure rate in, 32f, 293–94,
    295f
Democratic Republic of the Congo, 32f,
    171
Deng Xiaoping, 49
Denial of local production problems, 64,
    95b–96, 99, 108, 241, 390
Department for International Develop-
    ment (DFID) (UK), 352b
Derecho, Maximilliano, 234
Deterioration of drugs, See Degraded
    drugs
Deterrents, 76–77b, 79–81, 85, 148,
    149, 194
    See also Punishments
Diabetes drugs, 41b, 229
Dialek (company), 230
Diethylene glycol (DEG) and contamina-
    tion incidents, 17–18, 19–21, 333,
    337–38
DIGIMED, 235–36
Diluted foods/drugs, 62, 63, 231, 328,
    397
    See also Underdosed drugs
Dissolution (dissolving)
    in copy drugs, 41b
    definition, 38b, 259
    in drug rating systems, 142–43b
    testing, 261
Distribution chains
    Chinese control of, 73
    infiltrating, 139, 146, 148–52,
        207–8, 211–13

Distribution chains (*continued*)
   Middle East, 218, 219f, 221f
   Nigeria, 61
   overview, 15–16b
   and street markets, 76–78
   See also Supply and distribution
      chains
Distrust in modern medicine, *See* Confi-
   dence/trust in health care system
Diverted drugs
   ACT, 45–46, 117, 119–20b,
      122–24
   in AMFm program, 115b
   Angola, 117, 121
   and drug resistance, 47, 121
   East Africa, 5, 45–47, 118–20b,
      121–22
   in Nigeria, 46, 65–66, 89, 98
   trade in, overview, 45–47
   See also Organized crime
Dixon, Mark, xxi
Djibouti, 111b
Docetaxel, 39f, 41–42
Doctors, complicity of, 232–33
Doctors as gatekeepers, 334
Domestic producers, *See* Local produc-
   tion of drugs
Donated drugs
   diversion of, 65–66
   input *vs.* outcome measurement,
      123–24
   local markets affect on, 96–97b,
      343–44, 388
   local production affect on,
      92–93b, 94–95b
   theft of funds, Uganda, 108–9,
      113, 115
Dorgan, Byron, 254
Drug cartels, 49–50
Drug diversion, *See* Diverted drugs
Drug failure, resistance-driven, 22–24
   See also Drug resistance

Drug Importation Act (1848), 330
Drug resistance
   and degraded drugs, 115, 123,
      290
   and diverted drugs, 47, 121
   and formulation errors, 29
   and HIV drugs, 240b
   and international standardization,
      365, 389
   in malaria, 61–62, 63–64, 114b,
      115b, 239, 286
   prescription requirement as solu-
      tion, 334
   and TB treatments, 11, 21–24
   and underdosed drugs, 29, 154,
      218b, 364
Drug theft, *See* Diverted drugs
Drugs and Cosmetic Act of 1940 (India),
   169b
Drugs Controller General of India, 1
Dua, Rajesh, 152, 154–55
Dubai, UAE, 109
Duo-Cotexcin, 130
Durham-Humphrey Amendment, 333
Dye tests, 154, 198, 199–201b, 261, 289

East Africa
   AMFm program, 114–17b
   and diverted products, 5, 45–47,
      118–20b, 121–22
   Operation Mamba, 110–12b
   Rwanda, 32f, 110b, 171
   Tanzania, 32f, 110b, 114b, 124–
      26, 132, 171
   and trade route for fake drugs,
      171
   See also Kenya; Uganda
Eckard, Cheryl, 164–65b, 167
Economic analysis of results, 313–15,
   317–21, 323
Economic development and drug qual-
   ity, 393, 397–98

Economies of scale, 88–89, 95–96b, 139
Education
       and best practices, 202, 343, 345
       consumer, 141–42, 308–9, 347,
          351
       and local production, barriers to,
          94b
       on use of medicines, 61, 105–6
Egypt, 32f, 53f, 208, 219–22, 220, 288
Electronic chips, 82–83b
Eli Lilly, 365
EMA (economically motivated adultera-
    tion), 328
Embezzlement of donor funds, 113
Emerging markets sampling in, 54,
    266–67
Emirates airline, 209
Enforcement/regulatory efforts
       China, 188–89, 192–95, 217, 354
       importance of, 76–77b
       of MRA licensing requirements,
          43
       See also Legislation, progressive
"Ensuring the U.S. Drug Supply," 180
Environmental issues, 128–29
Epilepsy drugs, 40–41b
Erythromycin (antibiotic), 135, 143b
Escobar, Pablo, 49
Eske SRL (importer), 15b
Ethiopia, 32f, 92b, 111b, 119b
       See also Results, research
European Pharmacopoeia, 14
Europe/EU
       actions against Indian pharmaceu-
          tical industry, 172, 174
       Council of Europe, 358, 365–66,
          368, 379b
       deaths from contaminated drugs,
          14
       Internet purchase of drugs in, 50b
       proposed treaty by, 174
       seizures in, 34

Ex ante regulation vs. ex post liability,
    333
Ex post liability vs. ex ante regulation,
    333
Excipients
       definition ., 16b
       in generics, 38b
       importance of, 143b
       traceability of, improving, 337–38
Executions, 127–28, 193b, 194
       See also Death sentence
          punishments
Expired/expiring drugs
       black market trade in, 26, 132
       Colombia, 238
       dangers of, 26, 205
       and degradation, 26
       diversion of, 120b, 124
       and drug-resistant TB, 22
       Middle East market, 205, 207,
          208, 210, 221–22
       mismanagement of, 63, 108, 109,
          233
       South American market, 238
       TB drugs, 22
       Turkish market, 244
       See also Degraded drugs
Extermination, crime of, 376–77
Extortion, See Bribes
Extradition, issues with, 372–73
Extremely drug-resistant TB (XDR-TB),
    23
Ezeanyika, Emeka, 86

Failure rates
       in AMFm program, 114–15b,
          116b
       of BRIC countries, 31
       in Chinese drugs, 182
       mid-income nations vs. West,
          96–97b
       Niger delta market, 129–30

Failure rates (*continued*)
  of OECD countries, 31
  results, overview, 268–70
  of sampled areas by city, 31–32
  testing methodology, 52
  See also Results
Fake drugs
  contents of, research results,
    322–23b
  definitions and overview, 27–28b,
    28–29
  See also Counterfeit drugs
Fake/substandard drug market
  market values, 30–34
  percent of Chinese market, 178,
    192–94
  percent of Colombian market,
    237–38
  percent of Indian market, 156–57
  percent of Middle Eastern market,
    205–6
  percent of Russian market, 227
  percentage of Internet market, 54
  percentage of Nigerian market,
    61, 66, 78
  percentage of pharmaceutical
    market, 30
  percentage of pharmaceutical
    market, India, 150
  See also Routes, trade
Falciparum strain of malaria, 266, 291
False advertising, *See* Claims, fraudulent
Falsified medicines, definitions, 4, 382
  See also Counterfeit drugs
Familusi, Lanre, 76–77
FARC (Fuerzas Armadas Revolucionarias de Colombia), 219, 238
FDA (Food and Drug Administration,
  U.S.)
  as case study, overview, 327–28
  and China, 193, 337–39, 345
  on Colombian fake drugs, 237–38

and DEG incidents, 18, 20
and enforcing online purchase,
  254
ex ante regulation, evolution of,
  332–34
expansion of and timing issues,
  334–36
foreign production, inspections of,
  161–63, 339–40
foreign production, oversight of,
  336–40
and GSK incident, 164–65b
and heparin scandal, 11–13
historical profile and creation of
  FDA, 329–31
NAFDAC, partnership with, 72
on online jurisdictional problems,
  247
and Ranbaxy incident, 160–63
regulation and the market, 328–
  29, 331–32
role as MRA, 42
Fear as barrier to progress, 381–82
Federal Food, Drug, and Cosmetic Act,
  18
Federal Task Force on Counterfeit
  Drugs, Nigeria, 70–71
Federal Whistleblower Law, U.S., 165b
Ferane (company), 228, 229
Fidson (company), 136b
Field testing, 78–81, 85–88, 200b
  See also Dye tests; Minilab test
    system; Spectrometers
Films and public awareness, xxiii, 396–97
Fines
  GSK incident, 165b
  Jordan, 212, 213, 223, 225
  Massengill elixir incident, 18
  Nigeria, 66–67, 74
  overview of variables, 315
  and restitutions, 56
  Russia, 230

Finland, 50b
Firearms, Protocol on (CATOC), 384
First-line treatment, 23, 62
Food, Drug, and Cosmetic Act (U.S.),
    18, 335
Food, Drug, and Insecticide Agency,
    330–31
Food additives, 329, 330, 332
Food and Drug Act (1906), 330–31
Food and Drug Administration, U.S.
    (FDA), See FDA (Food and Drug
    Administration, U.S.)
Fountain market, Agra, 151
Framework Convention on Tobacco
    Control (FCTC), 378–80
Fraud
        claims, fraudulent, 44, 45f, 64,
            195, 331, 332, 394
        GSK whistleblower incident,
            164–65b
        humanitarian aid, bogus, 216
        insurance, 153–54
        mislabelling, 28, 169b, 173, 196,
            242, 369
        by pharmaceutical companies,
            160–63, 166, 336
        treatment schemes, 216
Free-trade zones, 125, 170–71, 194,
    243, 246
The Fugitive (film), 397
Fukushima nuclear plant, 192b

Gangs, criminal drug networks, See
    Organized crime
Gao Qiang, 337
Garbage, hospital, theft of, 220
Garcia, Elizabeth Carmelino,
    235–36
Garg, Pavel, 152–54
General Administration of Qual-
    ity Supervision, Inspection, and
    Quarantine (China), 190b

Generic drugs
        fake "Indian-made" products from
            China, 73–74, 196–98
        FDA approval scandal, 336
        markets for, 151
        overview, 38–41b
        quality variability, 387
        standards for, 38b, 259
        substitutions on Internet orders,
            251
        vs. "similars," 231, 232–33
        See also India
Ghana
        Accra, 32f, 114b, 116b, 117b,
            119b, 287–88
        AMFm program in, 114b
        Medicines Quality Monitoring
            program, 102–4b
        MeTA program in, 352b
        See also Results, research
Gieringer, D. H., 335
Glass in drugs, 137b
GlaxoSmithKline (GSK), 52, 164–65b
Glenny, Misha, 49
Glivec, 38b, 40b
Global Fund
        AMFm program, 114–17b
        and drug theft in Togo, 122–24
        and drug theft in Unganda, 108–9
        and drug theft/mismanagement in
            Uganda, 113
Global Pharma Health Fund, See Mini-
    lab test system
Glycerol (glycerine), 18, 19, 20, 337–38
Glycerol, contamination incidents, 19,
    20
GMP (good manufacturing practice)
        approaches to, market-specific
            strategies, 388–92
        in China, improved standards for,
            194–95, 202, 337–38, 354
        in China, substandard, 180–81

GMP (good manufacturing practice)
(*continued*)
in copy drug production, 38–41b
failures in, 12–13, 164–65b
importance of, 36–37, 40–42,
348
Good manufacturing practice (GMP),
See GMP (good manufacturing
practice)
Government complicity
China, 178, 190–93b, 197
India, 153
Kenya, 390–91
Nigeria, 65
See also Political corruption
Government Pharmaceutical Organiza-
tion (GPO) (Thailand), 240b
Government tenders, bidding on, 141
GPO-vir, 240b
Grants, mismanagement of, 108–9, 113
Great Depression, 381
GSK (GlaxoSmithKline), 52, 164–65b
Gulf War, 204
Gumustus, Cengiz, 243
Gupta, Dinesh, 152–53
GVS Labs, 73–74

Haiti, 20
Harm, as contingency for prosecution,
3, 140, 212, 352
Haryana State, India, 152–53, 154
"Hawkers," 105
Hawthorn berry, fake, 229
Health activism, anti-Western platform
of, 357
Health and Human Services (U.S.),
336–37
Heavy metal contamination, 17, 29
Heinz Company, 331–32, 389
Heparin scandal, 11–14, 16–17, 193b,
337
Herbal remedies, fake, 195, 229

Hess, Kimberly, 263
High, Jack, 331
High-performance liquid chromatography (HPLC), 13–14, 260, 262
Hilts, Philip, 328, 330, 332–33, 334,
335
HIV (human immunodeficiency virus)
drugs
diversions of, 121
GPO-vir in Thailand, 240b
international standards for, 389
IVIGLOB-EX, 150–51
Muslim fears and polio vaccine,
71b
and Ranbaxy scandal, 159–61,
166
scope of problem, 362
and theft of grant funds, 108–9
tier pricing for, 357
in Zimbabwe, xxi–xxii
Hogerzeil, Hans, 357
Holograms, 86–87b, 137b, 145, 200b,
241
Hospital refuse, stealing, 220
Hospitals, dangerous drugs in, 150, 179,
194, 215
Hostis humani generis, 376
Hourani, Yousef, 215–16
Hovione (company), 14, 180
Howarth, Bill, 387
HPLC (high-performance liquid chro-
matography), 13–14, 260, 262
Hu Jintao, 339
Hussein, Saddam, 204, 206
Hydrochlorothiazide (antihypertension),
212
Hypertension drugs, 20, 212

Illegality, debates over, 3, 145, 204,
361–62
Imatinib mesylate (leukemia drug), 38b,
213, 214, 215

IMPACT (International Medical Products Anti-Counterfeiting Taskforce)
  databank issues, 258
  function of, 361–62
  legislation templates, 358, 398
  opposition to, 172, 174
  and WADRAN, 100–101
  See also WHO (World Health Organization)
Import bans, U.S., 13, 21, 162–63
Importation of fake drugs, attempts to control, 68, 72–73, 95b, 330
Income level, effect on drug markets, 55, 393
  See also Economic analysis of results
Independent Newspaper, 98
India
  Africa, exports to, 168, 170–71
  Agra, 149–51, 152
  counterfeit drugs in, overview, 133–35, 138–43
  counterfeit drugs in, tracking, 143–46, 148–52
  deaths from contaminated drugs, 19
  Delhi, failure rate in, 32f, 293–94, 295f
  failure rates in, 269
  Indian views on dangerous drug subsets, 27–28b
  international cooperation, strategies for leadership in, 172–76
  large fake operations in, 152–55
  market share, overall, 196
  market share of fakes, 156–59
  Nigeria, relations with, 72, 73
  pharmaceutical industry, success of, 94b
  production oversight issues, Ranbaxy saga, 159–63, 166
  registration procedures in, 649

sampling breakdown by city, 266
sampling research methodology, 53–54, 158
substandard TB treatments, 22–23
whistleblowers in, 168, 169–70b
  See also Results, research
Indian Pharmaceutical Importers, Nigeria, 72
"Indian-made" (fake) drug production by China, 49, 73–74, 169, 172, 196–98
Infiltrations of legitimate market/authorities, 73, 98, 99, 139–40, 155
Informal drug market, 105–6
Informants, 154–55, 159, 212–13, 219–20
Injections, perceptions of, 61
Innovator drugs, 38–41b
  See also Brand protection; Intellectual property (IP) rights, protecting
Input *vs.* outcome measurement and consequences, 123–24
Insecticides, control over, 331
Insects and drug production, 17, 133
Inspections
  of foreign producers by FDA, 161–63, 339–40
  of foreign producers by Nigeria, 68, 72
  and MRA licensing, 43
  risk-based approach, 339–40
  third-party, 340
  visual, 199, 258, 261, 268, 291
Institute for Pharmaceutical Excellence, China, 202
Institute of Advanced Chemical Research (Colombia), 237
Insulin, substandard, 150, 229
Insurance fraud, 153–54

Intellectual property (IP) rights,
protecting
    and counterfeit drugs, 28–29, 301
    enforcement, lack of in China, 178
    and European pressure on Indian
        industry, 174
    future strategies, 392–95
    international argument over,
        356–58
    and knockoffs, non-drug, 139,
        140
    resentment toward, 367–68, 381
    trademark protection, 342, 393–
        94, 393–95
    vs. public safety, 144–45, 382
Intentionality and liability, 145, 368,
    378–79b, 383
Intergovernmental Working Group on
    Public Health, Innovation, and Intel-
    lectual Property (WHO), 174
Intermediates, definition, 92b
International cooperation, importance of
    Chirac Foundation efforts, 101,
        104
    to Indian pharmaceutical industry,
        172–76
    Nigerian efforts, 100–101
    and online drug market, 246,
        247–48
    Orhii's efforts and World Health
        Assembly, 101
    for quality standards, 163
    U.S./China agreements, 337–40
    See also Transnational approach,
        strategies for
International debate
    clinical trial procedures, 44
    death sentences, 75
    and definitions of "danger-
        ous drugs," 26, 30, 56, 173,
        368–71
    GMP standards, 37, 40

    illegality, 3, 145, 204, 361–62
    intellectual property (IP) rights,
        protecting, 356–58
    problem identification, 48
International Finance Corporation, 95b,
    96b
International Policy Network, 30
Internet drug sales
    banning of, 243
    Chinese oversight of, 195
    failure rates, 270
    Northern European buyers, 50b
    research overview, 54–55
    Russian fakes on, 231
    sampling breakdown, 243, 267
    Turkish-made, 242–43
    See also Online drugs
Interpol, 110–12b, 132
Iraq, 15b, 204–5, 205–6, 206–7, 225
Ireland, 50b
Isoniazid (antiTB), 143b, 182
Istanbul, Turkey, 32f, 242
IVIGLOB-EX (anti-cancer, HIV), 150

Jackson, Andrew, 231
Jail sentences, 66–67, 74, 223
    See also Arrests; Sentencing of
        criminals
Jänke, Richard, 80
Jarrar, Issam, 216
Jin, Ginger Zhe, 300
Jin, Shaohon, 178, 189, 192
Jingde, Gao, 187–88
Jordan, 208–11, 211–13, 223, 225,
    352b
Journal of Health Economics, 310
The Jungle (Sinclair), 331
Junk mail and online ordering, 252

Kafauver-Harris amendment, 335
Kamabare, Moses, 108, 109
Kamogra (Viagra), 148

Kampala, Uganda, 32f
Kano State, Nigeria, 70–71b
Karan, Vijay, 144, 153, 157–58, 456f
Karpov Pharmaceutical Plant, 228
Kashi, Ed, 128
Kathem Khawasiya, Sayed, 205
Kaur, Harparkash, 200–201b, 289
Kelsey, Frances, 334–35
Kenya
    AMFm program in, 114b
    failure rates in, 32f
    as hub for drug trade, 171
    Operation Mamba, 110b
    profile of metrics for MRA devel-
        opment, 341
    registration and quality results,
        271
    stockouts due to mismanagement,
        107–8
    unregistered drugs in, 348
Kessler, David, 177
Ketchup, 331–32
Kickbacks to doctors for referrals, 151
Kidnapping, 100, 128
Kidney dmaage/failure, 19, 20
Kigali, Rwanda, 32f
Kimadia (Iraq), 210–11
Knockoffs, non-drug counterfeiting,
    139, 140
Kodambo, Luke, 107–8
Kolkata, India
    failure rate in, 32f
Koutouzis, Michel, 168, 171
Krauss, Michael, 333
Kutta, 149
Kyrgyzstan, 352b

Labeling
    country-specific, 208–9, 335b
    legislation, 331, 334, 355
    relabeling, 15b, 62, 126, 150, 205
    See also Mislabelling

Lagos, Nigeria, 32f, 66, 287–88, 393
Lambo, Adeoye, 61
Lambo, Eyitayo, 66
Lancet, 121, 229–30
Large manufacturers, 152–55
Latin America, 20, 231–33, 246, 252
    See also South America
Lawsuits
    civil actions as solution, 55–56,
        341, 342
    GSK incident, 165b
    India against European Union,
        172
Leadership, 89
Leavitt, Michael, 337
Lebanon, 205, 219f, 221f, 223
Legislation, progressive
    anticounterfeiting, Nigeria, 74–75
    Brazil, 234
    for convictions, 315
    decriminalizing online purchase,
        254
    Drug Importation Act (1848), 330
    Food and Drug Act (1906),
        330–31
    IMPACT templates, 358, 398
    labeling, 331, 334, 355
    local production, support of,
        95b–96
    Malaysia, 242
    Middle East, 223, 225
    Peru, 236
    product safety testing, 18
    quality control, China, 202
Legitimate pharmaceutical companies
    counterfeits by, 141, 142–43, 227,
        230
    falsification of data by, 160–63
    negligence by, 142–43, 235–36
    role of in combating fake trade,
        226
Leishmaniasis, 208

Leukemia drugs, 38b, 40b, 213, 214
Li, Kenchun (Ken), 338
Li, Wen, 179, 183–84, 186
Li Keqiang, 192b
Liability and intent, 145, 368, 378–79b, 383
Licensing, export, 194–95
Licensing under MRAs, 43, 346
    See also Registration of health care products
Lifestyle drugs, fake market in, 34, 146
    See also Viagra, counterfeit/fake
Lipitor (statin), 162, 214
Listerine, 332
Literacy rate analysis, 313–14
Liver drugs, 187
LNG (liquified natural gas) Nigeria, 128
Local production of drugs
    advantages/disadvantages of, 88–89, 92–97b
    affect of donated drugs on, 92–93b, 94–95b
    Iraq, 206–7
    protection of, 88–89, 236, 350
    reticence of officials to admit problems, 64, 95b–96, 99, 108, 241, 390
Lonart (antimalarial), 73–74, 81
London School of Hygiene and Tropical Medicine, 200
Los Angeles Times, 225
Luanda, Angola, 32f
Lubumbashi, Democratic Republic of the Congo, 32f
Lukulay, Patrick, 104b
Lumefantrine (antimalarial), 2–3, 45f, 143b
    See also Coartem (antimalarial)
LuMether (antimalarial), 44, 45f
Lusaka, Zambia, 32f
Lymphatic leukemia, *See* Leukemia drugs

Madagascar, 114b
"Made in India" drugs faked in China, *See* "Indian-made" (fake) drug production by China
Mafia, 49
Magnetic resonance testing, 13
Majdalani, Atef, 223
Major manufacturers, 152–55
Malaria
    death rates from, 62, 122
    drug resistance in, 61–62, 63–64, 114b, 115b, 239, 286
    regional/seasonal differences, 266, 291–92
    self-treatment of, 25
    See also Antimalarial drugs
Malaysia, 241–42
Malinga, Stephen, 121–22
Mally, Komlan, 123
Manpower, lack of, 78–79, 89, 202, 241, 353–54
Markeih, Amjad, 222
Markeih, Mohammed, 213, 219–20
Markeih, Raed Abu, 212–13, 216, 222
Market segmentation strategies
    for counterfeiters, 141–42, 144, 185–86
    mixed-quality markets, 233–35, 389, 392, 398–99
Market share and "regulatory capture," 331–32
Market value of fake-drug industry, 30–34
Marketing, *See* Advertising
Masrouji Co., 215
Massengill elixir incident, 17–18, 333
Mathur, Aparna, 300
Mauritius, 170, 171
McMafia (Glenny), 49
Mecure Industries, 72
Médecins Sans Frontières, 65, 387
Medellín drug cartel, 49, 237

Media attention
    on Chinese counterfeits, 187–88
    and creating public awareness, 397
    films and public awareness, xxiii, 396–97
    health activism, 357
    kidnappings in Niger delta, 128
    and Massengill elixir incident, 18
    to medical shortages, Uganda, 113
    melamine in milk scandal, China, 190–91b
    mismanagement of drugs, Uganda, 113
    new technologies in Nigeria, 79
    Pavel Garg, 154
    and reliable data, 258
    and reporting of corruption, 98
    Thalidomide incidents, 335
    theft of drugs, Uganda, 108, 121–22
Medical regulatory authorities (MRAs),
    See MRAs (medical regulatory authorities)
Medicines Quality Monitoring Program (Ghana), 102–4b
Medicines Transparency Alliance (MeTA), 352–53b
Medicrime Convention, 358–59, 366, 368, 369–70, 379b
Meditag program, Malaysia, 241, 242
Mefloquine (antimalarial), 143b
Mekong Delta, 241, 257
Mekophar Chemical Pharmaceutical, 197
Melamine contamination in Chinese products, 188, 190–93b, 337
Meningitis drugs, xxiii, 15b, 63, 65–66, 69, 70–71b, 397
Mens rea, 145, 368
    See also Intentionality and liability
Merck (company), 393
Merck Darmstadt, 80

Mercury contamination, 17
Methodologies, research, 31–34
    See also Sampling research methodology
Methotrexate (leukemia drug), 235–36
Mexico, 233
"Miagra," 242
Middle East
    Chinese connection, 217
    Egyptian crackdown, 219–22
    infiltration of fakes, 207–8
    Iraq, 15b, 204–5, 205–6, 206–7, 225
    Jordan, 208–11, 211–13, 223, 225, 352b
    Lebanon, 205, 219f, 221f, 223
    legislation, progressive, 223, 225
    as market for Chinese fakes, 186, 209–10
    overview, 6, 204–6, 211
    Palestine, 214–17
    regional cooperation, need for, 226
    smuggling in, 204, 208–11
    Syria, 15b, 208–11, 213–14, 218–22, 223–24f
Mildenhall, Dallas, 17
Military in corrupt practices, 179, 194, 225, 339
Milk, melamine contamination scandal, 190–93b, 337
Miller, Michael, 336–37, 338
Minilab test system, 78, 80–81b, 198, 199b, 201b, 261–62
Ministry of Health and Family Welfare (India), 169b
Mislabelling
    fraudulent, 28, 169b, 173, 196, 242, 369
    legislation, 331, 334
    unintentional, 18, 164–65b
    See also Labeling; Packaging

Mismanagement of drugs
  expired/expiring drugs, 63, 108,
    109, 233
  Iraq, 210–11
  Kenya, 107–8
  Tanzania, 124
  Uganda, 109, 113
Mitra, Barun, 263
Mixed-quality markets, 233–35, 389,
    391, 392, 398–99
Mobile labs, 189, 192–94
  See also Minilab test system;
    TruScan spectrometer
Mogae, Festus, 99
Mombasa, Kenya, 171
"Monaco" (buyer), 219–20
Mondon, Annaliza, 113
Monotherapies (antimalarial), 114–15b,
    129-30, 143b, 286
  See also Artesunat/e (antimalarial)
Mooney, Lorraine, 263
"Moonshiner" (nickname), 228
Morality issues, 191b, 254
Morning sickness drugs, 334–35
Morphine, 144
Moscow, Russia, 32f
Movement for Democratic Change
    (MDC) (Zimbabwe), xxi–xxii
Movement for the Emancipation of the
    Niger Delta, 128
MPedigree, 8–843b, 342
MRAs (medical regulatory authorities)
  in China, 189
  development of, challenges to,
    340–43
  and good governance, 56
  implementation challenges, 351–55
  overreach, dangers of, 355b
  priority setting strategies, 344–47
  and private-sector support,
    144–45
  role and function, 42–44

role in registration process, 273,
    347–48, 348–51
  and WADRAN, 101
  See also FDA (Food and Drug
    Administration, U.S.); NAF-
    DAC (National Agency for
    Food and Drug Administration
    and Control) (Nigeria)
Mubarak, Suzanne, 220–21
Mubarak Mahal market, Agra, 149–50
Mugabe, Robert, xxi–xxii
Muhsin, Adil, 205–6
"Mules," 209–10
Muller, Mike, 365
Multilateral treaties, precendents, 366
Mumbai, India, 168
Muñoz, Felipe, 125
Muslims, perceived threat from Ameri-
    can medicine, 71b
Myeloid leukemia drugs, 38b, 40b
  See also Leukemia drugs
Mylan (company), 162

NAFDAC (National Agency for Food
    and Drug Administration and
    Control) (Nigeria)
  candor of, 64
  and Chinese/Indian relations,
    341–42
  and corruption issues, 89, 98–99
  in DEG incidents, 20
  as exemplar of MRA development,
    341–42
  and oversight over Indian produc-
    tion sites, 171
  progressive reform under
    Akunyili, 65–69
  progressive reform under Orhii,
    69–78
  technology, deployment of, 78–88
Nahamya, David, 131–32
Nairobi, Kenya, 32f

National Agency for Food and Drug Administration and Control (NAFDAC) (Nigeria), *See* NAFDAC (National Agency for Food and Drug Administration and Control) (Nigeria)

National Association of the Boards of Pharmacy, U.S. (NABP), 249, 250

National Drug Authority (Kenya), 107–8

National Institute for Pharmaceutical Technology and Education, U.S., 143b

National Institute for the Control of Pharmaceutical and Biological Products (China), 178

National Institute for the Supervision of Medications and Foods (Colombia), 237, 238

National Institute of Neoplastic Disease (Peru), 235

National Institutes of Health, U.S. (NIH) and heparin scandal, 13

National Nurses Association of Kenya, 107–8

Nationalism as barrier to reform
    and blaming foreign participants, 67–68
    in China, 338
    and diverted drugs issue, 89, 98
    Indian, 5, 158–59
    and local production , protection of, 88–89, 236

Nature Medicine, 170b

Nazis, 376

Near-infrared spectrometers, 189, 262

Negligence
    intentionality and liability, 145, 368, 378–79b, 383
    of legitimate drug companies, 142–43, 235–36
    mislabelling, 18, 164–65b
    willful, in copy drug production, 41–42, 185

New Vision, 122

New York Times, 247, 375

New Zealand, 17

Newton, Paul, 242, 257, 323b

Ngororano, Elizabeth, 113

Nicholas Priamal (company), 141

Niger, Republic of, 15b, 19–20, 65–66, 114b

Niger delta, 125–31

Nigeria
    AMFm program in, 114b
    authorities, attitude toward exposure, 5, 64
    bans on Indian drugs, 171
    corruption in, 60, 127
    deaths from contaminated drugs, 15b, 19
    diverted drugs intended for, 46
    historic review, 60–61
    international efforts, 100–101
    Lagos, 32f, 66, 287–88, 393
    leadership issues, 99–100
    malaria drugs and resistance, 61–64
    MRA evolution in, 64–67, 341
    Niger delta, 125–31
    unregistered drugs in, 348
    See also NAFDAC (National Agency for Food and Drug Administration and Control) (Nigeria); Results, research

Nigerian Compass, 105

Nigerian Newsworld, 77

"Night shifts," 141, 142–43, 227, 230

Noninvasive testing, 262–63
    See also Bar code scanning; Spectrometers

North Korea, 49

Novartis (company), 46, 63, 212, 213, 214, 231

Novo Nordisk (company), 229

Nursing practices, standardizing (China), 195

Odomodu, Joseph, 75–76
OECD (Organisation for Economic Copoperation and Development), 31, 33f, 363
Offshoring of drug production by U.S., 336–37
Ogon, Patterson, 127
Oil industry, exploitation by, 126–28
Okonkwor, Anselm, 100
Olamuyiwa, Adetoun, 72–73
Olympics, 2008 Beijing, 194
Oncology drugs, See Cancer drugs
Onitsha, Nigeria, 130–32
Online drugs
    cost advantages of, 248–49
    credentialing of web pharmacies, 249–50
    decriminalizing, U.S., 254
    international legislation, need for, 247–48
    overview, 6, 246
    results of research, 250–54, 268
    UK/European purchases, 50b
    verification schemes, 241
    See also Internet drug sales
Open-air markets, See Street markets
Operation Mamba, 110–12b
Organisation for Economic Copoperation and Development (OECD), 31, 33f, 363
Organized crime
    black market operations, 26, 63, 121, 130
    CATOC (Convention against Transnational Organized Crime, United Nations), 383–86
    Chinese control of drug trade in Africa, 129–30
    definitions, 384–85
    gangs/networks, 121, 183, 184–85, 246
    infiltrations, 73, 98–99

    methods/tactics overview, 49–50
    and need for transnational convention, 360
    and widespread and systematic concept, 375–77
    See also Middle East
Orhii, Paul
    and corruption issues, 89, 98–99
    international efforts, 100–101
    and local production issues, 88–89
    and NAFDAC progressive reform, 69–78
    and technology, deployment of, 78–88
Orphan Drug Act, 335
Osuoka, Asume, 127
Outcome vs. input measurement and consequences, 123–24
Overreach issues, 332, 355b
Over-sulfated chondroitin sulfate (OSCS), 12–14
Over-the-counter drugs, contamination of, 19

Packaging
    regional/cultural differences, 208–9, 215, 355b
    results overview, 268
    sophistication of fakes, 145–46, 147–48b, 363
    spotting fakes
        Artefan, 2–3
        Coartem, 103b
        holograms, 86–87b, 137b, 145, 200b, 241
        Plavix, 51b
        printing errors, 135
    suspicious, 211, 213, 214
    visual inspection, 199, 258, 261, 268, 291

Painkillers, 150, 184, 330, 393
    See also Acetaminophen
Palestine, 214–17
Panama, 20, 246, 252
Paonta Sahib plant of Ranbaxy, 161,
    162, 163, 166
Parallel trade, 248
Parasitic diseases, See Malaria
Paris principles, 353b
Partnership strategies, 356, 390
Pasteur Mérieux (company), 65
Patents, expiration of, 38b
    See also Intellectual property (IP)
        rights, protecting
Pathak, R. B., 155
Pathogenic contaminants, 29
Paul, Ron, 254
Peltzman, Sam, 329, 335
Penalties
    increases in, China, 194
    increases in, Malaysia, 242
    increases in, Nigeria, 66–67, 74–76
    increases in Colombia, 238
    need to increase and enforce,
        76–77b, 238
    See also Punishments
Penicillin (antibiotic), xxiii, 397
People's Liberation Army, 179, 339
Permeability, 38b, 142–43b, 259
Peru, 235–36, 352b
Pew Trust Group, 12, 180
Pfizer, 69–70
"Pharmaceutical and Medical Products
    in Iraq," 210
Pharmaceutical market value, global,
    30–31
Pharmaceutical Security Institute, 34,
    257
Pharmaceutical Society of Nigeria, 76–77
Pharmacists in drug trade, 207, 280–82,
    288–89
    See also Results, research

Pharmacopoeial monographs, 73
Pharmacy Checker, 249, 250
PharmaSecure (company), 83b,
    342–43
Phazir scanner, xxv, 263
Phenacetin (painkiller), 330
Philippines, 80b, 352b
Philipson, Tomas, 336
Pickles, 332
Pig products in drugs, 12
Pill production, 15–16b, 153f
Plavix (blood thinner), 50–51b, 214
PLoS ONE, 158, 252
"Poison squad," 330
Policy solutions
    and conflicting international
        views, 27–28b, 29
    political will/conviction, need
        for, 99–101, 104–5, 380–82,
        384
    suggested policies/activities,
        55–57
    treaties, need for, 173–76, 365–
        66, 398–99
    See also Legislation, progressive;
        Transnational approach, strate-
        gies for
Polio vaccine, 70–71b
Political corruption
    Chinese triads, 49
    and counterfeits by legitimate
        companies, 141
    Latin America, 232
    and MRAs, 49
    North Korean support of orga-
        nized crime, 49
    in registration/approval process,
        354
    See also Corruption; Government
        complicity
Political "patronage," 60–61
    See also Government complicity

Political will/conviction, need for, 99–101, 104–5, 380–82, 384

Pollen in investigations, 260

Poloola, Ade, 75

Poor quality drugs, overview, 25–26
　　See also Substandard drugs

Port Harcourt, Nigeria, 125–29

Portable testing systems, 189, 241–42
　　See also Minilab test system;
　　　Spectrometers

Porter, Karen, 250

Postmarketing surveys by MRAs, 43, 346–47

Poverty, 127–29, 138
　　See also Economic analysis of
　　　results; Economic development
　　　and drug quality

PQM (Promoting the Quality of Medicines) program (Ghana), 102b, 104b, 353b

Precursor chemicals, 181

Prequalification program of WHO, 73–74, 88, 96b, 97b, 159–60, 161

Prescription Drug User Fee, 336

Prescriptions, 158, 250–51, 333–34, 336

Preservatives, 330, 332
　　See also Additives, food

President's Emergency Plan for AIDS Relief (U.S.), 161

Pretesting requirements, U.S., 335

Price as driver of counterfeit brand choice, 197

Price as quality indicator
　　of fake products, 4
　　and government condoned "simi-
　　　lars," 234
　　misperceptions of, 35–36
　　results of research, 299–304,
　　　308–10, 310–12
　　of substandard products, 138

Price caps on medicines, 238, 248

Price regulation, 248–49, 316

Primary production process, 92b

Printing, *See* Packaging

Private sector efforts, 144
　　See also Donated drugs; Intel-
　　　lectual property (IP) rights,
　　　protecting

Production process, levels/stages of, 92b

Profit margins, 139, 148b, 198

Profit motives, xxiii, 184, 338

Promoting the Quality of Medicines (PQM) (of USP), 81b

Propolic, contamination of, 20

Prosecutions
　　in China, 189
　　Massengill elixir incident, 18
　　in Nigeria, 85
　　Russia, 229, 230
　　vs. extradition, 372–73 (*See also*
　　　Sentencing of criminals)

Prostate cancer drugs, 50b

Protectionist policies/legislation, 95, 206, 210, 350, 392

The Protector SS, 139

Protocols, manufacturing, 36–37
　　See also GMP (good manufactur-
　　　ing practice)

Psychotropic drugs, 40b

Public awareness, raising, xxiii, 396–97

Public drug programs, substandard drugs in, 165b, 187–88, 232

Public Library of Science One, 158, 252

Puerto Rico, drugs made in, 164–65b

Punishments, 76–77b, 188, 194
　　See also Penalties

Pyrimethamine (antimalarial), 114b, 143b

Quality assessments of research, *See* Results, research

Quality control, *See* Testing, quality

Quinine (antimalarial), 143b

Racial disparity issues, 60
Radiation, fake remedies for, 192b
Radio frequency identification (RFID), 82–83b
Rago, Lembit, 161, 240b, 365
Raids, 140f
    China, 191b
    India, 135, 144, 150
    Jordan, 211
    Malaysia, 242
    Nigeria, 66, 70
    Operation Mamba, 110b
    Palestine, 214–15
    Russia, 229–30
    and Suresh Sati, 135, 139
    Syria, 221, 223–24f
    Turkey, 243–44
    See also Seizures of drugs
Raijin trade zone (North Korea), 49
Raman spectroscopy, 79, 262, 264–65b
Ramsa, Jordan, 208
Ranbaxy (company), 160–63, 166
Rapid dye tests, 198
Rating systems for drugs, 142–43b
Rats in production facilities, 133
Reals Pharmacy (Nigeria), 75
Recalls, 14, 16, 43, 166, 347
Regional cooperation, 218–22, 226, 355b
Registration of health care products
    in China, 189, 194
    correlation to quality, research results, 271–78, 304f
    in Malaysia, 241
    MRA role in, 72–73, 345–46, 347–48
    in Peru, 235, 236
    procedures by country, 348–51
    slow pace of, Nigeria, 89
Regulatory authorities, medical,
    See MRAs (medical regulatory authorities)

"Regulatory capture," 331
Regulatory environment issues
    free-trade zones, 125, 170–71, 194, 243, 246
    India, central vs. state governments, 156, 169
    Iraq, 210
    Nigeria, 60–61
    and quality control, 51–52
    results, variables in, 315–17
    Russia, 227–28
    Turkey, 243
Reilly, Cynthia, 14, 16
Reimbursement schemes, 238
Relocation as avoidance scheme, 154
"Report on Countrywide Survey for Spurious Drugs" (CDSCO), 156–57
Reregistration processes, 349
Research approach and methodology
    data, dearth of, 257–58
    fake drug market value calculations, 31–34
    marketing new drugs, process of, 258–59
    Minilab protocols, 261–62, 264–65b
    quality testing procedures, 259–61
    See also Sampling research methodology
Resistant strains of disease, See Drug resistance
Restitutions, 55–56, 74, 341
    See also Civil actions as solution
Results, research
    Africa, 283–91
    dataset limitations, 270
    economic analysis, 313–15, 317–21, 323
    India, 291–94, 296–97
    interpretations, overview, 296–98
    local regulation variables, 315–17

Results, research (*continued*)
    by manufacturing class, 300f,
      301f
    overviews, 268–70, 294–95
    pharmacists survey, 280–82
    price as quality indicator, 299–
      304, 308–10
    registration status and correlation
      to quality, 271–78, 296
    spectrometry (variability analysis),
      278–80
Reverse engineering, 37
Rewards for whistleblowers, 74, 98,
    168, 169–70b
Reza, Saeed, 225
Richardson-Merrill (company), 335
Rifa i6 Kid (antiTB), 22, 23
Rifampicin (antiTB), 22–23, 154
Riggs, Michael, 161
Rimactizid (antiTB), 90–91b
Risk-based approach to inspections,
    339–40
Roll Back Malaria Partnership, 80–81b
Roosevelt, Theodore, 330, 332
Roszdravnadzor (Russian MRA), 229–
    30, 351
Routes, trade
    and diverted drugs, 45–47, 118b
    fake drugs and Africa, 53f
    India to Africa, 168, 170–71
    Middle East in, 205
Rubahika Kinungu, Denis, 113
Rueda, Miguel, 237
Russia, 227–31, 297, 348, 349–50, 351
Rwanda, 32f, 110b, 171
RxNorth.com, 246, 374, 376

Safety (personal) issues, *See* Violence
Salaxin (spurious antimalarial), 64,
    394
Samarra (company), 206
Samper, Ernesto, 49

Sampling research methodology
    AMFm program, 114b
    Niger delta market, 129–30
    online pharmacies, 250–51
    overviews by region/type,
      52–55
    sampling breakdown by region/
      type, 263–66
Sand flies, 208
Sanitation, lack of, 129, 133–35
Sanlu (company), 190
São Paolo, Brazil, 32f, 233
Saphire Lifesciences, 64, 394
Sarojini Naidu Medical College, market
    near, 151–52
Saro-Wiwa, Ken, 127–28
Sati, Suresh
    at Aligarh market, 149f
    background, 138–39
    on corruption issues, 155
    on counterfeiting by legitimate
      companies, 141
    on identifying fake drugs, 135,
      138–39
    and informants, 154–55
    and Minilab testing, 263
    and visit to production facility,
      133
Saudi Food and Drug Authority, 226
Scanning technology, 78, 82–84b,
    244–45
Schering do Brasil, 235
Schizophrenia drugs, 41b, 50b
Scientific Protein Laboratories, 12
S.E. Massengill Company, elixir incident,
    17–18, 333
Seasonality of malaria and sampling
    research, 54, 266, 291–92
Secondary production process, 92b
Second-line treatment, 23, 62
Sedatives, contamination incidents, 19
Seiter, Andreas, 61, 99

Seizures of drugs
  Bolivia, 15b
  Colombia, 237
  database of, 34
  global numbers, 34
  India, 153
  Malaysia, 15b242
  Mauritius, 171
  Nigeria, 66, 72–73
  Syria, 15b, 221–22, 223–24f
  Turkey, 244
  See also Raids
Self-correcting market, 328–29, 331–32, 391
Self-treatment, 22, 25, 62
"Semi-legal" businesses, 153
Sentencing of criminals, 74–76, 100, 315–17
  See also Convictions
Sentinel sites, definition, 81b
Sertraline hydrochloride (Zoloft), 251
Seychelles, 111b
SFDA (State Food and Drug Administration) (China)
  banning of DEG, 21
  enforcement actions by, 195
  establishment and roles of, 189
  execution of director for taking bribes, 193b, 194
  jurisdictional issues, 13, 184, 198, 202
  and melamine scandal, 193b
  and U.S. FDA, agreements with, 337–38, 345
Shah, Vidhyut, 137–38b
Shankar, Uday, 150, 151
Shao Mingli, 195
Sharma, Rajesh, 152, 154–55
Shell (oil), 128
Shenzhen, China, 178, 209
Sherley Amendment, 331

Shorja (company), 206
Shut-downs of operations
  China, 195
  Colombia, 237
  Iraq, 225
  Jordan, 223, 225
  Lebanon, 223
  Nigeria, 99
Sikka, Harinda, 141
Sildenafil citrate (Viagra), 147–48b, 184
Silk Street Market, Beijing, 184
"Similars," 231–32, 233–34, 234–35
Sinclair, Upton, 331
Singh, Malvinder, 162
Singh, Surinder, 156
60 Minutes, 167
Skimming profits, 142–43
Sky Park Co. Ltd, 209–10, 212–13, 216, 217
Sliding scale custom market, 152
SmithKline Beecham, 65
Smuggling, 89, 121, 125–26, 204, 208, 209–11, 285
  See also Black market operations
Social stigma of disease, 22
Solubility, 38b, 142–43b, 259, 261
Somalia, 111b
South Africa, 19, 23
South America
  Argentina, 20, 234–35, 383
  Brazil, 15b, 32f, 174, 232, 233–34, 297, 348
  Colombia, 49–50, 236–39, 237
  Peru, 235–36, 352b
  Venezuela, 232–33
Spain, 19
Spam and online ordering, 252
Spectrometers, 189, 262–63
  See also TruScan spectrometer
Sproxil (company), 83b, 84b, 342

Spurious drugs, 64, 156, 394
  See also Fake drugs
Stability testing, 160, 259, 261
Stage of production and quality standards, 181, 182b, 202
Standards, *See* GMP (good manufacturing practice); Registration of health care products
State Administration of Traditional Chinese Medicine, 195
State Drugs Control Authorities (India), 169b
State Duma (Russian assembly), 227
State Food and Drug Administration (SFDA) (China), *See* SFDA
Statin drugs, 162, 214
Stigler, George Joseph, 329
Stockouts, 14, 16, 47, 107–8, 113
Storage issues and deterioration, 26, 123, 126, 290
Street markets, 26, 67, 76–78, 87–88, 105–6, 123
Strempler, Andrew, 246, 247
Streptokinase, 41b
Substandard drugs
  definitions and overview, 4, 23–24, 27–28b, 28, 51–52
  and drug resistant TB, 21–23
  vs. counterfeits and prioritizing reforms, 48, 370, 388–92, 398–99
  See also Counterfeit drugs; Degraded drugs; Fake/substandard drug market; Underdosed drugs
Sudan, 111b, 112b
Sulfa drugs, 17, 333
Sulfadoxine-pyrimethamine (SP) (antimalarial), 114b, 143b
Sulfonamides, 17, 333
Sunday Monitor, 113
"Superbugs," 22

Supply and distribution chains
  complexity of, intentional, 187, 375
  criminal prohibitions along, 367
  GMP compliance along, 202
  online drug market, 247
  overview, 15–16b
  stockouts and fake drugs, 107, 121
  track and trace technology, 78, 82–84b, 244–45
  See also Distribution chains; Routes, trade
Surgery and fake anesthetics, 150
Suwankaesawong, Wimon, 239
Syria, 15b, 208–11, 213–14, 218–22, 223–24f

Taixing Glycerine Factory (China), 20
Talc as component of fakes, 322b
Tamiflu, 81b
Tanzania, 32f, 110b, 114b, 124–26, 132, 171
Tariffs, 95b, 206, 303, 313, 314f, 315–17
Tax fraud, 154
Taxes/levies, 95b, 206, 303, 313, 314f, 315–17
TB (tuberculosis), 11, 21–24, 90–91b, 143b, 154, 182, 269
Technology
  and counterfeit packaging, 145–46, 147–48b, 363
  HPLC (high-performance liquid chromatography), 13–14, 260, 262
  Minilab test system, 78, 80–81b, 198, 199b, 201b, 261–62
  mPedigree, 83b
  Nigerian deployment of, 78–81, 85–88
  scanning, 78, 82–84b, 244–45
  spectrometers, 189, 262–63

Technology (*continued*)
    TLC (thin-layer chromatography),
        81b, 199b, 261–62
    track and trace, 78, 82–84b,
        244–45
    TruScan spectrometer, 79–81,
        85–88, 131, 263, 265b
    See also Databanks; Online drugs
Technology transfer, 345
Teething medication, contaminated, 15b
Teething medication, contamination
    incidents, 15b, 19–20
Temperature deterioration, 26, 123,
    126, 290
Tertiary production process, 92b
Testing, quality
    advanced testing requirements,
        U.S., 333
    bogus, by pharmaceutical compa-
        nies, 157
    cheating with underdosed API,
        140, 154, 198, 200b
    Chinese efforts, 189, 192–94
    dye tests, 154, 198, 199–201b,
        261, 289
    flame test, 13
    HPLC (high-performance liquid
        chromatography), 13–14, 260,
        262
    incompetent, 215
    Minilab test system, 78, 80–81b,
        198, 199b, 201b, 261–62
    "semiquantitative," 261–62
    for stability, 160, 259, 261
    TLC (thin-layer chromatography),
        81b, 199b, 261–62
    toxicity, 18
    visual inspection, 199, 258, 261,
        268, 291
Text messaging in verification initiatives,
    83–84b, 342–43
Thailand, 32f, 239–41, 297, 349

Thalidomide, 334–35
Theft of donated funds, 108–9, 113, 115
Theft of drugs, *See* Diverted drugs
Theft of oil/petroleum, 127
Thin-layer chromatography (TLC), 81b,
    199b, 261–62
The Third Man (film), xxiii, 63, 397
Tiered pricing, 248, 357
Time magazine, 18
Timelines for registration, 349, 350f
Tips on dangerous drugs, 66, 74,
    154–55
    See also Whistleblowers
TLC (thin-layer chromatography), 81b,
    199b, 261–62
Tobacco control as example, 378–80
Togo, 114b, 115b, 122–24
Toothpaste, contamination incidents, 21
Toxic contaminants, 29
    See also Contaminated drugs/
        products
Track and trace technology, 78, 82–84b,
    244–45
Trade in diverted drugs, 5, 45–47
Trademark protection, 342, 393–94,
    393–95
    See also Intellectual property (IP)
        rights, protecting
Traditional medicines, fake, 195, 229
Trafic Mortel [Deadly Trade] (documen-
    tary), 168
Training
    and best practices, 202, 343, 345
    of chemists, Colombia, 237
    GMP protocols for, 37
    international assistance in, 343,
        345
    by Interpol, 110b
    lack of, 78, 260
    mandated, 195
    technology transfer, 345
    for testing, 78, 81b, 88f, 199b, 260

Transnational approach, strategies for
    argument over intellectual prop-
        erty protections, 356–58
    crimes against humanity concept,
        375–77
    criminalization of counterfeiting,
        359–60, 364–65
    extent of counterfeiting and effects
        of, 362–64
    extradition/prosecution issues,
        372–73
    international convention, need
        for, 358
    obstacles to national enforcement,
        360–62
    organized crime element, 360
    political will, need for, 99–101,
        104–5, 380–82, 384
    treaties, historic attempts, 365
    treaties, other forums/vehicles for,
        383–86
    treaties, precedents for, 366
    treaties, proposed strategies for,
        367–72
    treaties, WHO as forum/vehicle
        for, 377–80
    universal jurisdiction, 373–74
Transparency, commitment to
    Brazil, 232, 233–34
    Chinese reforms, 188–89
    Global Fund, 123
    MeTA alliance, 352–53b
    Nigeria, 65–69, 69–78
    Togo, 123
    Uganda, 113, 117
Treaties
    currency counterfeiting, 247,
        359–60, 367, 374, 381
    need for, 173–76, 365–66, 398–99
    tobacco control, 378–80
    See also Transnational approach,
        strategies for

Tren, Richard, 263
Trials, clinical, 44, 69–70, 259
    MRA oversight of, 44
TRIPS (Agreement on Trade-Related
    Aspects of Intellectual Property
    Rights), 392, 394
Trovan (antimeningitis), 69, 70–71b
TruScan spectrometer, 79–81, 85–88,
    129, 263, 265b
Trust in health care system, See Confi-
    dence/trust in health care system
Tuberculosis (TB), 11, 21–24, 90–91b,
    143b, 154, 182, 269
Turkey, 32f, 242–45

Udani, Samir, 72
Uganda
    AMFm program in, 114b
    Chinese controlled drug trade in,
        130–31
    corruption in, 108–9, 354
    in India's distribution chain, 171
    MeTA program in, 352b
    mismanagement of drugs, 109,
        113
    Operation Mamba, 110b
    progressive reform in, 113, 117
    theft of donor funds in, 113, 115
    theft of drugs and corruption in,
        108–9, 121–22
Ugandan Independent, 113
Ukraine, 231
Umar, Aliyu, 71b
UN Security Council Resolution 687, 206
Undercover investigations/operations,
    146, 153, 168, 219–21
Underdosed drugs
    African vs. Middle Eastern fake
        trade, 218b
    to cheat API testing, 140, 154,
        198, 200b
    China, 185

Underdosed drugs (*continued*)
 custom made fakes, 152–55, 168, 185–86, 220
 definitions, 29
 diluted foods/drugs, 62, 63, 231, 328, 397
 India, 144
 penicillin, xxiii, 397
 selling strategies for, 1
 spurious drugs, 64, 156, 394
 See also Drug resistance
Unisule (company), 152–54
Unit-dose level security measures, 82–83b
United Kingdom
 dangerous drug activity in, 50–51b
United Nations Conference on Trade and Development (UNCTAD), 94–95b
United Nations Convention against Transnational Organized Crime (CATOC), 383–86
United Nations Office on Drugs and Crime (UNODC), *See* UNODC (United Nations Office on Drugs and Crime)
Universal jurisdiction, 373–74
Universidad Nacional de Colombia, 237
UNODC (United Nations Office on Drugs and Crime)
 on corruption and criminals, 50–51
 on fake malaria drug market, 63
 on oil theft in Nigeria, 127
 as platform for transnational treaty, 383–84, 386
Unregistered drugs, 347–48
 See also Registration of health care products
U.S. Customs Service, 330
U.S. deaths from contaminated drugs, 11–12, 15b, 193b, 337

U.S. drug supply
 imports, 52, 177, 192b, 193b
 Indian products, distrust of, 158–59
 risks to from China., 14, 16–17
U.S. National Association of the Boards of Pharmacy (NABP), 249, 250
U.S. Pharmacopoeia (USP), *See* USP (U.S. Pharmacopoeia)
USA Today, 225
USAID (U.S. Agency for International Development), 117, 121, 210
 and PQM program, 102
USP (U.S. Pharmacopoeia)
 founding and function of, 329–30
 on inadequate testing in U.S., 14
 international assistance for MRAs, 345
 and Minilabs, 81b
 PQM (Promoting the Quality of Medicines) program (Ghana), 102b, 104b, 353b
 standards of, 330–31

Vaccines, 65–66, 70–71b
Valsartan (antihypertension), 212
Value, perception of, 140
Value of fake-drug market, 30–34
Van Wyk, Albert, 289
Venezuela, 232–33
Verification strategies, 83–84b, 241–42, 342–43
 See also Holograms; Track and trace technology
Vertical integration in counterfeit enterprises, 139
Viagra, counterfeit/fake, 17, 147–48b, 184, 239–40, 246, 251f
Vials, theft of, 220
Vietnam, 197, 348
Villax, Guy, 14, 180, 202

Violence
    danger to whistleblowers/wit-
        nesses, 160–61, 179, 188,
        216–17
    deaths of investigators/officials,
        69, 100
    See also Danger to investigators/
        officials
Vioxx (painkiller), 393
Visual inspection as test, 199, 258, 261,
    268, 291
    See also Holograms
Vivax strain of malaria, 266, 291
Von Eschenbach, Andrew, 337–38
VS International (company), 136–38b

Wall Street Journal, 127
Wang Zili, 184
Washington Post, 179, 190b
Waste, hospital, theft of, 220
Watkins, Harold, 18
Weapons, 149
Websites, control of, 195, 350–51
West African drug Regulatory Authority
    Network (WADRAN), 100–101
Whistleblowers
    on custom-made fakes, 168,
        170–71
    GSK incident, 164–65b
    inequity in treatment of, 167–68
    Ranbaxy company, India, 159–63,
        166
    strategies in India, 169–70b
    strategies in Nigeria, 74
    strategies in Uganda, 113
White, Nick, 257
Whitewashes, government, 156–59,
    164–65b, 235
WHO (World Health Organization)
    author's relationship with, 151
    and debate on intellectual prop-
        erty rights, 357
    definition of counterfeit drugs,
        369
    as forum for transnational treaties,
        377–80
    on obstacles to control, 360–61
    on online pharmacies, 249–50
    prequalification program, 73–74,
        88, 96b, 97b, 159–60, 161
    roles of in international assistance,
        343
    weaknesses of standards, 159,
        163
    See also IMPACT (International
        Medical Products Anti-Coun-
        terfeiting Taskforce)
Wholesale drug market, 50b, 149–51,
    266, 293–94, 295f
Widespread and systematic concept,
    360, 375–77
Wiley, Harvey, 330, 331
Williams, Roger, 14, 202–3, 331
Wine contamination with DEG, 19
Winnipeg Free Press, 246
Woods, Tom, 100
Working conditions in production facili-
    ties, 133–35
World Health Assembly, 101, 175
World Health Organization (WHO), *See*
    WHO (World Health Organization)
World Trade Organization (WTO), 172,
    356, 357, 358, 394
Wormwood, 198
Wu Xia, 209, 217

Yang Changjun, 184
Yehia, Ibrahim, 214

Zambia, 32f, 352b, 353b
Zamotina, Irina, 229
Zanu-PF party (Zimbabwe), xxii
Zanzibar, 110b, 170–71
Zhao Lianhai, 190b

Zhejiang Jinhuatailai Drug Company,
   187
Zheng Qiang, 202
Zhong-Yuan Yang, 193–94

Zidovudine (antiretroviral), 143b
Zimbabwe, xxi–xxii
Zoloft (antidepressant), 251
Zyprexa (schizophernia drug), 50b

About the Author

Roger Bate spent years on the trail of stolen counterfeit and substandard medicines in Asia, Africa, and the Middle East, learning the anatomy of the nebulous, far-reaching black market that has caused countless deaths and injuries around the world. He has undertaken field research on fake medicines using handheld spectrometers and laboratory research using basic and sophisticated techniques. He has studied the laws and economics affecting the medicine trade and has published widely in the peer-reviewed scientific, legal and economic literature, including in leading journals such as the *Lancet,* the *Journal of Health Economics,* the *Journal of International Criminal Justice* and the *Malaria Journal.* He has published nearly one hundred articles on the topic in popular media outlets including the *New York Times,* the *Washington Post* and the *Wall Street Journal.*